MEDIEVALISM

Volume V

# Medievalism
## Key Critical Terms

T0324240

ISSN 2043–8230

*Series Editors*
Karl Fugelso
Chris Jones

**Medievalism** aims to provide a forum for monographs and collections devoted to the burgeoning and highly dynamic multi-disciplinary field of medievalism studies: that is, work investigating the influence and appearance of 'the medieval' in the society and culture of later ages. Titles within the series will investigate the post-medieval construction and manifestations of the Middle Ages – attitudes towards, and uses and meanings of, 'the medieval' – in all fields of culture, from politics and international relations, literature, history, architecture, and ceremonial ritual to film and the visual arts. It welcomes a wide range of topics, from historiographical subjects to revivalism, with the emphasis always firmly on what the idea of 'the medieval' has variously meant and continues to mean; it is founded on the belief that scholars interested in the Middle Ages can and should communicate their research both beyond and within the academic community of medievalists, and on the continuing relevance and presence of 'the medieval' in the contemporary world.

New proposals are welcomed. They may be sent directly to the editors or the publishers at the addresses given below.

Professor Karl Fugelso
Art Department
Towson University
3103 Center for the Arts
8000 York Road
Towson, MD 21252–0001
USA

Dr Chris Jones
School of English
University of St Andrews
St Andrews
Fife  KY16 9AL
UK

Boydell & Brewer Ltd
PO Box 9
Woodbridge
Suffolk IP12 3DF
UK

Previous volumes in this series are printed at the back of this book

# Medievalism
## Key Critical Terms

*Edited by*
Elizabeth Emery *and* Richard Utz

D. S. BREWER

First published 2014
D. S. Brewer, Cambridge
Paperback edition 2017


ISBN  978 1 84384 385 6 hardback
ISBN  978 1 84384 455 6 paperback


D. S. Brewer is an imprint of Boydell & Brewer Ltd
PO Box 9, Woodbridge, Suffolk IP12 3DF, UK
and of Boydell & Brewer Inc.
668 Mt Hope Avenue, Rochester, NY 14620–2731, USA
website: www.boydellandbrewer.com




A CIP catalogue record for this book is available
from the British Library


  he publisher has no responsibility for the continued existence or accuracy
of URLs for external or third-party internet websites referred to in this book,
and does not guarantee that any content on such websites is, or will remain,
accurate or appropriate

To Kathleen Verduin

# Contents

# Illustrations

L. Birkedal-Barfod, O. Madsen, and S. Widding (Copenhagen and Leipzig: Wilhelm Hansen, 2nd edn. 1920), I, p. 254.

2    Thomas Laub's setting (1914) of N.F. S. Grundtvig's hymn *Kom, Gud*        219
*Helligånd, kom brat*. In: *Menighedens Melodier*, 2 vols, ed. by L. Birkedal-Barfod, O. Madsen, and S. Widding (Copenhagen and Leipzig: Wilhelm Hansen, 2nd edn. 1920), I, p. 253.

# Contributors

Nadia Altschul, Johns Hopkins University
Martin Arnold, University of Hull
Kathleen Biddick, Temple University
William C. Calin, University of Florida
Martha Carlin, University of Wisconsin–Milwaukee
Pam Clements, Siena College
Michael A. Cramer, City College of New York
Louise D'Arcens, University of Wollongong
Elizabeth Emery, Montclair State University
Elizabeth Fay, University of Massachusetts Boston
Vincent Ferré, Université Paris Est Créteil (UPEC)
Matthew Fisher, University of California, Los Angeles
Karl Fugelso, Towson University
Jonathan Hsy, George Washington University
Amy S. Kaufman, Middle Tennessee State University
Nadia Margolis, Mount Holyoke College
David Matthews, University of Manchester
Lauryn S. Mayer, Washington and Jefferson College
Brent Moberly, Indiana University
Kevin Moberly, Old Dominion University
Gwendolyn Morgan, Montana State University
Laura Morowitz, Wagner College
Kevin D. Murphy, Vanderbilt University
Nils Holger Petersen, University of Copenhagen
Lisa Reilly, University of Virginia
E. L. Risden, St. Norbert College
Carol L. Robinson, Kent State University–Trumbull
Juanita Feros Ruys, University of Sydney
Tom Shippey, St. Louis University
Clare A. Simmons, The Ohio State University
Zrinka Stahuljak, University of California, Los Angeles
M. J. Toswell, University of Western Ontario
Richard Utz, Georgia Institute of Technology
Angela Jane Weisl, Seton Hall University

# Making Medievalism: A Critical Overview

## Elizabeth Emery and Richard Utz

T HE FIELD OF medievalism studies owes a tremendous debt to Leslie J. Workman and Kathleen Verduin. They worked indefatigably throughout the 1980s and 1990s to foster critical academic interest in "medievalism," previously understood rather vaguely as a term describing a largely amateur nineteenth-century interest in what had since become the venerable twentieth-century discipline of "medieval studies." By 1979, Workman had published the first issue of *Studies in Medievalism*, the journal which would develop into a widely recognized peer-reviewed publication through an ongoing association with Boydell & Brewer. In 1981, he began collaborating with his wife, Kathleen Verduin, a professor of American Literature at Hope College in Michigan. By 1986, they had begun a conference series, now known as the International Conference on Medievalism, and a proceedings series, *The Year's Work in Medievalism*. Together, they created a nexus of medievalism studies in the English-speaking academy.[1]

We begin this introduction to *Medievalism: Key Critical Terms* with a tribute to Leslie Workman and Kathleen Verduin's achievements because the struggles they faced in bringing academic recognition to medievalism studies – tensions among "professionals" and "amateurs," Western Europeans and "Others"; debates about "pastism" and "presentism," memory and subjectivity; deconstructions of the concepts of authenticity, authority, and the academic disciplines and institutions reliant on them – reflect the development of the field as a whole. The idea of a dictionary or encyclopedia of critical terms in medievalism is also Leslie Workman's: a project left unfulfilled at the time of his death (2001). While the present volume does not seek to emulate the exhaustivity of such an encyclopedia, it does owe its existence to Workman's wish to engage with the contested terms used when

---

[1]  Kathleen Verduin produced a history of the *Studies in Medievalism* movement in "The Founding and the Founder: Medievalism and the Legacy of Leslie J. Workman," *Studies in Medievalism* XVII (2009): 1–27. For Workman's own recollections, see "Speaking of Medievalism: An Interview with Leslie J. Workman," in *Medievalism in the Modern World: Essays in Honour of Leslie Workman*, ed. Richard Utz and Tom Shippey (Turnhout: Brepols, 1998), 433–49.

speaking of medievalism. This introductory essay will provide a brief definition of "medievalism," as well as an overview of the development of medievalism studies, now so recognized that it warrants a book like this one.

## Medievalism: An Overview

Workman provided and spread the foundational notion of medievalism as the ongoing process of recreating, reinventing, and reenacting medieval culture in postmedieval times. But what is "medieval culture"? If by medieval culture we mean the cultural productions (art, literature, music, architecture, treaties, memoirs, etc.) produced during the period from the fall of the Roman Empire (476) to the fall of Constantinople (1453), the historical period roughly considered "medieval" by historians today, then medieval culture has always been "received": people of the sixth century discussed earlier events, texts, and works of art just as did people from the fifteenth century. The concept of a uniform period known as the "Middle Ages" is itself a construct, invented in the fifteenth century by human-ists seeking to glorify their own time as a superior "Renaissance" (see the entries on "**Authenticity**," "**Continuity**," and "**Middle**" in this volume). As a result, many of the stereotypes associated with the Middle Ages – knights, taverns, witchcraft, Crusades, plague – do not always have specific historical referents; they are simply accepted in popular culture as "medieval."

The term "medievalism" developed in the nineteenth century as a way of describing an engagement either with the historical period known as the Middle Ages or with what was perceived as belonging to this historical period. David Matthews has attributed the first published uses of "medievalism" in English to an anonymous journal article from 1844, thus updating the *Oxford English Diction-ary*'s previous attribution of the term to the cultural historian John Ruskin.[2] Regardless of the exact year and authorship of the term, it is in the Anglo-Saxon world and through English culture and language that "medievalism" was coined, very probably as one of the few -ism terms which responded to the veritable inva-sion of such progressive -ism words coming to Britain from the continent during the nineteenth century. Reacting against revolutionary continental coinages such as "republicanism," "democratism," "liberalism," "socialism," and "communism," the English "medievalism" in many ways represents an insular reaction against condemning and abandoning the premodern and the emerging temporal concept of the Middle Ages.[3] France, Italy, and some of the German-speaking regions identified medieval culture as a model against which a different future could be constructed, thus developing their own terminology for referring to the medi-eval past (see "**Lingua**" and "**Transfer**" in this volume) and to the development of distinct national approaches to the Middle Ages. Yet Britain and the United

---

[2]   "From Mediaeval to Mediaevalism: A New Semantic History," *Review of English Studies* 62 (2011): 695–715.

[3]   On the semantic history of these concepts, see Richard Utz, "Coming to Terms with Medievalism: Toward a Conceptual History," *European Journal of English Studies* 15.2 (2011): 101–13.

States (except for a short period following the "American Revolution") imagined their countries and communities as linked to the medieval past by a unique kind of continuity. Thus, in noted contrast to the violent break with the *Ancien Régime* constituted by the French Revolution, English politicians, historians, and artists celebrated political and legal traditions deriving from the Middle Ages as signs of an organically and peacefully progressing commonwealth.[4] Twenty-first-century medievalist movies and political discussions still draw upon this mostly nineteenth-century continuist mentality.[5]

Leslie Workman, whom William Calin once aptly called a "nineteenth-century man in the tradition of Carlyle, Mill, Ruskin, and above all, Scott," grew up and was educated in this continuist tradition, and his attraction to the general paradigm as well as his editorial predilection for British and North American medievalisms should come as no surprise.[6] Neither should be his published view that "medievalism, in origin and for the first hundred years" was "an English phenomenon."[7]

This Anglo-centric perspective was, for many years, foundational for medievalism studies, but it has been challenged in recent years through the work of colleagues studying other national traditions as well as by those with a postcolonial approach.[8] Such work calls into question temporal definitions of the Middle Ages, arguing that it was not a "global historical time," as Nadia Altschul puts it in "**Transfer,**" her contribution to the present volume, but a "local European time span." Such observations blur the previously accepted temporal divide between

---

4   See, for example, Clare A. Simmons, "Absent Presence: The Romantic-Era Magna Charta and the English Constitution," in *Medievalism in the Modern World*, 69–83. See Pamela S. Morgan, "'One Brief Shining Moment,' Camelot in Washington D.C.," *Studies in Medievalism VI* (1994): 185–208, as an example of "unique continuity" in U.S. history. On the role of the French Revolution for views of the Middle Ages in French education and historiography, see Jacques Heers, *Le Moyen âge, une imposture* (Paris: Perrin, 1999).

5   The English director Ridley Scott's 2010 *Robin Hood*, for example, reinforces similarly outspoken medieval roots, the birth of Magna C[h]arta under Richard the Lionheart and John Lackland, for British/Western democracy. In 2011, Republican lawmakers in New Hampshire proposed legislation which would have mandated direct citation from the medieval Magna C[h]arta to bolster contemporary individual liberties. See Karen Langley and Matthew Spolar, "Eight Hundred Years Later, an Inspiration," *Concord Monitor*, 25 December 2011, online: http://www.concordmonitor.com/news/4461339–95/raybuckley-bobkingsbury-timtwombly-lucienvita.

6   "Leslie Workman: A Speech of Thanks," in *Medievalism in the Modern World*, 451–2.

7   "Speaking of Medievalism," 439.

8   Seven of the first fourteen issues of *Studies in Medievalism* focused on medievalisms in England and North America, as do most essays in the journal's non-geographically defined volumes. For discussion of medievalism in Bulgaria, Denmark, France, Hungary, Italy, and Ukraine see, most recently, Patrick J. Geary and Gábor Klaniczay, eds., *Manufacturing the Middle Ages: Entangled History of Medievalism in Nineteenth-Century Europe* (Leiden: Brill, 2013). In France, *Modernités Médiévales* maintains an online database of scholarly work in medievalism (beginning in the nineteenth century), organized by author, theme, and date (see: http://www.modernitesmedievales.org/). For postcolonialism and medievalism see Kathleen Davis and Nadia Altschul, eds., *Medievalisms in the Postcolonial World: The Idea of "The Middle Ages" Outside Europe* (Baltimore: Johns Hopkins University Press, 2009).

"medievals" and "moderns" so often expressed as a requisite for medievalism (these issues are also discussed in entries for "**Modernity**" and "**Presentism**"). Despite his Anglo-centric approach, Workman himself consistently stressed the importance of presentism in medievalism – the fact that an individual's interpretation of the Middle Ages always reveals at least as much about that person's present concerns as about whatever the Middle Ages may actually have been.

A corollary to this often-expressed belief in the importance of presentism was his understanding that the scholarly writings of university professors and museum curators specializing in "medieval studies" were akin to the creations of amateurs fascinated with what they believed the Middle Ages to have been: "the *study* of the Middle Ages on the one hand, and the *use* of the Middle Ages in everything from fantasy to social reform on the other, are two sides of the same coin."[9] This was a particularly postmodern claim and one that called into question the professionalization of educational institutions. At the end of the nineteenth century, pressure to emulate the methods used by classical philology, medicine, and the natural sciences led to the rejection of the work of private enthusiasts, journalists, and antiquarians who had dominated work on "antiquities" from the Renaissance through the third quarter of the nineteenth century.[10] Professional scholars in the various national philologies and history thus performed a successful rhetorical turn, demarcating their own science-like work in academic "medieval studies" from that of "dilettantes" dabbling in "medievalism."[11]

Kathleen Biddick, who has written one of the most radical critiques of this process of academic institutionalization and demarcation, demonstrates how the practitioners of medieval studies built their discipline on "expulsion and abjection and [...] rigid alterity," not only withdrawing history and literary studies from public culture, but also separating medieval studies from co-disciplinary collaboration with other academic areas of specialization.[12] This divide between "professional" and "amateur" scholars continues today and is addressed in the present volume in the essays entitled "**Authenticity**," "**Co-disciplinarity**," and "**Reenactment**."

By the late 1960s, after often feuding waves of (old) historicist, philological, positivist, and scientist paradigms had dominated medieval studies, new critical theories gradually began to challenge by then tacitly accepted alteritist ways of understanding the Middle Ages. The rise of reception history and reception aesthetics, especially in the wake of the medievalist Hans Robert Jauss, demanded a balance between author- and authority-based approaches to literary and historical texts and audience-based ones, exposing existing readings of medieval texts as too static and essentializing, and opening an interpretive space between "modernity"

---

9    "The Future of Medievalism," in *Medievalism: The Year's Work for 1995*, ed. James Gallant (Holland, MI: Studies in Medievalism, 1999): 7–18 (12).

10    David Matthews, *The Invention of Middle English. An Anthology of Primary Sources* (University Park: Pennsylvania State University Press, 2000), 12.

11    On this process, see Monica Santini, *The Impetus of Amateur Scholarship. Discussing and Editing Medieval Romances in Late-Eighteenth- and Nineteenth-Century Britain* (Bern: Peter Lang, 2010), 15–23.

12    *The Shock of Medievalism* (Durham: Duke University Press, 1998), 16.

and "alterity" that academic and non-academic readers might inhabit together.[13] Paul Zumthor's *Parler du moyen âge* placed emphasis on the new medievalist's need for self-reflexivity; Umberto Eco situated his widely studied "ten little middle ages" within the broad non-academic cultural contexts of international politics; and Stephen G. Nichols and R. Howard Bloch proposed a New Medievalism/ New Philology that encouraged medievalists to abandon the "unexamined positivism" of their academic forebears and to celebrate the "irruption of a personalized subject in the otherwise dispassionate discourse of medievalism."[14]

Even relatively traditional historians such as Norman Cantor openly defined medieval studies as just one among the many forms the reception of medieval culture could take in postmedieval times; he, too, participated in conferences related to medievalism.[15] More than twenty years after Cantor was taken to task by many of his colleagues for revealing the necessity of reading medievalist research as deeply imbricated in the backgrounds and subjective predilections of its practitioners, national cultures, and academic traditions, major academic publishers of historiography, as well as their readers, now unhesitatingly embrace such projects.

Leslie Workman and Kathleen Verduin registered these paradigmatic shifts, connecting early on with the growing scholarship on medieval reception in the German-speaking world and establishing "medievalism" as a synonym for the somewhat more institutionalized "Mittelalter-Rezeption."[16] They also understood that the growing acceptance of the "medievalism" paradigm was to a large degree facilitated by the various ways in which gender studies championed the inclusion of subjectivity, and presentist approaches the study of medieval culture.[17] Gender and queer studies have subsequently constituted valuable new ways of approaching medievalism, as discussed in **"Co-disciplinarity"** and "**Love**," Jonathan Hsy's and Juanita Feros Ruys's contributions to the present volume. Aranye Fradenburg and Carolyn Dinshaw have showcased emotion, empathy, memory, subjectivity, resonance, affection, desire, passion, speculation, fiction, imagination, and positionality as contributing to a more comprehensive and self-aware engagement with the Middle Ages.[18] Such presentist engagements imply our common humanity as

---

[13]  One of the foundational texts in this history is Hans Robert Jauss's *Alterität und Modernität der mittelalterlichen Literatur* (Munich: Fink, 1977).

[14]  *Parler du moyen âge* (Paris: Éditions de Minuit, 1980). Umberto Eco, "Dreaming the Middle Ages," in *Travels in Hyperreality* (New York: Harcourt Brace Jovanovich, 1990), 61–72. R. Howard Bloch and Stephen G. Nichols, eds., *Medievalism and the Modernist Temper* (Baltimore: Johns Hopkins University Press, 1996), 5–6.

[15]  He presented a plenary, "Medievalism and Medieval Studies," at the Ninth Annual International Conference on Medievalism at Montana State University.

[16]  On the differences between "Mittelalter-Rezeption" and "medievalism" see Richard Utz, "Resistance to (The New) Medievalism? Comparative Deliberations on (National) Philology, *Mediävalismus*, and *Mittelalter-Rezeption* in Germany and North America," in *The Future of the Middle Ages and the Renaissance: Problems, Trends, and Opportunities in Research*, ed. Roger Dahood (Turnhout: Brepols, 1998), 151–70.

[17]  See Workman's "Medievalism Today," and Verduin's "Shared Interests of *SIM* and *MFN* (Vols. 22 and 23)," *Medieval Feminist Newsletter* 23 (1997): 29–33, and 33–5, respectively (available at: http://ir.uiowa.edu/mff/vol23/iss1/).

[18]  See, for example, Fradenburg's "'So That We May Speak of Them': Enjoying the

a foundational factor in bridging the temporal gap between postmedieval people and their medieval forebears and have raised questions about whether medievalism should, in fact, be expressed in the plural as "medievalisms."[19]

In his entry for "**Co-disciplinarity**," Jonathan Hsy notes that such flexibility is one of the hallmarks of medievalism; he praises its "capacity to transform and adapt: to explore both affective *and* intellectual modes of cross-identification with the past, and to facilitate intimate exchange between seemingly unlikely disciplinary bedfellows." Medievalism can encompass subjects as "seemingly unlikely" as those addressed in this volume: fourteenth- and twenty-first-century artistic interpretations of Dante's *Inferno* ("**Continuity**"), mimed twenty-first-century performances of medieval romance ("**Gesture**"), Viollet-le-Duc's architectural reconstructions of Gothic cathedrals ("**Gothic**"), ironic hindsight in the film *Monty Python and the Holy Grail* ("**Humor**"), the Mediaeval Baebes' performance of Latin lyric ("**Lingua**"), historians' use of the Middle Ages to commemorate a national past ("**Memory**"), blog posts from scholars specializing in the Middle Ages ("**Middle**"), thirteenth-century adaptations of Norse myth and twenty-first-century cinematic renditions ("**Myth**"), the appropriation of the medieval in video games ("**Play**"), the Ku Klux Klan and Nazi embrace of chivalry ("**Purity**"), Disney princesses and Las Vegas casinos ("**Simulacrum**"), and modern jousting ("**Reenactment**" and "**Spectacle**"). The present volume shows the extent to which medievalism has been embraced by recognized scholars in diverse areas of the humanities and social sciences, an indication that the once shunned term has reemerged from the academy's love affair with positivism and strict historicism, and has moved from margin to center.[20]

Yet while many aspects of medievalism studies have now been accepted into the mainstream of medieval studies, its inclusivity and recognition of subjectivity –particularly its willingness to discuss all kinds of engagements not only with the period from 476 to 1453, but with what has come to be considered "medieval" (i.e. chivalry, magic, crusades) – keep other aspects at the margins of academic legitimacy. This is most evident in the recent creation of new terminology – notably "neomedieval" – to differentiate the medievalism of popular culture.

Neomedievalism is not simply a new kind of medievalism, as its name might suggest, but, in fact, a completely different (and often irreverent) ahistorical approach to the medieval. Lauryn S. Mayer, Kevin and Brent Moberly, and Pamela Clements explore the neomedieval in the present volume ("**Simulacrum**," "**Play**," and "**Authenticity**," respectively), arguing that neomedieval creations appropriate and transform elements thought to be "medieval," often flaunting their historicity

---

Middle Ages," *New Literary History* 28.2 (1997): 205–30 and Dinshaw's *Getting Medieval: Sexualities and Communities, Pre- and Postmodern* (Durham: Duke University Press, 1999).

[19] This is the title of a 2009 issue of *Studies in Medievalism: Defining Medievalism(s)*.

[20] In "On the Margin: Postmodernism, Ironic History, and Medieval Studies," Lee Patterson capitalizes on Terry Eagleton's statement that a characteristic of the postmodern condition is the return to the center of what had previously been displaced to the margin. *Speculum* 65:1 (January 1990), 87–108.

or verisimilitude to achieve a particular aesthetic.[21] It is perhaps more akin to the technique of "sampling" in modern hip-hop music than to an attempt to perform medieval music in a modern context (see "**Resonance**" in the present volume). Neomedievalism is the perfect offshoot of postmodernism, but its fantastical leaps and juxtapositions make for an uncomfortable fit in classrooms where professors require students to understand the history, beliefs, and cultural productions of the period from 476 to 1453.

Despite its inclusion in the academy, then, medievalism studies is still considered as marginal to medieval studies or as busying itself with its *disjecta membra*. David Matthews has noted that:

> there is a strong suggestion […] that what tends to happen over time is that medieval studies passes into medievalism; as it ceaselessly updates itself, medieval studies expels what it no longer wishes to recognize as part of itself. Among late-twentieth-century works, we could consider the example of D. W. Robertson's *A Preface to Chaucer* (1962) and ask whether it is going the same way. In contemporary Chaucer criticism, Robertson's work is chiefly cited to point out where it went wrong, to highlight the follies of exegetical criticism.[22]

One generation's scholars are often the subject of the next generation's medievalism studies as older and less well-informed work is replaced by what science-like paradigms consider better-informed studies.[23]

Rather than seeing medievalism studies at the margin of medieval studies or as bringing up its rear, we see medievalism, the term and paradigm, as methodologically broad and flexible enough to comprise not only "dated" medieval studies scholarship, but also modern scholarship self-aware enough to recognize its role in the ongoing recreation – academic, artistic, popular, technological – of what is considered medieval culture. Over time, the stated professionalism of medieval studies tends to reveal itself as a subset of medievalism studies; research is always influenced by the present concerns of the individual scholar and his or her breadth of knowledge. For example, the journal *postmedieval: a journal of medieval cultural studies* (2010–), a publication which applies new critical methods to the study of medieval literature and history, is cutting edge for medieval studies, but it can also be studied in its own right as a work of medievalism, especially for the conscious and playful ways in which it conjoins the medieval, modern, and postmodern.[24]

---

[21]  See the 2009 and 2010 issues of *Studies in Medievalism* on *Defining Neomedievalism(s)* and the contributions in Carol L. Robinson and Pamela Clements, eds., *Neomedievalism in the Media: Essays on Film, Television, and Electronic Games* (Lewiston: Mellen, 2012).

[22]  "Chaucer's American Accent," *American Literary History* 22.4 (2010): 758–71, here: 758–9.

[23]  See Clare A. Simmons, *Medievalism and the Quest for the "Real" Middle Ages* (Oxford: Taylor and Francis, 2001): 12.

[24]  The Palgrave journal's specific goal is "to develop a present-minded medieval studies in which contemporary events, issues, ideas, problems, objects, and texts serve as triggers

In short, the term "medievalism," while defined in inclusive terms as the reception of medieval culture in postmedieval times, has long been contested and will continue to be contested as long as it remains distinct from "medieval studies." Above all, medievalism is much more implicated in theory than has previously been recognized. It is the need to explore the critical vocabulary used to discuss medievalism that has prompted this book.

### Medievalism: Key Critical Terms. A Reader's Guide

Medievalism studies has grown exponentially since the death of Leslie Workman in 2001, yet it still has no systematic theoretical map; the field of medievalism studies to date has been largely defined by thematic or historical works informed by specific national traditions. Since 2001, the journal *Studies in Medievalism*, first under the general editorship of Tom Shippey (2001–2005), then Karl Fugelso (2006–), abandoned Workman's largely national organizational principles and included volumes focusing more explicitly on theoretical concerns: *Scholarship, Politics, and Fraud*; *Reviewing the Middle Ages: Film and Fiction*; *Postmodern Medievalisms*; *Medievalism in Scholarship and the Arts*; *Medievalism in Technology Old & New*; *Defining Neomedievalism(s)* (2 vols.); *Memory and Medievalism*; and *Corporate Medievalism* (2 vols.). In addition, a book series, "Medievalism" (D. S. Brewer; 2010–), and an online review journal, *Medievally Speaking* (2009–), greatly expanded Workman and Verduin's original framework.

  Outside the Studies in Medievalism network, since 2001 organized as the International Society for the Study of Medievalism, a vast number of essays and at least thirty monographs have presented important case studies across a variety of geographical settings. These investigate topics such as the interplay of medievalism with English modernism (Michael Alexander), Middle Eastern politics (Muhammed Al Da'mi), Spanish and colonial philology (Nadia Altschul), Viennese women's convents (Cynthia J. Cyrus), multilingualism (Mary Catherine Davidson), Australian literature (Louise D'Arcens), fin-de-siècle France (Elizabeth Emery and Laura Morowitz), politics and popular culture (Tommaso Di Carpegna Falconieri), British romanticism (Elizabeth Fay), British orientalism (John Ganim), the Great War (Stefan Goebel), movies (Nickolas Haydock; Kathleen Coyne Kelly and Tison Pugh), the war on terror (Bruce Holsinger), Russia's Gothic Renaissance (Dina Khapaeva), Lacanian psychoanalysis (Erin Felicia Labbie), queer southern chivalry in the United States (Tyson Pugh), British Romanticism (Clare A. Simmons), Western European medicine (Zrinka Stahuljak), the Australian Gothic (Stephanie Trigg), and the "creole medievalism" of nineteenth-century France (Michelle Warren).[25]

---

for critical investigations of the Middle Ages" (http://www.palgrave-journals.com/pmed/about.html).

  [25] This survey of case studies is based on the "Timeline" of publications in medieval studies provided by *Medievally Speaking*: http://medievallyspeaking.blogspot.com/2009/09/timeline.html. In addition to these monographs, Tyson Pugh and Angela Jane Weisl recently published *Medievalisms: Making the Past in the Present* (New York: Routledge, 2012), the

The approaches behind these case studies, attentive as they are to a specific time period, nation, or theme, do not always explicitly address the critical underpinnings of medievalism itself. We seek to fill this lacuna with *Medievalism: Key Critical Terms*, by defining, exemplifying, and exposing problems with some of the essential vocabulary and ideas used when speaking of medievalism as the reception of medieval culture in postmedieval times. Although terms may seem transparent ("**Gothic**," "**Love**," "**Primitive**," or the word "medievalism" itself), they have a semantic history and often, an ideological agenda. The thirty essays included in this volume, written by leading international scholars in medievalism studies, seek to provide helpful definitions and illustrative examples from a wide range of cultural, linguistic, theoretical, and disciplinary areas. We specifically avoid terms that would coincide with existing major disciplinary areas (philosophy; hagiography) or approaches (Marxism; gender studies). Instead, we focus on problematic vocabulary related to such approaches, evoking terms such as "**Authority**," "**Love**," "**Middle**," "**Modernity**," or "**Reenactment**," which are often evoked as "givens" in discussions of the medieval period. Some of these, like "**Archive**," "**Gothic**," or "**Monument**," give a sense of the shifting meanings attributed to words over time. Others, like "**Feast**," "**Christianity**," "**Heresy**," "**Primitive**," "**Purity**," or "**Troubadour**," work with stereotypes that have been applied to the Middle Ages in different ways through the centuries. Terms such as "**Gesture**," "**Lingua**," and "**Transfer**" call into question assumptions about medieval and postmedieval communication. "**Continuity**," "**Modernity**," "**Myth**," and "**Presentism**" investigate the temporal medieval/modern divide. Yet others, such as "**Play**," "**Simulacrum**," "**Transfer**," and "**Trauma**," propose new modes of engaging with or interpreting the Middle Ages.

Although essays are presented from "A to Z" for ease of consultation, readers are invited to approach this book in a non-linear manner in order to take advantage of its many overlapping threads of thought. The most productive approach might be to consult it as an encyclopedia, or perhaps, more modestly, as a hyperlinked document (we make no pretense at encyclopedic comprehensiveness). In this way, the first topic chosen may lead to another on the immediately following list of "related essays." We hope such links will allow readers to engage in questions and themes not immediately apparent in the topic headings, but that resonate throughout. "**Heresy**," for example, treats, as the name might suggest, religious orthodoxy and martyrdom, but also raises important questions related to gender, cultural identity, love, nostalgia, "otherness," and the politics of writing history. It also includes a rich discussion of artistic, fictional, musical, and cinematic creations related to medieval history and literature.

We recognize that the choice of essay titles has excluded other possible key terms. We have thus developed the index as another way to access the volume; it picks up on themes and vocabulary that do not appear in the essay titles, but that weave in and out of the texts – geography, time travel, nostalgia for the past,

first attempt at a volume that could become a widely used introduction to medievalism studies.

magic, chivalry, sexuality, labor, animality, Dark Ages, translation, to name just a few – as well as historical figures, authors, and events making frequent appearances – Queen Elizabeth, Edmund Burke, Sir Walter Scott, Mary Shelley, John Ruskin, Mark Twain, J. R. R. Tolkien, C. S. Lewis, and, in a sign of this volume's own presentist bias, the ubiquitous George R. R. Martin.

*Medievalism: Key Critical Terms* is intended as an invitation to read across and through disciplines; the scholars contributing to this volume come from different backgrounds (art history, communication, history, literature, music, sociology, theology; those specializing in the Middle Ages or in postmedieval periods). Their differing approaches demonstrate how the contested vocabulary of medievalism studies may be implicated in theoretical considerations. We hope these engagements with some of the terms and concepts of medievalism studies will generate dialogue about the theoretical underpinnings of the field, the better to recognize our own presentist predilections when referring to the past. In reading these essays, our readers will themselves be reflecting on what – for them – constitutes medieval culture, its definition, and re-appropriation through the years, thus continuing to interpret and reinvent the period known as the Middle Ages. In the resulting dialogue, we carry on the work of Leslie Workman and Kathleen Verduin, to whom this book is dedicated.

# 1

# Archive

*Matthew Fisher*

I N CONTEMPORARY USAGE, an archive is a site for the unique and the excep-
tional. The value of the items preserved in an archive is commonly understood
to stand in relationship to their distinctiveness or rarity. The *Oxford English
Dictionary* exposes a challenging circularity in its definition of an archive as "a
place in which public records or other important historic documents are kept."[1]
Which documents are important, or, for that matter, historic, is rarely a judgment
that can be made before the fact. The value of the archive resides not, primarily, in
what is preserved. Rather, it is the potentialities the archive contains: the historical
record finds meaning in its range of uses in the present. In England, the idea of
"public records" came into focus around the documents of England's medieval
past, particularly as they entered private hands over the course of the sixteenth
and seventeenth centuries. The archives of the medieval past should be understood
as about use, not existence – as always suited to the present in which they are
deployed, rather than anchored in the past of their contents. This essay will trace
the development of the idea of the archive, and the ways in which the archive
was claimed to authorize its uses, from the creation of the medieval documentary
record, to the early modern use of the authority seemingly borne by medieval
documents, to contemporary projects digitizing the medieval past.

In 1291, the English King Edward I sent a request to the heads of cathedral
chapters and monasteries to reply to him with anything "touching the status of the
realms of England and Scotland and their rulers."[2] Edward was hoping to prove
that England rightfully held overlordship of Scotland, and that his broad call for
information would turn up useful results. Edward's investigation assumed these
institutions stored texts relevant to his purposes – that there was something to
be found in books of historiography and in documents, whether bound singly or
collected in rolls. Edward received many responses, and used the textual record

---

[1]  See the *Oxford English Dictionary*, archive, *n.*

[2]  See E. L. G. Stones, "The Appeal to History in Anglo-Scottish Relations between 1291
and 1401," *Archives* 41 (1969): 11–21 and 80–3, and *Anglo-Scottish Relations, 1174–1328*, ed.
and trans. E. L. G. Stones (1965; repr., Oxford: Clarendon Press, 1970).

of the past to make legal and political arguments about the present. Though some of the replies were to his advantage, seemingly attesting to Scottish kings of the distant or even fictional past paying homage to English kings, others were not. Regardless, the process was sufficiently promising for Edward to initiate in 1301 a second search for relevant texts through the dispersed archives of medieval England. Edward sought information, not merely documents; he desired arguments built upon abstractions to further his political purposes, not anything essential attached to the original text-bearing objects.

Although they had other purposes too, Edward's inquests were attempts to solve the perennial difficulty of searching for things: archival records are unevenly distributed, and the contents of any given archive likely to be quite heterogeneous. In our digital age, searching across multiple repositories is called "federated search," and Edward's attempt to find support for his political arguments was sensibly broad. The inquest exposes a tension at the heart of the archive, between uniqueness and plurality. A unique document may speak to a uniquely known truth, but a plurality of documents seems to offer the authority of confirmation and repetition. Before attempting what might be uncharitably described as a fishing expedition, Edward's clerks must have first searched their own records. Their initial consultation likely included narrative histories such as the chronicles of Bede, William of Malmesbury, Henry of Huntingdon, and John of Worcester. The clerks would also have searched the rolls of the Chancery and Exchequer. These searches, however, make clear that Edward's clerks knew the crown's records might *not* contain some important piece of information: if there was proof of English overlordship over Scotland, they did not have a copy of it. The libraries and document chests of the monasteries and cathedrals possibly contained something old that could be used to support a new argument.

At the other end of the chain of the inquest, the respondents understood that the king's request on a matter of (inter)national politics was not the place to innovate or challenge the statements of historiographical authorities. The medieval writers who replied to Edward's inquests copied the books and documents found in their own libraries. The materials they selected were almost entirely drawn from the most commonly available texts. Medieval historiographical authority was in some ways predicated upon repetition and conformity, rather than invention or innovation. For the respondents, repeating the schema of well-known and well-respected historians was more important than finding a unique document which did not accord with the historiographical tradition.[3] The replication at the center of medieval narrative history writing serves a larger rhetoric of authority; Edward's inquests largely turned up what he and his clerks already knew, even as they began to challenge how historiographical authority could be accrued and deployed.

Moving from history writing to deeds, charters, and financial transactions, it is interesting to note that Edward's clerks did not record the results of their inquiries in an appropriate roll. That is, they did not contribute to the main body

---

[3]   See Gabrielle Spiegel, *The Past as Text: The Theory and Practice of Historiography* (Baltimore: Johns Hopkins University Press, 1997), and Robert Hanning, *The Vision of History in Early Britain* (New York: Columbia University Press, 1964).

of the documentary archive that had been the centerpiece of the administration of the kingdom since at least the end of the twelfth century. The Chancery and the Exchequer copied into rolls the most important correspondence and business transacted.⁴ These rolls – large membranes of parchment, stitched together – were imagined as the definitive archive of the country's legal and financial doings. Possessing seemingly unimpeachable authority (although, of course, subject to the same misrepresentations and manipulations as all documents over time), the royal documentary archive served as a kind of Platonic ideal of the archive, comprehensive and authoritative in theory, though merely authoritative (not by nature, but rather by the supporting power structure) in practice. The earliest such royal documents were likely the rolls of "fines" – fines both in the punitive sense of modern administrative usage and something closer to a transaction or service fee for favors or privileges from the king.⁵ The records of these debts and privileges were recorded in the Fine Rolls, kept to this day in the National Archives (previously the Public Record Office).⁶ Along with the Fine Rolls, the Chancery and Exchequer clerks created a vast set of historical archives in the Close Rolls (containing copies of close letters), the Patent Rolls (letters patent), and the Pipe Rolls (a top-level audit of the year's transactions by the Exchequer).

Given the proliferation of rolls and historical records, if they are to be used, they must be both accessible and findable. Historical records are unwieldy, and finding aids are a necessity. Even in a world *with* digital indices and full-text search, the contents of medieval archives remain, and will probably forever remain, only partially described. The proposition recalls the famous challenge of measuring the coastline of Britain – the closer you look and the more finely you measure, the bigger the result. Archives hover at the uneasy interface of the known and the unknown, the identified but un- or under-described, the catalogued but not iterated. Archives can contain thousands of items, each of which itself may be a box containing a thousand more items. Even with a complete modern critical apparatus and the full range of finding aids and editions, the nature of the archive is overwhelming. The archive stores documents of potential value and also those without any particular value; it preserves a historical record definitive precisely for its shortcomings and omissions, its redundancies and its seemingly unnecessary details.

Records are bulky, and they accumulate alarmingly quickly. As it is impossible to know in advance if any given record may prove important, prudence dictates preserving as many records as possible. One solution for the flood of documents, devised during the particularly difficult administrative period of the Barons' Wars

---

⁴  See Reginald Poole, *The Exchequer in the Twelfth Century: The Ford Lectures Delivered in the University of Oxford in Michaelmas Term, 1911* (Oxford: Clarendon Press, 1912).

⁵  See the extremely helpful introduction to the rolls available through the Henry III Fine Rolls Project, http://www.finerollshenry3.org.uk/home.html (accessed August 2013). See also Richard Cassidy, "*Recorda splendidissima*: the use of pipe rolls in the thirteenth century," *Historical Research* 85 (February 2012): 1–12.

⁶  The National Archives were created by the 2003 merger of the Public Record Office and the Royal Commission on Historical Manuscripts, and the subsequent merger in 2006 of Her Majesty's Stationery Office and the Office of Public Sector Information.

in the middle of the thirteenth century, was the development of the so-called "rotuli pullorum," rolls assembled by removing dormant or low-value debts from the Pipe Rolls and re-enrolling them separately.[7] Although the *rotuli pullorum* went some way to making the Pipe Rolls more easily usable, the imperative to record all transactions continued to render the Pipe Rolls awkward for dealing with any particular transaction. Nonetheless, the Pipe Rolls were used to collect debts owed to the crown over surprisingly long periods of time – the year-in, year-out recopying of entries was not simply bureaucratic mindlessness. For example, in 1325, the Exchequer collected nearly £300 of debts first recorded in the Pipe Rolls over sixty years before, in 1260.[8] This is a remarkable demonstration of the use of the archive to render even the distant past present.

Edward II's treasurer, Bishop Stapeldon, was partly responsible for refining the archive into something still more usable, and thus valuable, for its (few) users in the early fourteenth century. Stapeldon reformed how the archives were organized by working to resolve the essential tensions between preservation and access and between conservation and use – issues that continue to be a challenge for modern archives. In 1320 Stapeldon began a large-scale effort to "calendar" (that is, summarize) and organize the Exchequer records, a project that took years to complete. Stapeldon also managed the centralization and sorting of a number of local and individual archives, including those of Wales, Scotland, and Ireland, and the records of the castles and barons who had led the opposition to the king.[9] For practical reasons, the records of the Exchequer had to be mobile, but Stapeldon was concerned about the danger posed by the potential loss of documents before they could be copied.[10] Such loss would compromise the comprehensiveness of the archive.

After a document has been copied, however, the nature of the original changes.[11] Copying can shift the value from the object itself to its exemplarity. That is, copying implies that a text's chief value is a matter of its contents, abstracted out of the historical and physical contexts of the parchment roll. The authority of the archive, then, becomes referential, rather than evidentiary: that there *is* such a document underlying political, legal, or financial claims is sufficient. There is no need to

---

[7] See C. A. F. Meekings, "The Pipe Roll Order of 12 February 1270," reprinted in *Studies in 13th Century Justice and Administration* (London: Hambledon Press, 1981), 222–53.

[8] See Cassidy, "*Recorda splendidissima*," 2. The debt was settled by the heirs of one William of Axmouth, who owed the crown £35 for the bishopric of Bath, and £284 from the tallage of the Jews (who had been expelled from England thirty-five years before the debt was collected).

[9] See Mark Buck, *Politics, Finance and the Church in the Reign of Edward II: Walter Stapeldon Treasurer of England* (Cambridge: Cambridge University Press, 1983), 168–70.

[10] On one occasion, while in Scotland along with his Chancellor and the Chancery, Edward I ordered a chest in London broken into, and certain rolls extracted and sent to him. The cost of issuing new keys for the broken locks was duly enrolled. See Lord Hanworth (Ernest Pollock), "Some Notes on the Office of Master of the Rolls," *The Cambridge Law Journal* 5 (1935): 313–31 (318).

[11] See V. H. Galbraith, "The Tower as an Exchequer Record Office in the Reign of Edward II," in *Essays in Medieval History Presented to T. F. Tout*, ed. A. G. Little and F. M. Powicke (Manchester, 1925), 231–47 (235–7).

wield the primary evidence of the document itself. Much like currency on a gold or silver standard, copies of the archive are backed by the existence of the archive.

As the archive shifted to authorizing arguments indirectly rather than directly, the contest over possession and access became more complex. The first English antiquarians were not long removed from the late medieval period, but they were keenly aware, in the light of the violent reshaping of the archival landscape that occurred during the Dissolution of the Monasteries, of the medieval as an endangered past.[12] Consider the precarity stressed in the earliest guide to accessing the archives, written by the Welsh lawyer Thomas Powell (d. c.1635), *Directions for the Search of Records Remaining in the Chancerie. Tower. Excheqver, with the Limnes thereof* (1622).[13] If there are records "remaining" in these archives, there are also records lost.[14] Powell's guide to the rolls of the Exchequer and the Chancery also reveals a deep concern about the ethics of the archive's use, an issue that accompanied increased access to the archives. In his dedication "To the Reader," Powell charges his audience that "Bookes, Medicine, and Lawes should never be publishet, or prescribed, but as Obiters, to meete with euils imminent; euer applied, and euer complying with the present necessitie." He declares he has published his guide to England's archives "only to such as shall make good use thereof and not arme and inable their purposes of prying into mens estates."[15] Powell is keenly aware of the possible misuses of the archive, particularly as "public" records were increasingly found in private hands. His interest in the archive as primarily a matter of what could (and should) be done with it marks a shift in the understanding of the medieval archive, and along with it, a shift in those actually using it.

Over the course of the seventeenth century, demand grew for access to the dispersed documents of the medieval past. Along with the exploration of the historical riches of the archive, however, came the increasingly complicated political implications of the archive itself. The uncovered traditions and newly discovered parliamentary and royal precedents were not innocent texts. The specifically medieval past was increasingly read as a text available to make arguments in the present. Sir Robert Cotton (d. c.1631) assembled the greatest private library of medieval manuscripts in England. Cotton, it is said, "always read the past for its direct applicability to the present moment."[16] Cotton exemplifies a more general trend in the period: the financial and transactional records of the past were used to make the political arguments of the day. The simultaneity of past and present

---

[12] See Eamon Duffy, *The Stripping of the Altars: Traditional Religion in England 1400–1580* (New Haven: Yale University Press, 1992).

[13] ESTC S115034. See Doris Mary Stenton, "The Pipe Rolls and the Historians, 1600–1883," *Cambridge Historical Journal* 10 (1952): 271–92 (275).

[14] Note that the most detailed descriptions of records in the opening pages of *Directions* concern the Dissolution, "The Cardinals Bundle, in which are contayned all Inquisitions ... of Abbeyes supprest and returned into the Chancerie" (8). See also Arthur Agard, *The Repertorie of Records: Remaining at Westminster* (London, 1631), ESTC S2396.

[15] Powell, *Directions for the Search*, 3.

[16] See Kevin Sharpe, "Introduction: Rewriting Sir Robert Cotton," in *Sir Robert Cotton as Collector: Essays on an Early Stuart Courtier and his Legacy*, ed. C. J. Wright (London: The British Library, 1997), 1–39 (25).

extended to the highest levels of society. In a private interview, Queen Elizabeth famously commented "I am Richard II. Know ye not that?" If she did say it (and scholars are divided on the point), she made this historic self-parallel to the anti-quarian William Lambarde. Elizabeth had appointed Lambarde Keeper of the Rolls the year before. Her Richard II remark was made in response to his present of a "pandecta rotulorum" – a summary of the rolls, a list of the contents of the archive.[17]

Late in Elizabeth's reign, perhaps 1602, Cotton presented her with a petition to create an "Academye for the studye of Antiquity and History founded by Queen Elizabeth," and a national library to support the academy. Of the examples he and the other members of the Society of Antiquaries cited to support their plan – to stress the value of the past to the present – the earliest was Edward I's appeal to history over the rule of Scotland.[18] The proposal gained no traction, and the politi-cization of the archive proceeded more quickly than antiquarians could navigate. King Charles I closed Cotton's library in 1629, supposedly because it contained a document advocating an absolute monarch (something Edward I would have appreciated uncovering). More generally, Charles suppressed the library because of the uses to which its many texts were being put. The Cotton library offered textual support for many arguments, and also facilitated networks of thought amongst those using it. Of further concern was Cotton's private ownership of offi-cial records, including many of the official state papers of the sixteenth century.[19] Cotton's library reshaped the expectations for the public nature of the record, with regards both to ownership and to access, while making increasingly visible the political cachet of the documentary past.[20]

Limitations on access, however, could be overcome by means of the same mechanism that had created the archive in the first place: copying. With the closure of Cotton's library came the proliferation of copies of its books, charters, and documents, and the medieval remnants of the country's past more broadly. A generation later, William Dugdale would write to Dr. Robert Plot (the first keeper of the Ashmolean Museum, d. 1696), "I can help you to a copy of them [the *Cartae*

---

[17] See Jason Scott-Warren, "Was Elizabeth I Richard II? The Authenticity of Lambarde's 'Conversation,'" *Review of English Studies* 64 (2013): 208–30. On Lambarde more generally, see Rebecca Brackmann, *The Elizabethan Invention of Anglo-Saxon England: Laurence Nowell, William Lambarde, and the Study of Old English* (Cambridge: D. S. Brewer, 2012).

[18] See Kevin Sharpe, *Sir Robert Cotton 1586–1631: History and Politics in Early Modern England* (Oxford: Oxford University Press, 1979), 27. See also Linda Van Norden, "Sir Henry Spelman on the Chronology of the Elizabethan College of Antiquaries," *Huntington Library Quarterly* 13 (1950): 131–60 (143–4).

[19] The 1887 edition of the *Oxford Dictionary of National Biography* observes, "A feeling was taking shape in James I's reign that there was danger to the state in the absorption into private hands of so large a collection of official documents as Cotton was acquiring," available through the *Oxford Dictionary of National Biography* Archive for Stuart Handley, "Cotton, Sir Robert Bruce, first baronet (1571–1631)," *Oxford Dictionary of National Biography*, http://www.oxforddnb.com/view/article/6425 (accessed August 2013).

[20] Thus, Cotton's contemporary William Howard "alone had more than twenty monastic cartularies in his hands," in May McKisack, *Medieval History in the Tudor Age* (Oxford: Clarendon Press, 1971), 75.

*Antiquae*] and save you the labour at the tower."[21] Copies of copies circulated, and fewer scholars needed to turn to the originals of the documents that supported their claims. Increasingly, interested scholars printed guides, calendars, indices, and eventually editions of the documents themselves. In the process of making these many copies, however, in some senses they obscured the historical artifacts themselves. There is no immediately clear benefit to the labor of going to the Tower and reading a charter written in Anglo-Saxon miniscule when it has been printed and its contents are already part of a larger legal and political debate. Yet, the tension between those types of intellectual labor would be the work of the scholars of medieval England from the seventeenth century to the last decade of the twentieth century.

After disappearing behind print for several centuries, the archive has resurfaced in the digital age. Digital photography offers the seemingly effortless reproduction of medieval documents (though, it should be stressed, at great expense).[22] In some cases, as with the exemplary Henry III Fine Rolls project, images of the documents of the archive are accompanied by transcriptions, translations, finding aids, and indices of people and places. Yet such comprehensive digital projects are rare. It remains far more common to encounter images of documents and manuscripts perhaps with some descriptive metadata, but not much more. Digital reproductions serve to protect the original documents from loss and damage, and to make them accessible to a vastly expanded audience. This function is an enormously significant one. But, as against print, digital content is differently divorced from historical context; its re-mediation of the medieval past, from parchment to pixels, has consequences. The medievalism of our own digital era again finds the present claiming the privileges of uniquely transparent access to the past. Digital reproductions of the medieval archive threaten to become simulacra, copies without an original, documents without a past. The medieval archive is more visible now than it has ever been, but the sense of the medieval as the ground of the arguments it was once used to make threatens to fade.

### Further Reading

McKisack, May. *Medieval History in the Tudor Age*. Oxford: Clarendon Press, 1971.
Ramsay, Nigel. "Libraries for Antiquaries and Heralds." In *The Cambridge History of Libraries in Britain and Ireland, Volume II: 1640–1850*. Ed. Giles Mandlebrote and K. A. Manley. Cambridge: Cambridge University Press, 2006. 134–57.

---

[21] Dugdale's letter to Robert Plot was printed in 1773, though Dugdale had died in 1686. See "Directions for the Search of Records, and making Use of them, in order to an Historicall Discourse of the Antiquities of Staffordshire," in *Select Papers Chiefly Relating to English Antiquities: Published from the Originals, in the possession of John Ives, F.R. & A.S.S.* (London, 1773), 34–7.

[22] The economic costs of such projects should not be underestimated. In some cases, private organizations have been funding such work, a situation not far removed from seventeenth-century concerns about Cotton's collection of official state papers.

Sharpe, Kevin. *Sir Robert Cotton 1586–1631: History and Politics in Early Modern England.* Oxford: Oxford University Press, 1979.

Stenton, Doris Mary. "The Pipe Rolls and the Historians, 1600–1883." *Cambridge Historical Journal* 10 (1952). 271–92.

Woolf, Daniel. *The Social Circulation of the Past: English Historical Culture 1500–1730.* Oxford: Oxford University Press, 2003.

**Related Essays in this Volume**

Authority, Authenticity, Memory, Presentism, Genealogy, Simulacrum, Feast

# 2

# Authenticity

*Pam Clements*

WHILE THE WORD *authentic* is cited in the *Oxford English Dictionary* (*OED*) as early as 1340, its first development as a noun, *authenticity*, does not appear until 1657, although the cluster of meanings is much the same as for the term *authentic*: 1) "being authoritative, or duly authorized," legal, worthy of respect; 2) "being in accordance with fact, as being true in substance"; 3) "being what [is professed] in origin or authorship, being genuine," really proceeding from the reputed source, of undisputed origin; and 4) "being real [or] actual."[1] The term *authentic* with its various meanings has great significance for medieval studies and medievalism, as these intertwined fields of scholarship are deeply concerned with the search for authenticity, albeit in a number of different, but overlapping quests. For the purposes of this article, *authenticity* takes on four intertwined definitions. These are, first, "authenticity as historical accuracy"; second, "the authentic as the original"; third, "the authentic as the authorized version"; and fourth, "authenticity as believability or verisimilitude."

From its inception as a field of study, medievalism has been identified as different from medieval studies – as it pertains to scholarship on texts, objects, and events created or occurring within the span of time historians have designated as *medieval* or *the Middle Ages*. Of course, even the designation *Middle Ages* is problematic in terms of periodization, and the dates of the said era are often in dispute.[2] *Medieval studies* is often described as the study of the "authentic" Middle Ages, that is, of authenticated artifacts and texts from the Middle Ages, while *medievalism* is said to be the study of artifacts and texts from later historical periods that make use of medieval matter. Created at a chronological distance from the historical Middle Ages, works that are described with the label *medievalism* are therefore seen as "inauthentic" interpretations of a supposedly authentic medieval world. Much scholarship on medievalism analyzes the ways such texts (in the broadest possible sense) transform allegedly authentic originals by infusing them with the obsessions, style, and tastes of their own eras.

---

[1]  http://www.oed.com, authentic, *adj.*
[2]  See David Matthews's entry for "Middle" in the present volume.

Medievalism, therefore, is in one sense the study of necessarily inauthentic "medieval" matter, filtered through a variety of eras, cultures, zeitgeists. This may include variations on medieval texts, along with appropriation of medieval settings, costumes, or artifacts to produce new works. The study of medievalism highlights differences between the medieval "originals" and more modern works imitating or exploiting their ideas and images. The texts in question, whether Edmund Spenser's *Faerie Queene*, Alfred Tennyson's *Idylls of the King*, the Kelmscott *Chaucer*, or George R. R. Martin's *Game of Thrones*, all appropriate images from, make reference to, or attempt to re-create "medieval matter" – though they are by definition *inauthentic* because of their historical distance from the period known as the Middle Ages. The *inauthenticity* of medievalism begins, then, at whatever point the Middle Ages is said to have ended.

During the later nineteenth century and the first half of the twentieth, however, medievalism and medieval studies were increasingly placed in opposition not by historical distance, but by scientific and professional affiliations and goals, as Clare A. Simmons has noted:

> Medieval Studies: Professional; within the academy; research-based, objective; committed to discovering the authentic past.
> Medievalism: Amateur; outside the academy; based on cultural preconceptions; subjective; shaped by the individual's needs and desires.[3]

Within medieval studies itself, one strain of scholarship is thus devoted to a professionalized "scientific" identification of whether certain texts or objects are authentic. Is a piece of writing correctly attributed to an author, or has it been misattributed over the years? Who is the "real" person behind the Muslim writer known as (one of the) pseudo-Aristotle? Does a reliquary contain any of the actual bones of the saint it purports to hold? Throughout the nineteenth and early twentieth centuries, textual provenance was a major theme of much linguistic and literary medieval scholarship, both professional and amateur. Tracing a text, along with its earlier versions, back to an *authentic* original was essential to the creation of an authoritative text.

Amateur folklore and ballad collectors also search relentlessly for "original" versions of stories and songs. In the nineteenth century this impulse, often conducted by non-specialists, was deeply connected with the Romantic ideal of cultural expression through nationalism.[4] While folklore collectors' efforts and methodology were eventually dismissed as medieval studies grew into a profes-

---

[3]   Clare A. Simmons, ed., *Medievalism and the Quest for the "Real" Middle Ages* (Oxford: Taylor and Francis, 2001), 12.

[4]   See, for example, *Folklore* 124.2 (2013): *The Ballad and its Paradoxes*; Suzanne Gilbert, "Alliance and Defiance in Scottish and American Outlaw-Hero Ballads," in *Scotland and the 19th-Century World*, ed. Gerard Carruthers, David Goldie, and Alastair Renfrew (Amsterdam and New York: Rodopi, 2012), 70–92; Jason Marc Harris, *Folklore and the Fantastic in Nineteenth-Century British Fiction* (Aldershot: Ashgate Publishing, Ltd., 2013); Scott B. Spencer, ed., *The Ballad Collectors of North America: How Gathering Folksongs Transformed Academic Thought and American Identity* (Plymouth, UK: Scarecrow Press,

sional field, linguists and historians contributed greatly to this search for authentic national origins.[5]

Infrared photography, carbon dating, and other more recent technologies have been indispensable in the chronological dating of material objects, but these do not supplant the importance of knowledge of material culture, contemporary chronicles, or historical linguistics. Recent archaeological finds, such as the Staffordshire Hoard of Anglo-Saxon gold[6] or the grave and skeleton of Richard III of England, are still in the process of chronological dating and provenance. The Richard III find is likely to challenge contemporary stories about that monarch's death and, potentially, his reign. Certainly the narrative about this king dramatized by Shakespeare (itself a work of medievalism) has long been seen as an example of history "written by the victors"; archaeological evidence and analysis of the surviving fifteenth-century writings both pursue the authentic, "real" Richard.[7]

One type of authenticity in medievalism is thus derived from academic professionalism. Yet even such scholarly or scientific "authenticity" is suspect. The New Historical criticism of the 1980s challenged the existence of an absolute, authentic Middle Ages. As Lee Patterson writes in *Negotiating the Past: The Historical Understanding of Medieval Literature*, "The appeal to 'history' so commonly made in current critical discourses of all varieties is necessarily only a reconstruction fabricated according to processes of interpretation that are identical to those applied to the 'not-history' of the literary text."[8]

Once periodization was recognized as a fictional construct, "the Middle Ages" also became a reconstruction, and scholars now realize that from our chronologically distant vantage point all medieval studies are intimately entwined with medievalism. Indeed, Simmons suggests that "one generation's medieval studies was the next generation's Medievalism" (12). By the 1990s, the concept of an *authentic* Middle Ages was coming under close scrutiny. Norman F. Cantor's *Inventing the Middle Ages* made it clear that this long era of European history is not one, but a collection of constructs, influenced by the circumstances and personalities of a series of influential scholars.[9] According to Clare Simmons, "*Inventing the Middle Ages* effectively shows how scholars like Schramm, Kantorowicz, Panofsky and Lewis injected their own personal circumstances into their reading of the Middle

Inc., 2012); David Atkinson, "The English Revival Canon: Child Ballads and the Invention of Tradition," *The Journal of American Folklore* 114: 453 (Summer 2001): 370–80.

5   See Monica Santini, *The Impetus of Amateur Scholarship: Discussing and Editing Medieval Romances in Late-Eighteenth- and Nineteenth-Century Britain* (New York: Peter Lang, 2009), and Timothy Baycroft and David Hopkin, eds., *Folklore and Nationalism in Europe During the Long Nineteenth Century* (Leiden: Brill, 2012).

6   See Alex Burghart, "Mud and Gold in Staffordshire: The Richest Hoard of Anglo-Saxon Treasure ever Discovered," *Times Literary Supplement* (14 October 2010), and Caroline Alexander, "Magical Mystery Treasure," *National Geographic* 220 (November 2011): 44.

7   See Richard Buckley, Mathew Morris, Jo Appleby, Turi King, Deirdre O'Sullivan, Lin Foxhall, "'The King in the Car Park': New Light on the Death and Burial of Richard III in the Grey Friars Church, Leicester, in 1485," *Antiquity* 87 (2013): 519–38.

8   Lee Patterson, *Negotiating the Past: The Historical Understanding of Medieval Literature* (Madison: University of Wisconsin Press, 1987), 42.

9   Norman F. Cantor, *Inventing the Middle Ages* (New York: William Morrow, 1991).

Ages; the book is thus a further nail in the coffin of the nineteenth-century model of scientific history" (16).

Can the Middle Ages, thus described, ever be considered *authentic* in the *OED*'s sense of "being in accordance with fact"; being real or actual? Laura Kendrick questions

> our distinctions between authentic and pseudo-medieval texts, between scholarly editions and amateur inventions, between history and fiction. The basic rule for becoming a professional medievalist has been that we must believe ourselves to be returning to, restoring and founding our criticism and literary history upon, authentic medieval texts that are as close as possible to authorial originals. Our erudition is fundamentally falsifying, our science a discipline of imposture – and this from the beginning, but increasingly so, and with less and less tolerance for such self-critical analysis, from the turn of the nineteenth century on.[10]

Leslie Workman, who was foundational to the field of medievalism studies, seconds this idea:

> The Middle Ages are virtually unique among major periods or areas of historical study in being entirely the creation of scholars. Since the term 'Middle Ages' in one of its many forms was first coined by Italian humanists, successive cultural revolutions down to and including the advent of Romanticism at the end of the eighteenth century found it desirable to adopt and enlarge the term for their own proposes. It is axiomatic that every generation has to write its own history of the past, and this is especially true in the case of the Middle Ages. It follows that medievalism, the study of this process, is a necessary part of the study of the Middle Ages. [...] [M]edievalism, being concerned with process rather than product, is a particularly fruitful area of several forms of postmodern criticism.[11]

According to Clare Simmons, "Perhaps one reason why the *Studies in Medievalism* series has prevailed since its founding in 1979 [...] is that by focusing on recreations of the Middle Ages, the journal has both avoided this problem of authenticity and has crossed disciplinary boundaries. [...] At least until the 1980s, Workman also saw Medievalism as distinct from 'scientific' medieval studies because it involves reading the past with a marked consciousness of one's own present" (14).

An underlying question about authenticity in medievalism thus becomes: "Whose Middle Ages are we studying?" This recognition, along with the development of cultural studies and related critical lenses, has led to acceptance of medievalism as a legitimate field of study. What seems to occur over time is that "medieval studies passes into medievalism; as it ceaselessly updates itself, medieval

---

[10] Laura Kendrick, "The Science of Imposture and the Professionalization of Medieval Occitan Literary Studies," in *Medievalism and the Modernist Temper*, ed. R. Howard Bloch and Stephen G. Nichols (Baltimore: Johns Hopkins University Press, 1996), 95–126 (95).

[11] Leslie J. Workman, "Medievalism," *The Year's Work in Medievalism* X (1995): 227.

studies expels what it no longer wishes to recognize as part of itself."[12] Indeed, many of the early works in medieval studies are now read as examples of medievalism, for instance, early scholarship on *Beowulf* that treated the epic as folklore.

In the 1970s and 1980s, when *Studies in Medievalism* was first established, medievalism was not readily accepted by many medieval scholars as legitimate scholarship; dealing with the not "authentically" medieval, the research, too, was held to be inauthentic scholarship, inadequately medieval. But there are other meanings for the term authenticity. If, for instance, one critiques a medievalist film like *Braveheart* for its anachronisms (a shallow form of criticism), one is demanding verisimilitude, another type of authenticity. The third *OED* definition, "being what [is professed] in origin or authorship, being genuine," seems appropriate here. The study of the anxiety of empire in *Idylls of the King*, and Tennyson's use of the Arthur stories to embody that anxiety, asks a particular kind of question about authenticity.

Another can be asked about the way the poet appropriates and transforms elements of the romances. How is the distance between the allegedly authentic original (if one can even consider twelfth- or thirteenth-century romances either original or authentic) and the modern recreation being employed? Another type of question is whether the medievalist work creates a sense of authenticity in terms of its integrity as a work; in this sense, *authenticity* is *integrity*. Is the medievalist artifact true to itself? Is it *genuine*? Does it create a believable (though obviously fictional) medieval world? This kind of verisimilitude, even as the reader or viewer or player is fully aware of the work's lack of historical accuracy, can create a sense of authenticity.

Many scholars of medievalism in film have analyzed at length "the illusion of medieval realism," the relationships between verisimilitude and authenticity. Indeed, in a well-known play on words, Kevin Harty titled his magisterial catalog of medieval films *The Reel Middle Ages*. In "Authenticating Realism in Medieval Film", William Woods writes:

> When viewers argue the authenticity of a film or the lack of it, they usually mean realism based on decorum or fittingness. [...] What is interesting is not how seldom Hollywood makes such a mistake (experts tell us that very little of what we see is historically accurate) but how unusual it is that a lapse of authenticity tears the fabric of the viewer's sense of the authentic.[13]

There are certain tropes (a "register," as Wood has it) in works of contemporary medievalism. These are not exactly symbols, but signposts or signifiers of "the medieval," sufficient to create enough of a sense of verisimilitude for audiences to

---

[12] David Matthews, "Chaucer's American Accent," *American Literary History* 22: 4 (Winter 2010): 758–72 (758).

[13] William Woods, "Authenticating Realism," in *The Medieval Hero on Screen: Representations from Beowulf to Buffy*, ed. Martha W. Driver and Sid Ray (Jefferson, NC: McFarland, 2004), 38–52 (47). Kevin Harty, *The Reel Middle Ages: American, Western and Eastern European, Middle Eastern and Asian Films About Medieval Europe* (Jefferson, NC: McFarland, 2006).

accept a work as "medieval." These signifiers need not be attached to any single era; for instance, a "medieval" castle can be architecturally Gothic, Frankish, Romanesque, Roman, even Byzantine in style, and still denote authentic "medieval." Other such signposts include matters of costume – tunics, tights and gowns, girdles and fantastic headgear; scenes of dirt and filth, of animals roaming at large in streets or halls; armor and weaponry. Region and date of origin matter less than that these signifiers of medievalism point to familiar images and tropes.

This casual approach to historical and regional accuracy is heightened in neomedievalism, where even the most relaxed medieval referents can be interposed with those from other time periods, and can be handled completely ahistorically. No matter which of the various scholarly definitions one follows, neomedievalism takes questions of authenticity to new levels. One definition of neomedievalism considers postmodern works that abandon any attempt at historical coherence in favor of a playful intermingling of themes, tropes, images, and referents from numerous time periods, thus reveling in historical inaccuracy. *Monty Python and the Holy Grail* is the quintessence of playful, anachronistic parody, but many other films (such as *A Knight's Tale*) and video games (such as *Arcanum*) have joyously mixed tropes from different historical eras and cultural milieux. Some of these also escape from the exclusively European settings of the old-fashioned, canonical "medieval period" and achieve a rapid-fire sense of *bricolage* through the constant shifting of historical referents. Indeed, John M. Ganim notes that "students' reactions to the medieval hero on the screen are mediated by […] medievalism itself, the self-conscious interpretation and reformulation of medieval themes, often ludic and performative."[14]

Bruce Holsinger points out that in contemporary journalism medievalist artifacts or referents can too easily be assumed to be authentically "medieval" and it does not seem to matter. He comments on a *New York Times* article about an organization called "Chivalry Today: Educational Program." An illustration for this article, described in the newspaper as "an 11th-century illustration," is clearly a modern (medievalist) drawing, which is copied to highlight the "medievalness" of this news article. Holsinger notes:

> In fact, if you do a quick search under "Lancelot" on the Lebrecht stock photography site you'll find that crucial qualifier "after" – as in "*after* miniature in 11th century manuscript." But it's always interesting when the visual register of contemporary medievalism augments its explicit argumentative dimension. Stock medievalism comes in many forms.[15]

It is such "stock medievalism," as Holsinger calls it, that allows neomedieval films and video games such license in creating neomedieval "authenticity."

---

[14] John Ganim, "The Hero in the Classroom," in *The Medieval Hero on Screen: Representations from Beowulf to Buffy*, ed. Martha W. Driver and Sid Ray (Jefferson, NC: McFarland, 2004), 237–50 (237–8).

[15] Bruce Holsinger, "Stock Medievalism," a 13 July 2013 post on the blog *Burnable Books*, http://burnablebooks.com/stock-medievalism/ (accessed September 2013).

Another definition of neomedievalism emphasizes the electronic nature of much contemporary medievalism, not only film and television, but also in the digital worlds of the Internet and video gaming. Since none of these electronic technologies were available during the historical Middle Ages, the mere existence of medievalism in these genres places them at an even greater remove from the original medieval material than those employing more traditional means (written text, paint, sculpture, song). Martha Driver notes that "With film, in particular, one is generally conscious (if one is watching consciously) of intentional and unintentional anachronism, and the imposing of contemporary social or political values on the past."[16] William Woods similarly writes, "Our sense of the typical in medieval life deserves special attention because it is the primary basis of cinematic medievalism – the way modern viewers conceive the Middle Ages" (47). Once again, the stock signifiers meaning "medieval" are enough, in many films, to convince the audience that it is dealing with the authentically medieval.

Those who use the term neomedievalism in yet another, political, sense often emphasize the fiercely nostalgic aspect of certain contemporary political movements – such as al-Qaeda's attempts to reconstruct an idealized and ideologically pure "medieval Islam." (The term medieval is also used in a pejorative sense, and often inaccurately, by Westerners as well.) In one sense, this is of course absurd; al-Qaeda makes effective use of modern digital technology to disseminate ideas and recruit new warriors. In terms of the Middle East, any view of medieval Islam that ignores its position on the cutting edge of science in the eleventh to the thirteenth centuries is a deeply inaccurate, perhaps *inauthentic*, one. Western cultural movements that similarly seek to re-create a somehow purer, "better" Middle Ages pursue the same nostalgic quest. The notion of "the medieval" attributed to such nostalgic movements is as much an inauthentic construct as any video game employing chain-mail-clad avatars bearing machine guns.

In "The Return of the King: Medievalism and the Politics of Nostalgia in the Mythopoetic Men's Movement," Susan Aronstein describes a movement which looks to the medieval past for its model of the ideal masculine, thus participating in what Umberto Eco calls our collective cultural "dreaming" of the Middle Ages. When we lose ourselves in medievalist fantasies, we engage in a politics of nostalgia, arguing for the return to a lost ideal that is paradoxically portrayed as both ahistorical and universal.[17] According to Aronstein, the narratives of the mythopoetic men's movement authors:

> represent a hodgepodge of motifs and stories in which every scene refers to a similar motif in another story, and all the pieces are put together in the service of rediscovering the psychological "ur" myth. In this way, the

[16] Martha W. Driver, "What's Accuracy Got to Do with It? Historicity and Authenticity in Medieval Film," in *The Medieval Hero on Screen: Representations from Beowulf to Buffy*, ed. Martha W. Driver and Sid Ray (Jefferson, NC: McFarland, 2004), 19–22 (19).

[17] Susan Aronstein, "The Return of the King: Medievalism and the Politics of Nostalgia in the Mythopoetic Men's Movement," in *Medievalism and the Quest for the "Real" Middle Ages*, ed. Clare A. Simmons (Oxford: Taylor and Francis, 2001), 144–59 (145).

mythopoetic writers are "medievalist" in their critical methodology as well as their choice of stories. (153)

Medieval studies began in the nineteenth century with a search for the authentic (original, factual, authoritative) Middle Ages. Medievalism, which now includes professional medieval studies within it, seeks other kinds of authenticity – and authority. The idea of medieval authenticity has therefore undergone several waves of variation: authenticity as historically accurate; authenticity as a search for cultural origins; authenticity as the authorized version of a medieval text or narrative; and authenticity as believability or verisimilitude, a sense of the genuineness of the "medieval" in a modern setting. Therefore, for medievalism the quest for medieval authenticity is always the search for a chimera.

## Further Reading

Cantor, Norman F. *Inventing the Middle Ages*. New York: William Morrow, 1991.

Eco, Umberto. *Travels in Hyperreality*. Trans. William Weaver. New York: Harcourt Brace, 1986.

Kendrick, Laura. "The Science of Imposture and the Professionalization of Medieval Occitan Literary Studies." In *Medievalism and the Modernist Temper*. Ed. R. Howard Bloch and Stephen G. Nichols. Baltimore: Johns Hopkins University Press, 1996. 95–126.

Nichols, Stephen G. "The New Medievalism: Tradition and Discontinuity in Medieval Culture." In *The New Medievalism*. Ed. Marina S. Brownlee, Kevin Brownlee, and Stephen G. Nichols. Baltimore: Johns Hopkins University Press, 1991. 1–27.

Patterson, Lee. *Negotiating the Past: The Historical Understanding of Medieval Literature*. Madison: University of Wisconsin Press, 1987.

Simmons, Clare A., ed. *Medievalism and the Quest for the "Real" Middle Ages*. Oxford: Taylor and Francis, 2001.

Woods, William. "Authenticating Realism." In *The Medieval Hero on Screen: Representations from Beowulf to Buffy*. Ed. Martha W. Driver and Sid Ray. Jefferson, NC: McFarland, 2004. 38–52.

Zumthor, Paul. *Speaking of the Middle Ages (Parler du moyen âge)*. Trans. Sara White. Lincoln: University of Nebraska Press, 1986.

## Related Essays in this Volume

Authority, Middle, Presentism, Modern, Simulacrum, Archive, Reenactment, Memory, Co-disciplinarity, Resonance

# 3
# Authority

*Gwendolyn Morgan*

EDIEVALISM IS INEXTRICABLY bound up with authority. The adaptation of, or appeal to, medieval tropes, whether philosophical, political,
artistic, or popular, frequently serves as an *auctoritee*, an unassailable
justification for the ideology and practices of the culture making the appeal. Such
practice is, of course, itself an adaptation (conscious or otherwise) of the medieval
appeal to ancient authority and hence a double practice of medievalism. In the
last 150 years, however, a sustained habit of inventing precedent, even for texts
that never existed in the Middle Ages, made such practice both more medieval
and more dangerous.

The appeal to ancient authority in medieval texts originally stemmed from
theological exigency to establish criteria and justification for the developing
Catholic dogma. In the early Middle Ages, the Bible served as the ultimate
authority (*auctoritee*), with God as the supreme *auctor* in religious and social
issues. However, when the scriptures did not supply specific direction – and with
a history of Roman political dominance – the mainstream Church came to rely on
classical texts evincing cultural didacticism as *auctoritees*. In the realm of literature, this manifested first as translation into the vernacular and interpretation
(frequently through glosses) of ancient texts and later as paraphrases of stories
and poetry. From there, it was a short step to poets merely adopting a classical
theme and claiming an ancient source to legitimize contemporary ideas. Such is
Benoît de Sainte-Maure's *Le Roman de Troie* (1154–60), a tale of *fin amor* primarily
of his own invention but claiming a classical heritage, cleansed (when it does peek
through) of "immoral" and non-Christian elements. By the fourteenth century,
poets following Benoît's lead merely nodded to the ancients, frequently inventing
classical authors and sources for their original work. Chaucer, for example, appeals
to an unnamed book, "*myn auctor*," and the muse Clio to lend credence to *Troilus
and Criseyde*, though, in fact, it is based on Boccaccio's *Il Filostrato* (c. 1336) and
no ancient account of the tale has ever surfaced.

In the centuries following the close of the Middle Ages, appeals to the era
in theology, philosophy, politics, and even simple tradition advanced the various
agendas of churchmen and rulers, forming and reforming the ideologies and

world-views of Western Europe. Nations and theology were created, rebels and heretics condemned, social orders devised, heroes and martyrs established based on medieval precedent or texts, rehabilitated and reinterpreted as necessary to reflect new intellectual and popular movements. The practice of medievalism has since ebbed and flowed for nearly a millennium, but never vanished, and in the twentieth and twenty-first centuries it surged stronger than ever and shows no signs of abating. It is with modern and postmodern use of medievalism as authority that this essay concerns itself.

Since the early twentieth century, medievalism has played a predominant role in learned attempts to define social practices and national identities. Umberto Eco credits this to locating the source of most significant modern problems and concerns in the Middle Ages and hence returning to our cultural "childhood" for their solutions. Yet, Norman Cantor has proven that we have largely invented that "childhood," thus appealing to an ancient authority that never really existed. In J. R. R. Tolkien's corpus of fantasy, medieval authorities justify and lend credence to modern fiction, rather than simply be part of it.[1]

Tolkien's hobbit tales create an undeniably medieval world, blending the languages, cultures, and mythologies of early England, in his own words a "recovery" of beauty destroyed by modernist "ugliness." Yet that world is already on the decline in *The Hobbit* (1937): the elves are leaving, ancient wisdom is forgotten, hobbits themselves (the modern British) eschew books unless they contain mundane things they already know. Repeatedly, especially in *Lord of the Rings* (1954–55), those defending Middle-earth against Sauron's forces turn to ancient and nearly forgotten books and legends, in effect to *The Silmarillion* (1977), to defeat him. *The Silmarillion*, which Tolkien considered his greatest work, provides a medieval history to his medieval world. Unable to complete sections of *Lord of the Rings* without repeatedly returning to his composition of *The Silmarillion* simply to explain to himself and to his characters why things were as they were, Tolkien essentially created his own *auctoritee*. Moreover, he professed his hope that it become a specifically *English* mythology independent of that of the rest of Europe. In other words, Tolkien located the authority for his hobbit stories outside them and referred to it for virtually everything which existed in the hobbit universe. That *The Silmarillion* is itself fiction in no way diminishes it as an *auctoritee* for the author and his other creations. This fact conflates medieval authors' practices of turning to classical texts proper as well as of claiming non-existent classical texts for their *auctoritees*, and it establishes the primacy of the medieval text as authority for modern fiction.

Umberto Eco, in the *Name of the Rose* (1980), addresses the same issues of authority, though with an utterly different approach and conclusion.[2] In Eco's tale, Brother William connects a series of murders to the sole copy of Aristo-

---

[1]   Umberto Eco, *Travels in Hyperreality*, trans. William Weaver (New York: Harcourt Brace, 1986. Norman Cantor, *Inventing the Middle Ages* (New York: William Morrow, 1991). J. R. R. Tolkien, "On Faerie Stories," in *Tolkien on Fairy-stories*, ed. Verlyn Flieger and Douglas A. Anderson (New York: HarperCollins, 2008), 27–84.

[2]   Umberto Eco, *The Name of the Rose* (New York: Houghton Mifflin Harcourt, 1995).

tle's *On Comedy*, secreted in a monastery library. The authority Aristotle carries in the medieval setting of the novel and the fear that his views would corrupt Christian morality lead a monk to murder those who seek the treatise, eventually burning down the largest library in Christendom to prevent its discovery. In short, the mystery reflects medieval obsession with classical authority and precedent. Yet, like Tolkien, Eco creates a fictional authority outside the main tale to lend credence to it. The book itself purports to be a late-twentieth-century discovery of a nineteenth-century clerical manuscript preserving a fourteenth-century death-bed record written by Adso, Brother William's assistant, fifty years after their attempt to recover a late Roman transcription of a classical Greek text. As if this were not enough, the narrator of the envelope tale rejects the nineteenth-century manuscript as corrupt, but believes Adso's tale has the ring of truth, despite the fact he has no access to the original account.

Obviously, the convoluted web of authority and authorship, which extends further outward to Eco's readers, problematizes the very idea of Truth – that an objective truth exists, or if it does, that it can be known, for even the aged Adso observes, "I leave this manuscript … I no longer know what it is about" (502). As a final, very postmodern comment on this impossibility, Eco precedes the entire story with the words "Naturally, a manuscript." Does he mean that readers should expect a manuscript? That they should reference the confusion of manuscripts and authors laid out in his fiction? Or that the manuscript and the story it contains are natural and exist independently of the author, a claim he makes in a later postscript to his novel? It is impossible to know. Moreover, Eco asserts he chose his title because the rose has been such a pervasive and loaded symbol that it has ceased to have any meaning at all. Ultimately, the subjectivity and fallibility of authors and readers confounds any Truth which may or may not be apprehended, not merely from *The Name of the Rose* but from any "manuscript." What is left is the text itself, completely unknowable. Such a conclusion is, of course, utterly opposed to medieval ideas of authority and authorship, but it nonetheless locates the authority to declare there can *be* no authority in the Middle Ages.

The genre of the "booklover's mystery" takes medieval authority a step further than even *The Name of the Rose*. In it, the author all but completely disappears, and the text itself develops into a quasi-sentient entity, the ultimate authority – or perhaps the ultimate *auctor* – that directs action in, and defines the world of, the fiction. Julie Kaewert's novels center on the exploits of independent British publisher Alex Plumtree and have at their heart a sense that life imitates art, that contemporary conditions and events within the fiction result from and follow the plots of much older texts. In only one of her novels – *Untitled* (1999) – is this explained as partially human contrivance; in all others, Plumtree observes the phenomenon, but it remains a shocking and mysterious law of nature. In short, the ancient text becomes God.[3]

*Unsigned* (2001) centers on the Anglo-Saxon manuscripts of *Beowulf* and *Judith*, originally of disparate origins but bound together with an assortment of short

---

3  Julie Wallin Kaewert, *Untitled* (New York: Bantam, 1999).

miscellanea in 1536.[4] Various modern authors whose work involves the medieval codex disappear or are murdered whenever attempts to subject the manuscripts to scientific scrutiny arise. After a number of twists and turns through libraries (public and private), medieval and Renaissance letters, and the scriptorium at Malcolmbury priory, Plumtree discovers that a monk employed by King James I altered the *Judith* manuscript to preserve the monarch's sense of kingship and religion. The monk hid the tale of his deception in the illuminated capitals of the monastery's chronicles, which Plumtree just happens to possess. The major alterations – that Judith's true victim was Nebuchadnezzar, not his general Holofernes, and that the events took place in the historical city of Shechem, not fictitious Bethulia – undermine contemporary religious authority, political stability, and the royal family, and are therefore left in secret. In addition to these bare bones of the formula, the issue of authority extends both to the manuscripts' original pairing and beyond, to *Beowulf* directing events in the fictional contemporary world.

On the pairing of *Beowulf* and *Judith* in a single codex, which also happens to include a life of St. Christopher, Plumtree noted that Judith may be seen as a "monstrous woman" as easily as a miracle worker, depending on context, and that the Anglo-Saxon audience of the seventh (or tenth) century may have seen the equation as logical. Similarly, the manuscript at one point refers to Christopher as a "monster" (48). In this light, *Beowulf* stands as the gloss that elucidates its companion texts. Plumtree goes on to observe that once *Beowulf* is thus accorded a level of credibility equal – or perhaps superior, given the epic's function as touchstone – to the scriptural account of Judith and the historical account of St. Christopher, it becomes the standard of Truth. That *Beowulf's* poet remains unknown removes human involvement in the creation or apprehension of that Truth; that it is the only pagan composition of the three negates both medieval and modern conceptions of God. The authorless text stands as the ultimate *auctoritee* and *auctor*.

Each chapter in *Unsigned* begins with a quote from *Beowulf*, or occasionally *Judith*, which seems to direct the action described therein. In other words, the modern story seems to act out earlier events. This is further confirmed by many of Plumtree's observations, such as "Grendel was knocking at my door," and "[un]like Beowulf, I couldn't slay Grendel alone." Moreover, any reader familiar with the ancient epic recognizes other parallels: the dangerous, misty moors haunted by monsters, the kingly havens set above them, the wise and kindly father figures inhabiting those havens who advise the adventurers, the series of three "monsters," and so forth. These links insidiously suggest that secrets and conspiracies Kaewert associates with its manuscript may extend beyond the fiction. This implication receives further reinforcement by the fact that real-world academic debates regarding the dating of *Beowulf*, both the physical manuscript and the poem itself, are what precipitate the action of the novel. Finally, the *Beowulf* manuscript itself is depicted as alive, suffering Truth, "ordaining" Plumtree's unraveling of the mystery, and somehow deliberately forming the foundation of the British National Library,

---

4   Julie Wallin Kaewert, *Unsigned* (New York: Bantam, 2001).

whose "books … presented too great a force for mere mortals to face." The text, not only independent of, but *in spite of*, authors and scribes, directs the fates of men. Freed of such constraints, the text approaches the rank of God, or perhaps more accurately, *wyrd*, that unknowable, unapproachable, ultimate force of the Anglo-Saxon universe which follows its own course heedless of humanity.

In *Untitled* (1999) a fifteenth-century incunable dubbed the Bedchamber Book holds nefarious secrets on several levels, from international politics to religion, to commercial and personal intrigue. Plumtree discovers the book in a secret compartment of the family library, and after news of its existence leaks out, it becomes the focus of a number of attempted thefts, most sustained by the Dibdin Club. The Dibdin Club, an aristocratic and self-styled protectorate of books and, through them, Knowledge and Truth, invites Plumtree to a weekend retreat on a member's estate, the price of entrance being the sharing of a unique text. At the club's insistence, Plumtree brings the incunable. It contains two irrefutable secrets which would destroy Britain's royalty and, more importantly, destabilize international politics and Britain's sovereignty. The first, that Richard and Saladin slept with and impregnated each other's wives, throws all subsequent ruling regimes of both nations into discredit, not to mention the religions which lionized one or the other. The second, that Richard formally traded the city of London for Jerusalem, threatens the nationhood of Britain and Israel and confounds claims by the Palestinians and other Arab peoples. Other secrets, including Richard's murder by his knight, bode less critical disasters. Ultimately, of course, the Bedchamber Book is again secreted – this time by a Muslim terrorist group – so that world order may continue unthreatened.

*Untitled* also posits another medieval text as both *auctor* and *auctoritee*: Boccaccio's *Decameron*. Several members of the Dibdin Club pattern the events of their weekend retreat on those of Boccaccio's text, an ultimately harmless practical joke which they cheerfully reveal after they have had their fun. However, one of Boccaccio's tales played out – a sultan's attempt to entrap a Jewish money-lender into heresy by demanding he decide which of the Old Testament religions is the truest – reverberates well beyond entertainment into the contemporary political situation of the novel, where disaster is evaded in an analogous manner. Moreover, it echoes through the resolution of the incunable's two more dire secrets. Just as the Bedchamber Book itself directs secret international negotiations in the novel, so does *The Decameron* orchestrate those of individuals, whether acting in private or public capacity. Thus, Kaewert offers two medieval texts as both *auctors* and *auctoritees* for present-day life. It can be no accident, for Plumtree notes that ancient texts stimulate "a near-religious experience." The equation of medieval texts with, and even perhaps as a substitute for, God, is unmistakable.

In 2003, Dan Brown's *The Da Vinci Code* presented a constructed medieval authority supporting a specific socio-political agenda and went to great lengths to ensure that his claims to veracity would derail any challenge.[5] It centers on a battle between, on the one hand, the Priory of Sion, founded by the Knights

---

5    Dan Brown, *The Da Vinci Code* (New York: Doubleday, 2003).

Templar in 1099 to protect secret documents tracing the human lineage of Jesus Christ and Mary Magdalene, and on the other hand Opus Dei, a secret sect affiliated with the Catholic Church and directed by a fanatical bishop, which seeks to destroy that evidence, which threatens established Christianity. The story gleans credibility from the historical facts of Church history sprinkled throughout the novel, but Brown's revisions and blatant misstatements rather outnumber these. However, while the booklover's mystery formula is evident throughout, more pertinent to the present discussion is Brown's attempt to validate his novel as "fact," through supplements which comment on major organizations and figures within the fiction. Unlike Eco, whose original front and back matter and later Postscript make it evident that *The Name of the Rose* is merely fiction, Brown allows his novel to masquerade as reality.

In the Preface titled, simply, "FACT," Opus Dei is identified as a real Catholic organization, and Brown probably did interview present and ex-members as he claims, but the organization has never in any way been connected with mysterious or criminal activities. The Priory of Sion, on the other hand, is not – as the Preface claims – a still-functioning organization founded in 1099, but a men's social club created in 1954 to promote rent control. It took its name from a nearby mountain and was dissolved three years later. Its more significant connection to Brown's novel is that the Priory's founder, Pierre Plantard, provided to a group of academics documents "proving" a bloodline descended from Mary and Jesus, through several French monarchs, and down to Plantard himself. The result was *The Holy Blood and the Holy Grail* (1982), by Michael Baigent, Richard Leigh, and Henry Lincoln, a book cited as evidence within *The Da Vinci Code*.[6] These appear to be the documents which Brown refers to as "Fact," yet he neglects to mention that Plantard – and hence *Holy Blood, Holy Grail* – was thoroughly debunked not long afterward, and Plantard admitted his forgeries and Priory of Sion scheme in court. The Bibliothèque nationale retains the forgeries used as sources by Baigent et al., as well as others discovered in a police raid of Plantard's home which "proved," among other things, the criminal to be the rightful king of France.[7]

In his "Acknowledgements," Brown continues his false authority. He first includes a dizzying list of the world-renowned authorities in art and architecture and the documents he references in his novel, but does not say in what capacity they assisted him. Moreover, a consultation of the resources from the Louvre, the Bibliothèque nationale, and the other authorities he mentions *disproves* the novel's assumptions. Brown also thanks his wife, "art historian, painter, and front-line editor," but never confirms her professional acceptance of his interpretations of Da Vinci's works, which, on the contrary, run afoul of accepted academic evaluation. Finally, Brown "encodes" in the synopsis of the novel on the book jacket the rather cryptic message "Is there no help for the widow's son," using discreetly bold letters that might well be taken as typesetting errors. The widow, it would seem, is Mary and her son Jesus. Other rather fantastic anagram solutions to

---

[6]   Michael Baigent, Richard Leigh, and Henry Lincoln, *The Holy Blood and the Holy Grail* (London: Jonathan Cape, 1982).

[7]   James Garlow, *Cracking the Da Vinci Code* (Colorado Springs: Victor, 2004), 112–13.

the bolded letters provided by Brown's fans offer equally suggestive messages. Whatever the "solution," if indeed there is one, what is important is that Brown has apparently hidden secret (and sacred) information, much as, in the *Da Vinci Code*, Leonardo encoded clues in his paintings. From the very core of the story to the front and back matter and even the book's cover, Brown maintains his false medieval authority to support present-day conspiracy theories, new-age Goddess worship, and disaffection with the Roman Catholic Church. The effectiveness of this technique lies in the fact that so many believed it that "Da Vinci Code" tours were set up, and people visited key locations in his fiction to confirm the book's assertions. Moreover, sales of *Holy Blood, Holy Grail* skyrocketed for several years after the publication of *The Da Vinci Code*. Since the former offers no disclaimers, the authors being victims of Plantard's forgeries, it continues to masquerade as an academic study of historical truth.

Practicing medievalism to construct false authority for patently non-medieval ideologies in fiction is likely to maintain its rapid pace, as the proliferation of medievally themed stories, graphic novels, and films indicates. Yet contemporary practice has become even further removed from the historical Middle Ages. Just as Dan Brown's novel has, without factual basis, become an authority on the period for popular audiences, so elsewhere in popular culture has neopaganism earnestly adopted early nineteenth- and twentieth-century re-imaginings of ancient Celtic beliefs as foundational, such as those presented in Marion Zimmer Bradley's *The Mists of Avalon* (1982).[8] In other words, conscious recreations of the era have bred further *un*conscious re-imaginings, beginning a chain of self-perpetrating self-deception in justifying contemporary beliefs by non-existent medieval roots. Whether one considers this acceptable or not, it is evidence of the effectiveness of medievalism as a practice for developing and understanding contemporary ideologies and of the Middle Ages' unbroken association with authority.

### Further Reading

Cantor, Norman. *Inventing the Middle Ages*. New York: William Morrow, 1991.
Eco, Umberto. *Travels in Hyperreality*. Trans. William Weaver. New York: Harcourt Brace, 1986.
Miller, Jacqueline. *Poetic License: Authority and Authorship in Medieval and Renaissance Contexts*. New York: Oxford University Press, 1986.
Morgan, Gwendolyn. *The Invention of False Medieval Authority as a Literary Device in Popular Fiction*. Lewistown, NY: Edwin Mellen, 2006.
Russell, Jeffrey Burton. *Dissent and Order in the Middle Ages: The Search for Legitimate Authority*. New York: Twayne, 1992.

### Related Essays in this Volume

Authenticity, Christianity, Play, Heresy, Memory, Lingua, Monument, Continuity, Transfer

---

[8]   Marion Zimmer Bradley, *The Mists of Avalon* (New York: Del Rey, 1982).

# 4

# Christianity

*William C. Calin*

W<small>E HAVE LEARNED</small> from structuralism that no intellectual construct can be comprehended as a monad, unique and self-sufficient, independent from all others. On the contrary, any such construct will be bound to other constructs, often in a binary position of identity or antithesis. Consequently, the notion of a Christian Middle Ages – simple, unproblematic, uniform, communal – is meaningful, indeed can exist, only when contrasted with its binary antithesis, the Renaissance, presumed to be complex, problematic, diverse, individual, and, most of all, secular. The Age of Faith set against the Age of Humanism.

Given that this notion – the simple, unproblematic, Christian Middle Ages – did not exist among the medievals, nor did it exist during the Renaissance, it can be deemed an example of medievalism. It is one of the most important medievalism phenomena, for it determines how many academics and the public at large view the Middle Ages – what it means to them. I propose that, for the most part, modern scholars launched this "myth," and it lives on today.

The people of the Renaissance did not think in these terms at all.

There was no humanist revolution in the Renaissance. The *umanisti* were, first and foremost, schoolteachers. They taught grammar, rhetoric, history, and aesthetics as the increments of a general education. The assumption was always that humanistic studies would develop virtue, would make one a better and more truly Christian person. These Renaissance humanists were all Christian; a number of them were ordained priests. They were, for the most part, apolitical; they relished the contemplative life and endorsed a hereditary or elective monarchy. Oriented toward the past rather than toward the future, to the extent that they held a personal philosophy, it was Christian Neoplatonism. They were text-centered, book people. Finally, they did not envisage the Middle Ages as different from their own time with regard to faith, nor did they either praise or denigrate a Christian Middle Ages.[1]

---

[1] See Hans Baron, *The Crisis of the Early Italian Renaissance*, 2 vols. (Princeton: Princeton University Press, 1955); William J. Bouwsma, *The Interpretation of Renaissance Humanism* (Washington: American Historical Association, 1959), and *The Culture of*

France was the land where great writers of the sixteenth century especially distinguished themselves, sometimes with scorn, from their "Gothic" forebears. François Rabelais denounced scholastic educational practices, and Michel de Montaigne preferred a "teste bien faite" to a "teste bien pleine" – in other words, the process, not the product. Joachim du Bellay and Pierre de Ronsard stated that, to write great literature, one must imitate the poetic forms of classical antiquity. In other words, tragedies and comedies in place of mystery plays and farces, or odes in place of ballades and rondeaux. Franco Simone has identified this sort of posturing as early manifestations of literary history; agreeing with Simone, I would also suggest that what we see are Bloomian strong sons, riddled with the anxiety of influence, eager to slay their fathers and to rely instead upon very distant, dead grandfathers.[2] However, these rebellious strong sons did not berate their forebears for being too Christian. How could they when they were Christian themselves?

The separation of the Middle Ages from the Renaissance – the break between two purportedly contrasting times – came in the later nineteenth century, along-side reaction to or in reaction to the medieval revival and as one result of the new German sense of *Historismus* (historism or historicism). Those who proclaimed or explored the break or separation in a serious manner were scholars – histo-rians whom today we might think of as gifted amateurs, but who, in their day, earned the respect of a relatively broad public for their scholarly and intellectual endeavors. Such were Jacob Burckhardt, Jules Michelet, and Henry Adams.[3]

On the Continent there was nostalgia for the Middle Ages, but quite often joy that at last those dark years were giving way to the first stirrings of Enlightenment coming from Italy. In the English-speaking world, apart from Ruskin, the most prevalent attitude was nostalgia for a premodern time which was, as Lee Patterson calls it, "universalist, institutional, and deeply conservative." Various major figures, including Scott, Coleridge, Wordsworth, Carlyle, and Disraeli, "celebrated the Middle Ages as a time when a harmonious society was held together by bonds of common faith and an unquestioned social order."[4]

Patterson cites a quatrain by one Sir John Manners:

> Each knew his place – king, peasant, peer, or priest –
> The greatest owned connection with the least;

---

*Renaissance Humanism* (Washington: American Historical Association, 1973); and Paul Oskar Kristeller, *Renaissance Thought: The Classic, Scholastic, and Humanist Strains* (New York: Harper and Row, 1961).

[2] Franco Simone, *Storia della storiografia letteraria francese* (Torino: Bottega d'Erasmo, 1969).

[3] Jacob Burckhardt, *Die Kultur der Renaissance in Italien: Ein Versuch* (Basel: Schweighauser, 1860), *The Civilization of the Period of the Renaissance in Italy*, trans. S. G. C. Middlemore, 2 vols. (London: C. K. Paul, 1878); Jules Michelet, *Histoire de France*, 19 vols (Paris: Lacroix, 1876); Henry Adams, *Mont-Saint-Michel and Chartres* (Boston: Houghton Mifflin, 1904).

[4] Lee Patterson, *Negotiating the Past: The Historical Understanding of Medieval Literature* (Madison: University of Wisconsin Press, 1987), 9.

From rank to rank the generous feeling ran,
And linked society as man to man. (9)

He relates this nineteenth-century *prise de position* to our modern, North American institution of medieval studies: "Whether a physical institution, center, or program, or simply a normative idea of the way work on medieval materials ought to be undertaken, it is by means of Medieval Studies that the fundamentally liberal modern university has accommodated a conservative, institutionalist, and universalist conception of culture" (37).

Patterson then cites Gerhart Ladner, who joys in the affiliation between "the universalist approach to medieval studies" and "the universalism of the Middle Ages" itself, and in the attractiveness of the "supra-individual and supra-political sense of community" purportedly of the Middle Ages (37). Looking at the evolution of medieval studies programs in North America, I believe one cannot but notice the privileging of Latin over the vernaculars, even over Old French, and the privileging of philosophy and theology over much of the rest.

Also related to the evolution of medieval studies programs in North America, in the second half of the nineteenth century the Catholic Church underwent a powerful turn to the Middle Ages, in reaction to modernity in general and, more particularly, to modernist tendencies in the Church. Hence, Pope Leo XIII's encyclical *Aeterni Patris*, which made Thomism – the thirteenth-century scholastic philosophy and theology of St. Thomas Aquinas – the official doctrine of Catholicism.[5] Aquinas's work was taught systematically in American Catholic colleges up to the Vatican II Council and beyond. Significantly, the first and still most important center for medieval studies in North America is the Pontifical Institute at the University of Toronto, its *genius loci* for many years the great Catholic Thomist philosopher and theologian Étienne Gilson.

Patterson also posits the deep affiliation of medieval studies as an institution to the allegorical or exegetical or Robertsonian approach to the study of medieval literature. The exegetical approach was dominant, in English departments, for a good two generations.[6] To paraphrase D. W. Robertson: because of the pervasive Christian culture of the Middle Ages, and more particularly, the pre-eminent position of St. Augustine, all serious medieval literature speaks for *caritas* and against *cupiditas* or *concupiscentia*. If a medieval book appears not specifically to promote *caritas*, either it really does and is meant to be read ironically, or it does not and consequently cannot be serious. On *fin'amor* he writes: "I have never been convinced that there was any such thing as what is usually called courtly love during the Middle Ages" and "The study of courtly love [...] has nothing

---

[5]  See Richard Utz, "Pi(o)us Medievalism vs. Catholic Modernism: The Case of George Tyrell," *The Year's Work in Medievalism* 25 (2010): 6–11.

[6]  The foundational texts are D. W. Robertson, Jr., *A Preface to Chaucer: Studies in Medieval Perspectives* (Princeton: Princeton University Press, 1962); and Bernard F. Huppé and D. W. Robertson, Jr., *Fruyt and Chaf: Studies in Chaucer's Allegories* (Princeton: Princeton University Press, 1963). See also Robertson, "The Concept of Courtly Love as an Impediment to the Understanding of Medieval Texts," in *The Meaning of Courtly Love*, ed. F. X. Newman (Albany: State University of New York Press, 1968), 1–18.

to do with the Middle Ages, and its use as a governing concept can only be an impediment to our understanding of medieval texts."[7] This must be the case because no medieval Christian author could possibly have encouraged his public to indulge in idolatrous passion, in irrational concupiscence. To quote Robertson: "the dominance of the church in the Middle Ages considerably simplifies the task of the historical critic" (cited by Patterson, 6).

The reaction against these assumptions came also from English departments. This took the form of denying the unicity, the privileged otherness, of the Middle Ages vis-à-vis the rest, and more specifically the Renaissance. C. S. Lewis stated openly, as a student and as a don, "I think I have succeeded in demonstrating that the Renaissance, as generally understood, never existed" and that "the Renaissance never happened in England. Alternatively that if it did, it had no importance."[8] By saying this, Lewis wished in no way to denigrate the sixteenth century. On the contrary, the Renaissance was, for him, a period which at its best prolonged and embellished so much of the best that is medieval. In sum, he exalted the Renaissance by emphasizing its medievalness.

Patterson observes that "the text produced by such an exegesis perfectly replicates the [purported] form of medieval culture as a whole, for it subordinates a wide range of disparate and potentially conflicting elements to the authority of an abstract *sententia*. And nothing of course, could be more totalizing than the fact that the *sententia* is always and everywhere the same ..." (32). This is what I would like to call the heresy of universal zeitgeist.

Here I speak not only as the chronicler of this dispute but also as a participant in it, as, if you will, the investigating subject of the subject of investigation. Inspired by Lewis, I have published meditations on the continuity between the Middle Ages and the Renaissance: traits presumed to be hallmarks of the new times – a passion for classical letters; the desire to embellish contemporary writing with Greco-Roman myth; a rich, lusty enjoyment of love, life, and nature; the exploration of subjectivity; and the exaltation of man in his secular destiny – these are all amply manifest in the twelfth and succeeding centuries. Quite a few so-called medieval practices – alchemy, astrology, allegory, typology, even witchcraft (especially witchcraft), not to speak of feudal loyalty, honor, chivalry, and heroism – extend well into the seventeenth century. Petrarchan love is nothing other than good old-fashioned medieval *fin'amor*, dressed up a little in Venetian carnival garb.[9] We have come to recognize the existence of the two cultures – the ecclesiastic and the feudal aristocratic – which influenced each other and which thrived together during the Middle Ages. I would suggest that they continued to thrive together until the Age of Voltaire.

---

[7]   Robertson, "Concept," 1, 17.

[8]   See Clive Staples Lewis, *English Literature in the Sixteenth Century (Excluding Drama)* (Oxford: Oxford University, Clarendon Press, 1954). The quotations are cited by William Calin, *The Twentieth-Century Humanist Critics: From Spitzer to Frye* (Toronto: University of Toronto Press, 2007), 86.

[9]   Calin, *In Defense of French Poetry: An Essay in Revaluation* (University Park: Pennsylvania State University Press, 1987), 154–7.

When would the break which separates Lewis's Old Western culture from our modernity have then occurred? Some propose 1650, others, including Lewis, say sometime in the nineteenth century, perhaps with the advent of Lord Byron and Charles Dickens, or, from a French perspective, with Gustave Flaubert and Charles Baudelaire. One paradigm of the *Annales* school of historians states that the end of the Middle Ages coincides with the French Revolution.

In French studies the Robertsonian approach never caught on, perhaps because there are so many obviously secular-feudal-aristocratic texts: many of the 100 *chansons de geste*, most of the over 100 courtly romances, all twenty-four branches of the *Roman de Renart*, all the 150 fabliaux, all twelve volumes of the late medieval farces, all the several thousand courtly lyrics. And perhaps because French medievalists read English only when they are forced to do so. If in France there is a popular stereotype concerning the Middle Ages, it would be that the Middle Ages is primitive (as in "medieval torture" or "medieval hygiene") rather than that it is universally Christian. This is the message of Régine Pernoud in *Pour en finir avec le Moyen Âge*.[10] Of course, it is possible that by positing the Middle Ages as primitive, Christianity can then be assumed as a matter of course.

So, Lewis debunks the myth of the uniquely Christian Middle Ages. Patterson debunks the myth. Even Calin debunks the myth. And Robertsonianism has gone the way of all flesh, nowadays discredited or, still worse, ignored. Yet, in North America at least, the myth persists. Why?

There are many explanations. I propose three.

First there is the inertia of received ideas. Scholars write for other scholars. It can take years, generations even, for their findings to reach the general public. The scholars are so specialized that even their close colleagues and friends will be unaware of what they are doing. For example, since the 1950s, we in the scholarly community have been aware of the extraordinarily rich literature, art, and music of the French Baroque. Has the average educated, cultured Parisian, or, for that matter, the average teacher of French, heard of the French Baroque? Most probably not.

Second, there is the continued influence of specialists in the Renaissance. In *Is Literary History Possible?* David Perkins argues that literary history must be structured by and according to an implied narrative.[11] The implied narrative proceeds from a beginning to an end, almost always underscoring the complexity of the evolution to the summit (the end) and oversimplifying the origins (the beginning) from which the evolution is derived. Most monographs or syntheses, for that matter, devoted to a century, a movement, or a current will attribute admirable qualities to the century/movement/current and significantly less admirable qualities to the preceding century/movement/current from which it arose. Add to this the fact that most scholars favor their own field of research while remaining to

[10] Régine Pernoud, *Pour en finir avec le Moyen Âge* (Paris: Seuil, 1977), *Those Terrible Middle Ages: Debunking the Myths*, trans. Anne Englund Nash (San Francisco: Ignatius Press, 2000).

[11] David Perkins, *Is Literary History Possible?* (Baltimore: Johns Hopkins University Press, 1992).

some extent uninformed about other fields, perhaps a generation or two out of date. Hence, the studies on the Renaissance or the early modern (for our purposes they are the same) which still proclaim any number of modern-seeming traits in the sixteenth century – subjectivity, agency, individual psychology, political and social awareness, consciousness of gender – set off against the Christian, unproblematic, uniform Middle Ages.

Finally, there is political and religious nostalgia. More than one conservative movement in the twentieth century exploited the notion of a simple, organic, and Christian society – the Middle Ages – as the justification for their movement and as the goal which they sought to attain. Examples would be the fetishization of racial purity in Nazi Germany, and in both Germany and Portugal the fetishization of sexual purity and the desire to attain a good, desirable primitive life, in contrast to the decadence in the French Republic. We saw above that for the Catholic Church the ideal was to be found in thirteenth-century scholasticism. Those who deplore the materialism, alienation, and secularization of contemporary society will quite often act on the assumption that at some time in the past society was spiritual, communal, and open to the sacred. For many Evangelicals this was the age of Luther and Calvin or the age of the Puritan settlements in America; for most others it was the Middle Ages.

And the future? One of the more exciting aspects of medievalism is the way our conception of the Middle Ages and our attitude towards it – for that matter, our conception of and attitude towards the historical past – evolve in time. For the American mass public, the Middle Ages lies in the Society for Creative Anachronism, medieval/Renaissance faires, and the cultural artifacts perpetrated by Hollywood. According to Michael A. Cramer, Benjamin Nugent:

> suggests that the Society for Creative Anachronism's creation of an alternate world with its own rules and hierarchies is quintessentially American: "The original American Dream, for the pilgrims, for the immigrant hordes, was to construct a new country that gave them the respect and possibility the old one couldn't. Isn't that what the SCA is doing?"[12]

I should add that North America offers a relatively affluent middle class with sufficient leisure to counter the alienation and reification of modernity by living the alternate world. So, too, for that other quintessentially American institution – Wicca.

Significantly, the index to Cramer's book contains no entry concerning religion, Christianity, and the churches (except for the Church of Satan). Also, at the American medieval faires are to be found a king and queen who are expected to speak with an English accent. There will also be dukes and duchesses, and knights and ladies, but rarely Christian monks, priests, or bishops. This Middle

---

[12] Michael A. Cramer, *Medieval Fantasy as Performance: The Society for Creative Anachronism and the Current Middle Ages* (Lanham, MD: Scarecrow Press, 2010), 13, where he discusses and quotes from Benjamin Nugent, *American Nerd: The Story of My People* (New York: Scribner, 2008), 180.

Ages is expanding and all-consuming. It devours the Renaissance/early modern, the Baroque, and the Classical – all periods which do not speak to the popular imaginary. One day it may well be The Past, the only historical past aside from the Bible and the American Revolution, in that imaginary. And because Hollywood is afraid of religion, and overtly hostile to Christianity, that Middle Ages may well be strictly heroic, chivalrous, aristocratic, and secular.

## Further Reading

Calin, William. "Defense and Illustration of *Fin'Amor*: Some Polemical Comments on the Robertsonian Approach." In *The Expansion and Transformations of Courtly Literature*. Ed. Nathaniel B. Smith and Joseph T. Snow. Athens: University of Georgia Press, 1980. 32–48

Cummings, Brian, and James Simpson, eds. *Cultural Reformation: Medieval and Renaissance in Literary History*. Oxford: Oxford University Press, 2010.

Davis, Kathleen. *Periodization and Sovereignty: How Ideas of Feudalism and Secularization Govern the Politics of Time*. Philadelphia: University of Pennsylvania Press, 2008.

Emery, Elizabeth. *Romancing the Cathedral: Gothic Architecture in Fin-de-siècle French Culture*. Albany: State University of New York Press, 2001.

Flanagan, Sabina. *Doubt in an Age of Faith: Uncertainty in the Long Twelfth Century*. Turnhout: Brepols, 2008.

Muldoon, James, ed. *Bridging the Medieval-Modern Divide: Medieval Themes in the World of the Reformation*. Aldershot, UK: Ashgate, 2013.

Simmons, Clare A. *Reversing the Conquest: History and Myth in Nineteenth-Century British Literature*. New Brunswick: Rutgers University Press, 1990.

## Related Essays in this Volume

Reenactment, Heresy, Purity, Primitive, Middle, Authenticity, Authority, Trauma, Gothic, Troubadour, Lingua, Love, Memory, Continuity, Modernity, Myth

# 5

# Co-disciplinarity

*Jonathan Hsy*

THINKING CRITICALLY ABOUT medievalism invites us to reassess the boundaries of modern academic disciplines and explore manifold conceptual approaches to the past. On their most basic level, studies of medievalism require cognitive multitasking – a sort of channel-flipping orientation toward time. That is, scholars who study medievalism enact modes of inquiry that sustain *at the very least* two temporal mindsets at once. First, they attend to how works (literature, art, music) were understood and used in their own time. Second, they investigate how people in *later* periods (including the present) engage with or recreate such materials.

In order to investigate a diverse range of cultural productions that engage with some notions of the past, academic studies of medievalism span a number of established disciplines and modes of inquiry: literary criticism, art history, and cinema studies, to name just a few. In this essay, I would like to posit "co-disciplinarity" as a key feature of medievalism studies within the academy but also outside of it. By this term co-disciplinarity, I do not simply refer to more familiar "multidisciplinary" or "cross-disciplinary" models of scholarly teamwork in which two or more people trained in different disciplines join forces to examine a shared object with the benefit of their respective interpretive skill sets. In this model of interaction, for instance, a literary scholar and an art historian might examine Pre-Raphaelite paintings that incorporate allusions to medieval narratives. For the purposes of this discussion, co-disciplinarity entails a shared intellectual and creative zone. Co-disciplinarity is a feature of any institutional, non-academic, or virtual space that allows an individual or a group of people to test the very conventions of academic disciplines and to experiment across diverse modes of artistic production.

This consideration of co-disciplinarity takes medievalism's conspicuous concurrence of temporalities as its conceptual starting point. Pivoting from a recent turn in medievalism studies that breaks down conceptual distinctions between professional (i.e., academic) medievalist scholarship and so-called "amateur" modes of medievalism, I emphasize the sense of "queer time" that medievalism so often engenders. In this essay, I reflect on current developments in medievalism scholarship, and also offer a kind of manifesto outlining unrealized possibilities. Namely, I posit that both medievalism *and* medievalism studies serve a shared, important function: they dynamically queer and reorient institutionalized academic disciplines and practices. In my view, the continued thriving of medievalism studies depends on its capacity to transform and adapt. Medieval studies explores both affective *and* intellectual modes of cross-identification with the past, and it facilitates intimate exchange between seemingly unlikely disciplinary bedfellows.

For people who are new to medievalism studies, the precise relevance of queer theory to this field might seem a little obscure. Queer theory, first of all, is a dynamic field of academic inquiry that has become increasingly invested in rethinking stable and safely partitioned notions of time. Queer theory's intense interrogation of temporality and the boundaries between historical periods is the main feature that makes it resonate so strongly with medievalism studies. Contemporary queer theorists, such as Lee Edelman, Judith (or Jack) Halberstam, José Muñoz, and Kathryn Boyd Stockton, have interrogated received histories of gender, sexuality, and desire.[1] In the process of analyzing literary works and other forms of popular culture, they encourage flexible notions of temporality that move beyond a normative, progressive unfolding of linear time. Other queer theorists, rather than positing new *models* of time, stress the fluidity of cross-temporal modes of identification and examine how a queer *experience* of time registers as multiple and heterogeneous.[2] In all its variety, contemporary queer theory amply demonstrates that time need not be conceived as entirely straight – in all senses of the word.

Participating in these ongoing conversations in queer theory, Carolyn Dinshaw has recently made an important intervention in rethinking the temporality of medieval studies itself. She elegantly posits that the amateur medievalist (that is, the non-academic non-professional) experiences time in a profoundly queer way. In her study, entitled *How Soon Is Now?* (2012), Dinshaw shows how the amateur's love of things medieval actually implicates the desires of professional medievalists.[3] While admitting she is well established in the academy as a tenured scholar "professionally trained as a medievalist," Dinshaw nonetheless confesses: "I feel a kinship with the amateur that I can only call queer" (32). This admission is not made solely on identitarian grounds. "I am a queer – a dyke and only sort of white," Dinshaw discloses, and "[b]ecause I am a medievalist ... studying the Middle Ages is, finally, about desire – for another time, for meaning, for life" (32). Dinshaw astutely observes that medievalism and medievalist scholarship are both always/already implicated in a deep desire to know, understand, and in many cases *experience* being in another time.

---

[1]    Lee Edelman, *No Future* (2004); Judith Halberstam, *In a Queer Time and Place* (2005) and (as Jack Halberstam) *The Queer Art of Failure* (2011); José Muñoz, *Cruising Utopia* (2009); Kathryn Boyd Stockton, *The Queer Child* (2009).
[2]    Elizabeth Freeman, *Time Binds* (2010); Sylvia Freccerco, *Queer/Early/Modern* (2006).
[3]    Carolyn Dinshaw, *How Soon is Now?: Medieval Texts, Amateur Readers, and the Queerness of Time* (New York: New York University Press, 2012).

In light of Dinshaw's observations, I would assert that co-disciplinarity functions as an interpretive and creative *orientation* that does not just mark an "affective turn" in the field of medievalism studies. Rather, it articulates how medievalism studies harnesses the *interpretive skills* of many academic disciplines concurrently. Inhabiting two temporalities simultaneously, medievalism studies seeks to "get inside the head" of medieval culture as much as it transforms modern understandings of that past. By enacting two-minded modes of cross-temporal analysis, medievalism studies can dynamically blur the boundaries of discrete academic disciplines as well.

In her influential work *Getting Medieval* (1999), Dinshaw adroitly enacts such a blurring of time and disciplinary orientations. She brings long-established historicist modes of medievalist training such as manuscript studies, close reading, and philology (study of the development of language) into conversation with conspicuously present-oriented approaches to reader reception, gay and lesbian cultural studies, and critical theory. One informative example of how a cross-temporal approach to medieval culture queers disciplinary approaches is Dinshaw's discussion of a late fourteenth-century Latin document recounting the confession of John (Eleanor) Rykener, a biologically male Londoner who dressed as a woman and was interrogated for prostitution and other transgressions at the Guildhall. Dinshaw begins consideration of this medieval text by placing it in conversation with texts of its "own" time, namely contemporaneous literary works by the medieval Londoner and poet Geoffrey Chaucer. Dinshaw's turn to literary analysis then pivots to a discussion of discourses of sexuality, and Dinshaw's conjoined analysis of literary texts and historical documents subsequently blurs the dividing line between the medieval past and the present. She reveals profound interconnections among medieval discourses of sodomy, the notoriously sexually ambiguous character of Chaucer's Pardoner, *and* political aspects of modern gay identity formation.

In traversing the past and present-day identity formations, Dinshaw evinces a "queer touch" and "'felawshipe' across time" that encompasses both the "queer historian" *and* her/his archive of medieval texts.[4] Studies of medieval culture like Dinshaw's thus engage in a cross-temporal simultaneity. They enact modes of historicist forms of scholarship mindful of past cultures and states of mind while also engaging with the most cutting-edge trends in critical discourse in the present. More profoundly, such work demonstrates how cross-temporal engagement can only be achieved once disciplinary approaches and a wide range of analytical tools are co-implicated and work to inform one another.

This dynamic co-operation of disciplinary orientations within one academic monograph not only blurs the perceived boundaries between past and present. It also renders porous the boundaries between a research-oriented academy and an activist political world outside of it. Rather than enacting a form of literary criticism that stays safely within its institutional and disciplinary confines, Dinshaw's queer

---

[4] Carolyn Dinshaw, *Getting Medieval: Sexualities and Communities, Pre- and Postmodern* (Durham: Duke University Press, 1999), ch. 2, "Good Vibrations: John/Eleanor, Dame Alys, the Pardoner, and Foucault," 101–42.

and co-disciplinary orientation generates a new concurrent mode of engaging with the past. It powerfully inhabits the medieval past while also resonating with a community of present-day gay, lesbian, and queer readers.

The pervasive co-disciplinarity of medievalism studies is perhaps most noticeable in *collaborative* multi-voiced endeavors, including essay collections that widen their scope beyond literary texts to other forms of media. In *Queer Cinema Medievalisms* (2009), co-editors Kathleen Coyne Kelly and Tison Pugh conjoin queer theory, film studies, and textual analysis of medieval works. They assert that "bad cinematic history" can expose how cultural adaptations and modern storytelling strategies reenact the past, and such "cinematic representations of the Middle Ages provide [insights] into contemporary understandings of gender, sexuality and identitarian forms." More importantly, such cinema can create another "Middle Ages," a flexible and ludic "space for reflection and reinvention unfettered from the demands of historical accuracy and charges of anachronism."[5] In charting new theoretical territory, Kelly and Pugh yoke together the two seemingly nonrelated terms *queer* and *movie medievalism*, and they show how "queer theory is a useful mode" for interrogating modern engagements with the past. This is "in part because queer theory has the power to disrupt our notion of linearity and of a differentiating temporality (that is, how difference might be experienced as past/present/future)" (1–2).

Such manifold queer medievalisms can reveal how professional medievalists construct the past through conditions of their own lived experience, including (at times) identitarian politics. Even conventional historicist approaches offering an apparently straight analysis of medievalist scholarship can nonetheless disrupt disciplinary expectations. Through a form of biographical criticism that accommodates a non-specialist reading audience, Norman F. Cantor shows in his study *Inventing the Middle Ages* (1991) how prominent twentieth-century scholars envisioned the medieval past by drawing from their own respective historical circumstances.[6] Each scholar *invents* (constructs) his or her own vision of the Middle Ages in a way that is deeply informed by gendered, national, religious, and political influences. The devoutly Christian C. S. Lewis and J. R. R. Tolkien worked in the wake of wars that radically transformed Britain and found in medieval literature a route for imagining ethically inspiring alternate worlds; David Knowles, Catholic convert and later Benedictine monk, delved into pre-Reformation monasticism in England; Marc Bloch, a French Jew who died in the Resistance against Nazi occupation, questioned medieval systems of class and power; Eileen Power, one of the few prominent female medievalists of her time and a woman of middle-class ancestry, attended in sensitive ways to the lived experiences of medieval women and other everyday people. In writing these compelling accounts of "the great medievalists," Cantor interweaves textual traces that cut across the personal and professional domains a scholar's life story. The construction of a scholar's life

---

[5]    Kathleen Coyne Kelly and Tison Pugh, eds., *Queer Cinema Medievalisms* (Farnham: Ashgate, 2009), xi.
[6]    Norman F. Cantor, *Inventing the Middle Ages: The Lives, Works, and Ideas of the Great Medievalists of the Twentieth Century* (New York: William Morrow, 1991).

disrespects any perceived partition between private letters and business correspondence, or between academic scholarship and creative fiction. Cantor's wide-ranging archive yields a multitasking narrative voice, and he creates a style that flows across the modalities of the historian, literary critic, and even the armchair psychoanalyst.[7]

Cantor's study might appear quite straight in that each chapter unfolds in a linear chronological sequence. Nonetheless, the work's ambitious scope and use of a promiscuous archive models its own kind of co-disciplinary orientation toward the past, and its fluid style resonates at times as queer and unbounded. Cantor's study sets out to uncover how scholars "invented" the Middle Ages, and his orientation toward his archive enacts a deeply *medieval* understanding of the term "invention." The Latin *inventio* is of course derived from *in* + *venire* ("to come across" or discover), and in this context inventing suggests not a spontaneous generation of something entirely new but rather an intimate encounter with materials of the past. In other words, Cantor's seemingly straight and conventional study tracing how modern scholars invented the Middle Ages enacts its own kind of "queer touch" with the past. The project of uncovering how scholars invented the Middle Ages produces a new creative space in the form of Cantor's study. It is a work that presents itself in a straight historicist mode while displaying its own fictive and imaginative features.

What might an appreciation for co-disciplinarity contribute to our discussions of medievalism writ large? For one, co-disciplinarity posits a manifold engagement with the past that does *not* simply re-entrench academic disciplines as we know them. Works in medievalism studies, for instance, can traverse literature and history, or literary criticism and creative fiction. Terms like "inter-disciplinary" and "cross-disciplinary" are useful on practical and administrative levels, but they still have the effect of reinstating the very disciplinary boundaries they strive to transgress. A truly *co*-disciplinary approach to medievalism is a mode of being *with* disciplines that allows for disciplinary orientations to *flow into and through* one another. It is also a mode that queers relations within academic departments and institutional structures. Such a queering process renders more porous the disciplinary and professional communities that take shape within academy, as well as what lies outside of or adjacent to it.

One mode of toying with the notion of what lies inside and outside of disciplinary conventions is creative medievalist fiction and academic parody. In "Parchment Ethics" (2010), a work first delivered as an oral presentation at the Seventeenth Biennial Congress of the New Chaucer Society in Siena, Italy, in July 2010, Bruce Holsinger – informed by animal rights perspectives – provocatively constructs an alternate history for important objects from the medieval past.[8] As if a reporter at a press conference, Holsinger (or rather Holsinger's narrating persona) claims

---

[7]  See for instance Cantor's florid account of the "retarded Oedipal maturation" and "homoerotic disturbance" of the monk and medieval Catholic historian David Knowles (312).

[8]  Bruce Holsinger, "Parchment Ethics: A Statement of More than Modest Concern," *New Medieval Literatures* 12 (2010): 131–6.

he will "announce the results of a series of laboratory experiments on a number of the *Canterbury Tales* manuscripts and other works by Geoffrey Chaucer" (131). He introduces a "leader of my genetics team," a certain "Dr. Lollius" who is "one of the world's experts in paleo-DNA" (133). Dr. Lollius reveals, with "his face pale [and] his hands trembling," that the parchment of these manuscripts derives not from hides of sheep or other creatures (as one would expect) but the skin of *humans* (133). When the presenter goes on to assert that the "original plan to go over the results of our genetic experiments" and thereby "raise a number of ethical questions about parchment vis-à-vis the field of animal studies" has now been effectively derailed, the fictional narrative readily implicates anthropocentric mentalities that *unthinkingly* privilege human lives over those of (nonhuman) creatures.

This playful and provocative fictional narrative interweaves allusions to medieval literature (namely Chaucer's fictive source "Lollius" in *Troilus and Criseyde*) and enacts a satire of academic disciplines: codicology (the scientific study of manuscripts) and historical genetics, most noticeably. All the while, this work inspires ethical reflection in the present moment. Holsinger's forthcoming book on the use of medieval Norse sagas by amateur and professional paleo-climatologists provides another example of co-disciplinary medievalism that resonates strongly in the modern world. This project exposes the scientific appropriation of medieval texts about Arctic (North Atlantic) travel while also challenging those who would deny human agency in global climate change.[9]

Such global orientations demonstrate how readily the medieval past can animate cross-disciplinary work, and other strands in medievalism studies work to break out of narrow national and linguistic frameworks to wider comparative vistas. An increasing number of scholars, for instance, investigate how medievalism takes shape in cultural settings around the globe that do *not* trace their origins back to the medieval West. Postcolonial cultural appropriation of medieval material requires scholars to remain sensitive to *alternate* cultural and political timelines: to adopt, on a local level, a nuanced orientation to far-flung cultures across the globe (Africa, Asia, the Caribbean, Oceana) that did not necessarily experience a "medieval" past in the same way as the nation-states of Western Europe.[10]

Despite all its rich possibilities, one of the significant challenges of co-disciplinarity for any scholar of medievalism is combatting perceptions of dilettantism: the notion that any individual scholar who seeks to traverse disciplinary conventions far beyond his or her perceived disciplinary home is a "Jack of all trades, master of none." When genuine gaps in knowledge or training pose a challenge to the scholar, collaboration and cooperation among people with different

---

[9]   This book is tentatively entitled *The Medieval Optimum: Climate Change and the Making of Denial.*

[10]   See for instance Kathleen Davis and Nadia Altschul, eds., *Medievalisms in the Postcolonial World: The Idea of "the Middle Ages" Outside Europe* (Baltimore: Johns Hopkins University Press, 2009); Michelle R. Warren, *Creole Medievalism: Colonial France and Joseph Bédier's Middle Ages* (Minneapolis: University of Minnesota Press, 2010); and "Transfer," Nadia Altschul's contribution to the present volume.

specialized knowledge domains and different analytical skills become tantamount. The *co-* in the term co-disciplinary can thus foreground the rich positive potential of cooperation, collaboration, and collectivity. An individual scholar lacking the specific linguistic fluencies, relevant cultural background, technical expertise, or archival access to certain materials can combine forces with one or more people who have complementary skills and jointly create and transform knowledge.[11]

While collaboration increasingly characterizes co-edited collections and journal issues, the most radical co-disciplinary endeavors to challenge and remake institutional academic structures have not yet been realized. One encouraging para-academic development is the proliferation of online blogs and social media that create community *precisely* by bridging the Middle Ages and modern world: *In The Middle*, a group medieval studies blog and online community; the BABEL Working Group, a virtual and real-life collective that seeks non-hierarchical forms of association and interaction; *Modern Medieval*, a group blog composed of literary scholars and historians; *Sexy Codicology*, a blog of manuscript studies and digital media with a savvy social media presence and an avid following across platforms; and the online forum associated with *postmedieval: a journal of medieval cultural studies* tied to the journal's multidisciplinary issues on topics such as "Cognitive Alterities/Neuromedievalism" (*postmedieval* 3.3 [Fall 2012]) and "The Medievalism of Nostalgia" (*postmedieval* 2.2 [Summer 2011]). Such a burgeoning of new venues for discussion traverses professional scholarship, contemporary popular culture, and broader issues facing the academy, and they explore ever-expanding frontiers in collaborative digital media and critical theory.

Amateur and para-academic endeavors, meanwhile, uncannily continue to mimic and expose the operations of institutionalized academic methods. Some of the most provocative, avant-garde forms of recreating the Middle Ages in the present effectively repurpose the medievalist's toolkit: for instance, philology inclines away from conventional historicist scholarship and bends toward creative experiments in literary craft, contributing to a multimedia neomedievalism of speculative play that taps into the transformative potentiality of art and language. The Confraternity of Neoflagellants, a visual arts collective, explores such extradisciplinary, speculative practice in *thN Lng folk 2go* (2013). Sporting a title that reinvents Middle English in text-messaging format, this work "draw[s] its heterogeneous approaches from studies in medievalisms, international relations, literary theory, actor-network theory, anthropology, hypereconomics, art history, aesthetics, ecology, cultural theory, cultural geography, ambience, speculative realism and future studies," and was published by punctum books, an open-access and print-on-demand independent publisher directed by Eileen Joy.[12] In a

---

[11]  One example of such a project might be the Global Chaucers project, which seeks to locate, digitally catalog, and analyze all modern translations and adaptations of Chaucer produced in non-Anglophone settings: http://globalchaucers.wordpress.com.

[12]  Confraternity of Neoflagellants (with preface by Simon O'Sullivan), *thN Lng folk 2go* (Brooklyn: punctum books, 2013), http://punctumbooks.com/titles/thn-lng-folk/. In a manifesto published in the open-access journal *continent*, Eileen Joy explains how punctum press – an endeavor initiated by medievalists and early modernists – seeks to

similar media-crossing experiment in medievalism, French-Norwegian language poet Caroline Bergvall has crafted an oeuvre that includes books, performance art, audio recordings, and art installations. Published in the form of printed books and audio recordings, her poetry in "Meddle English" occupies a literary zone between languages. It exhibits a *melding and commingling* of modern English with traces of Middle English, French, and Latin.[13]

Such endeavors demonstrate the sheer range of venues through which inventive medievalism flows, generating new artistic media in an ever-shifting present. What co-disciplinarity enacts as a critical orientation and a strategy of creative engagement with the world is a generative simultaneity of modes and media. It is a lively phenomenon that slips around the many boundaries (disciplinary, linguistic, and vocational) that shape and constrain our everyday lives. In its most utopian manifestations, medievalism studies can foster a capacious notion of community that not only sustains diverse orientations toward the past, but also strives towards ethical, intellectual, and artistically fulfilling transformations in the world(s) we currently inhabit.

## Further Reading

Altschul, Nadia. "Introduction: Creole Medievalism and Settler Postcolonial Studies." In Altschul, *Geographies of Philological Knowledge: Postcoloniality and the Transatlantic National Epic*. Chicago: University of Chicago Press, 2012. 1–30.

Biddick, Kathleen. *The Shock of Medievalism*. Durham: Duke University Press, 1998.

D'Arcens, Louise. "Europe in the Antipodes: Australian Medieval Studies." In *Studies in Medievalism X: Medievalism and the Academy*. Ed. David Metzger. 2000. 13–40.

Eileen Joy. "Disturbing the Wednesday-ish Business-as-Usual of the University Studium: A Wayzgoose Manifest." *continent* 2.4 (2012). 250–68. http://continentcontinent.cc/index.php/continent/article/view/119.

Kelly, Kathleen Coyne, and Tison Pugh. "Queer History, Cinematic Medievalism,

---

"occupy [a] more fluid space [and] also de-territorialize the University itself, disturbing and disrupting … protocols of both the generic university *studium* and its individual cells and holding tanks, [and] extending the very important work of the University into new and often untended [para-academic] spaces" (266). Eileen Joy, "Disturbing the Wednesday-ish Business-as-Usual of the University Studium: A Wayzgoose Manifest," *continent* 2.4 (2012): 250–68, http://continentcontinent.cc/index.php/continent/article/view/119. On the potential *vulnerabilities* of co-disciplinarity and the uncertain forms of co-dependence that can characterize such efforts, see Jonathan Hsy, "Let's FAIL Together, yeah yeah YEAH!" *In The Middle*, 5 October 2012, http://www.inthemedievalmiddle.com/2012/10/lets-fail-together-yeah-yeah-yeah.html.

[13] Caroline Bergvall, *Meddle English: New and Selected Texts* (Callicoon, NY: Nightboat Books, 2011). Voice recordings can be accessed on PennSound: http://www.writing.upenn.edu/pennsound/x/Bergvall.php.

and the Impossibility of Sexuality." In *Queer Cinema Medievalisms*. Ed. Kelly and Pugh. Farnham: Ashgate, 2009. 1–17.

Salih, Sarah. "A Response: Queer Medievalism: Why and Whither?" *Medieval Feminist Forum* 36, 1 (2003). 31–3.

### Related Essays in this Volume

Transfer, Play, Presentism, Love, Humor, Lingua, Archive, Authenticity, Gesture, Reenactment, Trauma

# 6

## Continuity

*Karl Fugelso*

To qualify as a legitimate focus for the study of medievalism a subject must refer to the Middle Ages, yet stand apart from the period. This may seem self-evident, but it glosses over many potential problems with regard to continuity, as demonstrated by illustrations of Dante's *Inferno* 13 in the fourteenth-century Italian manuscript Holkham Miscellanae 48 (Fig. 1), in a watercolor series William Blake began in 1824 and left unfinished at his death in 1827 (Fig. 2), and in Seymour Chwast's 2010 graphic novel *Dante's Divine Comedy* (Fig. 3). All three of these images, which depict harpies roosting on anthropomorphic trees that represent the suicidal, come from series that have been discussed in publications such as *Medievally Speaking: Medievalism in Review* and *The Year's Work in Medievalism*.[1] Yet all three of these illustrations portray a text (Dante's *Commedia*) that may not be medieval, and they do so in ways that depart from even the broadest stereotypes about medieval art, which is almost as controversial as the Middle Ages itself.

David Matthews proposes that the Middle Ages is ultimately a series of post-medieval constructs.[2] The start of the period is often associated with the collapse of the Roman Empire, but that fall is itself open to interpretation and has been linked to events as far apart in time as the accession of the emperor Diocletian in 284 and the capitulation of the emperor Romulus Augustus in 476.[3] Nor is there a clear end to the Middle Ages, as feudalism and many other traits associated with the period did not go out with a bang, much less in synchronicity.

---

[1]  See, for example, Karl Fugelso, "Chwast, *Dante's Divine Comedy*: A Graphic Adaptation," *Medievally Speaking* (28 January 2011), http://medievallyspeaking.blogspot.com/2011/01/chwast-dantes-divine-comedy-graphic.html, and Karl Fugelso, "Time and Influence in Illustrations of Dante's *Divine Comedy*," *The Year's Work in Medievalism* 21 (2006): 140–54.

[2]  David Matthews, "Middle," in the present volume. See also Karl Fugelso, "Problems with Continuity: Defining the Middle Ages for Medievalism Studies," *Perspicuitas*, http://www.uni-due.de/imperia/md/content/perspicuitas/fugelso_continuity.pdf.

[3]  For a survey of 200 sources on theories about the collapse of the Roman Empire, see Alexander Demandt, *Der Fall Roms: Die Auflösung des römischen Reiches im Urteil der Nachwelt* (Munich: Beck, 1984).

1. The Suicides, *Inferno* 13, by an anonymous Italian, c. 1350–75.

2. William Blake, *The Wood of the Self-Murderers: The Harpies and the Suicides*, 1824–27.

3. Canto 13 in the *Inferno*, from Seymour Chwast's *Dante's Divine Comedy: A Graphic Adaptation.*

(Indeed, some writers claim that the Middle Ages continues in places like Mali and Bangladesh,[4] and many scholars have defended the continuity thesis, which holds that the intellectual development of the Middle Ages carried on through at least the Renaissance and/or early modern period.[5]) Moreover, few, if any, traits have been unanimously identified as medieval.[6] While William Manchester recently characterized the era as "A World Lit Only by Fire," other writers portray it as a highly heterogeneous period enlightened by a wealth of inherited knowledge, a great desire to expand on it, and considerable progress in doing so.[7]

More than one of these scholars at least partly bases that interpretation on the *Commedia*, which was begun after its author's exile from Florence in 1302 and presumably completed by his death in 1321.[8] Though this is rather late to qualify for the Italian Middle Ages, Dante echoes *Tundale's Vision* (c. 1150) and other quintessentially "medieval" works in which the protagonist experiences the divine but does not necessarily do so in the flesh.[9] Moreover, as Dante privileges the Christian community over himself by repeatedly and overtly submitting himself to the will of God, he deploys a trope long characterized as medieval.[10] In blatantly alluding to many earlier texts, he also participates in a literary tradition that took root in antiquity but greatly expanded during the twelfth and thirteenth centuries.[11]

Yet Dante worked during the age of Giotto, who visually articulated the *Inferno* in the Arena Chapel (1305) and is celebrated in Giorgio Vasari's *Lives of the Artists* (1550) as the first truly modern artist.[12] Moreover, Dante wrote the *Commedia* not

---

[4]   For interesting examples of such characterization with regard to Mali, see Rabia Gregory, "Our own Orientalism: Why Medievalists are Complicit when Manuscripts Burn and Ruins Crumble," posted 10 February 2013 on *Modern Medieval: The Middle Ages Still Have Something to Say*, http://modernmedieval.blogspot.com/2013/02/our-own-orientalism-why-medievalists.html (last accessed 23 July 2013), and posted 12 February 2013 on *ISLAMi Commentary*, http://islamicommentary.org/2013/02/rabia-gregory-our-own-orientalism-why-medievalists-are-complicit-when-manuscripts-burn-and-ruins-crumble/ (last accessed 29 July 2013).

[5]   See Arun Bala, *The Dialogue of Civilizations in the Birth of Modern Science* (New York: Palgrave Macmillan, 2006).

[6]   See Fugelso, "Problems with Continuity."

[7]   Manchester's phrase is the title of his enormously popular survey of the Middle Ages (New York: Little, Brown and Company, 1992), which resists more progressive views found in other recent surveys of the period or of some aspect of it, such as Henry Luttikhuizen and Dorothy Verkerk's second edition of *Snyder's Medieval Art* (Upper Saddle River, NJ: Prentice Hall, 2006).

[8]   See, for example, Michael Camille, *Gothic Art: Glorious Visions* (New York: Harry N. Abrams, 1996), 145–6.

[9]   *Visions of Heaven and Hell before Dante*, ed. and trans. Eileen Gardiner (New York: Italica Press, 1989).

[10]   Such treatment of the trope is found throughout many surveys of one or more aspects of the Middle Ages, such as Luttikhuizen and Verkerk, *Snyder's Medieval Art*.

[11]   See, for example, the discussion of those centuries in Alastair Minnis, *Medieval Theory of Authorship: Scholastic Literary Attitudes in the Later Middle Ages* (1984; 2nd ed. Philadelphia: University of Pennsylvania Press, 1988).

[12]   For a highly accessible English version of Giorgio Vasari's "Vita di Giotto," see George Bull's translation in *Lives of the Artists*, 2 vols. (1965; repr. London: Penguin, 1987), I: 57–81.

in Latin, but in the vernacular, which was unprecedented for such an ambitious work about such a lofty subject.[13] Within the discourse allowed by his format, he often dwells on politics, economics, and other matters far from the religiosity that dominates earlier post-classical writing.[14] He departs in important ways from even the broadest characteristics of the Middle Ages as a whole and of medieval literature in particular.

Nor does the Middle Ages fully explain Figures 1–3. By favoring clarity and expression over illusionism in Figure 3, Chwast parallels a great deal of art often classified as medieval. Indeed, he closely echoes many tenth- to twelfth-century miniatures in stripping his subjects to their most essential iconography and portraying it through heavy outlines, black blocks, and occasional patterns of dots or short strokes that simulate texture. But his figures are correct in their proportions, strike feasible poses, overlap in a logical manner, and are often set against a backdrop that revolves around a single vanishing point.

The same cannot always be said for Blake, but he, too, does not entirely privilege clarity and expression over realistic anatomy and convincing space. His extraordinarily muscular protagonist in Figure 2 may seem histrionic as he recoils from a bleeding tree, but neither the figure's pose nor his proportions are impossible. Although some of the background in this and many of Blake's other illustrations is blank, his landscapes are otherwise highly detailed, diminish at a roughly consistent rate into the distance, and revolve around a single vanishing point. Moreover, though his shading is not entirely illusionistic, it is not far from it, and his illustration as a whole is not nearly as linear or monochromatic as Chwast's.

It is also less linear and monochromatic than the Holkham illustration (Figure 1), though the latter joins the Blake and Chwast illustrations in not fully conforming to traditional definitions of medieval art, especially the privileging of expressiveness over illusionism. The third quarter of the fourteenth century is often considered a part of the Italian Middle Ages; the Holkham artist painted this illustration in ink on parchment, a technique often associated with medieval illuminators; his figures sway like those in such stereotypically Gothic works as the Hours of Jeanne d'Evreux (1325–28); and he executed much of it in a rather flat, artificial manner, as his nine harpies line up at almost the same angle in a horizontal row of trees against a blank background. But despite this and the fact that his figures are only a few centimeters high, they have fairly correct proportions, their clothes have realistic folds that somewhat convey the anatomy of the bodies beneath them, and their faces, as well as the bare body of the centaur Nessus at left, are shaded in a consistent manner that approaches Renaissance illusionism.

Yet, even if these illustrations parallel works widely considered in some regard medieval, that parallel may still not represent continuity with the Middle Ages. As in the earlier cases of expressiveness, the category could be too broad (not to mention too subjective) to establish meaningful conclusions. Many works from

[13] Peter Dronke, *Dante and Medieval Latin Traditions* (Cambridge: Cambridge University Press, 1986).

[14] Joan M. Ferrante, *The Political Vision of the "Divine Comedy"* (Princeton: Princeton University Press, 1984).

many different periods, such as the Hellenistic sculpture *Laocoön and His Sons*, could be considered highly expressive, and all art can be considered at least somewhat expressive.

Moreover, even the narrowest parallels, such as (in this instance) particular techniques for favoring two dimensions over three, are often not limited to the Middle Ages. Though the composition of some neolithic paintings accommodates the stone on which they are painted, almost all of their backgrounds are otherwise as empty as those in the Chwast and Holkham illustrations (Figures 3 and 1). Ancient Near Eastern, ancient Egyptian, classical, and Renaissance reliefs, such as Tullio Lombardo's panels for St. Antonio in Padua (c. 1500), favor foreground friezes like that of the Holkham illustration. Mannerist paintings such as Jacopo Pontormo's *Deposition* (1525–28), not to mention Romantic and post-Impressionist works, often privilege effect over anatomically correct proportions and humanly possible poses. And many Western works, such as Käthe Kollwitz's early twentieth-century prints, join Chwast's illustration in limiting their descriptiveness to bold outlines, monochromatic "coloring," symbolic texturing, and other abbreviated, non-illusionistic detailing.

Nor are any of the practices and effects mentioned above, or any others of which I am aware, found in absolutely every known work that is widely seen as medieval. Though this conclusion ultimately rests on the definition of "widely" and "medieval" (not to mention my awareness), the Lewis Chessmen (twelfth century) and Isenheim Altarpiece (1512–16), for example, may be as far apart as any works in any other commonly defined period. And this does not even take into account the fact that many works from the Middle Ages, however we define that period, are no longer extant or recognized as such.

Finally, even if all of these criteria are met, even if there is a highly specific parallel exclusive to every known (and presumably unknown) work ascribed to the Middle Ages, that parallel may still not represent continuity with the period. Instead, it could spring from an identical response to identical circumstances, such as two Western artists illustrating the same text (as is likely the case here). Or it could represent broader anthropological common denominators, such as the fact that most people see two focal points from two eyes approximately an inch apart and five to six feet from the ground. Or it could represent nothing more than coincidence.

Indeed, a combination of these factors would seem to explain the many artistic parallels these three illustrations share not only with medieval art, but also with each other. Beside privileging two-dimensionality and expressiveness, all three depict Virgil and Dante standing at the center of the forest as some of the anthropomorphic trees gaze towards them and as the harpies shriek or chew leaves they have ripped from the suicides. But there are profound differences among the illustrations, such as their media, and none of the artists are likely to have directly known the other works in this series. Though the Holkham illustration appears in a widely disseminated 1969 survey of *Commedia* miniatures,[15] and though Blake's

---

[15] *Illuminated Manuscripts of the "Divine Comedy"*, ed. Peter Brieger, Millard Meiss, and Charles Singleton, 2 vols. (Princeton: Princeton University Press, 1969).

watercolor appears in multiple sources that have been distributed even more widely than that survey,[16] Chwast gives no direct indication in his illustrations, writings, or interviews of having known either predecessor. (In fact, when asked to name all his sources for the illustrations, he mentioned only Henry Francis Cary's early nineteenth-century translation of the *Commedia* and Gustave Doré's mid-nineteenth-century engravings of it.[17]) It is also extremely unlikely that Blake knew the Holkham miniature, for though it was in the Earl of Leicester's library by the early nineteenth century and Blake lived in England at the time, he did not have access to that collection, and, to my knowledge, the miniature had not been reproduced or overtly copied in other images that he could have seen.[18] As may be true of the stylistic parallels these illustrations have with art that has been characterized as medieval, their similarities to each other do not seem to represent even subconscious influence, much less deliberate allusion.

Far easier to prove would seem to be discontinuity, for no two works are exactly the same. Indeed, I have already mentioned numerous ways in which these three illustrations depart from each other and from earlier works as they privilege clarity and expression over illusionism. Moreover, instead of echoing Musée Condé MS 597, whose fifty-nine miniatures date to 1327–28 and treat Dante's narrative as an actual journey through the afterlife, the Holkham artist joins his contemporaries in treating the *Commedia* as a didactic tool, with stiff friezes that unfold from left to right beneath double-line borders and copious labels;[19] Blake paints on paper in a highly layered, rather impressionistic manner with watercolors that appear more viscous than those used by most artists identified as medieval; and Chwast's pen-and-ink drawings on paper join other graphic novels in embedding all text in the images, as he casts the *Commedia* as a film noir, as he portrays Dante in a trench-coat and fedora meeting gangsters, molls, and hucksters while tramping through nightclubs, theaters, and funeral homes.[20]

Yet though these differences clearly distinguish one work from another, they do not necessarily mark the departure of a work from an entire era. As we have seen, the characterization of a period and what has led or may lead to its demise are open to debate.[21] Though the trench-coat and fedora on Chwast's protagonist may not fit many definitions of the Middle Ages, that does not mean they could

---

[16] For example, David Bindman's *The Divine Comedy: William Blake* (Paris: Bibliothèque de l'Image, 2000).

[17] From a private email to me on 13 May 2013.

[18] On the provenance of the Holkham miniatures, see Marcella Roddewig, *Dante Alighieri, "Die göttliche Komödie": Vergleichende Bestandsaufnahme der "Commedia"-Handschriften* (Stuttgart: Hiersemann, 1984), 151–2.

[19] For more on the Musée Condé miniatures in relationship to later fourteenth-century miniatures, including those in Holkham Misc. 48, see my "Historicizing the *Divine Comedy*: Renaissance Responses to a 'Medieval' Text," *The Year's Work in Medievalism* 15 (2000): 83–106.

[20] For details on the film-noir aspects of Chwast's illustrations, see Fugelso, "Chwast."

[21] For a discussion of the linguistics associated with these issues, see Richard Utz, "Coming to Terms with Medievalism," *European Journal of English Studies* 15:2 (2011): 101–13 (103–6).

not fit any, particularly if the Middle Ages is seen as having survived until at least the invention of those accessories. And the very fact that many elements of the *Commedia* fit well with film noir suggests that, at least in some sense, the Middle Ages did indeed last until cinematic anti-heroes started dressing like Sam Spade.

This brings us back to the ways that Figures 1–3 can represent continuity and be considered medievalist. The fact that three such disparate artists who were apparently unaware of each other's portrayal of *Inferno* 13 not only chose to depict it, but also did so in such similar ways demonstrates the enduring legacy of the *Commedia*, of its illustration tradition, and of many tenets in Western art. And though these parallels may not represent direct or deliberate references to the Middle Ages, they and other aspects of the illustrations may nevertheless respond to the Middle Ages via the *Commedia* or other sources. Though Dante's text may not be completely medieval, it participates in many literary and other trends that, as we have seen, stretch back through preceding works often characterized as fully medieval, and unless we are to believe that Chwast, Blake, and the Holkham artist could respond so selectively to the *Commedia* as to avoid this influence, then they, too, must engage the latter. They, too, must have at least some continuity with the Middle Ages.

They may even represent continuity, if not medievalism, in their departures from each other and from "medieval" sources. Continuity can not only coexist with discontinuity, as noted by Stephen Nichols in his introduction to *The New Medievalism*,[22] but also overlap with it, as demonstrated by many of the essays in *Early Modern Medievalisms* and *Resonances*.[23] All changes can be broken down into constituents small enough to have continuity within them, and all changes that revolve around a common denominator, such as responding to the *Commedia*, can be said to constitute a continuity of change. Though Chwast, Blake, and the Holkham illuminator may differ from each other in the expressivity with which they illustrate the *Commedia*, they are linked not only by expressively illustrating it, but also by the very fact that they do not completely agree with each other (or any other illustrators). Their departures from each other and from their apparent sources can be seen as a series that, like all series, represents a degree of continuity.

Finally, we must address the question of whether studying medievalism can, in fact, be considered medievalism. Many scholars maintain that analyzing medievalism is entirely different than practicing it, than responding directly to the Middle Ages.[24] But this presumes that one can study the past without being influ-

---

[22] Stephen G. Nichols, "The New Medievalism: Tradition and Discontinuity in Medieval Culture," in *The New Medievalism*, ed. Marina S. Brownlee, Kevin Brownlee, and Stephen G. Nichols (Baltimore and London: The Johns Hopkins University Press, 1991), 1–27.

[23] *Early Modern Medievalisms: The Interplay between Scholarly Reflection and Artistic Production*, ed. Alicia C. Montoya, Sophie van Romburgh, and Wim van Anrooij (Leiden: Brill, 2010), especially the introduction and first section, "Continuities and Discontinuities"; and *Resonances: Historical Essays on Continuity and Change*, ed. Nils Holger Petersen, Eyolf Østrem, and Andreas Bücker (Turnhout: Brepols, 2011).

[24] Much of this debate has revolved around terminology and has been discussed by, among others, Richard Utz, most notably in "Coming to Terms"; Nils Holger Petersen in, for example, "Medievalism and Medieval Reception: A Terminological Question," in

enced by it linguistically, rhetorically, and otherwise, or at least presumes that one can distinguish between such influence and the study of the past. Moreover, this position does not address the issue of how we would define links in a chain of reactions that lead back to a direct response to the Middle Ages, how we would treat the traces of medievalism that survive not only around, but also within direct analysis of it.[25] Even as we discuss how our subjects are continuous and discontinuous with the Middle Ages, we ourselves participate in these (sorts of) relationships; even as we study medievalism, we become valid subjects for continued (scholarship on) medievalism.

## Further Reading

Brownlee, Marina S., Kevin Brownlee, and Stephen G. Nichols, eds. *The New Medievalism*. Baltimore and London: The Johns Hopkins University Press, 1991.

Fugelso, Karl. "Problems with Continuity: Defining the Middle Ages for Medievalism Studies." *Perspicuitas*, http://www.uni-due.de/imperia/md/content/perspicuitas/fugelso_continuity.pdf.

Montoya, Alicia C., Sophie van Romburgh, and Wim van Anrooij, eds. *Early Modern Medievalisms: The Interplay between Scholarly Reflection and Artistic Production*. Leiden: Brill, 2010.

Petersen, Nils Holger, Eyolf Østrem, and Andreas Bücker, eds. *Resonances: Historical Essays on Continuity and Change*. Turnhout: Brepols, 2011.

Utz, Richard. "Coming to Terms with Medievalism." *European Journal of English Studies* 15:2 (2011). 101–13.

## Related Essays in this Volume

Middle, Authenticity, Primitive, Troubadour, Genealogy, Resonance, Authority, Co-disciplinarity, Christianity, Gesture, Modernity, Transfer

---

*Studies in Medievalism* XVII: *Defining Medievalism(s)*, ed. Karl Fugelso (2009), 36–44; and Elizabeth Emery, "Medievalism and the Middle Ages," in *Studies in Medievalism XVII*, 77–85.

[25] See Fugelso, "Neomedievalism as Revised Medievalism in *Commedia* Illustrations," *The Year's Work in Medievalism* 22 (2008): 55–61, as well as the essays on defining neomedievalism in volumes XIX and XX of *Studies in Medievalism*.

# 7

# Feast

*Martha Carlin*

WHEN ANTIQUARIANS OF the eighteenth and nineteenth centuries first began to investigate the history of medieval food and eating, they stared in appalled fascination at the menus they discovered. It was not the number of dishes that disturbed them, or the heavy preponderance of meat, poultry, game, or fish, for these features remained typical of European dining in wealthy households and on grand occasions. Rather, they were horrified at what they saw as a promiscuous jumble of foods served in a distastefully foreign form. Richard Warner, for example, who in 1791 published an edition of the medieval English recipe collection called the *Forme of Cury*, commented that the fashionable French cooks of Richard II's court, to whom the collection was attributed, "appear to have equaled their descendants of the present day, in the variety of their condiments, and in their faculty of disguising nature, and metamorphosing simple food into complex and non-descript gallimaufries."[1] The French antiquary Alfred Franklin (1830–1917), who published extensively on daily life in medieval Paris, believed that the various dishes that made up each course in a formal medieval meal were heaped together helter-skelter on enormous platters in a "hideous salmagundi" (*affreux salmigondis*).[2]

Such views were not wholly abandoned by scholars until late in the twentieth century, and they continue to color depictions of medieval feasts in popular culture to the present day. So, too, does the Victorian idealization of medieval feasting as representative of a pre-industrial age of gallant knights and beautiful ladies, and the modern belief that medieval feasts were uninhibited food-fights, in which diners slurped, slobbered, belched, fought, and gobbled their way through enormous joints of meat and massive flagons of wine and ale. From Victorian novels to Hollywood films, and from Gary Larson's *Far Side* cartoons to themed restaurants featuring "medieval banquets" complete with jousting, the medieval

---

[1]  Richard Warner, *Antiquitates Culinariae, or Curious Tracts Relating to the Culinary Affairs of the Old English* (London, 1791), xxxii–xxxiii.

[2]  Alfred Franklin, *La Vie privée d'autrefois*, 27 vols. (Paris: E. Plon, 1887–1902), 3 (*La Cuisine*): 47–8.

feast has served as a lens through which people could view the past either as a symbol of lost aristocratic splendor, or as a barbarous but entertaining spectacle.

In medieval Europe, rich and poor alike took a strong interest in feasts. Great feasts were historic occasions, marking major public events such as coronations, royal weddings, or the enthronements of bishops. The cult of celebrity was strong, and people of all ranks enjoyed hearing about the luxuries enjoyed by the wealthy and powerful. In 1354, for example, Henry, duke of Lancaster, wrote that he delighted in devising and recalling feasts, and in hearing descriptions of those that he had not attended.[3] The lavish displays of splendid clothing and jewelry, food and drink, decorations and entertainments were dazzling events for onlookers and guests. To tradespeople and workers, feasts represented profit and employment; to the poor, they offered hope of a distribution of leftovers. Feasts were recorded in chronicles, stories, and songs; they were painted on glass, on walls, and in books; they were declaimed by poets, and derided by moralists.

One of the most spectacular celebrations of medieval England was the enthronement in September 1465 of George Neville as archbishop of York. Pages of menus for the gargantuan meals were copied into at least three cookery collections.[4] Around 1570, during the reign of Queen Elizabeth I (1558–1603), accounts of Neville's feasts were printed in the form of a paper roll together with similar records, including those of the installation of Ralph de Bourne as abbot of St. Augustine's, Canterbury (1309), and the enthronement of William Warham as archbishop of Canterbury (1505). It may have been Archbishop of Canterbury Matthew Parker (1559–75), an antiquarian and collector of medieval manuscripts, who was behind the publication of this roll, which represents one of the earliest postmedieval evocations of medieval feasting.[5] However, Queen Elizabeth herself may have been interested in such matters, for on 27 July 1586 Edward, third baron Stafford, evidently hoping to ingratiate himself with the queen, presented her with a vellum roll of c. 1420–25 containing the *Forme of Cury*, the recipe collection attributed to the master cooks of Richard II (1377–99).[6]

---

[3]    Henry, duke of Lancaster, *Le Livre de seyntz medicines: The Unpublished Devotional Treatise of Henry of Lancaster*, ed. E. J. Arnould, Anglo-Norman Text Society 2 (1940; rpt. 1967), 20, 48.

[4]    The three cookery collections are: Holkham Hall, Norfolk, MS 674, fols. 5v–11r; Society of Antiquaries, London, MS 287, fols. 26v–33r; and *A noble boke of festes royalle and Cokery* (London: Richard Pynson, 1500; STC 3297), sig. a ii, fols. 4–5.

[5]    This was suggested by the English antiquary Thomas Hearne, in *Joannis Lelandi antiquarii de rebus Britannicis collectanea*, ed. Thomas Hearne, 2nd edn., 6 vols. (London, 1770–74; rpt. Westmead, Farnborough, Hampshire: Gregg International Publishers, 1970), 6: 2–40. For a discussion of Hearne's account, see Christopher M. Woolgar, "Fast and Feast: Conspicuous Consumption and the Diet of the Nobility in the Fifteenth Century," in *Revolution and Consumption in Late Medieval England*, ed. Michael A. Hicks (Woodbridge, Suffolk: The Boydell Press, 2001), 7–25 (7, 23–5).

[6]    Stafford added an obsequious note at the foot of the roll (now London, British Library, Additional MS 5016, fol. 4v), recording his gift of "this ancient muniment" to the queen (*Antiquum hoc monumentum oblatum et missum est majestati vestræ vicesimo septimo die mensis Julij, anno regni vestri fœlicissimi vicesimo viij ab humilimo vestro subdito,*

In France, another great fourteenth-century culinary collection, known as the *Viandier* and ascribed to the French royal cook "Taillevent" (Guillaume Tirel, c. 1315–95), went through at least fifteen printed editions between c. 1490 and 1604. The fact that these editions were so full of errors that the recipes would have been incomprehensible to anyone who tried to cook from them suggests that the *Viandier*'s popularity lay more in its antiquity than its utility.[7] In the culinary transformations underway in sixteenth-century Europe, the royal recipes of the *Forme of Cury* and the *Viandier* were rapidly becoming quaint curiosities.

The interest of antiquarians and scholars in medieval food was stimulated by the publication, beginning in the 1690s, of printed catalogues of the manuscripts housed in the great libraries of Europe, including medieval culinary manuscripts.[8] It was probably the English antiquary Thomas Hearne who pioneered the study of medieval cookery around 1727, when he made a transcript of the medieval roll containing the *Forme of Cury* that Lord Stafford had given to Elizabeth I in 1586.[9] Samuel Pegge published his own edition of this in 1780, together with an addendum called "Ancient Cookery" containing a collection of recipes from a commonplace book of c. 1381.[10] In 1790, the Society of Antiquaries of London published a compilation called *A Collection of Ordinances and Regulations for the Government of the Royal Household ... from ... Edward III to ... King William and Queen Mary. Also Receipts in Ancient Cookery*. The following year Richard Warner published a collection of household account rolls and appended to it a copy of Pegge's edition of the *Forme of Cury* and "Ancient Cookery," under the umbrella title of *Antiquitates culinarie; or Curious Tracts Relating to the Culinary Affairs of the Old English*.[11]

---

vestræq[ue] majestati fidelissimo), and signed it "E[dward], Lord Stafford, heir of the ruined house of Buckingham" (*E ᴰ Stafford/Hæres domus subversæ Buckinghamiens[is]*). Constance B. Hieatt and Sharon Butler, eds., *Curye on Inglysch: English Culinary Manuscripts of the Fourteenth Century (Including the Forme of Cury)*, Early English Text Society [hereafter EETS], Supplementary Series 8 (1985), 21. Hieatt and Butler date the roll to "the end of the first quarter of the fifteenth century" (24).

7  For the incomprehensibility of the recipes in these early printed editions of the *Viandier*, and for the number of editions, see [Baron] Jérôme Frédéric Pichon and Georges Vicaire, eds., *Le Viandier de Guillaume Tirel dit Taillevent* (Paris: Techener, 1892), Introduction, iii–iv, lii–lxviii.

8  For citations of medieval cookery manuscripts in catalogues published before 1800, see Constance B. Hieatt, Carole Lambert, Bruno Laurioux, and Alix Prentki, "Répertoire des manuscrits médiévaux," in *Du manuscrit à la table*, ed. Carole Lambert (Paris: Champion-Slatkine, and Montréal: Les Presses de l'Université de Montréal, 1992), 325 (no. 15), 329 (no. 26), 335 (no. 48), 337 (no. 54), 338 (nos. 56–7), 339 (nos. 59–61), 340 (nos. 62–3), 351 (no. 100), 352 (nos. 102–4).

9  At least eight medieval copies or partial copies of this cookbook survive, of which the most complete is London, British Library, Additional MS 5016. See Hieatt and Butler, eds., *Curye on Inglysch*, 20–30.

10  Hieatt and Butler, eds., *Curye on Inglisch*, 17–18.

11  London: Blamire, 1791. On Warner's reprint of Pegge's edition, see Hieatt and Butler, eds., *Curye on Inglysch*, 22. In 1797 John Nichols published a collection of financial accounts that contain many incidental references to the purchase, preparation, and consumption of food, in *Illustrations of the Manners and Expences of Antient Times in England, in the Fifteenth,*

On the Continent, the publication of medieval cookery texts began in the early nineteenth century in Denmark (1826),[12] and then spread to Germany (1844),[13] France (1846),[14] Italy (1863),[15] Belgium (1872),[16] and Spain (1881–82).[17] In England, nineteenth-century antiquarians published an avalanche of medieval household accounts, both private and institutional, from the 1830s on.[18] Studies of table manners and ceremony followed,[19] as did further editions of medieval cookery collections.[20] While such publications were of interest to scholars, middle- and upper-class interest in the Middle Ages grew in response to different trends, including an easing of Protestant suspicion of pre-Reformation culture, resistance to the ubiquitous dominance of Classicism in the arts, and the beginnings of the Industrial Revolution. As the eighteenth century rolled into the nineteenth, as the expanding industrialization, urbanization, and commercialization of society took hold, and as revolutions and revolutionary politics began to shatter age-old monarchical paradigms, the fashion for medievalism as a nostalgic response to the "future shock" of a rapidly changing world spread and grew.

The explosive growth of the popular novel was deeply influential in popular-izing and romanticizing the Middle Ages as a "golden age" that embodied the

---

*Sixteenth, and Seventeenth Centuries, Deduced from the Accompts of Churchwardens, and Other Authentic Documents* (London, 1797; rpt. New York and Millwood, New Jersey, 1973).

[12]   Christian Molbech, *Henrik Harpestrengs Danske Lægebog fra det trettende Aarhundrede* (Copenhagen, 1826) [now Copenhagen, Kongelige Bibliotek, MS Ny kgl. Samling, nr. 66 R, 8v°].

[13]   [Johann Andreas Schmeller, ed.], *Ein Buch von guter Speise*, Bibliothek des literarischen Vereins in Stuttgart 9 (Stuttgart, 1844).

[14]   Baron Jérôme Pichon, ed., *Le Ménagier de Paris*, 2 vols. (Paris, 1846) [now Brussels, Bibliothèque royale, MSS 10310–10311; and Paris, Bibliothèque nationale, MS nouv. acqu. fr. 6739].

[15]   Francesco Zambrini, ed., *Il libro della cucina del sec. XIV* (Bologna, 1863) [now Bologna, Biblioteca universitaria della Università di Bologna, MS 158].

[16]   Constant Antoon Serrure, ed., *Keukenboek uitgegeven naar een handschrift der vijftiende eeuw* (Ghent, 1872) [now Ghent, Universiteitsbibliotheek, MS 1035].

[17]   Serrano Morales, "La cocina española. El libre del Sent Soví," *Revista de Valencia* 2 (1881–82): 171–5 [now Valencia, Biblioteca de la Universidad de Valencia, MS 216].

[18]   E.g., John Gage, "Extracts from the Household Book of Edward Stafford, Duke of Buckingham," *Archaeologia* 25 (1834): 311–41; Beriah Botfield, ed., *Manners and Household Expenses of England in the Thirteenth and Fifteenth Centuries*, Roxburghe Club (1841); and John Payne Collier, ed., *Household Books of John Duke of Norfolk and Thomas Earl of Surrey, temp. 1481–90*, Roxburghe Club 61 (1844). The Botfield and Collier volumes are now largely reprinted in Anne Crawford (intro.), *The Household Books of John Howard, Duke of Norfolk, 1462–1471, 1481–1483* (Stroud, Gloucestershire, and Wolfeboro Falls, New Hampshire: Alan Sutton, 1992).

[19]   See, e.g., Frederick J. Furnivall's editions of Caxton's *Book of Curtesye*, EETS, Extra Series 3 (1868), *Early English Meals and Manners*, EETS, Original Series 32 (1868), and *Early English Treatises and Poems on Education, Precedence and Manners in Olden Times*, EETS, Extra Series 8 (1869).

[20]   See, e.g., Richard Morris, ed., *Liber cure cocorum* (Berlin: A. Asher, for the Philological Society, 1862); Mrs. Alexander [Robina] Napier, ed., *A noble boke off cookry ffor a prynce houssolde* (London, 1882); and Thomas Austin, ed., *Two Fifteenth-Century Cookery Books*, EETS, Original Series 91 (1888, rpt. 1964).

essence of national culture and tradition. In Britain, the Scottish novelist Sir Walter Scott was a key figure in the growth of popular interest in the medieval past, and feasts figure prominently in Scott's idealized depictions of this world. Scott used feasts as metaphors for true and false nobility, and of just and unjust governance: a good lord uses his power to provide bounty for all, while a wicked lord uses seeming hospitality as a ruthless exercise in power. Thus, in *Ivanhoe* (1819), set in the reign of Richard the Lionheart (1189–99), the stalwart Anglo-Saxon franklin, Cedric, welcomes two haughty Norman guests to his home and offers them supper, modestly describing the meal as "homely fare." In fact, it is a lavish but simply prepared feast of local foods, and all guests, whatever their rank and background, are given a courteous reception. By contrast, when the villainous Prince John hosts a grand feast at Ashby Castle, his principal guests are the Norman nobility and gentry of the district, but he includes "a few distinguished Saxon and Danish families" for self-serving political reasons. Having used his royal authority to requisition all the luxury provisions in the neighborhood, Prince John serves a meal designed to awe and embarrass these despised guests, rather than to put them at ease:

> With sly gravity, interrupted only by private signs to each other, the Norman knights and nobles beheld the ruder demeanour of Athelstane and Cedric at a banquet, to the form and fashion of which they were unaccustomed. And while their manners were thus the subject of sarcastic observation, the untaught Saxons unwittingly transgressed several of the arbitrary rules established for the regulation of society. Now, it is well known, that a man may with more impunity be guilty of an actual breach either of real good breeding or of good morals, than appear ignorant of the most minute point of fashionable etiquette. Thus Cedric, who dried his hands with a towel, instead of suffering the moisture to exhale by waving them gracefully in the air, incurred more ridicule than his companion Athelstane, when he swallowed to his own single share the whole of a large pasty composed of the most exquisite foreign delicacies, and termed at that time a "Karum-Pie". When, however, it was discovered, by a serious cross-examination, that the Thane of Coningsburgh (or Franklin, as the Normans termed him) had no idea what he had been devouring, and that he had taken the contents of the Karum-pie for larks and pigeons, whereas they were in fact beccaficoes and nightingales, his ignorance brought him in for an ample share of the ridicule which would have been more justly bestowed on his gluttony.[21]

In *Castle Dangerous* (1831), set in 1306, Scott – himself a baronet – again uses the

---

[21]  Sir Walter Scott, *Ivanhoe* [1819], ed. Francis Hovey Stoddard (New York: American Book Company, 1904), ch. 4, p. 39; ch. 14, pp. 148–9, 151–2. The modern French film *Le Dîner de Cons* (1998; written and directed by Francis Veber from his play of the same title) is very similar in theme to Prince John's malicious feast in *Ivanhoe*: a smug group of elite Parisian men amuse themselves by inviting men of modest background to dinner and then sneering at their gauche behaviour. An American version of this film was released in 2010 as *Dinner for Schmucks*.

theme of medieval hospitality to uphold the ideal of a society led by a paternalistic aristocracy that uses the rich abundance of its estates to ensure the well-being of the less fortunate. "What use," asks the heroine, Lady Augusta de Berkeley, "of the mountains of beef, and the oceans of beer, which they say our domains produce, if there is a hungry heart among our vassalage ...?"[22]

Other leaders of the medieval revival movement, including Robert Southey, Thomas Carlyle, Augustus Pugin, Benjamin Disraeli, and John Ruskin, similarly romanticized the Middle Ages as a time of bounty and splendor. They mourned the loss of "a society held together by mutual bonds of feudal rights and duties,"[23] and saw "the prosperity of medieval England – feasts, roast beef, merriment –" as a sharp contrast to "the penury and drabness" of their own industrial age.[24]

Nineteenth-century debates over the rise of capitalism and the role of labor, most notably by Karl Marx (1818–83), together with the expanding availability of sources concerning the economy and society, helped to awaken scholarly interest in the history of daily life. The rise of economic and social history was canonized in Britain and France by the foundation of the English journal *Economic History Review* (1927–) by the medieval historian Eileen Power, and of the French journal *Annales* (1929–) by the medieval historian Marc Bloch and the early modern historian Lucien Febvre. This new focus on daily life eventually led a number of scholars to turn their attention to the role of food. Since the 1970s, scholarship on food in medieval Europe has investigated such subjects as diet, nutrition, standards of living, household management, religious observance and spirituality, markets, public health, food costs, ceremony, hospitality, cookery, the senses, and technical writing (*Fachliteratur*).[25]

In modern popular culture, interest in the Middle Ages has spread not only through books, but also through the new media and entertainments of the twentieth and twenty-first centuries, including film, animation, television, Renaissance faires, live-action role-playing games, reenactment societies, themed restaurants and events, video games, and the rapidly expanding resources of the Internet. Feasts have played a lively role in these popular modern conceptualizations of medieval life, which often echo the earlier dichotomy between nostalgia for a lost time of nobility and honor, and fascination with the exciting but shocking customs of a barbaric age. In the new media and entertainments, as well as in modern popular literature, medieval feasts emblematize wealth and power, aristocratic grandeur, and the acquisition of honor. They serve as occasions for portraying dazzling magnificence and farcical crudeness, and as settings for keynote scenes

---

[22] Sir Walter Scott, *Castle Dangerous* [1831], The Edinburgh Waverley, vol. 48 (Edinburgh: T. C. and E. C. Jack, 1903), ch. 1, p. 12.

[23] W. A. Speck, "Robert Southey, Benjamin, Disraeli, and Young England," *History* 95.318 (2010): 194–206 (195).

[24] Alice Chandler, "Sir Walter Scott and the Medieval Revival," *Nineteenth-Century Fiction* 19:4 (1965): 315–32 (332), http://extensionstyluspapyrus.wikispaces.com/file/view/Sir+Walter+Scott+-+Medieval+revival.pdf (accessed 15 August 2013).

[25] For a pan-European overview of the scholarly literature, see the Notes and Bibliography in Melissa Weiss Adamson, ed., *Regional Cuisines of Medieval Europe: A Book of Essays* (New York: Routledge, 2002).

of romance, comedy, eroticism, heroism, and treachery. Such scenes epitomize the contrast between the excitements of life in an idealized or fantasized past and the ordinariness of life in the present day. Examples can be found in the series of medieval-themed fantasy books by George R. R. Martin called *A Song of Ice and Fire* (1996–), serialized on television as *Game of Thrones* (HBO, 2011–); these have inspired spin-offs, including a board game (currently in its second edition), and numerous fan-fiction communities (www.fanfiction.net/tv/Game-of-Thrones/). Medieval-themed restaurants, fairs, weddings, and other entertainments are popular worldwide. The Society for Creative Anachronism (www.sca.org) is a leading international organization for medieval reenactors. Video games that feature medieval feasts, realistic or fantasized, include *Sims Medieval, Stronghold 2, Skyrim, Assassin's Creed,* and *World of Warcraft.*[26]

Even scholars have not been immune to the sheer entertainment potential of medieval food and feasting. A recent example is the purported discovery of a fourteenth-century manuscript in the British Library that features illustrated recipes for hedgehogs, blackbirds, a fish stew called "codswallop," and grilled unicorn.[27] Enjoy this April Fool's Day joke – a delightful example of comic medievalism.

## Further Reading

Bynum, Caroline Walker. *Holy Feast and Holy Fast: The Religious Significance of Food to Medieval Women.* Berkeley: University of California Press, 1987.

Furnivall, Frederick J., ed. *Early English Meals and Manners.* Early English Text Society, Original Series, 32 (1868).

Henisch, Bridget Ann. *The Medieval Cook.* Woodbridge, Suffolk: The Boydell Press, 2009. Ch. 5 ("The Staging of a Feast"), 134–63.

Winter, Johanna Maria van. *Spices and Comfits: Collected Papers on Medieval Food.* Totnes, Devon: Prospect Books, 2007. Ch. 19 ("Feasting in Earlier Times"), 293–302, and ch. 20 ("A Wedding Party at the Court of Holland in 1369"), 302–17.

Woolgar, Christopher M. "Fast and Feast: Conspicuous Consumption and the Diet of the Nobility in the Fifteenth Century." In *Revolution and Consumption in Late Medieval England.* Ed. Michael A. Hicks. Woodbridge, Suffolk: The Boydell Press, 2001. 7–25.

## Related Essays in this Volume

Reenactment, Spectacle, Play, Humor, Archive, Troubadour, Presentism, Gesture, Memory, Authenticity, Resonance, Simulacrum

---

[26] I am grateful to Tyler Scott Smith for much helpful information on Martin's books and these video games.

[27] http://britishlibrary.typepad.co.uk/digitisedmanuscripts/2012/04/unicorn-cookbook-found-at-the-british-library.html. For this reference I am grateful to Mary Beth Emmerichs and Sharon Emmerichs.

# 8
# Genealogy

*Zrinka Stahuljak*

P ERHAPS THE MOST influential, and the most contested, of writings on genealogy is Michel Foucault's 1971 essay "Nietzsche, Genealogy, History."[1] Its
definition works against all expectations: genealogy is opposed to sanguinity,
continuity, and tradition because it is defined against the notion of the survival
of transhistorical essences. It likewise stands in contrast to the notion of evolution that would establish a fixed origin, a time of an immutable and uncorrupted
truth, which can only be the matter of metaphysics and myth. Nevertheless,
Foucauldian genealogy does not refute transmission; rather, it acknowledges
transmission that operates through violent interruptions and (re)emergences, and
is neither dependent nor calqued on the biological sequence of human generations and linear time that traditionally serve as narrative frameworks for history.
Foucauldian history traces the transmission of singularities, their (dis)appearance
and return under different guises, through an analytics of discursive shifts in the
apparatus (*le dispositif*), a system of relations between the elements of a heterogeneous ensemble consisting of various discursive and non-discursive mechanisms,
techniques, and knowledge structures (discourses, institutions, architectural forms,
regulatory decisions, laws, administrative measures, scientific statements, philosophical, moral and philanthropic propositions). Finally, it considers sanguinity
– that is, blood – to be a symbolics rather than a physiology.[2]

Genealogy has been a central notion in the study of medieval literature, culture,
and society for several decades, yet medievalists have deployed genealogy at the
other extreme from the Foucauldian method of "genealogical analysis." They have
focused on genre definition and classification of source material, rather than on
discursive or epistemological issues. In its most restrictive meaning, "the Middle

---

[1] Michel Foucault, "Nietzsche, Genealogy, History," in *Language, Counter-Memory,
Practice: Selected Essays and Interviews*, ed. Donald F. Bouchard, trans. Donald F. Bouchard
and Sherry Simon (Ithaca, N.Y.: Cornell University Press, 1977 [1971]), 139–64.
[2] Michel Foucault, "The Confession of the Flesh," in *Power/Knowledge Selected
Interviews and Other Writings*, ed. and trans. Colin Gordon (New York: Pantheon Books,
1980 [1977]), 194–228; and *The History of Sexuality, Volume I: An Introduction*, trans. Robert
Hurley (New York: Vintage Books, 1990 [1976]).

Ages called *Genealogia* … a self-standing work, written or drawn to present a filiation of one family or individual," a work "that establishes the ascendancy of one personage or lineage, and nothing more."[3] For the discipline of history, genealogy is a written or hand-drawn document of filiation that forms a clear-cut genre, and thus provides a model for reading the medieval historical mindset. But the dilemma of how exactly to read medieval genealogy can be summarized in two questions: Can medieval genealogy be narrowly identified with filiation, primogeniture, and bloodline? Does its narrative reflect a historical reality of medieval practices of kinship or is it an effect of discourse?

Genealogy as object of study in the work of medievalists – anthropologists, historians, and literary historians – can be traced to Georges Duby's 1953 landmark social history of the Mâconnais region. Drawing almost exclusively on diplomatic sources and cartularies, virtually all ecclesiastical, because of the "dearth of [local] narrative sources" that he calls "literary testimonials," Duby described a reorganization of the medieval family from an amorphous horizontal kin group to vertical and linear patrilineage, and he grounded this transformation in the social and political changes in the aftermath of the year 1000, especially the institution of castle lordship.[4] Lords imposed the vassality bond on smaller lords and exercised tighter fiscal controls on the peasantry. In order to preserve, rather than disperse, their patrimony and power, the nobles then began restricting the transmission of inheritance, patronymic, and marriage rights to the eldest son, creating the institution of primogenital patrilineage. This first age of feudalism was supported by genealogy, itself understood as filiation that secured transmission from fathers to first-born sons, and from which sisters or younger brothers were excluded. In other words, the backbone of a new social-economical regime was the patrilineal family structure. This shift from an amorphous horizontal, highly unstructured kin group to a sudden appearance of a rigid primogenital patrilineage, Duby claimed, was once again reversed in the thirteenth century and replaced with a relatively fluid structure more accepting of daughters and younger sons. This was the second age of feudalism. By virtue of the selection of his sources, Duby conveyed to documents the status of witness to a historical reality, without interrogating them as narratives. This identification of the archive with social reality lent an immediate aura of authenticity and transparency to the genealogical genre.

Duby offered a patrilineal model of medieval "family" – a term that in the Middle Ages corresponded to "household" – that resonated with the nuclear family of the bourgeois paternalist order of modern nation-states. Such a historically transparent model of the medieval aristocratic lineage had broad appeal and dominated modern historians' and literary historians' work into the twenty-first century. For literary history, best represented in R. Howard Bloch's work, the natural and the social order were equated because they rested on a genealogi-

---

[3]  Léopold Génicot, *Les généalogies*, Typologie des sources du Moyen Âge occidental 15 (Turnhout: Brepols, 1975), 11, 12. All translations from the French are mine, unless otherwise noted.

[4]  Georges Duby, *La société aux XIe et XIIe siècles dans la région mâconnaise* (Paris: A. Colin, 1953), xi.

cally defined linguistic model. Patrilineage lent an organic cohesion to linguistic structures and their cultural production, which in turn sustained the system of patrilineal primogeniture.[5] In a major corrective to Duby, Bloch made literary narratives corroborating historians' archives the center of an anthropology and history of the Middle Ages. But because this approach presupposed that language and lineage – etymology and genealogy – were connatural, and therefore did not question from what structures genealogy itself made meaning, it further strengthened the underlying notion that medieval genealogy equaled generation or procreation, that it necessarily meant biological, blood filiation.

Gabrielle Spiegel's influential 1983 article, published the same year as Bloch's literary anthropology, cemented the idea that medieval genealogy was biological: "Genealogy functioned to secularize time by grounding it in biology, transforming the connection between past and present into a real one, seminally imparted from generation to generation." Genealogy served as a metaphor for the relatedness of historical events, a sort of humanization of historical time, in contrast to ecclesiastical universal history, where "events stand in a filiative relation to one another … mirror[ing] the reproductive course of human life."[6] The seminal, biological link between father and son naturalized such social constructs as history and causality. In stark contrast to Foucault, genealogy and history became mirrors of biology, and it was "small wonder that the historian dedicated to understanding the form and function of medieval genealogy would find Foucault's genealogical conspectus illegible."[7]

Interestingly, Duby anticipated this kind of conflation between genealogy and biology when he highlighted repeatedly the difference between medieval kinship and modern-day genealogy. Historians' genealogies, he argued, are "biological," "those *reconstructed after the event* by historians patiently uncovering evidence of consanguinity and intermarriage.… This kind of genealogy, necessarily incomplete, and often uncertain, gives us a *true*, one might almost say a *biological*, picture of the family group throughout its existence." But medieval genealogies are "*psychological*" and offer "evidence of family psychology, and the reactions which at that period the ties of kinship produced."[8] In recent years, scholars have nuanced this distinction between the psychological and the biological in two areas: first, they have interrogated the incongruity of primogenital patrilineage as the emblem-

---

5   R. Howard Bloch, *Etymologies and Genealogies: A Literary Anthropology of the French Middle Ages* (Chicago: University of Chicago Press, 1983).

6   Gabrielle M. Spiegel, "Genealogy: Form and Function in Medieval Historiography," in *The Past as Text: The Theory and Practice of Medieval Historiography* (Baltimore: Johns Hopkins University Press, 1997 [1983]), 99–110 (107, 108).

7   Gabrielle M. Spiegel, "Foucault and the Problem of Genealogy," *Medieval History Journal* 4.1 (2001): 1–14 (12).

8   Georges Duby, "The Nobility in Medieval France," in *The Chivalrous Society*, trans. Cynthia Postan (Berkeley: University of California Press, 1980 [1961]), 94–111 (99); "The Structure of Kinship and Nobility," in *The Chivalrous Society* [1967], 134–48 (134–5); "French Genealogical Literature," in *The Chivalrous Society* [1967], 149–57 (149); "Lineage, Nobility and Knighthood: The Mâconnais in the Twelfth Century: A Revision," in *The Chivalrous Society* [1972], 59–80.

atic model of medieval family organization and second, they have pointed to the anachronistic and erroneous identification of medieval lineage with our modern idea of genealogy, conceptually defined as blood lineage and visually identified with genealogical trees.

In challenging the primacy of patrilineage, historians have concentrated on two geographical areas that were the cradle of Western medieval aristocracy: the county of Champagne and the lands of the Loire. In Champagne, it is striking that the term "lineage" appears only infrequently in twelfth-century sources, and in one instance where lineage clearly means descent – Chrétien de Troyes's hero Cligés belongs to King Arthur's lineage – "lineage carries a general sense of kinship rather than patrilineal descent."[9] The sources from the Loire refute Duby's model of patrilineage and primogeniture exclusive of all other kin and show that "there was no fundamental shift in family structure during [...] the eleventh through twelfth centuries."[10] When taking the *longue durée* view of the evolution of kinship, from the Middle Ages to the twentieth century, historians now observe that the shift to patrilineal devolution of property appears to occur only at the passage to the early modern period and is less general than earlier research had assumed. It is also "more specifically related to modes of linking political power to the possessions of certain goods such as castles, titles and offices."[11]

Put differently, succession of rights and titles was more strictly regulated than other property that was inheritable by all children. Women were not marginalized in medieval family histories or in medieval family organization, and in marrying men of less distinguished ancestry they could bestow pedigrees and titles on their children.[12] Among anthropologists, research on lineage as kinship has helped define medieval lineage as descent through both the maternal and paternal line, that is, as cognatic bilateral kindred, reinforcing the idea that the importance of agnatic lineage had been exaggerated in the study of medieval genealogies. For instance, the medieval Latin term *cognatio* does not differentiate between the matrilineal and patrilineal lineage, or between spiritual, "*cognatio spiritualis, cognatio spiritus*," and "biological" kinship.[13] Other terms like *propinquus* and *parentela* refer to a mixture of "biological" and "alliance" relationships. *Consanguinitas*, paradoxically,

[9] Theodore Evergates, *The Aristocracy in the County of Champagne, 1100–1300* (Philadelphia: University of Pennsylvania Press, 2007), 85–6.

[10] Amy Livingstone, *Out of Love for My Kin: Aristocratic Family Life in the Lands of the Loire, 1000–1200* (Ithaca: Cornell University Press, 2010), 3.

[11] David Warren Sabean and Simon Teuscher, "Kinship in Europe: A New Approach to Long-Term Development," in *Kinship in Europe: Approaches to Long-Term Development (1300–1900)*, ed. David Warren Sabean, Simon Teuscher, and Jon Mathieu (New York: Berghahn Books, 2010 [2007]), 1–32 (6).

[12] Constance Brittain Bouchard, *Those of My Blood: Constructing Noble Families in Medieval Francia* (Philadelphia: University of Pennsylvania Press, 2001); Christiane Klapisch-Zuber, *L'ombre des ancêtres: Essai sur l'imaginaire médiéval de la parenté* (Paris: Fayard, 2000).

[13] Jack Goody, *The Development of the Family and Marriage in Europe* (Cambridge, UK: Cambridge University Press, 1983); Anita Guerreau-Jalabert, "La désignation des relations et groupes de parenté en latin médiéval," *Bulletin du Cange* 46–7 (1988): 65–108; Anita Guerreau-Jalabert, "*Spiritus* et *caritas*. Le baptême dans la société médiévale," in *La parenté*

refers to degrees of proximity whether by biology or affinity. The case in point is the 1215 Lateran Council's prohibition of marriage in the fourth degree applied to both blood and spiritual kinship. The Middle Ages had, on the one hand, a functional view of lineage that fluctuated over the lifetime of an individual and of a lineage and, on the other, a social-juridical definition of consanguinity, shaped on the basis of need with relative disregard for blood relations: "'Family' does not and did not reside only in biological connections."[14]

Some literary historians took Bloch's cue that genealogy belongs to the general problematics of the sign, arguing that genealogy is not just embedded in linguistic structure, but is itself a linguistic structure and a narrative genre. Genealogy is a cultural and discursive construct, and discourses – not fluids – organized the medieval social and mental space. Transmission of patronym, lands, titles is only seemingly linked to a seamless, uninterrupted continuity of the bloodline, from the founding ancestor to the present heir, but this continuity is not biological, rather it is naturalized through narrative. Historical documents and "literary testimonials" are similarly emplotted as narrative.[15]

Others pointed out that genealogical imaginary taken at the level of medieval cultural discourse, of which the Judeo-Christian tradition is exemplary, always posits the logic of supersession of the past by the present, a fantasy of a cut between Christian Ecclesia and Jewish Synagoga. Group identity was grounded in a temporality of supersession – then versus now – out of which the discourse of biological unity and difference began to emerge.[16]

Such discursive analyses reveal that medieval lineage was not necessarily about biological filiation and that genealogy may not have been identical with a bloodline; rather, blood served primarily as a metaphor naturalizing an alliance, giving history a linear temporality and making periodization possible. The Lateran concept of consanguinity referred both to blood kin and kin by alliance; treated as equal, these consanguinary concepts could not be grounded in blood as a natural given, but rather in a concept of "blood" naturalized by discourse. Indeed, the development of the genealogical concept of blood, "blood *as definition of kinship* in the aristocracy appears ... only very late. Starting only in the fourteenth century, direct descendants of kings are called 'princes by blood.' And only at the end of the fifteenth century does the notion of 'blood purity' appear in Spain, in opposition to the Jews."[17] In the treatises on consanguinity and marriage prohibitions from the twelfth through the fourteenth century, there are "far fewer

*spirituelle*, ed. Françoise Héritier-Augé and Élisabeth Copet-Rougier (Paris: Éditions des archives contemporaines, 1995), 133–203.

[14] Bouchard, *Those of My Blood*, 3, 4.

[15] Zrinka Stahuljak, *Bloodless Genealogies of the French Middle Ages: Translatio, Kinship, and Metaphor* (Gainesville: University Press of Florida, 2005).

[16] Kathleen Biddick, *The Typological Imaginary: Circumcision, Technology, History* (Philadelphia: University of Pennsylvania Press, 2003).

[17] Jacques Le Goff (with Nicolas Truong), *Une histoire du corps au Moyen Âge* (Paris: Éditions Liana Levi, 2003), 40; David Nirenberg, "Mass Conversion and Genealogical Mentalities: Jews and Christians in Fifteenth-Century Spain," *Past and Present* 174:1 (2002): 3–41.

references to shared blood than one might expect."[18] The Old French word "*sanc*" can include blood-related kin, but this usage seems to have developed particularly at the end of the Middle Ages," and a far more frequent term designating familial relationships is "flesh" (*char*), as in expressions such as "cognatio carnalis, carnis" and "ami charnel."[19] The prevalent metaphor of kinship in the literature of the twelfth and thirteenth centuries is the body, "the body of kinship."[20]

Hence, while it is certain that the Middle Ages had a notion of blood kinship, it is also true that kinship could be constituted in ways that were not identical to a bloodline. Through discourse, lineage could be organized, rearranged, and reconstructed as needed. The family structure was permanently in production as it assimilated new individuals, even whole lineages, into preexisting structures. These strategies of incorporation and representation resembled less a bloodline than a "web of alliance and blood-relationship."[21]

Only in the late Middle Ages did a regime of nature, grounded in blood and race, begin to emerge. But when nature makes history and biology mutually intelligible, the discipline of history has trouble questioning the very ground it stands on, writing its own genealogy. Few have been willing to examine the origin of the conflation between medieval "psychological" – a picture of its mental field – and modern "biological" definitions of genealogy. Yet the origin of the definition of medieval genealogy as a patrilineal bloodline lies in our modern nation-state discourses on family and nation and, specifically, in nineteenth-century medicine of heredity and consanguinity.[22]

Hereditarianism was the scientific theorization of the permanence of form, meaning organic reproduction of physical and mental traits transmitted over generations of blood descendants, "the tendency toward the regular transmission of traits [...] a legacy transmitted more or less loyally across an infinitely long chain of generations."[23] Nineteenth-century laws of hereditary transmission were also derived from pathological deviations from normal heredity. Heredity, healthy or morbid, was known to be transmitted by blood, but medicine could identify the reproduction of form and the laws of heredity only over an extended period of time in an uninterrupted succession of descendants. Doctors naturally turned to the documentary evidence of medieval and *Ancien Régime* genealogies. But while these pre-Revolutionary genealogies were grounded in law, the juridical concept of kinship subject to social convention and canonical prescription, the result of such scientific study of history was the medicalization of the very concept of genealogy now grounded in blood: "Knowing the hereditary antecedents of his clients, [the

---

[18]    Christiane Klapisch-Zuber, "Le Corps de la parenté," *Micrologus* 1 (1993): 43–60 (48).
[19]    Anita Guerreau-Jalabert, "Sang," in *Dictionnaire du Moyen Âge*, ed. Claude Gauvard, Alain de Libera, and Michel Zink (Paris: Presses universitaires de France, 2002), 1280–1.
[20]    Klapisch-Zuber, "Le Corps de la parenté."
[21]    Bouchard, *Those of My Blood*, 178.
[22]    A detailed analysis of what follows can be found in Zrinka Stahuljak, *Pornographic Archaeology: Medicine, Medievalism, and the Invention of the French Nation* (Philadelphia: University of Pennsylvania Press, 2013), 25–68.
[23]    Charles Letourneau, "Hérédité," in *Dictionnaire encyclopédique des sciences médicales*, ed. Amédée Dechambre, 4e sèrie, t. 13 (1888), 588–605 (589).

doctor] will be able to foresee what their children will be; in his perspective, the adage: *Pater est quem morbi filiorum demonstrant* will offer many more guarantees than the famous saying of Roman law: *Pater est quem nuptiae demonstrant.*"[24] The identity between the children's and father's disease(s), and not marriage, confirms the father's biological paternity and charts the bloodline. Juridical and medical paternity were now two separate paradigms, subjects of two distinct discourses of law and medicine. Moreover, doctors argued that consanguineous marriage – among blood kin – enhanced morbid heredity. The long debate on the degenerative effects of consanguinity and the even longer reign of hereditary medicine into the twentieth century sealed the notion of consanguinity as uniquely biological and finalized the discursive and conceptual shift from kinship to blood kinship, from lineage to bloodline, from blood symbolics (proximity among kin) to biological materialism (blood kin). This difference between juridical and medical conceptualizations of consanguinity split the notion of kinship in a radical way, between old genealogies established on the basis of marriages that guaranteed filiation through the juridical (that is, potentially affiliative and fictional) bond and modern genealogies identified as a bloodline of hereditary characteristics (that is, biological and objective).

In short, while "blood" had been a psychological (and not physiological) concept in the Middle Ages, denoting both juridical filiation and biological bloodline, nineteenth-century hereditarianism and the consanguinity debate narrowed its semantic field to an exclusively naturalized, medical concept of biological bloodline. This in turn means that our modern understanding of medieval genealogies and their deployment has been grounded in the nineteenth-century biological understanding of genealogy as bloodline. This misunderstanding has had a long-lasting effect on the disciplines of history and literary history and on their analytical models of the medieval family, kinship, and the disposition and structure of medieval history, time, and narration, and it is only in the last decade that scholars have begun providing a corrective to the study of medieval genealogy (Biddick, Guerreau-Jalabert, Evergates, Livingstone, Stahuljak), while, in another monumental effort, other medievalists (Holsinger, Labbie, Warren) have started excavating intellectual genealogies that, alongside the nineteenth-century scientific bias, have shaped our medievalism.[25]

---

[24] Dr. Fernand Debret, *La sélection naturelle dans l'espèce humaine. Contribution à l'étude de l'hérédité convergente* (Paris: G. Steinheil, 1901), 72.

[25] Kathleen Biddick, *The Shock of Medievalism* (Durham: Duke University Press, 1998); Bruce Holsinger, *The Premodern Condition: Medievalism and the Making of Theory* (Chicago: University of Chicago Press, 2005); Erin F. Labbie, *Lacan's Medievalism* (Minneapolis: University of Minnesota Press, 2006); and Michelle R. Warren, *Creole Medievalism: Colonial France and Joseph Bédier's Middle Ages* (Minneapolis: University of Minnesota Press, 2011).

## Further Reading

Bloch, R. Howard, *Etymologies and Genealogies: A Literary Anthropology of the French Middle Ages.* Chicago: University of Chicago Press, 1983.

Duby, Georges, *The Chivalrous Society.* Trans. Cynthia Postan. Berkeley: University of California Press, 1980.

Sabean, David Warren, Simon Teuscher, and Jon Mathieu, eds. *Kinship in Europe: Approaches to Long-Term Development (1300–1900).* New York: Berghahn Books, 2010 [2007].

Spiegel, Gabrielle M., "Genealogy: Form and Function in Medieval Historiography." In *The Past as Text: The Theory and Practice of Medieval Historiography.* Baltimore: Johns Hopkins University Press, 1997 [1983]. 99–110.

Stahuljak, Zrinka, *Pornographic Archaeology: Medicine, Medievalism, and the Invention of the French Nation.* Philadelphia: University of Pennsylvania Press, 2013.

## Related Essays in this Volume

Continuity, Transfer, Trauma, Christianity, Presentism, Archive, Heresy, Purity, Authenticity, Co-disciplinarity, Lingua

# 9
# Gesture

*Carol L. Robinson*

ESTURES, WHETHER MEDIEVAL or contemporary, formal, ritualistic, or informal, are socially codified movements of body parts or vocalized sounds that, even in a formal setting, can send a uniquely personal message. Consider the smile: that gesture has held different meanings in different times, in different places, for different individuals, within different social situations. Yet, the written description – or drawing – of a damsel smiling in the Middle Ages is understood by contemporary readers. Context is crucial to the meaning of a particular gesture. Consider the medieval romance *Sir Gawain and the Green Knight*: a damsel smiling at a Christmas party in King Arthur's court holds distinct meaning if that smile is maintained as the Green Knight chops off his head. Outside the context of a literary work full of narrative details, it can be difficult to know a smile's meaning; even within the context of a literary work the lack of description (or even mention) of a gesture constitutes a lack of meaning. Thus, knowing who is gesturing and for what reason(s) is crucial information often lacking in medieval literary, performative, and other artistic works.

The word *gesture*[1] was apparently first used in the sixteenth century, derived from Anglo-French and Medieval Latin,[2] and referred to little more than a sound and/or bodily movement that had not been formally assigned meaning as part of a language. Jody Enders points out, "[f]rom Greco-Roman antiquity to modern (or even postmodern) literary theory, it has been a cultural commonplace to

---

[1]  The Middle English word *geste* (which is, as with gesture, derived from Old French but its Latin derivation is *res gestae*) is not associated with the later medieval-early modern word gesture; however, it is still noteworthy to examine it as the sound-cousin to visual-physical gestures. Karl Reichl points out that the term *geste* has "a number of different senses, which cannot always be clearly identified in a given context," and seems to denote "any deeds, in particular of memorable kind, and consequently also their recording in narrative," such as in the *Legend of Good Women* (Text G) in which Geoffrey Chaucer states in the Prologue "that he will give the 'naked text in English' of 'many a gest'" (ll. 85–8). "Comparative Notes on the Performance of Middle English Popular Romance," *Western Folklore* 62.1–2 (Winter and Spring 2003): 63–81 (64).

[2]  *Oxford English Dictionary*: gesture; also jester, jesture, gester; first used as a verb in 1542.

acknowledge the existence of an entity called 'body language.'"[3] The term *language* as used in this context, however, does not refer to the strict linguistic definition of a systemized structure of communication; rather, it refers to a broader, more colloquial, conception of patterned communication.[4] Prior to the late twentieth century, the word *gesture* was applied to any form of non-verbal expression, including visual-physical expressions that had been systematized into (sign)-languages. Non-verbal languages were not recognized officially as languages until the mid-twentieth century.[5] However, even as the term *language* has broadened to include systemized gestures, thus leading to significantly less biased appreciation for non-verbal languages, *gesture* is still recognized as distinct from *language*. Furthermore, gesturing often drove medieval communication and played a grammatical part in a (yet to be discovered) language system of visual-physical signs and as an emphatic marker of communication.[6]

Gestures are crucial supplements to conveying the meanings of linguistic (if not also narrative) structures, and yet they are difficult to record, know, and fully comprehend. It is important, furthermore, to remember that not all gestures that we associate with the medieval actually are *medieval*. Gestures representing the medieval, in other words, are more likely to represent contemporary times (post-1800s), and yet, because of ritualistic gestures that have become institutionalized (such as within a church or a castle), it is possible to appreciate what gestures might have been (or still remain). Vocal and visual-physical gestures vary widely, even in the twenty-first century, even among twenty-first-century Christian clergy: from the formal, ritualistic gestures of some contemporary Roman Catholic priests to the passionate, spontaneous expressions associated with some Southern African-American Baptist ministers. The former clergy are steeped in ritual expressions, that may have come down from medieval European practices: from kissing relics to kneeling, bowing, and crossing the hands across the chest. The latter clergy may be steeped in a cultural blending of European-American ritual gestures and African-American ritual gestures: from "Uh-huh" added in with other linguistic

---

3   Enders, "Of Miming and Signing: The Dramatic Rhetoric of Gesture," in Clifford Davidson, ed., *Gesture in Medieval Drama and Art* (Kalamazoo: Medieval Institute Publications, 2001), 1–25 (2).

4   "In recent decades, the field of sign-language linguistics has established itself as one of the most yeasty, contentious and promising branches of cognitive science." Margalit Fox, *Talking Hands* (New York: Simon & Schuster, 2007), 3.

5   Margalit Fox summarizes the situation well: "In the popular imagination, to the extent that anyone thought about it at all, a signed language was one of two things: at best, it was a word-for-word version of spoken language, simply rerouted onto the hands. At worst, it was a set of rude imitative gestures, devoid of grammar and good for discussing only the most concrete essentials of daily living. Nearly all scholars, and even many deaf people themselves, held with one or the other scenario" (17).

6   See also M. J. Toswell's entry on "Lingua" in the present volume. There is no question that gesture may have been more predominately used internationally than even Latin (as one of the editors of this volume, Elizabeth Emery, has suggested in a private conversation). Even today, when interpreters are absent or when the vast range of communication technology fails, we resort to gesture, a *smiley* on the Internet speaks a thousand words in any language.

expressions (such as "Say it like it is, Brother!") to deeply personal and individual-ized (non-ritual) bodily and vocalized gestural expressions of soulful experiences.

Clifford Davidson writes of the influences and sources of gesture upon medieval British drama, such as monastic sign language: "Sign language served to preserve the quiet of monasteries generally and established gesture alone as a means of communication at times when speech was prohibited."[7] Consider, for example, the gesture of kissing, which has been "shown to have been a common gesture for showing veneration, and indeed still remains in use today, as when viewing a holy relic such as the Holy Blood at Bruges, the cross on Good Friday, or a holy image such as a bronze statue of St. Peter at the Vatican."[8] In an analysis of "Statutes, Ordynances, & order of Service concernyng the state of an Earles household," a set of late-medieval household regulations and ordinances, Kim M. Phillips has shown how the kiss was used in the fifteenth-century secular world to express or demand power.[9] This document illustrates to what extremes such manners and rituals might have been taken. Such rituals were, Phillips argues, "lay liturgy" created to rival "ecclesiastical ritual."[10]

In making a comparison between medieval gestures and contemporary Amer-ican Sign Language, Dunbar H. Ogden makes a strong case for the importance of blending body and hand expressions with spoken English to make a performance's communication complete. For example, Geoffrey Chaucer's Pardoner (and hence, Geoffrey Chaucer) knew this: "Myne handes and my tonge goon so yerne / That it is joye to se my bisynesse."[11] He used his hands to add gestural meaning to the language he spoke. Ogden goes so far as to argue that "American Sign Language used by today's deaf community encompasses this distinction between a gestural sign and an attitude conveyed along with it."[12] He singles out "two categories of gesture in the rubrics of the liturgical drama," for example: "the stage directions calling for hand, head and body movements that derive directly from the liturgy,

---

[7]   Clifford Davidson. "Gesture in Medieval British Drama," in *Gesture in Medieval Drama*, ed. Davidson, 66–127 (70).

[8]   Davidson, "Gesture in Medieval British Drama," 72.

[9]   Kim M. Phillips, "The Invisible Man: Body and Ritual in a Fifteenth-Century Noble Household," *Journal of Medieval History* 31 (2005): 143–62. "London, British Library, Harleian MS 6815 ('Heraldical miscellany'), fols 25re56v, 16r. The latter folio, which is the final leaf of the first copy, has become detached from the rest and misbound in the manuscript. This discussion will refer to the first copy, bound in folios 25re41v, 16r. The second copy lacks a final leaf" (144, n.1). "Christopher Woolgar dates their composition to between c. 1470 and c. 1500, or possibly c. 1460 and c. 1510, on the basis of its references to Pre-Reformation liturgy and dietary calendar, types of furniture – especially trestle rather than dormant tables –, the use of spoons and knives but not forks, the large size of the household (all of which place the document more securely in the fifteenth rather than sixteenth century), and the drinking of beer rather than ale (which locates it in the later fifteenth century rather than earlier)" (144, n.2).

[10]   Phillips, "The Invisible Man," 158.

[11]   "The Pardoner's Prologue," *The Canterbury Tales*, lines 112–13.

[12]   Dunbar H. Ogden. "Gesture and Characterization in the Liturgical Drama," in *Gesture in Medieval Drama*, ed. Davidson, 26–47 (34).

such as bestowing a blessing or opening or folding the hands in prayer," and gestures that come "from daily life, such as prayer."[13]

Indeed, it is possible that more formal gestures may be more closely tied to medieval (or earlier) contexts, such as formal ritualistic gestures; it is also possible that less formal gestures are more timeless and culture-less in that they change in meaning as they appear in various times and various places. Both mime and gesture were a fundamental part of medieval drama. As Jody Enders observes, "Gesture was so powerful that it encompassed the linguistic denotation, ideological connotation, grammar, emotion, physical demonstration, theatrical representation, speech acts, and even cross-cultural communication."[14] Davidson affirms, "The principles of classical rhetoric were also known in England, and here as on the Continent the gestural traditions of classical Roman actors also were not lost (though inaccurately understood)."[15]

Yet, while there is clearly a timelessness to the use of gestures, the actual meanings of certain gestures in particular points of time seem to elude those of later eras. In contemporary media, gesture has taken on new forms. A computer programmer, for example, responds to various tones of beeps made by the computer to correct a program she is writing; the beeps of a computer are in no way medieval, and yet one might hear similar audio gestures when installing or playing a medievalist computer video game. In text-messaging, the letter $X$ is a gesture for a hug and the letter $O$ is a gesture for a kiss; in some chat programs, variations of these symbols (that date back to mid-twentieth-century letter writing) have been adapted to turn automatically into cartoon-like faces that gesture the expressions of a kiss, or a hug, or a sad face. Davidson concludes, "Whatever the source and scope of the gestures used in the vernacular British plays in the late Middle Ages, the result was not, we can be sure, the kind of primitive theater that formerly was often assumed by critics."[16]

Within the confines of contemporary media, both positive and negative cultural attitudes toward gestural expression continue to exist. The television show *Seinfeld* relied heavily upon both vocal and physical gestures as a source of comedic antics of inarticulateness, and we often see exaggerative movements that are intended to replicate modern conceptions of medieval gesturing (particularly in terms of manners) at Renaissance and medieval faires. Indeed, speech-making and acting are all about the successful combinations of sound and visible-physical gestures, used to supplement language with further meaning. "It has been understood for a long time," writes William C. Stokoe, "that movements, gestures among them, have semantic interpretations."[17] He makes note of the structural differences between

---

[13] Ogden, "Gesture and Characterization," 34.

[14] Enders, "Of Miming and Signing," 1.

[15] Davidson, "Gesture in Medieval British Drama," 69.

[16] Davidson, "Gesture in Medieval British Drama," 110.

[17] William C. Stokoe, *Language in Hand: Why Sign Came before Speech* (Washington: Gallaudet University Press, 2001), 176. Stokoe argued that his Deaf students at Gallaudet University were actually communicating in a physical-visual gesture system of language (now known as American Sign Language) and suggested "that we should look for the beginning of language in the actions of other living things, even the housefly evading a

sound gestures and visual-physical gestures: "Sounds can alarm, warn, beckon, threaten, and so on, but unaided by convention they cannot represent nounlike or verblike concepts."[18] Although we cannot know entirely, there is nonetheless a consistent logic behind them.

Gesture is a fundamental aspect of serious performance art, that of American Deaf storyteller Peter S. Cook, for example, who relays his adaptation of the stories of Sir Gawain and Dame Ragnell almost completely through mime and gesture (with a few expressions of American Sign Language and voiced-over English). Indeed, he boasts of this method in text projected during the video recording of his performance: "The story of Sir Gawain & Lady Ragnelle is told by Peter Cook using the universal language of gestures and pantomime with minimal voice interpretation needed."[19] At one point in the story, the hag insists upon the ritualistic sealing of the marriage with a kiss (a gesture perhaps more modern than medieval). Cook mimes this formal gesture, however, in a very informal manner, one that is more closely tied to contemporary American culture than to medieval British culture (Figure 4). In telling his story, Cook's gestures constantly remind the audience that this medieval tale is being told in a contemporary context: King Arthur uses a cell phone to call Sir Gawain, and he shows Lady Ragnell a photo album of knights (possibly for her to marry in exchange for the secret to what women want most).[20]

While gestures are often universal (and there are also universal gestures), gestures of medieval European times – most of which are presumably lost to us – are the meanings missing, or merely implied (even through description and image), in the carefully preserved written expressions of medieval spoken words and drawings. It is easy to assume that gestures are always sensible, as well as both timeless and universal, but this is simply not the case. *I am smiling as I write this conclusion.* A gesture can be spontaneous, made without any intended meaning, and yet be understood to be full of meaning. "Indeed," suggests C. Nadia

---

swatter. The connection is unmistakable. Not just flies but all creatures with functioning eyes interpret what they see to survive" (19). This analogy is not quite accurate. House flies only successfully evade a swatter when they feel the small amount of air pressure that eludes the tiny holes that make up this unique invention: the reason fly swatters are so successful is that they exert far less air pressure in the direction of the little bug than does a hand. One might argue that air pressure is a gesture and that the action of the little fly interpreting the meaning of that moving air might be a form of making meaning; however, does anyone truly know what goes on in the mind of a fly? And yet, Stokoe has been successful in making and re-making his argument: "speech is sufficient for language, but not necessary" (ix).

[18] Stokoe, *Language in Hand*, 176–7. This is not completely true. One might make a motion with the hands, for example, to signify movement from one room into the next. One might make the same gesture with sound volume. However, other verbs are easier to express visually than with sound: desire, hatred, love, hunger, pleasure – these expressions can be made with a series of grunts, hums and sighs, but not at all as clearly as with a series of pantomimes and/or facial expressions.

[19] Peter Cook, "Sir Gawain and Lady Ragnelle," *Sir Gawain and Other Finger-licious Stories*. PC Production, 2007. (http://deafpetercook.com/home/DVD_Sales.html)

[20] Cook, "Sir Gawain and Lady Ragnelle."

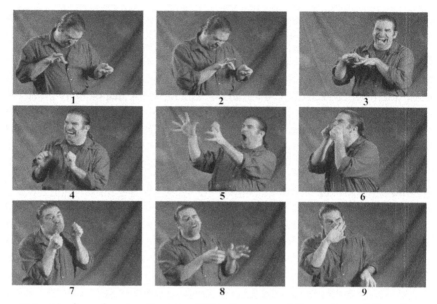

4. Peter Cook performing the tale of "Sir Gawain and Dame Ragnelle" in the DVD *Sir Gawain and Other Finger-licious Stories.*

Seremetakis, "the involuntary gestures of the body, which, for social scientists, are emblematic of the rural or archaic, are, in the cinema of Charlie Chaplin, the dramaturgy of Bertolt Brecht and Samuel Beckett, and the literature of Franz Kafka, the exemplary representation of failed subject formation."[21] *I release a small, snorting chuckle with my smile.*

It is likely that the art of the involuntary gesture, however, can be associated with the medieval; thus, by such processes of elimination, it might be possible to identify what is uniquely *medieval* in the descriptions, drawings, or other record-ings of postmedieval works. *Are my smile and chortle medieval gestures or contem-porary gestures; regardless, what do they mean? Being at the "right" time in the "right" place is crucial to understanding gesture.* Most often, however, a gesture can be intended to have meaning while also failing to convey any meaning what-soever. *Sometimes (as with the proverbial Freudian cigar), a smile is just a smile, with or without the chortle, with or without the context.* A gesture can, in fact, be deeply tied to cultural (or even small community) context and/or be formed with uniquely individualistic characteristics. *Those who know me, know the complex meanings of my smiles.* To those outside the culture or community, to those who do not know the individual, it can be tied to nothing and thus be meaningless. *I continue to smile, as I pick up a shield in one hand, wield a sword in the other hand, and slightly bend the knees, ready for action.*

[21] C. Nadia Seremetakis, "Divination, Media, and the Networked Body of Modernity," *American Ethnologist* 36.2 (2009): 337–50 (348).

## Further Reading

Davidson, Clifford, ed. *Gesture in Medieval Drama and Art.* Kalamazoo, MI: Medieval Institute Publications, 2001. 66–127.

Fox, Margalit. *Talking Hands.* New York: Simon & Schuster, 2007.

Seremetakis, C. Nadia. "Divination, Media, and the Networked Body of Modernity." *American Ethnologist* 36.2 (2009). 337–50.

## Related Essays in this Volume

Lingua, Play, Spectacle, Reenactment, Christianity, Humor, Co-disciplinarity, Feast, Primitive, Resonance

# 10
## Gothic

*Kevin D. Murphy and Lisa Reilly*

O NCE A TERM used to deride the ecclesiastical architecture of the late Middle Ages, and now an omnibus label for counter-cultural phenomena imbued with mysticism and a vague historicism, the word "Gothic" has been characterized by its apparent elasticity; its scholarly usefulness is debatable. Although "Gothic" originally designated certain kinds of architecture, and to a lesser degree painting produced between the decline of Roman antiquity and the Renaissance, the word has been applied increasingly liberally since the eighteenth century, not only to works of material culture, but even to emotions and sensations apparently opposed to classical rationality and reason. The influential eighteenth-century critic Horace Walpole (1717–97) – a leader of the then-nascent "Gothic Revival" – may well bear a good deal of responsibility for the expansion of the word's connotations, for in 1762 he wrote that "One must have taste to be sensible of the beauties of Grecian architecture; one *only* wants *passions to feel Gothic*."[1]

Given the flexibility in the use of the term Gothic, already in evidence in the mid-eighteenth century, it is not surprising that its utility for the history of architecture has been continually debated, notwithstanding its association with particular building materials and formal attributes, from stone vaulting to pointed arches. As a review of some of the major theorists of the Gothic will demonstrate, its meanings have been in near constant flux and contestation, especially in connection with its applicability to the scholarly study of medieval architecture. At the same time, the term's place in popular culture has been secure since the eighteenth century, and it has been used to describe a literary genre closely associated with horror stories, as well as a counter-cultural movement signaled in personal style by darkly dramatic fashions and outlandish makeup.

The origins and meaning of the term "Gothic" are deeply problematic. While sometimes used as a chronological term to describe the late Middle Ages or the period roughly from the mid-twelfth century to c. 1500 in Western Europe, Gothic is more commonly understood as a stylistic term often applied to sculpture and

---

[1]   Horace Walpole, *Anecdotes of Painting in England* (1762), i, 107–8; quoted in Nick Groom, *The Making of Percy's Reliques* (Oxford: Oxford University Press, 1999), 241.

painting, but mainly referring to architecture. The *Oxford English Dictionary* (*OED*) offers a definition in line with most perceptions of Gothic: "A term for the style of architecture prevalent in Western Europe from the twelfth to the sixteenth century, of which the chief characteristic is the pointed arch."[2] Historically, Gothic architecture has been defined largely according to the characteristics of the cathedrals of the Île-de-France, such as Reims and Amiens, which are characterized not only by pointed arches, but also by flying buttresses, quadripartite vaults, tremendous height, and expansive stained-glass windows.

Such a style-specific definition was not, however, part of the term's early history. Its association with a particular set of buildings and elements has been historiographically problematic, as Marvin Trachtenberg demonstrates.[3] This focus on ecclesiastical Île-de-France architecture of the thirteenth century led to the near-exclusion until recently of secular examples, as well as the marginalization of churches that do not conform to this model, such as Florence Duomo or Albi Cathedral, which tended to be either ignored or denigrated.

The term "Gothic" is partly problematic since it emerged out of Renaissance discussions that attempted to differentiate the classical period of ancient Greece and Rome and the Renaissance from what is perceived as a middle period in between. A break with the antique past was not a part of medieval consciousness, although there seems to have been an acknowledgment of difference between what we now call Romanesque and Gothic. The architecture commonly referred to as Gothic today was sometimes called *opus francigenum* during the Middle Ages and *lavori moderni* in the Renaissance.[4] Burchard von Hall's well-known *Chronicle* of c. 1280 discusses the construction of Wimpfen Church (c. 1269–1300) and describes it as being built in the "French style" or *opus francigenum* by an architect who came from Paris; the *Chronicle* makes it clear that Wimpfen is distinct in its piers and windows, for example, from other churches in the area. Earlier, Gervase of Canterbury, in his account of the rebuilding of the choir following the fire of 1170, offered a comparison of the old and new building which highlights the differences between the two, recording discrepancies in their height, decoration, and vaulting. He clearly acknowledges that the master mason, William, came from Sens, France.[5] So, while the later Middle Ages understood the French associa-

[2]   Gothic, *adj.* and *n.*, *OED Online*, June 2013: http://www.oed.com/viewdictionaryentry/Entry/80225?p=emailAeVaT2ziHylgc&d=80225.

[3]   Marvin Trachtenberg, "Gothic/Italian Gothic: Toward a Redefinition," *Journal of the Society of Architectural Historians* 50.1 (March 1991): 22–37.

[4]   Paul Frankl, *The Gothic: Literary Sources and Interpretation through Eight Centuries* (Princeton: Princeton University Press, 1960), 55–6, 256, 858. This text is also discussed in Trachtenberg, "Gothic/Italian Gothic," 22. Yet E. S. de Beer cites a seventh-century text that describes the church of St. Ouen at Rouen as *constructa artificis gothis*: "Gothic: Origin and Diffusion of the Term; The Idea of Style in Architecture," *Journal of the Warburg and Courtauld Institutes* 11 (1948): 143–4.

[5]   Discussed in Frankl, *The Gothic*, 24–35. A more complete text can be found in William Stubbs, ed., *The Historical Works of Gervase of Canterbury*, 2 vols. (London: Longman & Co., 1879–80). See also Robert Willis, *The Architectural History of Canterbury Cathedral* (London: Oxford: Longman, W. Pickering, and G. Bell; Parker, 1845).

tions of what was seen as a new kind of architecture in the twelfth and thirteenth centuries, the term Gothic was not used.

Nor was it commonly employed during the Renaissance when the concept of differing degrees of interest in classical forms between this middle period and antiquity, on the one hand, and the Renaissance, on the other, was promoted.[6] In these early discussions, the construction of the period's chronology was imperfect, but it was understood to include a time of destruction at the hands of Germanic tribes, including the Goths. Manetti, writing what might be considered a survey of architectural history (c. 1460), acknowledges a period of decline following antiquity, which was replaced by a Carolingian rediscovery of Roman buildings, which in turn was replaced by a period of German rule and building until the age of Brunelleschi.[7] The actual term Gothic appeared twice in the fifteenth century, once in an Italian text of Alberti in which he discussed sculpture, and once in a text by Laurentius Valla who described letters as Gothic (*gothice*) rather than Roman.[8] In both cases the term is used derisively. Vasari, who is frequently cited as the first to connect the Goths with what we understand as Gothic architecture, refers to *il lavoro tedesco* as from the time of the Goths.[9] Anne-Marie Sankovitch points out, however, that while the terms Gothic and Vasari's *la maniera tedesca* or *il lavoro tedesco* have been conflated and discussed as if they were one and the same, this reading is highly flawed, in part due to the unstable use of the term *la maniera tedesca* by Vasari.[10] *La maniera tedesca* came to mean the architecture of the entire Middle Ages, largely treated with contempt by Italian Renaissance writers and artists. As was often the case subsequently, in the Renaissance, medieval architecture was defined in ways that enhanced the prestige of contemporary work.

Over time, the meaning of the term was refined and acquired more positive associations. Philibert de l'Orme, whose volume *Architecture* (1567) was roughly contemporary with the second edition of Vasari's biography, describes what we would identify as Gothic in positive terms and as part of his discussion of French architecture, labeling rib vaults as *voûtes modernes*. De l'Orme was partly interested in recovering a history of French architecture separate from that of Italy and understood the architecture of the period preceding the Renaissance in France as worthy of his approval. Unlike his Italian contemporaries, he does not describe it as German. Seventeenth-century French authors following de l'Orme continued his interest in medieval architecture in France, sometimes describing features as Gothic. While some, such as André Duchesne and Sébastien Rouillard, are full of praise for the cathedrals of Notre-Dame in Paris and Chartres respectively, while not necessarily using the term Gothic to describe them, others such as Molière used the term negatively to describe art produced by ignorant

---

[6] Petrarch subdivides the history of the world to include a period called the middle ages. In Frankl, *The Gothic*, 242.

[7] Frankl, *The Gothic*, 255.

[8] Frankl, *The Gothic*, 259–60.

[9] De Beer, "Gothic: Origin and Diffusion," 145–7.

[10] Anne-Marie Sankovitch, "The Myth of the Medieval: Gothic Architecture in Vasari's *Rinascita* and Panofsky's *Renaissance*," *RES* 40 (2001): 29–50.

barbarians.[11] By the eighteenth century in France, a "Graeco-Gothic" ideal of an architecture combining Gothic lightness and structural sophistication with classical clarity would take root, in part as a result of the 1753 publication of Marc-Antoine Laugier's *Essai sur l'architecture*.[12]

English writers also began to use the term in the early seventeenth century, initially to describe language but soon thereafter to describe non-classical architecture, a practice apparently drawn from French examples.[13] John Evelyn's diaries frequently describe Gothic buildings throughout Europe. At approximately the same time, William Dugdale and Roger Dodsworth undertook a massive study of English medieval architecture, which they published in several volumes. Best known of these is the three-volume *Monasticon Anglicanum*.[14] Their detailed illustrations in particular continued to make these volumes, together with Dugdale's *History of St. Paul's Cathedral* (1658), critical sources for scholars of medieval architecture and reflected a growing interest in understanding Gothic architecture as part of a national history.[15] At this point, the chronology in place for medieval architecture was still problematic, with little understanding that much of what was being described as Gothic – Notre-Dame in Paris for instance, or Westminster Abbey – was not contemporary with the Goths seen as the destroyers of the Roman Empire in late antiquity.[16] It was not until the nineteenth century that the differentiation of medieval architecture into stylistic phases with a clearer understanding of the dating of individual buildings emerged. The term Romanesque gained wide acceptance in the early nineteenth century and Thomas Rickman's landmark study, *An Attempt to Discriminate the Styles of Architecture in England from the Conquest to the Reformation* (1817), established the terminology and sequence still used today, a comparative method of classification typically described as scientific. Ultimately, Gothic was associated with architecture of the later Middle Ages, French in particular, and disassociated from the marauding Germanic tribes considered responsible for the destruction of the classical world.

This interest in architectural description and dissemination was paralleled by a more Romantic concern with the emotions provoked by medieval architecture as witnessed, most famously by the writings of Johann Wolfgang von Goethe, in particular his essay of 1772, "Von Deutscher Baukunst."[17] Here Goethe analyzes

---

[11] Frankl, *The Gothic*, 338–40.

[12] Harry Francis Mallgrave, *Modern Architectural Theory: An Historical Survey, 1673–1968* (New York: Cambridge University Press, 2005), 19–23.

[13] Gothic, adj. and n., *OED Online*, June 2013: http://www.oed.com/viewdictionaryentry/Entry/80225?p=emailAeVaT2ziHylgc&d=80225.

[14] Vol. 1 published in 1655, vol. 2 in 1661 and vol. 3 in 1673 – the latter two after Dodsworth's death.

[15] John Hopkins, "Dugdale,William," *Grove Art Online, Oxford Art Online*, Oxford University Press: http://www.oxfordartonline.com.proxy.its.virginia.edu/subscriber/article/grove/art/T023964 (accessed 13 August 2013).

[16] See, for example, Christopher Wren's description of Westminster Abbey cited in Frankl, *The Gothic*, 364.

[17] Susan Bernstein, "Goethe's Architectonic *Bildung* and Buildings in Classic Weimar," *MLN* 114.5 (1999): 1014–36.

his reaction to Strasbourg Cathedral, recording how he initially approached the building with a rational knowledge that as a Gothic structure it would be in poor taste, a reaction which he then discarded for a more experiential one, which led him to appreciate the building as an organic whole provoking a more emotional response. In his later writings, particularly *Wahlverwandtschaften*, he describes the experience of Gothic revival architecture in a language distinctly reminiscent of Suger's description of St. Denis, with its focus on the transformational experience of light that moves us to a higher, more spiritual realm. This interest in the transformative, perhaps irrational, power of Gothic architecture, with its emphasis on the emotional and the sublime, aligns with late eighteenth-century literature described as Gothic, like that produced by Ann Radcliffe, Matthew Lewis, and Mary Shelley, among others.

The modern interest in Gothic architecture, as both a subject of historical inquiry and as a model for new building, coincided with the emergence of a new consciousness of the past that many critics and scholars have associated with the French Revolution. In overturning the Ancien Régime, the Revolution drew a conceptual line between a past that was definitively over and a new, modern age built on a foundation of more democratic institutions. At the end of the eighteenth century, the past became the subject of increasingly passionate interest, and physical objects that had been handed down through the generations were given new importance as reliable evidence of previous eras.[18] With the emergence of nation states in North America, Great Britain, and on the Continent, associations between architectural styles and political regimes became the subjects of great concern as antiquarians in various countries sought to describe the evolution of a national patrimony in buildings. The Gothic was central to many of these narratives and numerous countries attempted to lay claim to it as a particularly national style.

This effort was signaled by both historical writings and medievalizing buildings. Horace Walpole's rebuilding of a modest house, Strawberry Hill, in Twickenham, beginning in 1749, occupied a number of architects and builders who collaborated with him to create a pastiche of Gothic architectural forms. With some of its exterior and interior details based on published elements of both ecclesiastic and secular Gothic buildings, Strawberry Hill has been considered by some to represent the beginning of the Gothic Revival. The well-known house, along with Walpole's most celebrated literary work, *The Castle of Otranto* (1764) – subtitled in some later editions "A Gothic Story" – popularized Gothic aesthetics in architecture as well as in literature. In 1796, the architect James Wyatt began work on William Beckford's house, Fonthill Abbey in Wiltshire, the most famous element of which was a soaring central tower, so daring in its conception and hasty in its construction that it collapsed in 1825. Beckford, too, authored Gothic fiction, in his case, the novel *Vathek*, begun around 1782. In Gothic literature, vast fictional spaces mirrored the sublimity that was associated with Gothic architecture at the

---

[18] Barrett Kalter, *Modern Antiques: The Material Past in England, 1660–1780* (Lewisburg: Bucknell University Press, 2012).

time, and evocations of dark and mysterious places contributed to passionate and gripping tales.

Moreover, the effort to describe a Gothic style in England was closely connected with the identification of national literary traditions: "The wide popularity [...] of the architecture of the middle ages, and of 'Medievalism' in general, which accompanied the peace [following the French and American revolutions], must be ascribed to the works of one appropriately called the 'Great Wizard of the North,' Sir Walter Scott,"[19] the popularizer of the historical novel. Scott's interest in vernacular literary traditions complemented his awareness of earlier architecture; furthermore, he cemented an association between Gothic buildings and literature that had been established by other writers in the eighteenth century. Scott's home, Abbotsford (1816), was among a handful of eighteenth- and nineteenth-century historicist houses that popularized the Gothic as a building style and established a connection between Gothic architecture and a kind of sensationalist literature that often used medieval settings to heighten drama and suspense.

By the middle of the nineteenth century, associations between Gothic architecture and mysticism and sublimity, which had been established during the Romantic period, were complemented by new ways of thinking about medieval architecture. This intellectual transformation took place in both Anglo-American and Continental architectural theory. Throughout the West, theorists and critics conceptually linked Gothic architecture with national identity. For the French architect and theorist Eugène-Emmanuel Viollet-le-Duc, the solution to the central problem he believed to have motivated medieval builders – the construction of large covered meeting spaces – had arrived in the form of the great vaulted churches and cathedrals, and had coincided historically with the emergence of the French nation. His was a secular interpretation of the Gothic that conceptually detached it from Christianity and anchored it in what previous theorists had identified as a specifically French capacity when it came to building in stone. Further, Viollet-le-Duc saw the elements of Gothic architecture not so much as responding to liturgical requirements or theological concerns, but as expressions of a structurally rational approach to design on the part of medieval masons, whose engagement with the challenges of stone-vaulted construction had led, teleologically, from the Romanesque to the "High" Gothic of the Île-de-France where the pointed-arched ribbed vault made possible the most soaring and transparent architecture.

Scholars have typically set Viollet-le-Duc's concept of the Gothic in opposition to that of the influential British art critic John Ruskin whose books, *The Seven Lamps of Architecture* (1849) and *The Stones of Venice* (1851–53), advanced a moral interpretation of architecture, especially of the Middle Ages, that had been advocated by A. W. N. Pugin and other writers in the early decades of the nineteenth century.[20] Like Pugin's *Contrasts* (1836), Ruskin's writings compared modern

---

[19]  Sir Walter James, "On the Influence of Some Contemporary Writers on Architecture of the Day," *Civil Engineer and Architect's Journal* 30 (1867): 205.

[20]  Ruskin was one of the first English authors to use the term "medievalism," in his *Lectures on Architecture and Painting* (1854); medievalism, *n.*, in *OED Online* (accessed 29 August 2013).

5. Eugène-Emmanuel Viollet-le-Duc, "Septième Entretien" in *Entretiens sur l'Architecture*, I: 269.

6. John Ruskin, Plate II of *The Seven Lamps of Architecture*.

and medieval building methods while promoting a return to some earlier traditions. Ruskin interpreted the Gothic not so much in structural terms, as Viollet-le-Duc did, but instead saw it as the expression of builders and craftsmen who were morally superior to alienated modern construction workers. Further, while Viollet-le-Duc had vaunted French Gothic for its supposed structural rationality, Ruskin praised the Venetian Gothic for – among other qualities – its decorative richness. Where Viollet-le-Duc and other French writers analogized the Gothic building to an animal's skeleton, thereby conceptually turning the wall into a set of bones over which a skin of colored glass was stretched, Ruskin praised what he called the "wall veil" – a tapestry of polychrome materials he found in the medieval architecture of Venice. (See Figures 5 and 6)

Both of these interpretations of the Gothic – the structural generally associated with France and the moral or ethical with Great Britain[21] – gained widespread acceptance in the second half of the nineteenth century. The positive moral associations of Gothic architecture undergirded its ongoing reuse in church building throughout the West, while those same connections made the Gothic an appropriate choice for domestic architecture during a period in which the middle-class home became increasingly understood as a moral refuge from contemporary industrialization, urbanization, and the social conflicts they engendered. At the same time, the structural interpretation of Gothic architecture meant that it could be used with some justification as a style for tall commercial buildings: hence, the Skyscraper Gothic best embodied in the Woolworth Building in New York City, designed by architect Cass Gilbert and completed in 1913. By that time, the analogy between medieval masons and modern engineers was a familiar trope and it suggested that both were motivated by structural concerns, were outside of academic tradition, and were intent on pushing the capacities of the materials with which they worked – be they metal or masonry – to achieve the tallest and most impressive results.

The fact that the concept of the "Gothic" could be applied equally to buildings that evidenced pre-modern construction techniques and spirituality and to soaring monuments to modern capitalism and engineering process underscores how elastic a term it has been. The critical fortunes of the Gothic, always central to images of the architecture of the Middle Ages, illustrate how medievalism has always constituted a response to present-day concerns and conditions.

## Further Reading

Frankl, Paul. *The Gothic: Literary Sources and Interpretation through Eight Centuries.* Princeton: Princeton University Press, 1960.

Germann, Georg and Gerald Onn. *Gothic Revival in Europe and Britain: Sources, Influences and Ideas.* Cambridge: MIT Press, 1973.

Lewis, Michael J. *The Gothic Revival.* London: Thames and Hudson, 2002.

---

[21] The classic statement of this point of view is Nikolaus Pevsner, *Ruskin and Viollet-le-Duc: Englishness and Frenchness in the Appreciation of Gothic Architecture* (London: Thames and Hudson, 1969).

Mallgrave, Harry Francis. *Modern Architectural Theory: An Historical Survey, 1673–1968*. New York: Cambridge University Press, 2005.

Sankovitch, Anne-Marie. "The Myth of the Medieval: Gothic Architecture in Vasari's Rinascita and Panofsky's Renaissance." *RES* 40 (2001). 29–50.

### Related Essays in this Volume

Monument, Troubadour, Authenticity, Christianity, Continuity, Primitive, Middle, Presentism, Simulacrum

# 11
# Heresy

*Nadia Margolis*

**M**ORE THAN ANY other term, "heresy" may well signify the quintessential medievalistic moment within the modern popular imagination, conjuring forth visions of D. W. Griffith-like pageants of intolerance, showcasing defiant dissenters at the fiery stake in the name of God, for "purification," with Carl Orff's music in the background. Such repressive brutality toward heretics, as with witches, lepers, and Jews, also evokes the religious zealotry and irrationalism often associated with the so-called "Dark Ages," preceding the avowedly more enlightened Renaissance and modern centuries. Examining heresy may offer a prime example of a medieval term useful in understanding our current culture's attitudes toward difference, despite our era's self-image as far more tolerant.

The existence of any type of heresy presupposes some sort of incumbent orthodoxy, whether in religious-philosophical, artistic, or scientific belief systems, from which the heresy born within defines itself by willfully differing in some way. This aspect of perceived choice is crucial: people are not born heretics, they choose to be such. Since the prevailing orthodoxy purports to represent the most correct tenets of its domain, any real challenge to this supremacy, whether by dissenting with or surpassing, constitutes a heresy and not just a renunciation (apostasy) or irreverence (blasphemy) since it *de facto* threatens that orthodoxy's inherent self-image of perfection, often supported by political power, thus necessitating the heresy's and its practitioners' expulsion, even destruction, and not merely its refutation. Apparently, the more seductive a heresy's teachings the more ruthless and definitive its persecution by the orthodoxy, whether in religion, science, or the arts. Since many heresies first arose simply by being different, without any rigorously systematic philosophical or theological underpinnings, verbal persecution, in the form of methodically argued written refutations by the early Church Fathers, actually benefited orthodoxy's doctrinal development. Later, however, such efforts to discredit or harass heretics often proved counterproductive – what did not doctrinally/physically kill them made them stronger – back then as today, beyond converts' initial psychological thrill of "questioning authority" (to use a late 1960s term).

Although the word is used quite freely these days to connote any deviance from any orthodoxy, the original context of the term heresy is religious. When we consider the multitude of heresies throughout the world's religions, those in early and medieval to Renaissance (Reformation) Christian history appear the most seminal in their theological and social impact. Little matter that Christians, too, were once mercilessly persecuted as a dangerous religious and political sect by the then-prevailing orthodoxy, pagan Rome, with even the first Christian emperor, Constantine the Great (r. 306–37), condemning those deviating from his brand of the faith as heretics, and fledgling Christianity as a whole requiring a theological defender no less than St. Augustine, in his *De civitate Dei contra paganos* (*The City of God against the Pagans*, early fifth century), to counter accusations that this new faith had brought about the Empire's fall. The international primacy of Christian heretical history, or heresiology, may be ascribed to abundant documentation: the Catholic Church's records and reformers'/dissenters' tracts supplied profuse reportage – and with it, the impact of public performance, enhancing the roles of both persecutors and heretics alike.

After isolating and briefly examining a few highly significant medieval religious heresies and adjudged heretics whose case histories continue to speak to our own time – Gnosticism, the so-called Cathar Heresy, the Béguines/Beghards, and the case of Joan of Arc – we hope to glean from these examples a postmedieval paradigm of heresy as a model for rebellion and/or reform within any discipline, religious or secular, artistic or scientific, and so forth.

Heresy as a notion and term pertaining to deviants from the Christian faith gained its first known broad recognition in a five-volume treatise in Greek, soon translated and abbreviated into Latin as *Adversus haereses* (*Against Heretics*, c. 180), by Irenaeus, bishop of Lyon, attempting to refute the teachings of the Gnostics. Simply explained, the Gnostics (Gr. *gnosis* = "[spiritual] knowledge, insight"), a sect existing in multiple subgroups, threatened the nascent orthodoxy by claiming a secret, mystical knowledge of God surpassing that attained through orthodox Christian belief and practices. In addition, Gnostics envisioned many aspects of the Gospels quite differently while invoking similar authorities.[1] Socio-politically speaking too, Gnosticism is in a sense the mother of all heresies: at least, the "Gnostic impulse" would self-replicate under other names throughout the Middle Ages into modern times, and has been related to all the other heresies treated here.

In attacking their teachings, Irenaeus keenly earned his renown as Church Father in reinforcing and developing Church doctrine while sabotaging the Gnostics' actual beliefs by exaggeration, calumny, and outright misrepresentation of their ideas and customs. This is especially ironic in light of Irenaeus's and others' accusing the Gnostics of perpetrating "false knowledge." Fate would further help Irenaeus by allowing the bishop's polemic to survive as one of the

---

[1]   See Mark Jeffrey Olson, *Irenaeus, the Valentinian Gnostics, and the Kingdom of God* (*A.H. Book V*): *the Debate about 1 Corinthians 15:50* (Lewiston, NY: Edwin Mellen Biblical Press, 1992), 11–14. For an overview of the Gnostics and on Irenaeus's treatise: http://en.wikipedia.org/wiki/On_the_Detection_and_Overthrow_of_the_So_Called_Gnosis#Main_arguments (accessed 8 August 2013).

very few extensive works describing Gnostic beliefs – most primary Gnostic texts presumably having been destroyed – until the 1945 discovery of the Nag Hammadi Library made the most complete collection of true primary Gnostic texts available to scholars for the first time. Amidst analyses of the wealth of real information reaped from these treatises, one observes that the argumentative arsenal mustered toward combatting Gnosticism's privileged knowledge – beginning with St. Paul's admonition to "avoid the godless chatter and contradictions of what is falsely called knowledge" (1 Timothy 6:20) – greatly enriched Christian doctrine by imposing a closer, more rigorous study of the Gospels and Paul's Epistles for evidence against heretical teachings, but somehow we do not find any grateful acknowledgement of this Gnostic contribution in Irenaeus and other orthodox defenders. If the early Gnostics endured slanderous characterizations – especially of their indulging in bizarre sexual practices and orgies – without suffering much physical persecution, their codices certainly did endure mutilation and burning. That modern editions and translations of the arcane Nag Hammadi texts attracted major commercial publishers attests their enduring interest, together with Elaine Pagels's widely read and acclaimed 1979 general exposé, *The Gnostic Gospels*.[2] Such honest yet approachable scholarship has rescued Gnosticism from its early detractors' distortions, particularly concerning Gnostics' sexuality. On the other hand, current popular groups professing Gnostic faith nurture similar weird notions indiscriminately while merging them with others, albeit reverently. As a lofty example of this marginal movement's influence in Western thought and the arts, Richard Wagner's *Parsifal* embodies a "phantasmagorical evocation" of medieval Gnosticism.[3]

Inflicting physical suffering as a means of persecution evolved over the period extending from late antiquity to the High Middle Ages (the thirteenth century). Yet paradoxically, heresy came to thrive in what R. I. Moore has labeled this "persecuting society."[4] Some principal milestones in this transformation include the 1022 burning of heretics at Orléans, then at Milan and Goslar shortly afterward; the 1184 bull *Ad abolendam* (To abolish [the depravity of various heresies]), issued by Pope Lucius III and Emperor Frederick Barbarossa at Verona, the first such edict against heretics and their abettors on a pan-European scale; and the

---

[2]    These twelve Coptic codices, likely translated from Greek (one was once owned by Carl Jung), were reproduced in facsimile edition (1972–84) and twice translated into English: James M. Robinson, et al., eds., *The Nag Hammadi Library in English* (1977; 3rd rev. ed. San Francisco: Harper Collins, 1990), and Bentley Layton, *The Gnostic Scriptures* (Garden City: Doubleday, 1987). For an outline of the codices' contents, see http://en.wikipedia.org/wiki/Nag_Hammadi_library (accessed 8 August 2013). Elaine Pagels, *The Gnostic Gospels* (New York: Random House, 1979).

[3]    For example, see the blogs for World Pantheism: http://www.pantheism.net/paul/history/gnostic.htm and Halexandria: http://www.halexandria.org/dward269.htm (accessed 2 September 2013). For Wagner, see Enrique Gavilán, "The Gnostic Imprint on *Parsifal*, an Illumination of Ruins," *Romanic Review* 103.1–2 (Jan–Mar 2012): 133–53 (133).

[4]    *The Formation of a Persecuting Society: Power and Deviance in Western Europe, 950–1250* (Oxford: Blackwell, 1987).

Fourth Lateran Council's decree of 1215, defining "Christian community" so as to defend "the Catholic faith against its perceived enemies."[5]

Chief among those enemies by then was the Cathar or Albigensian heresy (Gr. *Kathari* = "pure ones"; Albi was an important Cathar center in southern France) – also referred to by various other names – focused mainly in southern France (Languedoc, or, more poetically, Occitania), whose obscure yet widely diverse roots some historians trace back to Gnosticism, along with other sources and analogues in Bulgaria, North Africa, and Italy. Partly because of the above-characterized era during which it rapidly flourished and also because it threatened France's – moreover Christendom's – political unity by dividing northern (pro-papal) and southern Europe (pro-Cathar), even more than its radical theological rejection of Catholicism, Catharism remains the supreme, and most dangerous, heresy of the Middle Ages.[6]

Its dualist theology, like the earlier Manicheans', contended that the universe consisted in a constant rivalry between good and evil, light and dark. Like the Gnostics, the Cathars taught that evil functioned as an independent force in the universe, that in fact Satan – a fallen angel, rival to God, or younger brother to Jesus – had created the universe in which the human body imprisoned the soul, whose salvation was attainable only through an upward scale of reincarnations until free of Satan's influence.

By contrast, the Cathars deplored normal human sexual intercourse for producing more imprisoned souls, and thus the sacrament of marriage for legitimizing it. Therefore, to earn their souls' holier transmigration, the most rigorous Cathar practitioners, or *perfecti*, emphasized strict asceticism, eschewing Roman Catholic rituals of salvation, and devoted themselves to prayer and preaching. These "perfects" were aided by a less ascetic but pious class known as the "believers," or *credenti*, among the general public, who came to admire the *perfecti*'s extreme spiritual devotion, which far outshone that of their richly attired Cistercian adversaries.[7] But for the more easy-going majority of converts unschooled in Neoplatonism, this new faith refreshingly sanctioned extra-marital liaisons enjoyed by the aristocracy, men and women alike, confident that they could still redeem their souls after leading self-indulgent lives by taking the *consolamentum* prior to dying. Such laxness was probably just as well, since, had *perfecti*-level Cathar doctrine – virtually a heresy against nature – predominated everywhere, human populations would have died out. Instead, among the refined, pleasure-seeking southern-European aristocracy, the heresy also functioned as the religion of troubadour *fin'amor* ("courtly/fine love") via a spiritual-artistic erotic connection, which explains the Cathars' unique popularity in refined, tolerant Languedoc. It was another means of asserting this region's autonomy from the dour, more orthodox

[5]   Moore, *Persecuting Society*, 6–9 (6–7); also Moore, *The War on Heresy* (Cambridge, MA: Belknap/Harvard University Press, 2012), chs. 1–9, esp. pp. 13–15, 204–5.

[6]   In Moore's *War on Heresy*, e. g., Catharism figures as the central episode for the entire Middle Ages, see esp. xii.

[7]   Richard Landes, "Cathars" and "Heresy," in *Medieval France: An Encyclopedia*, ed. William W. Kibler and Grover A. Zinn (New York: Garland, 1995), 182–3, 447–9, resp.

northern regions that would crusade against them and remains so to this day, at least symbolically, among recurrent Occitanist separatist movements hoping to reenact their twelfth-century glory days.[8]

Many commoners also converted to the heresy, which gradually constructed its own ecclesiastical administrative hierarchy throughout parts of Europe, separate from that of the Catholic Church, to accommodate its alarmingly rapid growth. Beginning with Innocent III, the popes thus felt compelled to declare war on them – the lengthy, bloody Albigensian Crusade; so redoubtable an enterprise that at least one other heresy, the Waldensians, offered to join forces with the Church against the Cathars[9] – following this with an inquisition to root out numerous remaining sympathizers, well after the legendary siege, massacre, and burning of some 200 heretics at their last stronghold at Montségur, high in the Pyrenees (1244), an episode recounted by the French historian Zoé Oldenbourg in her classic *Bûcher de Monségur* (*Massacre at Monségur*, 1961). Yet sixteenth-century Church polemicists resurrected the Cathars during the Protestant Reformation, depicting them as Protestant ancestors and deliberately infusing their teachings into Luther's and Calvin's so as to adulterate and discredit both latter reformers. This served as only the beginning in a long posterity for Catharism as the ultimate rebel religion.

As with the Gnostics, although some primary Cathar texts have recently been recovered, most documentation is contained in Church records from the Inquisition, invectives preached against them, and crusade chronicles.[10] Though they often make for captivating reading on this most dramatic of heresies, these pro-orthodox sources are inevitably biased. Even more than Gnosticism, the "Cathar experience" has inspired numerous modern historical accounts – notably Emmanuel Le Roy Ladurie's monumental study of a Cathar village, Montaillou, based on Inquisition records (1975) – not to mention fictional ones. Historians continue to dispute Catharism's true nature and origins, even its name. As if studying heresy begets heresy, the historiographical debate is no less exciting, and usually devoid of any persecuting element, as the various sides scrupulously re-examine primary sources and contexts more broadly than the Annales School's microcosmic methodology exemplified by Le Roy Ladurie. The latest viewpoints include Mark Pegg's questioning and then overt denial of the heresy as described above, contending instead that it was a "fiction constructed by increasingly sophisticated, repressive

---

[8]    René Nelli, chief of the pro-Cathar, Occitanist-revival scholars, in such classic works as *L'Érotique des troubadours* (Toulouse: Privat, 1963) and *Le phénomène cathare – perspectives philosophiques et morales* (Toulouse: Privat, 1988) – a little romantic for many current historians. See also Emily McCaffrey, "Memory and Collective Culture in Occitanie: The Cathars in History and Popular Culture," *History and Memory* 13 (2001): 114–38.

[9]    Landes, "Cathars," 183. Distrusting the Waldensians, however, the Church clerics refused their support. This instance illustrates the frequently complex politics of coexistence among heresies and orthodoxy. See also Moore, *War on Heresy*, 222–4.

[10]    Landes, "Cathars," 182; Moore, *War on Heresy*, esp. chs. 12–18. Antoine Dondaine discovered and published the first authentic Cathar texts in 1939 (McCaffrey, "Memory and Collective Culture," 115). For the texts themselves, see http://gnosis.org/library/cathtx. htm –posted by the Gnostic Society Library (accessed 10 August 2013).

secular governments and religious institutions in the High Middle Ages."[11] R. I. Moore also supports this thesis, adding that the heresy never existed until the Church retrospectively linked various events over the eleventh and twelfth centuries.[12] Claire Taylor's work represents a more moderate position.[13]

Within the realm of popular history and historical fiction, Henri Gougaud has produced many volumes: photo essays of Cathar ruins and evocations of their culture as "living myth," translations of pertinent literary works pro (troubadour lyrics and political poems) and con (*Chanson de la croisade albigeoise*), but most intriguing may be his novel recreating the life of the last "perfect," Bélibaste, burned in 1324 but now resuscitated as a popular cult figure through Gougaud's works.[14] Later, and more outlandishly, Languedoc and its Cathar castles – as a crucible mixing this heresy with other currently favored medieval mysteries involving martyrdom, chivalry, and sanctity like the Holy Grail, the Knights Templar, and their supposed modern counterpart, arguably representing medievalism at its most nefarious, the Nazis[15] – have furnished the backdrop for such bestsellers as Kate Mosse's well-researched *Languedoc Trilogy* and, of course, Dan Brown's more fantastic, vastly popular *Da Vinci Code*. Not surprisingly, these books have fostered a booming new tourist trade for "Cathar Country" as they represent the factual liberties – though not all are ridiculous – taken by postmedieval enthusiasts for this region's heretical heritage while boosting the local economy.[16]

The Beguines (women) and Beghards (men), alternative religious communities of northern Europe, particularly Flanders and the Rhinelands, may be considered an offshoot of the so-called apostolic heresies: popular heresies that were really ultra- rather than counter-orthodox, in that their followers sought to emulate the lives of the Apostles by choosing lives of poverty, chastity, manual labor, and preaching the Gospel. These movements incurred the displeasure of the twelfth-to-thirteenth-century Church by according too much power to lay communities at the expense of the clergy, whose pampered version of the holy life was often put to shame by the heretics' ascetic ardor, an awe-inspiring self-mortification that would also spawn such Church-approved mendicant orders as the Franciscans and Dominicans.[17]

---

[11] Quoted from Lawrence W. Marvin, review of Claire Taylor, *Heresy, Crusade and Inquisition in Medieval Quercy*, in *TMR* 13.03.07 (7 March 2013): 1; Mark Gregory Pegg, *The Corruption of Angels: The Great Inquisition of 1245-1246* (Princeton University Press, 2003) and *A Most Holy War: The Albigensian Crusade and the Battle for Christendom* (New York: Oxford University Press, 2008), esp. 190-1.

[12] Moore, *War on Heresy*, 332-3, 343.

[13] *Heresy, Crusade and Inquisition in Medieval Quercy* (York: York Medieval Press, 2011).

[14] See, e.g., the photo-essay and bande-dessinée biography of Bélibaste at http://paratge. wordpress.com/2012/12/21/belibaste/ (accessed 3 September 2013).

[15] For Hitler's attitude toward the Middle Ages, see, e.g., Albert Speer, *Inside the Third Reich*, trans. Richard and Clara Winston (New York: Simon & Schuster, 1970; repr. 1997), chs. 1-12, passim.

[16] See, e.g., http://www.creme-de-languedoc.com/Languedoc/activities/sentier-cathar-trail.php (accessed 11 August 2013).

[17] Landes, "Heresies, Apostolic," in *Medieval France*, 446-7.

The Beguines proved especially necessary because, given the demographic glut of women emerging around 1200 in the wake of relentless crusades and other warfare, these single women had difficulty finding acceptance in established convents. This new movement enabled laywomen to lead equally devout and austere communal lives, or as solitaries, within an urban setting, into which they could venture at will, outside the walls of the *béguinage*. Some Beguines could also affiliate themselves with established orders. Such freedom, especially for women, rankled with the clergy – the Beguines'/Beghards' reputation was also tarnished by popular confusion with the Brethren of the Free Spirit, who *were* openly dissident and anarchic, which fueled many a misogynistic satirical reference in major thirteenth-century authors like Jean de Meun and Rutebeuf.

Contrary to these prejudiced portrayals, Beguine spirituality in fact attained the highest level, which, through its mystical intensity expressed via the "fine love" locution of the courtly poets – in an erotico-spiritual fusion resembling René Nelli's modern linking of Catharism with troubadour poetics – challenged Church spirituality, again by claiming a more personal union with God. One Beguine, Marguerite Porete, suffered burning at the stake in 1310 by the Inquisition for her enthralling mystical meditation *Le Mirouer des ames simples* (*Mirror of Simple Souls*), yet now is reborn in her own scholarly society, whose bibliography attests that she is quite widely taught in college classrooms.[18]

Modern-day Beguines have persisted, at least until recently, in Germany and Belgium. Cole Porter's famous big-band tune "Begin the Beguine" (1935) inadvertently commemorates the negative tradition of the Beguines' medieval detractors, mixed with later colonial racism (from the Creole usage meaning "white woman" [a minority in the Caribbean], then a slow dance [another sacrilege: white girls can't dance]) to produce an exhilarating tune nevertheless.[19] But more current, favorable allusions have arisen: for example, current Italian feminist theorists, eager to break the perceived "gridlock" caused by American feminist theorists' excessive typologizing (e.g. labeling as French, American, essentialist), have proclaimed themselves "modern Beguines" as they assimilate and develop ideas of sexual difference into a new, workable strategy.[20]

The case of Joan of Arc harks back to the Gnostics, since she too was condemned for "false knowledge." Her accusers adjudged her professed angelic visions and

[18] See Renate Blumenfeld-Kosinski, "Beguines," in *Women in the Middle Ages: An Encyclopedia*, ed. Katharina M. Wilson and Nadia Margolis (Westport, CT: Greenwood Press, 2004), I: 76–9; Dyan Elliott, *Proving Woman: Female Spirituality and Inquisitional Culture in the Later Middle Ages* (Princeton: Princeton University Press, 2004), esp. ch. 2; for the Marguerite Porete Society, http://margueriteporete.net/ (accessed 2 Sept 2013).

[19] For the (supposedly) last Beguine: http://www.youtube.com/watch?v=8vuJgoxx-9w; for Porter's tune: http://www.youtube.com/watch?v=zNcPnEc99UE (accessed 11 August 2013).

[20] Carol Lazzaro-Weis, "The Concept of Difference in Modern Italian Feminist Thought: Mothers, Daughters, Heretics," in *Italian Feminist Theory and Practice: Equality and Sexual Difference*, ed. Graziella Parati and Rebecca J. West (Cranbury, NJ: Associated University Presses, 2002), 31–49. For Beguines in modern American feminist thought, see *Signs* 38.4 (Summer 2013) devoted to "Intersectionality", with considerable mention of the Beguines.

voices heretical because through them she dared bypass the reining orthodoxy known as the Church Militant (church on Earth) – in this case, the pro-English French clergy of the University of Paris and Inquisition – to instead communicate directly with the Church Triumphant (God and His angels in heaven). For refusing to submit to the Church Militant and deny her angelic voices she was condemned for heresy. But her true "heresy" lay in being a woman in male dress who militarily and verbally defied the pro-Anglo-Burgundian cause still governing the University of Paris, whose corrupt theologians ran the 1431 trial. At this time Paris was still occupied by the English, but upon their expulsion in 1452–56, King Charles, Joan's beloved Dauphin, could finally "save" her by ordering the so-called Rehabilitation Trial leading to her exoneration as heretic.

Joan herself was not above damning her share of heretics during her mission, in language and motive similar to her persecutors'. This is most evident in her letter to the Hussites – a radical Catholic, pre-Protestant heresy founded by Jan Hus in Bohemia – warning them to flee their "false and vile superstition" and return to orthodoxy lest she join a crusade against them. Even in her letters to the Anglo-Burgundians and their allies, she speaks to them as if they were "heretics" toward King Charles's legitimacy: for Joan, God was on Charles's and France's side exclusively. As the trial record also reveals, her testimony to this effect infuriated the English, who of course asserted the contrary in condemning her. Bob Dylan's Vietnam-era protest song "With God on Our Side," though limiting its historical scope to nineteenth- and twentieth-century America, speaks for this syndrome in heretics and persecutors alike.

In her mystical communion with heaven and as a woman transcending orthodox boundaries, Joan connects with several Beguines: if the Beguines escaped the cloister's walls to fulfill their pious lives, she escaped the confinement of women's clothing once her voices appointed her to accomplish her mission. This was not "cross-dressing" in the modern sense, but rather a practical choice, as she transformed herself from sweet country girl to soldier: an enduring facet of her iconography finding direct and indirect replication in films and war posters.[21] Even more disconcerting to her ecclesiastical inquisitors, her male clothing symbolized her obedience to her voices, and thus to God. Like the Beguines, she encountered accusations of lewd, wanton behavior or witchcraft because of this new freedom, accusations contrived by her detractors, especially the English, humiliated after her miraculous Orléans victory.

As with the Gnostics and Cathars, though much was and continues to be written about her, we have little by Joan in her own words, except for her trial testimony, although this, too, was somewhat tainted by transcription and translation from French to Latin by pro-English clerics; the original French record was then destroyed. Apparently, her speech alone was so charismatic that they changed much of her direct discourse into indirect discourse to dampen its effect. As with

---

[21] See, e.g., Susan Crane, *The Performance of Self: Ritual, Clothing, and Identity during the Hundred Years War* (Philadelphia: University of Pennsylvania Press, 2002), ch. 3, p. 177.

the Cathars, the nature of her reality (virgin? royal bastard? really burned? Armagnac propaganda fiction?) continues to trigger dispute.

Finally, like most illustrious condemned heretics (including Jan Hus), Joan was burned at the stake. As many of today's political prisoners know, such martyrdom guarantees immortality in collective memory, which is why captors avoid such potentially "glorious" punishments. This holds true for Joan's afterlife most of all. Her executioner would experience grave remorse, and 489 years before her 1920 canonization an anonymous Englishman allegedly declared, "We are all lost! We have burned a saint!" Such utterances, mostly recorded during her Rehabilitation Trial, would furnish the stuff of her legend, a reception history powerful and multidimensional enough to outlast the Church's – and France's – embarrassment at having burned her, and finally begin the process of her canonization in the 1850s. Although the French nineteenth century famously reveled in rediscovering the Middle Ages as a whole, cultivating Joan's image responded to Gallic pride, then seriously endangered by German incursions on multiple fronts, more than that of any other medieval figure. Soon thereafter, this patriotic identification with her spread to other countries suffering foreign invasion. For example, one of some forty film-makers worldwide who would recreate Joan's story according to their diverse cultural contexts, Cecil B. DeMille, in his *Joan the Woman* (1916–17), hoped to stir America out of its pre-World War I isolationism via Joan's heroic example. To proclaim the above-quoted sanctifying words, DeMille borrowed a fictitious amorous English soldier, Trent – from the character Lionel in Schiller's "romantic tragedy" *Die Jungfrau von Orleans* (*The Maid of Orleans*, 1801), a remarkably influential play, despite its having Joan perish on the battlefield instead of at the stake. These are but two examples of how Joan's story as the supreme virginal martyr-warrior has arguably inspired more international literary, historical, visual, and musical rewrites than that of any spiritual figure except Jesus,[22] emblematizing every cultural context and ideological affiliation, whether positively or negatively, regardless of the author's gender, be it Christine de Pizan's patriotic feminist paragon (*Ditié de Jehanne d'Arc* [*Song of Joan of Arc*, 1429]), Shakespeare's "foul accursed minister of hell" (*Henry VI: 1*, V: iv, 93 [1592]), Mark Twain's pseudo-memoir subject (1896), and, well after the canonization, countless others, such as Japanese novelist Ishikawa Jun's anti-war icon (1939). She was French collaborator Robert Brasillach's idol right up to the Liberation firing squad (1944), and conversely, American leftist Lillian Hellman's during the McCarthy hearings, thus motivating her translation of the right-wing Jean Anouilh's *L'Alouette* (*The Lark*, 1956). Another alumnus of the infamous House Un-American Activities Committee trials, exiled German Marxist playwright Bertolt Brecht, had already recast her as a naïve labor-union organizer in his *Heilige Johanna der Schlachthöfe* (*Saint Joan of the Stockyards*, 1929). But after 1994, she was reappropriated by the right as official symbol of Jean-Marie Le Pen's Front National party. But less politically and more personally, movies about her continue to be made, novels

---

[22] Liz-Ann Bawden asserts this for film alone in *The Oxford Companion to Film*, ed. Bawden (London: Oxford University Press, 1976), 369.

and plays written, images painted and sculpted.[23] All center on an inexhaustibly multi-purpose notion of her defiant spiritual purity – as heretic *par excellence* – whatever the cause.

By this point the working paradigm, or "recipe," for the typical heretical episode should be self-evident: an exotic setting and/or origins; dissenters or reformers seeking to recapture a given faith or discipline's bygone purity despite merciless, often physically cruel, persecution by an orthodoxy (itself once a heresy) feigning religious/moral rectitude instead of actual political reasons; orthodoxy's destruction of all objective or primary texts, leaving just enough information to stimulate a rich afterlife within collective consciousness, even for those eradicated sects, guaranteed by modern scholarly disputes and/or literary and artistic recreations reflecting the heresy's enduring appeal – indeed the appeal of medievalism in general – to yet another milieu. Most significantly, even though history's chief persecutor has labeled itself the Catholic Church, human failings have usually been the true perpetrators.

Although ensuing centuries have claimed to have become more tolerant and enlightened, it has not been a linear progression, as demonstrated by the sixteenth-century Renaissance's burning more witches than ever before, and Galileo's persecution (1633) for what are now hallowed concepts of the solar system, right on up to the 1925 Scopes Monkey Trial in Tennessee, whose victory has since been compromised by recent advocates of the teaching of creationism alongside Darwinism in certain schools. Despite our wishful thinking, often thanks to medievalistic simulations of past events, that we live in more progressive times, injustices nevertheless recur, causing us to repeat Joan's question as it concludes George Bernard Shaw's *Saint Joan* – no less poignant in this otherwise sacrilegiously witty 1923 Protestant rendering – "O God that madest this beautiful earth, when will it be ready to receive Thy saints? How long, O lord, how long?"

## Further Reading

Astell, Ann W. *Joan of Arc and Sacrificial Authorship.* Notre Dame: University of Notre Dame Press, 2003.

Elliott, Dyan. *Proving Woman: Female Spirituality and Inquisitional Culture in the Later Middle Ages.* Princeton: Princeton University Press, 2004.

Lambert, Malcolm. *Medieval Heresy: Popular Movements from the Gregorian Reform to the Reformation.* Oxford: Blackwell, 1992.

Moore, R. I. *The Formation of a Persecuting Society: Power and Deviance in Western Europe, 950–1250.* Oxford: Blackwell, 1987.

——. *The War on Heresy.* Cambridge, MA: Belknap/Harvard University Press, 2012.

---

[23] Nadia Margolis, *Joan of Arc in History, Literature and Film* (New York: Garland, 1990) and Ann W. Astell, *Joan of Arc and Sacrificial Authorship* (Notre Dame, IN: University of Notre Dame Press, 2003).

## Related Essays in this Volume

Trauma, Purity, Christianity, Transfer, Co-disciplinarity, Love, Myth, Troubadour, Authenticity, Authority, Presentism, Primitive

# 12
# Humor

*Clare A. Simmons*

E VEN THOUGH MEDIEVALISM gained some respectability as a cultural and artistic phenomenon and as a state of mind in the mid-nineteenth century, those who aspire to return to medieval ways have not infrequently provoked laughter: the chivalric dreams of Don Quixote, after all, have given the English language the word *quixotic*. Moreover, there can be little doubt that many of its leading proponents (including John Ruskin and A. W. N. Pugin) were more earnest than humorous. This earnestness sometimes unintentionally prompted laughter, leaving those who tried to recreate a medieval world open to ridicule and parody. I would suggest, though, that intentional humor is an important strategy for medievalism because medievalism depends upon a consciously articulated comparison between "then" and "now." Many medievalist works include characters who provide comic relief, often in combination with a side commentary on the action: for example, Wamba the Jester in Scott's *Ivanhoe* is able to use his position as a "fool" to speak comic truths about race and class divisions.

I focus here on two commonly used varieties of humor compatible with an affection for the Middle Ages, namely incongruity dependent on received cultural impressions of what the medieval period should be like; and a related medievalist trope, ironic hindsight. Both of these forms draw attention to the double consciousness of "then" and "now." Helping readers understand how these forms of humor work can be a means of appreciating that medievalism is not just a style, but a way of looking at the world. Humor, then, is a means of acknowledging both the retrospective and the introspective characteristics of medievalism.

A working definition of "humor" posits that what is seen or heard prompts the initial emotion of feeling amused, a cheerful state of mind expressed almost involuntarily by smiling or laughter. My interest here is when the laughter is prompted not merely by ridicule based on a sense of superiority, but by some more introspective consciousness. As early as 1776 James Beattie suggested that "laughter seems to arise from the view of things incongruous united in some assemblage";[1]

---

[1] James Beattie, "Essay on Laughter, and Ludicrous Composition," in *Essays* (Edinburgh, 1776), 3: 344.

he also suggests that a primary "cause of laughter is something compounded; or something that disposes the mind to make a comparison, by passing from one object or idea to another" (345). Later definitions tend to agree that incongruity and economy of expression are frequent elements of humor. In *Jokes and their Relation to the Unconscious*, Freud quotes Kuno Fischer's observation that "a joke is a judgement which produces a comic contrast."[2] Freud himself also associates the joke with the kind of economy of expression found in dreams (46); a good joke enables the hearer to make multiple connections of sound and meaning. More recently, Elliott Oring has proposed the term "appropriate incongruity," something that hearers may recognize even if the message of the humor is "far from self-evident."[3] If much humor consists of the bringing together of two seemingly unrelated ideas in an unexpected way, the "past and present" and the "others" and "self," modes so central to medievalism, seem ripe for humor. Perhaps a person who is interested in the Middle Ages is enacting some kind of wish-fulfillment, looking for a world where adventure is still possible; or where social order prevails; or where artistry serves to glorify the divine; or where good triumphs over evil. Humor may serve as a means of confronting these expectations, making the subconscious conscious and causing readers to question their preconceptions. With some justification, then, W. C. Sellar and R. J. Yeatman claim their comic spoof of English historiography *1066 and All That* as the only "Memorable History of England, because all the History that you can remember is in this book" (Preface).[4]

The main action of *Monty Python and the Holy Grail* begins: "Mist. Several seconds of it swirling about. Silence … After a few more seconds we hear hoof-beats in the distance. They come slowly closer. Then out of the mist comes KING ARTHUR followed by a SERVANT who is banging two half coconuts together."[5] The incongruity arises from the moral earnestness of King Arthur as played by Graham Chapman, which stands metonymically for notions of a decorous Middle Ages as a whole, and the use of coconuts to suggest the idea of the horses that King Arthur and his servant, the prosaically named Patsy, do not possess.[6] As the scene continues, the soldiers on the castle walls debate with King Arthur not about why he is using coconut shells but about the likelihood of finding coconut shells in eighth-century Mercia and about the migratory habits of swallows. Most

---

[2]  Sigmund Freud, *Jokes and their Relation to the Unconscious*, trans. James Strachey (New York: Norton, 1960), 6.

[3]  Elliott Oring, *Jokes and Their Relations* (Lexington: University of Kentucky Press, 1992), 14.

[4]  Walter Carruthers Sellar and Robert Julian Yeatman, *1066 and All That* (London: Methuen, 1930).

[5]  Terry Jones and the Monty Python Group, *Monty Python and the Holy Grail (Book)* (London: Methuen, 1977, rpt. 1999). Shooting script p. 1. Page references cited in text by script page number. See also the 1975 movie, directed by Terry Gilliam and Terry Jones.

[6]  Critics have justifiably analyzed this scene and many others in terms of Mikhail Bakhtin's idea of the carnivalesque (see *Further Reading*). I suggest here, however, that incongruity may also function at the level of detail. See also Brian Levy and Leslie Coote, "The Subversion of Medievalism in *Lancelot du Lac* and *Monty Python and the Holy Grail,*" *Studies in Medievalism* XIII (2004): 98–126.

viewers will find this very funny; even though they will be aware at some level that the story is commenting on its status as story, they will probably not stop to analyze whether King Arthur's demeanor echoes their preconceptions both of the Middle Ages and of how the Middle Ages is represented in film.

Through bringing together the incongruous elements of King Arthur, coconuts, and castle guards with knowledge of ornithological facts, the scene is playing on audience expectations and encouraging viewers to compare what they think they know about King Arthur and the Middle Ages with what they see. Of course *Monty Python and the Holy Grail* contains many other forms of humor; scenes parody other films, medievalist (such as *Camelot*) and non-medievalist alike (such as the Peckinpah parody with the killer rabbit).[7] Class humor (for example, the villagers see no reason why they should accept Arthur as their king) draws both on medieval feudalism and on the Britain of the 1970s. Yet the incongruity between viewers' preconceptions of the Middle Ages and how it is represented here is a central element of the humor. To take a straightforward example, if viewers find it humorous that "an impressive wizard figure," played by the very tall John Cleese, who can conjure up fire from the ground should be named Tim (69), they are economically comparing their preconceived notions of what a Merlin-like enchanter should be called with their own sense of what somebody called Tim should be like.[8]

Incongruity can also function as a combination of image and text. For example, early issues of *Punch* magazine, begun in the 1840s, often feature elaborate illuminated capital letters in the medieval style, which contrast amusingly with the everyday articles that follow. Richard "Dicky" Doyle was the most consistently medievalist illustrator in *Punch*'s first decade; his series "Manners and Customs of Ye Englyshe in 1849" gave a medieval style to society events in 1849. Even though the dozens of figures in the drawings wear contemporary dress, the style imitates the Bayeux Tapestry. During the craze for medievalism as the Gothic-styled new Palace of Westminster was built and decorated, *Punch* offered a number of tongue-in-cheek suggestions for medieval illustrations. A series labeled "Our Barry-eux Tapestry" suggests that Charles Barry adopt designs in the style of the Bayeux Tapestry illustrating a current French diplomatic mission to Britain to decorate the new House of Lords. A letter from Punch himself offers his wife and daughter to work the tapestry and promises that it "will be strictly in character with the building, 'bran-new and intensely old.' ... As you have raised a middle-age building for modern senators, with middle-age decorations for modern debates, and middle-age characters for modern inscriptions, I beg to offer my middle-age

---

[7]    The cartoonish violence of *Monty Python and the Holy Grail* has a nineteenth-century predecessor in R. H. Barham's *Ingoldsby Legends*, where medieval violence is narrated in a casual tone using contemporary diction. For example, in "The Ingoldsby Penance," the crusader Sir Ingoldsby Bray dismembers Saracens until "Twenty and three, Of high degree,/ Lay stark and stiff on the crimson'd lea, All – all save one – and he ran up a tree!" Barham, *The Ingoldsby Legends* (c. 1840; T. Nelson and Sons, n.d.), 299–30.

[8]    John Cleese and Graham Chapman were long-time friends of Tim Brooke-Taylor, who often played a good-natured and very un-wizard-like naïve character in comedies.

7. Richard Doyle, "Here ye Frenche are seene crossynge ye Brytyshe Channele," *Punch, or the London Charivari* XIV (1848): 33.

representation of a modern event – if that may be called modern which is yet in the bosom of the future."[9] Six panels of tapestry design by Richard Doyle follow, the first bearing the inscription "Here ye Frenche are seene crossynge ye Brytyshe Channele" (Figure 7). Boatloads of seasick French, including King Louis-Philippe's son, the Prince de Joinville, are at the center of the image, being followed by a smaller steamboat of sick dogs, labeled, "Here are Poodles."

A new French invasion on the scale of the Norman Conquest might be a cause for alarm, but here the grandeur of the diplomatic mission is undercut by the incongruity of seasickness, especially as experienced by French poodles. At first consideration this is parody, but Doyle's work continually reminds *Punch's* readers that their time and behavior will become history, and what is more, when he can even medievalize poodles, his affection for the medieval style is clear. Doyle was also among the artists responsible for elaborately illuminated initial letters commencing prose articles. For example, an initial D for "Dear Mr. Punch," which begins a short piece on the royal visit to Stratford-on-Avon, contains not only the figure of the young Queen Victoria but a politician (probably Lord Brougham) laying his jacket in front of her and Mr. Punch himself mounted on a hobby-horse.[10]

Often, however, medievalist humor will require more conscious work on the part of the reader or viewer. Thomas Carlyle's *Past and Present* (1843) is a key example of the double consciousness of medievalism that compels the reader to make comparisons. By contrasting the chronicle of the medieval monastery

---

9   *Punch, Or The London Charivari* 14 (1848): 33.
10   *Punch* 12 (1847): 187. Doyle was to part ways with *Punch* in 1850 because he disapproved of the magazine's treatment of Roman Catholicism.

of Croyland with his own age's lack of social awareness, Carlyle creates a tone of melancholy. Even in this most serious of works, however, there are darkly humorous moments. *Past and Present* represents the monks of Croyland as in a world strangely different from the present's preoccupation with materiality – "they are in fact so very strange an extinct species of the human family."[11] At the same time, however, by exposing the monks' human foibles, the narrative shows that human beings are much the same. Probably because the idea of the human function of eating seems incongruous set in the very different world of the Middle Ages, a number of humorous references in *Past and Present* involve food. King John himself visits the monks, "tearing out the bowels of St. Edmundsbury Convent (its larders namely and cellar) in the most ruinous way" and paying only thirteen pence for the hospitality (51). Jocelin himself tries to pull a prank on Abbot Sampson by switching his food-plate (101).

Readers may remain unconvinced of the humorous rhetoric of incongruity in *Past and Present*; they will probably concede, though, to having smiled at references to food and eating in other medievalist works. Tolkien's hobbits may live in a world where the medievalist quest is still very much a possibility, along with battles alongside and against elves, dwarves, goblins, orcs, and other creatures of the world of the medievalist imagination. Yet in *The Hobbit* Bilbo's adventure starts with a chaotic visit at tea-time and ends with the promise that although "tea is at four" his fellow adventurers are "welcome at any time."[12] Given the epic dangers of their adventures, the hobbits' concern with regular meals is a form of incongruity that blurs the line between romance and realism. Paradoxically, then, medievalist incongruity often reminds the reader of shared humanity: while it seems out of keeping with the lofty aims of medievalism that characters should eat snacks, readers or viewers can more readily identify with those characters, leading to the conclusion that the medieval is not so different after all.

*The Hobbit* also provides useful examples of the narrative method that I am calling "ironic hindsight," where readers and listeners are encouraged by the narrative to become conscious of the similarities and differences between their own experience and those of the medieval or medievalized world of the story. The narrator of *The Hobbit* observes, "I suppose hobbits need some description nowadays, since they have become rare and shy of the Big People, as they call us" (4). The gentle humor of the quasi-anthropological account of what hobbits are like may possibly trick the reader into thinking he or she should have heard of hobbits, and at the same time sets up the incongruity of hobbits as "normal" and the reader as one of the "Big People."

Another moment in *The Hobbit* where ironic hindsight combines with incongruity is at the death of Smaug the Dragon, who falls on the town of Esgaroth. The people lament the loss of their town, but the narrator comments with an incongruous matter-of-factness, "they had really much to be thankful for, had they thought of it, though it could hardly be expected that they should just then"

---

[11] Thomas Carlyle, *Past and Present* (1843), ed. Richard D. Altick (New York: Gotham, 1965), 49.

[12] J. R. R. Tolkien, *The Hobbit* (1937; Boston: Mariner Books, 1995), 266.

(229). *Past and Present* contains a similar moment of grim ironic hindsight. When the frail Abbot Hugo sets off to the shrine of St. Thomas of Canterbury, "near Rochester City, his mule threw him, dislocated his poor kneepan, raised incurable inflammatory fever; and the poor old man got his dismissal from the whole coil at once." Then the narrator seemingly cannot resist adding, "St. Thomas à Becket, though in a circuitous way, had *brought* deliverance!" (67).

If ironic hindsight is a narrative strategy, it may still have equivalents in non-textual media. To return to *Monty Python and the Holy Grail*, a present-day "Very Famous Historian" looking suspiciously like A. J. P. Taylor attempts to provide a commentary on the status of the search for the Holy Grail. Yet just as the historian is explaining King Arthur's state of mind and providing a narrative link to the individual "tales" that follow, "A KNIGHT rides into shot and hacks him to the ground" (29). Past and present have come into violent contact, but violence in the viewer's present is differentiated from Arthurian violence in having consequences: the historian has a wife who calls the police, and at the end of the movie the police arrest King Arthur and his knights. The use of the historian (amusingly played by the same "old man" who is "not dead yet" in the plague scene) adds the kind of narrative complexity where the Monty Python troupe shows genius. A BBC-type historian seems to validate the story of King Arthur as history, but his death and the knights' subsequent arrest remind viewers that they have been watching the Monty Python troupe act out the quest for the Holy Grail.

Story and history work in a similar combination in T. H. White's cycle *The Once and Future King*, where ironic hindsight becomes a central trope. First, at the level of plot, Merlyn tells the Wart that he "unfortunately was born at the wrong end of time," so he has to live "backwards from in front, while surrounded by a lot of people living forwards from behind."[13] Merlyn knows the story that must be told – but at the same time, so does the reader with an awareness of the writings of Thomas Malory. White creates an alternative history that, somewhat like Malory's account that inspired it, combines elements of the mythic Arthurian conflicts with elements from the fifteenth century – hence the narrator can remark, "Seven hundred years ago – or it may have been fifteen hundred according to Malory's notation – people took dreams as seriously as the psychiatrists do today" (328).

The constant structuring, after even the less pleasant parts of the Arthurian story as constructed by Malory, could result in a heavy-handed sense of inevitability, but in the earlier parts of the tale in particular the tone is frequently lightened by the seemingly matter-of-fact narration of the strange. For example, Merlyn's chamber is a magical hodgepodge of anachronisms that remind readers of the limitations of their ideas about time; the Wart and Merlyn end up eating "the most perfect breakfast" that conveniently clears itself away (27). Yet the strangeness of this world is tempered by the narrator's repeated comparisons with the reader's world.[14] For example, when a character suggests to Sir Ector over a glass of port that he send his boys to Eton, the narrator explains that "It was not really Eton

---

[13]  T. H. White, *The Once and Future King* (1939–40; New York: Putnam's Sons, 1958), 20.

[14]  White's first readers in 1939–40 would have been fully aware of the reality of war,

that he mentioned, for the College of the Blessed Mary was not founded until 1440, but it was a place of the same sort. Also they were drinking Metheglyn, not Port, but by mentioning the modern wine it is easier to give you the feel" (4). The narrator also has the power to advise the reader to consult Malory for details (364) or not to trust Tennyson. But as King Arthur ages, the humor is increasingly tinged with melancholy; *The Once and Future King* is not alone in medievalist multi-volume works in beginning with the gently comedic and moving towards the elegiac. Kathleen Biddick has suggested, as a way of thinking predicated on loss, that medievalism has its sorrows and traumas.[15] At some of its most memorable moments, though, the humorous double consciousness prompts readers and viewers to laugh not at the past but at our own attitudes towards it, the final effect being a deeper understanding of both past and present.

## Further Reading

Altick, Richard D. *Punch, The Lively Youth of a British Institution, 1841–1851.* Columbus: Ohio State University Press, 1997.

Bakhtin, Mikhail. *Rabelais and his World.* Trans. Helene Iswolsky. Cambridge: MIT Press, 1968.

Harty, Kevin J., ed. *King Arthur on Film: New Essays on Arthurian Cinema.* Jefferson, NC: McFarland, 1999.

Levy, Brian and Leslie Coote. "The Subversion of Medievalism in *Lancelot du Lac* and *Monty Python and the Holy Grail.*" *Studies in Medievalism* XIII (2004). 98–126.

Nellis, Marilyn K. "Anachronistic Humor in Two Arthurian Romances of Education: *To the Chapel Perilous* and *The Sword in the Stone.*" *Studies in Medievalism* II:iv (1983). 57–77.

Yeager, R. F. and Toshiyuki Takamiya, eds. *The Medieval Python: The Purposive and Provocative Work of Terry Jones.* New York: Palgrave, 2012.

## Related Essays in this Volume

Troubadour, Presentism, Middle, Feast, Gesture, Authenticity, Trauma, Co-disciplinarity, Continuity, Modernity, Myth

and the text to some degree reflects White's personal objection to military solutions of any kind.

[15]  See Kathleen Biddick, *The Shock of Medievalism* (Durham: Duke University Press, 1998). See also her contribution on "Trauma" in this volume.

# 13

## Lingua

*M. J. Toswell*

FROM THE FOURTH century onward in most of Western Europe the language of thinking and writing was Latin. There were areas where that language was Greek, and there were certainly other languages and other modes of thinking at work in the early Middle Ages, but the basic linguistic worldview from 300 to 1500 CE in Europe was Latin. A student could start his education at Heidelberg in Germany, could then attend lectures at the Sorbonne in Paris, could finish with the lectures of a famous legal thinker at Bologna, and submit himself for examination in Oxford. After that, he could set himself up to teach anywhere in Europe. Even a century after the supposed end of the Middle Ages, Shakespeare could craft a Hamlet, a Danish prince just returned from university in Germany at Wittenberg, and another nobleman at the same court, Laertes, who was doing his further education in France. Both were learning in the same language.

Latin offered the rich and the powerful and the literate and the religious a common language, a vocabulary, and a construction of the European world which was both stable and permanent. Moreover, from the seventh century the basic religious worldview became Roman Christianity with its fully developed sense of hierarchy, its process for determining theology and heresy, and its preference for incremental change. Other languages and other religions battered against these central pillars of Europe, but without significantly affecting the hegemony of either Latin or Christianity. And the liturgy, crafted in Latin for all Christians, offered a daily ground bass to support the life and thought of every individual in the Middle Ages. If it was the week after Easter, then the triple "Alleluia" was to be sung at every liturgical service. The Great "O" Antiphons were sung in the last few days before Christmas, the "Sorrows of Mary" were to be sung on the Friday after the third Sunday in Easter, and Michaelmas was near the end of September, marking the beginning of harvest season. Of such everyday and festal details were the roots and branches of medieval life constructed.

In the modern era, while the religious worldview remains largely the same – if not Roman Christianity itself, then certainly inflected by a Christian culture – the linguistic worldview has shifted to English, at least for my purposes here. While medievalism in the sixteenth to nineteenth centuries was plurilingual and pluricultural, and tended to involve a rich intermixing of ideas and tropes and images, medievalism in the twentieth and to date in the twenty-first century starts with English. Other linguistic worldviews certainly exist,[1] but the central strand of modern medievalism involves the reception of King Arthur and his knights as some kind of chivalric ideal, fights with monsters and dragons and orcs and Muslims in a multitude of Hollywood-based movies that provide tropes and symbols for medievalism in other languages, and the neomedieval engagement with a medieval that both never existed and also remains resolutely Anglocentric. Thus, the non-English-speaking medieval character is generally the villain, and the character without the Hollywood-approved accent has to demonstrate virtue, rather than be taken at face value.

Moreover, the Anglocentric patterning of modern medievalism means that even where a rich tradition of indigenous medievalism exists, at least some of its modern expression becomes a reaction against the hegemonic approach. Thus as early as the 1960s French television presented a very popular Robin Hood series entitled *Thierry la Fronde* and more recently Francophones have enjoyed another television series (2005–09), this one a fantastic and putatively realistic version of Arthurian legends called *Kaamelott*.[2] Even if these examples of medievalism offered superb and original modern interpretations, they are still interpretations which engage with Anglocentric materials and offer "new" ways to think about Hollywood-style texts. In short, although the sonorous bass notes of Christianity continue today as the unnoticed backbone of Western religious thinking, the elegant and soaring polyphony anchored in Latin has given way to the funkier polyglot harmony that is English. Although other languages and other religions representing other worldviews might consider themselves as autonomous or independent or as having their own modern medievalism, these few hints of other instruments in the orchestra only serve more fully to highlight the main theme of English dominance – both as *lingua franca* and as the master narrative.

It seems best to demonstrate this point more fully starting with the periphery, to consider a language and a worldview that arguably could indeed separate it from the monolithic hegemony indicated here: Spain. During the central Middle Ages, Spain enjoyed or suffered a deeply mixed set of influences, with large parts of the peninsula ruled by two successive caliphates, during much of which there developed a *convivencia*, or co-living, involving the Moor or Muslim, the Jew, and the Christian. Thus, while by the end of the Middle Ages Spain was thoroughly Catholic and thoroughly Christian, having expelled both the Jews – except to some extent the *conversos* or "converted" – and the Moors, its influences during

---

[1]    See, for example, the papers in *Medievalisms in the Postcolonial World: The Idea of "the Middle Ages" Outside Europe*, ed. Kathleen Davis and Nadia Altschul (Baltimore: Johns Hopkins University Press, 2009), which investigate medievalism in Mexico, Latin America, the Orient, Africa, and elsewhere.

[2]    I am grateful to Richard Utz and to Elizabeth Emery for sharpening this point and many others. See also Richard Utz, "Robin Hood, Frenched," in *Medieval Afterlives in Popular Culture*, ed. Gail Ashton and Daniel T. Kline (New York: Palgrave Macmillan, 2012), 145–58.

the period included elements of Hebrew and Arabic as well as Latin. Medical texts, for instance, arrived in Spain in Arabic translations from the Greek of Hippocrates, Galen, and Dioscorides, and could find themselves translated again into Hebrew and from there into Latin, or directly into Latin in the translation school of Alfonso X el Sabio (the Wise). A rich cultural intermingling took place. The literary and social influences were very diverse for the *Libro de Buen Humor* by the Arcipreste de Hita (the "Book of Good Love" by the Archpriest Juan Ruiz of Hita), a complex text which loosely follows the adventures of the narrator through a number of love relationships moving in fits and starts from *loco amor* to *buen amor* (mad or silly love to good or useful love). Those influences include Ovid, the Bible, and troubadour poetry, but they also include Islamic love poetry and spiritual materials. On the face of it, then, medieval Spain had a rich intermingling of several cultures, a kind of *convivencia* that led not just to the word for butter being *mantequilla* from Arabic roots rather than the Latin *butyrum* which underlies the butter of most Romance languages, but also to a continuing sense through the ages of Hispanic exceptionalism.

Consider, then, the quite extraordinary fact that the towering figure of twentieth-century literature in the Spanish language remains Jorge Luis Borges, a poet and thinker who learned English and Spanish equally as a child in Buenos Aires, read voraciously in both languages, and maintained a fascinating and deep-seated lifelong link to the Middle Ages of northern Europe. His tombstone in Geneva has Old English words incised upon one side along with a northern image of warriors shaking spears, and on the obverse has a Viking ship and a quotation from the *Völsungassaga*. Other than his name, the one indication of Borges's Latin origins on his tombstone is a private inscription using pet names to indicate his love for his partner María Kodama. Borges taught and lectured on Old English and Old Norse, and one might well argue that his lifelong literary search was for the hero and the skald, the poet who could both speak and act.

Often mistranslated as "be not afraid," the words on Borges's tombstone, from the opening section of the Old English *Battle of Maldon*, are actually *and ne forhtodon na* – "and they were not at all afraid." For Borges, courage, and poetry come when fear is acknowledged but set aside. And for Borges, engagement with the medieval was something that came as naturally as engagement with philosophy, or with the Romantic poets, or with Kafka or Góngora or *porteño* stories from the Buenos Aires of his youth, or indeed with westerns or crime novels. The medieval was a familiar stranger. Moreover, the medieval was a stranger encountered first in English, with the William Morris translation of the Norse sagas. Medievalism was neither a national nor a linguistic concept: it was an engagement with an "other" common to all inhabitants of the twentieth century and available to them all, though not adequately accessed by more than a few. Like many twentieth-century creators of medievalist texts, Borges set Christendom aside in favor of a generalized secular medieval world, but his medievalism was founded in Egil and Beowulf, in Sigurd and Arthur, not in the *Cid* or the *romance* of Spanish medieval chivalry. He loved Dante, not the Arcipreste de Hita.

At the same time, Borges also serves as a perfect example of modern deracination, a true citizen of the globalized and disconnected twentieth century. In his own reading in several languages as a teenager and young adult, he modeled the polylingualism of the Middle Ages, or at least the mutual comprehensibility offered by the *lingua franca* that was Latin. He brought the Spanish ideas of *ultraísmo* to the literary circles of Buenos Aires and he founded or co-founded several literary magazines in his chosen city, but at the same time most of his fabulations are famously devoid of specificity, of the localism that might have been expected of a proud *porteño*. One of his earliest works was a biography of his mentor, the poet of gauchos and dives in Buenos Aires, Evaristo Carriego, and he co-edited anthologies of Argentine poetry and literature. But, he also wrote a detailed and careful study of early medieval Germanic literatures, including Old English, Old Gothic, Old Norse, and Old High German.

Borges, as has often been said, defied classification. He was fascinated by medieval dream visions, including in his *Nueve ensayos dantescos* (*Nine Dantean Studies*), an essay on the Christian visions of Fursey and Drihthelm described by Bede in his *Historia Ecclesiastica* in the eighth century. He was also a collaborator for two *bestiaros*, volumes of fantastic animals which rival medieval bestiaries for sheer imagination and allegorical play, though not for their profound Christianity. Language, and the way it connected to laws and to culture, fascinated Borges. Questioned once about this point, he described German as the most beautiful language and quoted some verses from Heine, which he then stated as something he was quoting in the German of Austria, more melodious than that of Germany. He compared the difference to the Castilian of Spain as against that of America, and then concluded: "Lo mismo pasa con el anglosajón o con el inglés, son las vocales más abiertas lo que hace una lengua más melodiosa" (The same thing happens with Anglo-Saxon and English; the more open vowels are the ones that make a language more melodious).[3] Borges's engagement with Old English is alive and precise; his principal concern is the sound of the language, and when given the opportunity he connects languages to their nations and their literatures.

In the Middle Ages, language did not have an indelible connection to nationhood, or even to the potentiality of nationhood. The Angevin kings of England spoke French, as it was their mother tongue, and Richard the Lionheart spent barely six months of his life in the northerly land which called him king; his famous lyric, if indeed he wrote "Ja nus hons pris," is in French not just because it is the language of love and of music, but because it is his language. The Provençal or Occitan poets produced their work for nobles and prelates who spoke Occitan, or French, or Italian, or Spanish, or Catalán. It might not have been the case that languages were as readily comprehensible, one to another, as some might hope, but it was certainly the case that language was only rarely a barrier in the Middle Ages. Latin was generally always available.

The modern *rapprochement* to the medieval functions quite differently. Language is, in some respects, the central issue in current debates about what

---

[3]   *Las Obsesiones de Borges: Una Entrevista de Dante Escobar Plata* (*The Obsessions of Borges: An Interview with Dante Escobar Plata*) (Buenos Aires: Editorial Distal, [1989]), 18. My translation.

medievalism is or might be. The hegemony enjoyed by English bleeds into a hegemony for North American and British scholarship, and a sense by scholars in other languages who also construct the medieval differently that they must contend against this simplistic hegemony according to which medievalism is a neomedievalism engaging happily and anachronistically and superficially with a medieval that was never really there. In continental Europe, and to some extent in the United Kingdom, medievalism is a lived engagement in daily life and language, a continual and continuous ground bass of history and attitude and approach. The very language spoken every day sonorously and savagely recalls the historical and political foundations of the nation, the geographical and linguistic boundaries of the individual in society. Thus, the hegemony of the *lingua franca*, the constant irritation that is the engagement with medievalism in English: these are sour notes in the orchestra, tunes and tones that hurt.[4]

Addressing the issue of *lingua*, the tongue and the language that trips off the tongue, with respect to medievalism today is a particularly fraught endeavor. In some respects, the medieval is mined for linguistic goodies, for metaphors and symbols. It offers a linguistic tickle trunk, a toy box from which to extract a word that looks attractive, or an idea that appeals. Thus, for example, a group of homosexual and homophile individuals in 1950 could decide to form in Los Angeles a fraternal order, somewhat Masonic in its structure as a set of cells (or, perhaps, Marxist, as both groups found secrecy useful). The stated purpose of the group was advocating for the rights and freedoms of homosexuals, and the work was accomplished through legal challenges as well as through the foundation of a journal. The group called itself the Mattachine Society, seizing for its central metaphor the figure from the *commedia dell'arte* tradition called the *mattaccino*. Dancers and burlesque figures who serve as the fool in the *commedia*, the *matachin* or *mattaccino*, would engage in great leaps wearing masks and, their greatest characteristics, bells on their legs. Their origin was earlier than the *commedia dell'arte* tradition, though many of the depictions of them in dance, music, and play-text appear to start in the sixteenth century. Grotesque figures of buffoonery, the *mattaccini* took their name from *matto*, the Italian word meaning "mad" or "crazy."[5] The Mattachine Society of Los Angeles, which previously referred to itself as the "Society of Fools," clearly chose the capering *matachin* as its focus in order to establish ludic and subversive connections. James Gruber selected the name, apparently presenting it as following in a medieval French tradition. In other words, Harry Hay and his audacious and now-famous friends chose a name for their society which played up their secrecy, their subversive approach, their upheaval of "normal" order, a name whose origin in medieval Italian *commedia* tradition was largely unknown to them – but would not have been unwelcome.[6] In other words, the ludic nature

---

4   The likelihood that a *lingua franca* will last for centuries is, of course, very low; see Nicholas Ostler, *The Last Lingua Franca: English Until the Return of Babel* (New York: Walker & Company, 2010).

5   See McDowell E. Kenley, "*Il Mattaccino*: Music and Dance of the Matachin and its Role in Italian comedy," *Early Music* 40.4 (2012): 659–70.

6   For the Mattachine Society see John D'Emilio, *Sexual Politics, Sexual Communities:*

of the dancing grotesque, and the name of the Mattachine, was all that they needed of this medieval tradition for their new and forward-thinking foundation.

However, in other respects the question of language holds a place in the center of modern medievalism. In France in recent years the field has come to be termed "le moyen âge moderne" or "le moyen âge dans la modernité," a locution that avoids the complications of using the Latin *medium aevum*, the "middle years," as its base. It thereby avoids the teleological effect of the traditional approach to Caucasian history, literature, and culture, framing the Roman era as the origin, Europe from around 300 to around 1500 as a middle, and the modern/early modern era now constructed as from the Renaissance on to the postmodern. Clearly language matters.

Other locutions like the French are certainly on the way, reflecting both the temporality and the spatiality of the Middle Ages, or accessing the modern reception of the medieval as always already a matter of negotiation. Some, of course, are already here in various guises: neomedievalism, New Medievalism, the post-medieval, *Mediävalismus, Mittelalter-Rezeption*. Others use participles to impart a more active sense to the engagement with the Middle Ages in the modern era: "getting medieval," "reimagining the Middle Ages," "engaging with the medieval," "replaying the Middle Ages." There are nouns ("the shock of medievalism" and even "the schlock of medievalism," "memory and medievalism," "the nostalgia of the medieval") and adjectives ("the digital medievalist," "the reel/real medievalist," "the cyber medievalist"). The language of self-definition holds firm to the attention of the modern-day student of the reception of the medieval. And then there is the problem with the supposed progenitor field. The language of medievalism, the tongue we all use as medievalists, is the same organ whether we are engaging in medievalism or in "real" medieval studies, editing medieval texts, engaging with their sociocultural milieu, rethinking their stylistic accomplishment. For some medievalists these practices are one, the language precisely the same though its fine calibrations might differ. And for others – some of them on promotion and tenure committees – the language of engagement with the medieval today is a lesser entity, an easier engagement, somehow an inferior school of thought. The dialect we use for medievalism needs adjustment.

Umberto Eco adverts to this definitional, linguistic, and originary problem when he refers to a tenth- or eleventh-century Arab version of the myth of Babel, which argued that the single language, the perfect language, originally made available by the divine, was "so rich in synonyms that it *included every possible language*."[7] What happened, therefore, was a fragmentation of the original language, save for the Koran, as all the imperfect languages fell away. In the world of medievalism,

---

*The Making of a Homosexual Minority in the United States, 1940–1970* (Chicago: University of Chicago Press, 1983), and for Harry Hay himself see Stuart Timmons, *The Trouble with Harry Hay: Founder of the Modern Gay Movement* (Boston: Alyson, 1990). The story about the name is widespread, including on Wikipedia: see http://en.wikipedia.org/wiki/Mattachine_Society (accessed 21 May 2013).

7  Umberto Eco, *Mouse or Rat? Translation as Negotiation* (London: Phoenix, 2003), 174. Italics are authorial.

that falling away continues. Perhaps it could even be said that we are enjoying our own Babelistic moment, a time of heteroglossia or polyglossia or xenoglossia or even glossolalia. Some argue that our language must always be historical, perhaps nostalgic, taking into account that every generation remakes the Middle Ages in its own image, engages with different issues, interprets with new eyes. Thus race, gender, vernacular theology, class, and sexual orientation have become the lenses of the modern era. Others argue that the Middle Ages are literally re-made, given new limbs and consciousness in every generation, such that the languages of the medieval today are the languages of film, television, Twitter, Facebook, and the re-creation of the era "as it ought to have been" by its more fervent admirers. Clothes might be authentically made of linen or wool, but not the scratchy stuff. Baked lamprey is on the menu, but with less lard. Jousting is available to all classes, genders, ages, and abilities, but with extensive padding and blunted blades. Such are the physical languages of modern medievalism.

The languages and terms of medievalism range widely. In some countries the term medievalism applies to works produced in the seventeenth and even the eighteenth centuries; in others, very much earlier indeed. In some countries the English, and perhaps properly speaking the North American, term "medievalism" has only just come into transliterated usage, while in others a different political or sociocultural stance pertains. Medievalisms are many, though the tongue of medievalism is largely an English one. It seems fitting, then, to end by addressing the question of language that has been emptied of all meaning, reduced to a floating and fleeting signifier. The Mediæval Bæbes, a modern British troupe of six female singers, delivers a Latin song in five stanzas breathily entitled "Veni veni bella." Their song adapts a version of a *Carmina Burana* text (*Tempus est iocundum*), from a previously adapted version by the German medieval-music group Qntal. Qntal calls the lyric "Flamma" and has a solo female voice on the melody with an electropop beat and heavy organ background, and an admixture of other instruments; it has something of a Goth vibe.

The Mediæval Bæbes go in a different and fascinatingly salacious direction, starting with the last line of the song, "Veni veni bella," and using that line as a very frequent refrain. They revise the rest of the song into very short lines which they deliver as a torch ballad in slow motion, with two instrumental interludes in which one of them plays a descant on the violin while two others dance and one accentuates the slow rhythm with a tambourine. Their video version, shot in St. John at Hackney Church, in the chancel and rather strikingly close to the altar, offers pouty lips, the breathy delivery of Taylor Swift, long and clingy gowns, and a tendency to gaze meaningfully at or through the camera. Above them, in a window embrasure, one male musician plays a drum set, while the women below intertwine slowly and sing to the camera, with individual close-up shots only. Their goal seems to be predatory virginity, which probably accords with the lyric's publication as part of their recent CD "The Huntress."[8] The sexy Middle

---

[8] The video can be seen at http://www.youtube.com/watch?v=tov7nv2s3tQ&feature=yo utube (accessed 21 May 2013). For the website see http://www.mediaevalbaebes.com/index. html (accessed 21 May 2013).

Ages are here. The medieval tongue has become a modern *lingua*, a postmodern signifier of Latin as a language still in existence, though now only for marking sexual commodity. As the Mediæval Bæbes strut at center stage, they use Latin as a foreign and exotic language with which women erotically seduce the watcher, and English becomes the pragmatic language, the lingua with which those watchers buy and pay for the commodity on offer. No longer a tongue, perhaps just a transaction.

## Further Reading

Cantor, Norman F. *Inventing the Middle Ages: The Lives, Works, and Ideas of the Great Medievalists of the Twentieth Century.* New York: William Morrow, 1991.

Dahood, Roger, ed. *The Future of the Middle Ages and the Renaissance: Problems, Trends, and Opportunities for Research.* Turnhout: Brepols, 1998.

Ferré, Vincent, ed. *Médiévalisme: Modernité du Moyen Âge.* Paris: L'Harmattan, 2010.

Ostler, Nicholas. *Empires of the Word: A Language History of the World.* London: HarperCollinsPublishers, 2005.

## Related Essays in this Volume

Gesture, Transfer, Co-disciplinarity, Authenticity, Memory, Gothic, Troubadour, Love, Christianity, Continuity, Feast, Middle, Modernity, Reenactment, Presentism, Simulacrum, Resonance

# 14

## Love

*Juanita Feros Ruys*

I N CONTEMPLATING THE likelihood of sexual activity in the Garden of Eden, medieval thinkers looked to the two distinct sets of genitalia that differentiated man and woman. Arguing that since God, as perfect being, could create nothing superfluous, and since woman was good for no function that a man could not perform except procreative sexual intercourse, they determined that God had ordained the sexually active heterosexual couple. This medieval idea of the heterosexual couple as necessary construct has been replicated by medievalists who have seen the Middle Ages as the originary point of the heterosexual couple and the ideal of romantic love. At work here is one of the defining mechanisms of medievalism, which posits the Middle Ages as productive of postmedieval cultural constructs.[1]

To C. S. Lewis, writing *The Allegory of Love* in 1936, courtly love was a presentist concern, since "an unmistakable continuity connects the Provençal love song with the love poetry of the later Middle Ages, and thence, through Petrarch [...] with that of the present day." Lewis situates the invention of romantic love in eleventh-century Provence, its constructed nature evident "if we imagine ourselves trying to explain this doctrine to Aristotle, Virgil, St. Paul or the author of *Beowulf*."[2] Mary F. Wack's investigation of the advent of the disease of "lovesickness" in medieval Europe via translations of earlier Greek and Arabic medical texts similarly suggests that erotic love developed a high cultural currency in the High Middle Ages. Working together, lovesickness and courtly love both fettered and fostered erotic impulses, so that "romantic ideology" became "a social practice."[3] Yet the

---

[1]  See Gayle Margherita, *The Romance of Origins: Language and Sexual Difference in Middle English Literature* (Philadelphia: University of Pennsylvania Press, 1994), 1; and Jeffrey Jerome Cohen and Bonnie Wheeler, "Becoming and Unbecoming," in *Becoming Male in the Middle Ages*, ed. Cohen and Wheeler (New York and London: Garland, 2000), vii–xx (xi).
[2]  C. S. Lewis, *The Allegory of Love: A Study in Medieval Tradition* (Oxford: Oxford University Press, 1936; reprinted with corrections 1938), 3.
[3]  Mary F. Wack, *Lovesickness in the Middle Ages: The* Viaticum *and its Commentaries* (Philadelphia: University of Pennsylvania Press, 1990), 30, 174, see also 50.

true cultural work done by courtly love has been interrogated by R. Howard Bloch, who sees it rather as permitting the denigration of the feminine, paradoxically through the idealization of the same.[4] A partner to more open forms of clerical misogyny, then, courtly love functioned as "a competing mode of coercion" that used the seductions of courtesy to hide its misogynistic functions, in this way dominating Western discourses of love.[5]

These explorations into the creation of romantic love in eleventh- and twelfth-century Europe rely, however, on the *idea* of courtly love, or "amour courtois," which itself has a history, dating from late nineteenth-century France. E. Talbot Donaldson argued that courtly love was so amenable a concept through which to study an era preoccupied with love "that if it had not existed scholars would have found it convenient to construct it – which [...] they have, at least partially, done."[6] In fact, David F. Hult has shown that Gaston Paris's coinage of the term "amour courtois" in an article in *Romania* in 1881 (though it is more widely known from his 1883 publication in the same journal) was a reaction against the type of medi-evalism informing the work of his father, Paulin Paris, and figured a move away from what Gaston saw as the subjective, affective, and effeminate medievalism of his father's generation to the scientific and objective medieval studies of his own. "Courtly love" then became ossified as a means of approaching medieval texts and became "the expression designating *the* ideal of love and desire in refined medieval society."[7] More recently, Zrinka Stahuljak has shown how courtly love and chivalry were used in the late nineteenth century as nationalist markers of France's civilizing mission to the world.[8] At the same time, courtly love, which is supposed to be an adulterous love in its medieval context, was medicalized by physicians to reinvent marital love and circumvent the need for new divorce laws. As a consequence, the idea of courtly love "continued to be socially productive."[9]

By the last decades of the twentieth century, the Middle Ages had begun to prove productive of queer, homosocial, and/or homosexual relationships as well as heterosexual ones. The flagship study was John Boswell's *Christianity, Social Tolerance, and Homosexuality* (1980) in which Boswell argued that "The twelfth-century 'revival' of love included gay people and their passions no less than others. 'Courtly love' occurred between women and between men just as between women and men."[10] This study was followed by Boswell's *Same-Sex Unions in Premodern Europe* (1994), which argued that premodern churchmen recognized and celebrated

---

[4]   R. Howard Bloch, *Medieval Misogyny and the Invention of Western Romantic Love* (Chicago: University of Chicago Press, 1991), 194.

[5]   Bloch, *Medieval Misogyny*, 197.

[6]   E. Talbot Donaldson, "The Myth of Courtly Love," in Donaldson, *Speaking of Chaucer* (London: Athlone, 1970), 154–63 (155).

[7]   David F. Hult, "Gaston Paris and the Invention of Courtly Love," in *Medievalism and the Modernist Temper*, ed. R. Howard Bloch and Stephen G. Nichols (Baltimore: Johns Hopkins University Press, 1996), 192–224 (193–4).

[8]   Zrinka Stahuljak, *Pornographic Archaeology: Medicine, Medievalism, and the Invention of the French Nation* (Philadelphia: University of Pennsylvania Press, 2013), 19.

[9]   Stahuljak, *Pornographic Archaeology*, 164.

[10]   John Boswell, *Christianity, Social Tolerance, and Homosexuality: Gay People in*

same-sex friendships/homosexual relationships with religious rites approximating heterosexual marriage ceremonies.[11] A number of chapters of *The Boswell Thesis* (2006) catalogue how profoundly Boswell's scholarship influenced the contemporary discussion of homosexual love, particularly within Christian contexts. Carolyn Dinshaw has noted how Boswell's work, and especially his championing of a "transcendent" form of love over a narrowly "biological" one (in the words of Bernard Schlager), inspired personal communications from correspondents widely divergent in age, sex, ethnicity, and sexual orientation. Indeed, Mark D. Jordan has described Boswell's lecture series following the publication of *Christianity, Social Tolerance, and Homosexuality* as a "ministry."[12] Since Boswell's groundbreaking studies, multiple publications have proclaimed the existence and, moreover, foundation of queer loves and sexualities in the European Middle Ages.[13]

Lewis's claim for the Eurocentric foundation of romantic love[14] has been investigated by the emotionologist William M. Reddy, who agrees that non-European cultures such as twelfth-century Bengal and Orissa, and Heian Japan, comprehend ideas of love that are not contingent upon the distinction that courtly love makes "between love and lust ... a sublime emotion and a bodily appetite."[15] Yet C. Stephen Jaeger has questioned the need to see sex at the heart of love/s in the Middle Ages, arguing that this is a function of a post-Freudian reader. Rather, Jaeger asserts, we need to understand that "[t]he attachment of love to sexuality has a history," and the ennobling love of the High Middle Ages uncoupled love from sexuality, in the process subordinating binary oppositions such as man–woman, hetero–homosexual, or normal–abnormal. Ennobling love could be expressed in Latin or the vernacular, between men and/or women, precisely because it was indifferent to sex and gender, and far more concerned with social ranking.[16]

Karma Lochrie takes this theorization one step further, observing that if desire in medieval texts is not called into being by the sex of the object of desire, then the existence of heteronormativity itself, so long presumed to be an artefact of

---

*Western Europe from the Beginning of the Christian Era to the Fourteenth Century* (Chicago: University of Chicago Press, 1980), 209.

[11]  Boswell, *Same-Sex Unions in Premodern Europe* (New York: Villard, 1994).

[12]  Mathew Kuefler, ed., *The Boswell Thesis: Essays on Christianity, Social Tolerance, and Homosexuality* (Chicago and London: The University of Chicago Press, 2006); see especially Carolyn Dinshaw, "Touching on the Past," 57–73; Bernard Schlager, "Reading *CSTH* as a Call to Action: Boswell and Gay-Affirming Movements in American Christianity," 74–87 (82–3); and Mark D. Jordan, "'Both as a Christian and as a Historian': On Boswell's Ministry," 88–107 (88).

[13]  See, for example, Glenn Burger and Steven F. Kruger, eds., *Queering the Middle Ages* (Minneapolis: University of Minnesota Press, 2001); Glenn Burger, *Chaucer's Queer Nation* (Minneapolis: University of Minnesota Press, 2003); Tison Pugh, *Queering Medieval Genres* (New York: Palgrave Macmillan, 2004); and Anna Klosowka, *Queer Love in the Middle Ages* (New York: Palgrave Macmillan, 2004).

[14]  Lewis, *The Allegory of Love*, 4.

[15]  William M. Reddy, *The Making of Romantic Love: Longing and Sexuality in Europe, South Asia, and Japan, 900–1200 CE* (Chicago: University of Chicago Press, 2012), 223, 291.

[16]  Jaeger, *Ennobling Love: In Search of a Lost Sensibility* (Philadelphia: University of Pennsylvania Press, 1999), 17.

the courtly Middle Ages, must be questioned.[17] By the same token, "more hetero-geneous categories of sexual desire" can become available. This is not to deny the enforcement in medieval times of regulations around sexuality, but to see these as "less 'heteronormative' [...] than they are 'desiro-skeptical,' that is, deeply suspicious of the mobility, disruptiveness, and affiliations of all forms of desire."[18] Similarly, James A. Schultz argues that studies focusing on norms of medieval sexuality fail to interrogate courtly love and thus allow the heterosexuality it repre-sents to occupy a central position from which it appears as "natural, normal, and unquestionable."[19] Reddy has asked whether courtly love itself represents "a type of queer performativity" insofar as romantic love constitutes "a kind of surreptitious dissent, a shadow religion, a queer performance."[20] From these reconsiderations, argues Lochrie, not only does a new Middle Ages become possible, one "that is not structured along the heterosexual/homosexual axis and is also not saturated with modern heternormativity," but skepticism can also be brought to bear on contem-porary categories of sexual identity.[21] Dinshaw has similarly viewed the heteroge-neity of medieval desire as having presentist ramifications, since "a historical past can and does provide material for queer subject and community formation now."[22]

Yet this theoretical reconsideration of courtly love is predicated upon vernac-ular texts and operates by constructing Latin as the monolithic and monovocal enforcer of all that is prescriptive and repressive in sexuality, against which the vernacular can productively and innovatively transgress. This has silenced the erotic and non-conformist in medieval Latin, which has had, in turn, to be redis-covered in the course of the twentieth century. The fact that there exist love letters from the twelfth century such as the Regensburg and Tegernsee collections,[23] that the *Carmina Burana* contains over a hundred love lyrics,[24] and that monastic men and women collaborated in the exchange of sexually charged correspondence[25] has forced a recognition that the expression and experience of erotic love in the Middle Ages were not confined to the vernacular world of romance, troubadour, and trobairitz. Once again, the Middle Ages is constituted as an originary point, with Thomas C. Moser, Jr. positing twelfth-century Western Europe as offering a

---

[17] Karma Lochrie, *Heterosyncrasies: Female Sexuality When Normal Wasn't* (Minneapolis: University of Minnesota Press, 2005), xiv.

[18] Lochrie, *Heterosyncrasies*, xxi.

[19] James A. Schultz, *Courtly Love, the Love of Courtliness, and the History of Sexuality* (Chicago: University of Chicago Press, 2006), xvii.

[20] Reddy, *The Making of Romantic Love*, 387, 389.

[21] Lochrie, *Heterosyncrasies*, xxii, xix.

[22] Carolyn Dinshaw, *Getting Medieval: Sexualities and Communities, Pre- and Postmodern* (Durham: Duke University Press, 1999), 22.

[23] Peter Dronke, *Medieval Latin and the Rise of European Love-Lyric* (Oxford: Clarendon Press, 2nd ed., 1968).

[24] P. G. Walsh, ed. and trans., *Love Lyrics from the* Carmina Burana (Chapel Hill and London: University of North Carolina Press, 1993).

[25] Gerald A. Bond, *The Loving Subject: Desire, Eloquence, and Power in Romanesque France* (Philadelphia: University of Pennsylvania Press, 1995).

new "freedom and inspiration to write an amusing, scholarly, sexy little lyric" in Latin.[26]

Yet pressing questions still remain for scholarship. While the nineteenth-century myth of the "goliards" or wandering scholars devoted to wine, women, and song has been discarded, Andreas Capellanus's Ovidian-inspired *De amore* (*On Love*) remains an academic bone of contention, with no consensus to date on whether its advice is to be read as prescriptive or deeply satiric with regard to the courtly love tradition.[27] Similarly, scholars remain divided over whether medieval Latin letters professing love are authentic or merely school exercises. Controversy in this matter has centered upon the *Epistulae duorum amantium* (*Letters of Two Lovers*), which Constant J. Mews claimed in 1999 as genuine letters exchanged between Abelard and Heloise.[28] He found these letters to be deeply concerned with the nature of love, with the female correspondent in particular conceiving of love as an ideal expressed through a melding of Ciceronian friendship and Scriptural forms of love.[29] Mews's attribution of the letters has been contested, not least because it has been thought that such discussion of love in learned Latin *must* be a rhetorical exercise.

Undoubtedly an invention of the Middle Ages is the expression of Christian religious love through discourses of physical love, first in Latinate mysticism, and then in the erotic mysticism of later medieval vernacular writers. The proposition "amor ipse intellectus est" (love itself is understanding) became central to conceptions of the relationship between humanity and God, while the fact that Latin had multiple nuanced terms for love (*amor, dilectio, caritas*) allowed writers to express devotional gradations of love ranging from the carnal to the familial to the holy. The biblical book of the Song of Songs was central to these exegetical contemplations of love, most particularly for the Cistercians Bernard of Clairvaux and William of St. Thierry.[30] Love was also explored within the Victorine context, most famously in Richard of St. Victor's *De quatuor gradibus violentae caritatis* (*On the Four Degrees of Violent Love*). He predicated each form of divine love upon its human counterpart, of which, however, it proved the inversion, capable of achieving satiety where none could be possible in human relationships. Richard posited sexual union as figuring the third of these stages of love.

Women mystics whose experiences were recorded in the vernacular particularly employed the imagery of erotic physicality to express divine love. Caroline Walker Bynum has pointed out that these women's mystical union with Christ

---

[26] Thomas C. Moser, Jr., *A Cosmos of Desire: The Medieval Latin Erotic Lyric in English Manuscripts* (Ann Arbor: University of Michigan Press, 2004), 8.

[27] See Don A. Monson, *Andreas Capellanus, Scholasticism, & the Courtly Tradition* (Washington, DC: The Catholic University of America Press, 2005), and Kathleen Andersen-Wyman, *Andreas Capellanus on Love? Desire, Seduction, and Subversion in a Twelfth-Century Latin Text* (New York: Palgrave Macmillan, 2007).

[28] Constant J. Mews, *The Lost Love Letters of Heloise and Abelard: Perceptions of Dialogue in Twelfth-Century France* (New York: Palgrave Macmillan, 2nd ed., 2008).

[29] Mews, *The Lost Love Letters*, 113.

[30] See Denis Renevey, *Language, Self and Love: Hermeneutics in Richard Rolle and the Commentaries of the Song of Songs* (Cardiff: University of Wales Press, 2001).

was frequently described "in images of marriage and sexual consummation; it sometimes culminates in what appears to be orgasm."[31] She suggests that both the emerging vernaculars and secular love poetry offered these women the freedom and vocabulary "to speak of the highest of all loves."[32] Valerie M. Lagorio has similarly characterized women mystics like Hadewijch of Antwerp, Mechthild of Magdeburg (*The Flowing Light of the Godhead*), and Beatrice of Nazareth (*The Seven Manners of Loving*) as fusing "the poetry of courtly love, Latin sequences from the liturgy, and love mysticism."[33]

Not all scholars have been satisfied with this representation of erotic mysticism, however. Nancy F. Partner has contested the "disciplinary" (academic and erotic) silencing of medieval women mystics in the way that the patently sexual has been anachronistically subsumed into religious discourse, such that "the blunt word 'sex' is absent, replaced by the politely distant 'erotic'; the act of intercourse is euphemized as 'marriage', or disembodied as 'union', and there are no orgasms at all."[34] Karma Lochrie has gone further in her critique of scholarly approaches to erotic mysticism, arguing that "a master narrative" of heteronormativity works to restrict "what we regard as sexual in mystical texts."[35] Interrogating the vaginal imagery by which the wound in Christ's side has been represented in artwork, Lochrie suggests that a queering of medieval mystical sex, and its severance from masculinist fantasies, will reveal that "the desire of the female mystic often strays from the heterosexual realm she is assumed to inhabit."[36]

Two phenomena further challenge the relationship between love and sexuality in the Middle Ages. Lifelong virginity was an expression of the truest love of the adherent for God, a love so pure that the devotee would forego human sexual relations to savor instead the ineffable delight of union with God. As Lochrie has asserted, "[a]rmed only with the heterosexual/homosexual divide and a presumption of heteronormativity, we cannot even begin to sort out such categories as … virginity."[37] Even more confronting was the medieval concept of chaste marriage. By the High Middle Ages, marriages were understood to be contracted through both consent and sexual consummation, and a certain *affectio maritalis* (marital love) was expected to exist within them. Dyan Elliott's study of the distrust with which influential Church leaders, such as Bernard of Clairvaux, viewed chaste

---

[31] Caroline Walker Bynum, *Fragmentation and Redemption: Essays on Gender and the Human Body in Medieval Religion* (New York: Zone, 1991), 133.

[32] Bynum, *Fragmentation and Redemption*, 134.

[33] Valerie M. Lagorio, "The Medieval Continental Women Mystics: An Introduction," in *An Introduction to the Medieval Mystics of Europe*, ed. Paul E. Szarmach (Albany: State University of New York Press, 1984), 161–94 (176).

[34] Nancy F. Partner, "Did Mystics Have Sex?" in *Desire and Discipline: Sex and Sexuality in the Premodern West*, ed. Jacqueline Murray and Konrad Eisenbichler (Toronto: University of Toronto Press, 1996), 296–311 (302).

[35] Lochrie, "Mystical Acts, Queer Tendencies," in *Constructing Medieval Sexuality*, ed. Karma Lochrie, Peggy McCracken, and James A. Schultz (Minneapolis: University of Minnesota Press, 1997), 180–200 (181).

[36] Lochrie, "Mystical Acts, Queer Tendencies," 186.

[37] Lochrie, *Heterosyncrasies*, xv.

marriages reveals that love and sex were seen as inevitable and unavoidable corre-
lates for a cohabiting male-female couple.[38]

Although the Middle Ages has proven a fertile matrix for the production of
erotic loves (whether courtly, queer, Latinate, or mystic devotional), it has also
been depicted as antecedent to parental love, the flowering of which has been
located rather in the modern world. This claim came to prominence in Philippe
Ariès's *L'Enfant et la vie familiale sous l'ancien régime* (1960),[39] which argued that
there was no concept of childhood in the Middle Ages and that parents saw their
offspring only in instrumental terms, not as emotional beings or individuals
worthy of love. While later twentieth-century studies by Boswell[40] and Shulamith
Shahar[41] recovered a sense of childhood as an identifiable stage of life in the
Middle Ages, the concept of parental "love" did not appear as a term of enquiry
in either of these texts. More recently, many of the chapters in Albrecht Classen's
edited volume *Childhood in the Middle Ages and the Renaissance* have addressed
the existence of love relationships between premodern parents and their children,
finding these expressed in both the literary and didactic texts of the Middle Ages.[42]
This recuperative move once again, however, discovers an originary point for love
– in this case, parental love – in the Middle Ages.

Finally there remains medievalism itself as a form of love, with the academic as
lover and the medieval world as the beloved or love object. The exemplar of such
medievalism must be Henry Adams, the pages of whose *Mont-Saint-Michel and
Chartres* (1904) are suffused with nearly 200 references to "love" and throb with
nostalgia.[43] John M. Ganim has observed how productive this nostalgic love is for
the study of medieval literature, to the extent that the "sentimental romance of
the period precedes any response to any particular work."[44] The love relationship
of scholar to subject has been analyzed by Nicholas Watson who has proffered as
an analogy the medieval concept of *appropinquatio* – an "approaching near to."[45]
Watson argues that "there are continuities between our desire to understand the
medieval past and that past" which can be productive, for "to write emotionally

[38] Dyan Elliott, *Spiritual Marriage: Sexual Abstinence in Medieval Wedlock* (Princeton: Princeton University Press, 1993), esp. ch. 4.

[39] Philippe Ariès, *L'Enfant et la vie familiale sous l'ancien régime* (Paris: Plon, 1960); trans. Robert Baldick as *Centuries of Childhood: A Social History of Family Life* (New York: Knopf, 1962).

[40] Boswell, *The Kindness of Strangers: The Abandonment of Children in Western Europe from Late Antiquity to the Renaissance* (New York: Pantheon, 1988).

[41] Shulamith Shahar, *Childhood in the Middle Ages* (London and New York: Routledge, 1990).

[42] Albrecht Classen, ed., *Childhood in the Middle Ages and the Renaissance: The Results of a Paradigm Shift in the History of Mentality* (Berlin: Walter de Gruyter, 2005).

[43] Henry Adams, *Mont-Saint-Michel and Chartres* (first published privately Washington, 1904; first trade edition Boston: Houghton Mifflin, 1913).

[44] John M. Ganim, "The Myth of Medieval Romance," in *Medievalism and the Modernist Temper*, ed. Bloch and Nichols, 148–66 (149).

[45] Nicholas Watson, "Afterword," in *Maistresse of My Wit: Medieval Women, Modern Scholars*, ed. Louise D'Arcens and Juanita Feros Ruys (Turnhout: Brepols, 2004), 185–8 (186).

about the past is not necessarily to displace it in solipsistic self-enjoyment, but to allow it to live again in constructive textual engagement with the present."[46]

### Further Reading

Jaeger, Stephen C. *Ennobling Love: In Search of a Lost Sensibility*. Philadelphia: University of Pennsylvania Press, 1999.

Lochrie, Karma. *Heterosyncrasies: Female Sexuality When Normal Wasn't*. Minneapolis: University of Minnesota Press, 2005.

Lochrie, Karma, Peggy McCracken, and James A. Schultz, eds. *Constructing Medieval Sexuality*. Minneapolis: University of Minnesota Press, 1997.

Mews, Constant J. *The Lost Love Letters of Heloise and Abelard: Perceptions of Dialogue in Twelfth-Century France*. New York: Palgrave Macmillan, 2nd ed., 2008.

Reddy, William M. *The Making of Romantic Love: Longing and Sexuality in Europe, South Asia, and Japan, 900–1200 CE*. Chicago: University of Chicago Press, 2012.

Schultz, James A. *Courtly Love, the Love of Courtliness, and the History of Sexuality*. Chicago: University of Chicago Press, 2006.

Watson, Nicholas. "Desire for the Past" and "Afterword." In *Maistresse of My Wit: Medieval Women, Modern Scholars*. Ed. Louise D'Arcens and Juanita Feros Ruys. Turnhout: Brepols, 2004. 149–84 and 185–8.

### Related Essays in this Volume

Co-disciplinarity, Troubadour, Purity, Trauma, Heresy, Christianity, Genealogy, Feast, Myth, Presentism, Memory

---

[46] Watson, "Desire for the Past," in *Maistresse of My Wit*, ed. D'Arcens and Ruys, 149–84 (162).

# 15
# Memory

*Vincent Ferré*

A ccording to Paul Zumthor, the Middle Ages occupies a specific position in our collective memory since this period provides the most obvious term of comparison for readers from the end of the twentieth century and the early twenty-first century.[1] Modern medievalism grew in Europe and the United States at the end of the twentieth century, when Western societies began to feel the uncertainty of the future and the distance of the medieval past. According to Pierre Nora, since the 1970s and 1980s, "our present time [has been] promoted and doomed to memory, that is fetishism of traces, of historian obsession, of patrimonial capitalization [...] Everything [has] become historical, deserves to be remembered, and to be kept in memory."[2] Are these two phenomena – the growing importance of memory and medievalism – connected?

*Memory* (Latin *memoria*, Greek *mnēmē*) may be defined as the faculty to preserve and evoke representations of past and absent things – facts or states of mind – and bring them to the present: to *presentify* and actualize them; or, to put it briefly, to keep information in mind and recall it. Still, *memory*, as "conceptual crossroads,"[3] belongs to multiple fields and possesses multiple applications: in biology (heredity, neurophysiology), history and psychology, social sciences and humanities, modern technology (computers). Throughout the twentieth and the twenty-first centuries, the concept has expanded by analogy and metaphor.

As Pierre Nora has remarked, it is not possible to reduce memory to a mere opposition to oblivion or to a shared experience.[4] *Memory* is best understood in conceptual pairings: present and past, present and future, cause and effect, spontaneity and will, private and public, remembering and forgetting, praise and criticism, orality and writing. Memory is both a cause and an effect; it is a synonym of *remembrance*, like vestige, remnant, trace, or *remanence*. More precisely, it is

---

[1] Paul Zumthor, *Speaking of the Middle Ages* [1980], trans. Sarah White (Lincoln: University of Nebraska Press, 1986).

[2] Pierre Nora, *Présent, nation, mémoire* (Paris: Gallimard, 2011), 25. Unless otherwise indicated all translations from the French are mine

[3] Jacques Le Goff, *Histoire et mémoire* (Paris: Gallimard, 1988), 11.

[4] Nora, *Présent, nation, mémoire*, 27.

usually conceived, after Aristotle, either as *mnēmē* – a spontaneous remembrance, close to an *affection* (Ricœur) – or *anamnesis*, that is the result of a voluntary effort to recall.[5]

Nevertheless, these related concepts are not antonyms; they are to be understood in a dialectics with forgetting. Memory is also made of oblivion because it is sometimes discontinuous, as the fortune of texts, writers, or motives reveals: their history is made of disappearances.[6] Besides, memory is torn between preservation of the past and creation of an image, always risking that the latter will become a delusion. Since memory, both individual and collective, is not inherited, but is the result of a construction, one may try and define the nature of the relationship between memory and medievalism: is memory a staple of history and medievalism, or is it a construction? Can we indeed "remember" the Middle Ages, and if so, *what* Middle Ages do we "remember" since we cannot rely on a personal and direct experience of the Middle Ages? The issue is particularly acute in literature and the arts, which offer a form to express memory: since medievalism is forced to rely on *images*, which are the mode of appearance of the "representation of the past,"[7] what is it but a form that is another (further) mediation? What is the limit between *image* and *imagination*, and where does invention, or *fiction*, begin?

Given its importance in education and learning, or as a literary *topos*, the Middle Ages is associated with memory.[8] In keeping with techniques inherited from antiquity, memory was indeed at the core of medieval teaching, as Frances Yates argues;[9] and the celebration of a glamorous past, of the Arthurian court or of ancient Greece, is a commonplace in fictional and "historical" works by medieval writers such as Wace, Geoffrey of Monmouth, Layamon, and Chrétien de Troyes, to name only a few.

Even though the term seldom appears as a separate entry in literary companions, lexicons, or encyclopedias, memory is of great importance not only for the Middle Ages, but also for medievalism defined as a study and a *recreation* of the past, learned and creative activities – hence a sort of *mise en abyme*, since medievalism deals with the "memory" of an era itself engaged with memory. This dual approach is sometimes viewed as corresponding to rival kinds of memories, a learned memory (aiming at authenticity) being challenged by a creative memory so to speak, associated with representation, image, and freedom from accuracy. The latter considers the past as an aesthetic category, a pool of images that the

5   Paul Ricœur, *Memory, History, Forgetting* [*La mémoire, l'histoire, l'oubli*, 2000], trans. Kathleen Blamey and David Pellauer (Chicago: University of Chicago Press, 2006), 4. See also Michèle Gally, *La Trace médiévale et les écrivains d'aujourd'hui* (Paris: P.U.F., 2000), 1.

6   For a general reflection, see Ricœur, *Memory, History, Forgetting*.

7   Ricœur, *Memory, History, Forgetting*, 5.

8   See Elma Brenner, et al., eds., *Memory and the Commemoration of Medieval Culture* (Farnham: Ashgate, 2013), and Bernard Andenmatten, Panayota Badinou, Michel E. Fuchs, Jean-Claude Mühlethaler, eds., *Lieux de mémoire antiques et médiévaux. Texte, image, histoire: la question des sources* (Lausanne: BSN Press, A contrario Campus, 2012).

9   Frances Yates, *Art of Memory* (New York and London: Routledge and Kegan Paul, 1966).

mind may use.[10] Nevertheless, it is possible to argue that these two aspects belong to the same impulse, as Jeff Rider suggests:

> The Middle Ages are, today, a body of artifacts [...] and, more importantly, the worlds we imagine based on these artifacts. Imagining these past worlds, whether from a historicist, academic point of view or from an anachronistic, popular point of view is useful because it helps us discover new modes of being-in-the-world, new capacities for knowing ourselves, and improving our abilities to understand and to configure the experiential world and our lives.[11]

Is memory a staple of learned and creative medievalism, as it is of history, according to Jacques Le Goff; or is memory created, instead of inherited, by medievalism? Le Goff argues against those who tend to identify memory and history, and even tend to "prefer, so to speak, memory that is allegedly more authentic, more 'true' – history being artificial, and, above all, a falsification of memory." He continues to note that the hierarchy is much different: "Memory is the staple [*matière première*] of history. Whether spiritual, oral, or written, memory is the breeding ground" for historians.[12] Should one follow this suggestion, at least in the case of the learned side of medievalism, and consider that anything like *memory* exists in itself, that could be used as *matière première*?

In *Lieux de mémoire*, Pierre Nora defines "realms of memory" as objects, places, landscapes, symbols, institutions, or characters.[13] Medieval and postmedieval *lieux de mémoire* include, in the three-volume project, monasteries, royal sanctuaries, cathedrals and churches such as Notre-Dame de Paris and Vézelay, medieval cities such as Reims (site of coronations), feudal borders, Viollet-le-Duc's restorations, and medieval people such as Joan of Arc. This list shows that *memory* is close to *legacy*, and that patrimony is often used for commemoration. Two comments are to be made with regard to the historical context and the cultural frame. First, the issue of *memory* was especially relevant at the end of the twentieth century: Nora establishes a parallel between the nineteenth century's discovery of Gothic art and patrimony and the last decades of the twentieth century, "obsessed" by the Middle Ages and memory and characterized by an expansion of the concept of patrimony.[14] Second, *Lieux de mémoire* focuses on French history, but Nora contemplates the possibility of exporting the notion not only to other European

---

[10] Gil Bartholeyns, "Le Passé sans l'Histoire. Vers une anthropologie du temps," in *Médiévalisme. Modernité du Moyen Âge*, ed. Vincent Ferré (Paris: ILTC, 2010), 47–60.

[11] Jeff Rider, "L'utilité du Moyen Âge," in *Médiévalisme. Modernité du Moyen Âge*, ed. Vincent Ferré (Paris: ILTC, 2010), 35–46 (35–6).

[12] Le Goff, *Histoire et mémoire*, 10.

[13] Pierre Nora, ed. *Lieux de mémoire* [1984–92], 3 vols. (Paris: Gallimard, 1997); abridged transl.: *Realms of Memory*, trans. Arthur Goldhammer (New York: Columbia University Press, 1996–99).

[14] Nora, ed. *Lieux de mémoire*, 2(3): 657.

countries, but also to the United States; and the fact is similar endeavors have been undertaken in the Netherlands, Germany, Italy, and Spain.[15]

In the same essay, whose title (*Présent, nation, mémoire*) insists on the relation between present and memory, Nora explores the value judgments common to all statements about memory. Such judgments have varied in the course of centuries. In ancient Greece, memory was symbolized by the goddess Mnemosyne, who was herself the mother of the nine muses: Calliope (eloquence and epic poetry), Clio (history), Erato (elegy), Euterpe (music), Melpomene (tragedy), Polyhymnia (lyricism), Terpsichore (dance), Thalia (comedy), Urania (astronomy); this genealogy is another proof of the link between imagination and memory. Plato's *Phaedrus* reflects a positive judgment on (oral) live memory and the criticism against writing, accused of being a "dead" and useless memory. This legacy from antiquity was reinterpreted through the Middle Ages, when Thomas Aquinas and Albert the Great (among other philosophers and theologians) commented upon theories by Plato, Aristotle, Augustine: Aristotle's *De memoria et reminiscentia* (in a Latin translation) was viewed as an "art of memory" (*ars memoriae*) like the *Ad Herennium*, erroneously attributed to Cicero.[16]

Although memory as a faculty has sometimes been criticized, the memory of the medieval past, that is the image of the Middle Ages, was in the nineteenth century instrumental in the construction of a national conscience and of a "collective memory" – in the sense conveyed by Maurice Halbwachs[17] – even though the phenomenon appeared earlier, as soon as "postmedieval" times began (the sixteenth century).[18] It is well known that in England, Italy, Germany, and France a certain image of the Middle Ages has regularly been summoned by partisans of a national, and even nationalistic, sentiment. A "national memory" emerged – according to Pierre Nora – between 1820 and 1840 in France; and as history became both a "science" and an institution at the end of the nineteenth century, it subjugated this memory, which gave birth to official history, to the authority of the state. Nora suggests the phrase "nation-mémoire" (nation-memory) to comment upon the association of memory, state, and nation in France.[19] The medieval past was later evoked in England and Germany to explain historical events, as Stefan Goebel has shown, to understand, and overcome, the disaster of the Great War, which was perceived by a general audience as a Crusade and whose soldiers were viewed as knights.[20]

---

[15]   See Nora, *Présent, nation, mémoire*, 373–4, and Pim den Boer and Willem Frijhoff, eds., *Lieux de mémoire et identités nationales* (Amsterdam: Amsterdam University Press, 1993).

[16]   Yates, *Art of Memory*, 67–81.

[17]   Maurice Halbwachs, *La mémoire collective* [1950]; *On Collective Memory*, trans. Lewis A. Coser (Chicago: University of Chicago Press, 1992).

[18]   See for instance Richard Utz's essay on the "invention" of Arthur by sixteenth- and seventeenth-century authors: "*Hic iacet Arthurus?* Situating the Medieval King in English Renaissance Memory," *Studies in Medievalism XV: Memory and Medievalism* (2007): 26–40.

[19]   In his conclusion to the section on *Nation*, in the second part of *Les Lieux de mémoire*.

[20]   Stefan Goebel, *The Great War and Medieval Memory: War, Remembrance and*

But what is the impact on the general idea of the Middle Ages in such a case, when a model of a "Middle Ages" that has never existed is created from a modern point of view and for political purposes? Not only is this model used to "explain" the Great War, but it also contributes to the creation of a biased image of the Middle Ages, of a medieval reference that does not exist in itself, but is a construction.

Literature and the arts – and particularly epics – were objects of political interest at the turn of the nineteenth century. In keeping with medieval epics, loaded with a political and "national" purpose,[21] readings of *The Song of Roland* or of the Nibelungen tradition included biased interpretations in France and Germany, influenced by the context of the Franco-Prussian war. Fifty years later, in Germany, the Nazi regime used such interpretations to try and legitimate its power – as did the fascist regime in Italy with the Roman Empire.

To mention a less known example, the singer Yvette Guilbert, Elizabeth Emery has shown how the manipulation of medieval heritage may take over the desire for preservation in less literary genres like songs. Renowned for her performance of "medieval songs" at the turn of the nineteenth century, Guilbert was viewed as an embodiment of France, despite the fact that "the art of performing medieval song ha[d] been lost over the years."[22] What would constitute an aporia for a modern reader was not perceived as such at the time; Guilbert's audience appeared receptive to her attempt "to make the characters and emotions of old songs come alive for audiences unfamiliar with them."[23]

More generally, literary works of the twentieth century configure the relation between the medieval past and political or national issues. According to historians such as François Hartog, the first quarter of the past century underwent a crisis of temporality reflected in its literature.[24] It is not surprising that Hartog should mention Proust in his analysis and present *À la recherche du temps perdu* (*In Search of Lost Time*) as a symptom of this historical moment when memory came to the foreground, as it did again at the end of the same century, suspending the movement and the projection toward the future. One may add that the Middle Ages play a great part in this novel and are present through characters – the Guermantes family as well as Françoise, the servant, who is called a "medieval peasant (a survivor in the nineteenth century)" – places (Combray), names, and stories as examples of the plurality and complexity of memory with regard to the Middle Ages.[25]

---

*Medieval Memory in Britain and Germany: 1914–1940* (Cambridge: Cambridge University Press, 2007), 14ff. on memory.

[21] Paul Zumthor, *Essai de poétique médiévale* (Paris: Seuil, 1972).

[22] Elizabeth Emery, "From Cabaret to Lecture Hall: Medieval Song as Cultural Memory in the Performances of Yvette Guilbert," *Studies in Medievalism XV: Memory and Medievalism* (2007): 3–25 (3).

[23] Emery, "From Cabaret to Lecture Hall," 10.

[24] François Hartog, *Régimes d'historicité. Présentisme et expériences du temps* (Paris: Éditions du Seuil, 2003).

[25] Marcel Proust, *À la recherche du temps perdu*, 4 vols. (Paris: Gallimard [Bibliothèque de la Pléiade], 1987–89).

In Proust's novel, memory is both individual and collective. A distinction between voluntary and involuntary memory lies at the core of "Combray," the first part of the first volume, and is theorized in *Le Temps retrouvé* (*Time Regained*), the last volume; the volumes in between progressively constitute a memory for the reader, who follows the thread of the hero's life and benefits from the help of the narrator. *À la recherche du temps perdu* also appears as a shrine for the memory of an epoch: the turn of the twentieth century, characterized by the rise of the *bourgeoisie* and the end of aristocratic rules, aristocrats being, in the novel, remnants of a medieval heritage.

In literature, in cinema (and also in games and video games), in fantasy works less canonical but typical of the end of the twentieth century, memory is at stake as a reinterpretation of medieval *topoi* or elements and in imitation of Tolkien's *Lord of the Rings* (1954–55). First, with the influence of George R. R. Martin's cycle, *A Song of Ice and Fire*, fantasy novels have recently claimed fidelity to the "real" Middle Ages, either medieval mentalities or medieval weapons.[26] For instance, Mary Gentle's *Book of Ash* (2000), which describes the life of a female warrior and gives many details about her armor, appears as a byproduct of war studies, studies in military history; and many contemporary writers are involved in associations aiming to recreate medieval scenes and battles.[27] Memory is also common to the many rewritings of the Arthurian matter of the end of the twentieth and the beginning of the twenty-first century.[28]

Second, since the end of the 1960s imitators of the prominent features of Tolkien's romances and epic poems have flourished: the last March of the Ents (against Saruman), the desperate challenge of Sauron's armies by Aragorn, the death of Théoden, King of Rohan, and the outcome of Frodo's journey, among other examples, are all celebrated by songs created to commemorate these deeds, which become "the brave things in the old tales and songs," as Sam says on the Stairs of Cirith Ungol.[29]

On a deeper level, memory is not only a motive but also the foundation of *The Lord of the Rings*, since Tolkien creates – for the reader, who does not have a "direct" experience of the Middle Ages, not even through contact with medieval artifacts such as manuscripts – an artificial (fictional) memory by means of allusions to poems or narratives that he has previously written and which are referred to by the narrator; and those texts themselves are based on a rich intertextuality that is a way of conveying a literary patrimony. Memory has many aspects in this work, especially since one of Tolkien's originalities is intimate contact with medieval texts, as a philologist: it has been shown (by Tom Shippey in particular) that

---

[26] George R. R. Martin, *A Song of Ice and Fire* (New York: HarperCollins, 2012).

[27] Mary Gentle, *Ash: A Secret History* (London: Gollancz, 2013). These remarks follow Anne Besson's analysis in her volume on *Fantasy* (Paris: Klincksieck, 2007).

[28] Anne Besson, "Le *topos* de la mémoire dans les réécritures arthuriennes contemporaines," in *Histoires des Bretagnes 4. Conservateurs de la mémoire*, ed. Hélène Bouget, Amaury Chauou, and Cédric Jeanneau (Brest: CRBC/UBO, 2013), 56ff.

[29] J. R. R. Tolkien, *The Lord of the Rings*, 50th Anniversary Edition (New York: Houghton Mifflin, 2004), 711.

Tolkien's literary achievement may be seen as a kind of fictional philology,[30] in keeping with his own definition of philology, explained in the *Valedictory Address to the University of Oxford* (1959): "Philology rescued the surviving documents from oblivion and ignorance, and presented to lovers of poetry and history fragments of a noble past that without it would have remained forever dead and dark."[31]

More broadly speaking, Tolkien's entire work might be examined from the perspective of memory and in relation to political interpretations of medieval heritage and memories. His essays on *Beowulf* underline the importance of *lof* (praise) in the poem; a shorter work like *The Homecoming of Beorhtnoth* (1953), a sequel to the medieval *Battle of Maldon* in the form of a dramatic dialogue, exemplifies the danger of memory, through the description of the fascination exerted by literary models on Beorhtnoth, an Anglo-Saxon chief who wishes to imitate Beowulf. In Tolkien's interpretation (Tolkien develops historical facts and transforms the character), Beorhtnoth dies because he wants to remain in memories and to behave according to literary (epic) memory, as does Don Quixote. The political role of Beorhtnoth is a sign of the fundamental issue at stake for this English writer who, in his youth, had a mind to make "a body of more or less connected legend, ranging from the large and cosmogonic, to the level of romantic fairy-story – the larger founded on the lesser in contact with the Earth, the lesser drawing splendour from the vast backcloths – which I could dedicate simply: to England; to my country."[32]

Does Tolkien's work represent a degree further in the "democratization" of memory, this time through the appropriation of Western memory by the common reader? Most of his work was created between World War I (1916) and after the end of World War II (1955), at a time of methodological change in historical studies. Step by step, history as a field became less subjugated to national discourses; with the help of the humanities and social sciences, it offered an alternative narrative of modern societies. Still, one should never forget that because "medievalists have often based their interpretations on post-medieval sources," both in the academic field and in literature or the arts, their achievements have often resulted in manipulating, transforming, and even creating, memory or, to be more accurate, "metamemories."[33]

---

[30] See Ferré, "Tolkien ou la philologie fictionnelle: du mot à la fiction," *Fabula LHT* 5 (2009), http://www.fabula.org/lht/4/ferre.html (accessed September 2013).

[31] J. R. R. Tolkien, *The Monsters and the Critics* (London: HarperCollins, 1997), 235.

[32] J. R. R. Tolkien, *Letters* (London: HarperCollins, 1995), 144.

[33] Karl Fugelso, "Editorial Note," *Studies in Medievalism XV: Medievalism and Memory* (2007), 2.

## Further Reading

*Studies in Medievalism* XV: *Memory and Medievalism*. 2007.

Goebel, Stefan. *The Great War and Medieval Memory: War, Remembrance and Medieval Memory in Britain and Germany: 1914–1940*. Cambridge, Cambridge University Press, 2007.

Brenner, Elma, et al., eds. *Memory and the Commemoration of Medieval Culture*. Farnham, Ashgate, 2013.

## Related Essays in this Volume

Monument, Modernity, Authenticity, Authority, Simulacrum, Middle, Co-disciplinarity, Genealogy

# 16
# Middle

*David Matthews*

THE TERMS WE use to describe periods of time are obviously crucial as they do not simply describe a period but impute a character to it. It is not possible to refer to a "renaissance" or "the Dark Ages" without suggesting something about the nature of the designated period. Indeed, these terms are obviously more precise about the *character* of the periods designated than their chronological limits. It is for this reason that we hear more about the "early modern period" in scholarship today than the "Renaissance," and in the same vein, scholars have stopped using "Dark Ages," preferring the more chronologically oriented "early Middle Ages." But even the language of "early" and "late" is not without wider implications than the simply chronological: when we speak of the "High Middle Ages" it is difficult not to think that this must be the Middle Ages *par excellence*, while by contrast, an "early" Middle Ages is possibly primitive, and a "late" Middle Ages possibly decadent.

Another reason for wariness about periodizing terms is that, having established when they came into use, we can often privilege that moment as originary, when in truth the moment is usually one of confirmation or culmination rather than inauguration. For example, the adjective "medieval" was first used in print around 1817, appeared sporadically in the 1820s, and was standard in the 1830s. But this should not be taken as suggesting that something new was going on. Quite the opposite: a new word had been found to describe a very precise phenomenon which had been in evidence for some decades. Likewise, the precise moment at which it became possible to discuss the "Middle Ages" was not the end of a process, and still less the beginning: it was simply a stage in a long process of the fashioning of the idea of a historical period.

With these things in mind, I want to summarize here some of the key moments for the terminology surrounding medieval studies, medievalism studies, and their objects of inquiry. I hope to bring some clarity to the field by gathering together the salient aspects in one place. Naturally, I draw heavily on and am gratefully indebted to the *Oxford English Dictionary* (*OED*) in its online edition (though I do not draw on it uncritically).[1] Other classic interventions on the topic (such as work by George

---

[1] www.oed.com (accessed April 2013).

Gordon, Theodor Mommsen, and Fred C. Robinson) are mentioned in the *Further Reading* section. In an era such as ours when vast amounts of text can be rapidly searched, their findings can be updated with more recent additions and modifications.

One thing is unequivocally clear about the terminology of the Middle Ages and medievalism. This is the inescapable implication of "middleness." This middleness refers, of course, to the construction of the Middle Ages as a period *between* two other periods: the period of classical antiquity and the renaissance. The neo-Latin term *medium aevum* means "Middle Age"; the adjective derived from it, "medieval," inescapably refers to the "middle" character of the age. The stages by which this terminology entered the English language (and other European vernaculars) from Latin are well understood and can be summarized as follows.

We know that it was in the fifteenth century that some humanists, looking to revive the learning of classical antiquity, began thinking of the period immediately prior to their own as a form of "middle" time. Petrarch is thought to be the originator of a tripartite view of history in which he looked back to the light of classical learning, thought of himself as living in a dark age, and could envisage a future time of light.[2] The *OED*'s earliest instance of "dark age" in this sense dates only from 1686 but there is no question that the concept of a recent darkness counterposed to present light was a standard metaphor in the later Middle Ages and early sixteenth century.[3] Opening *A Necessary Doctrine and Erudition for any Christian Man* (which appeared under Henry VIII's name in 1543), Archbishop Thomas Cranmer contrasted "the time of darckenesse and ignorance" with the present "tyme of knowledge" which had been achieved by the "openynge of goddes truthe."[4] This is just one prominent example of a whole genre.

In the fifteenth century, as well as the notion of a dark time, there also arose the sense that the period intervening between classical antiquity and the present (whenever that present happened to be) was a "middle" time. As the *OED* makes clear, there were several variations on this idea:

> *media tempestas* (1469, Rome), *media aetas* (1522), *media antiquitas* (1519), *media tempora* (1531), *medium tempus* (1534; 1586 in a British source), *medium aevum* (1604; *aevum medium* 1610 in a British source).[5]

Inevitably, these Latin terms made their way into the European vernaculars. Noting that Spelman, in 1625, used both *medium seculum* and *media secula*, the *OED* points to the comparison with French *siecles moyens* (1668), *siecles metoyens* (1656), *siecles mitoyens* (1659), and also the German *die mittleren Zeiten* (Lessing 1774), *das mittlere Zeitalter* (Wieland 1777), and *Mittelzeit* (Goethe 1812). In English, it was "Middle Age"

[2]  Theodor E. Mommsen, "Petrarch's Conception of the Dark Ages," *Speculum* 17 (1942): 226–42.
[3]  *OED*, s.v. dark, *adj.* S3 dark ages.
[4]  *A necessary doctrine and erudicion for any chrysten man set furth by the kynges maiestye of Englande. &c.* (London: Thomas Berthelet, 1543), A.iir
[5]  *OED* s.v. middle age, *n.* and *adj.*

(later more commonly in the plural) that became standard (with "middle time" as a lesser competitor). The *OED* attributes the first known use of "Middle Age" in this sense to the second edition of John Foxe's *Acts and Monuments* in 1570:

> Thus thou seest (gentle reader) sufficiently declared, what the Moonkes were in the primitiue tyme of the church, and what were the Moonkes of the middle age, and of these our latter dayes of the church.[6]

For Foxe, the primitive time of the Church is that immediately after the apostles, hence of late antiquity. This in turn suggests that what he means by the middle age here is the time between late antiquity and the Reformation (in the light of which he is explicitly writing). After Foxe, and more particularly William Camden (to whom we will turn in a moment), the idea of a middle age was, seemingly, espoused as a general period of history. This was the case in Germany by the early seventeenth century, according to Reinhart Koselleck, and in France by 1640; Koselleck adds that, "It was only in the eighteenth century that the term, primarily still in its pejorative sense, was generally accepted ..."[7]

However, while there is no doubt that the Latin concept of a *medium aevum* was available to Foxe and his readers, it is not at all clear that what he intended was reference to a general historical period. The quotation above, placed in context, almost certainly refers to a middle age *of the Church* rather than a general period. The *OED* does not mention at this point the *first* edition of *Acts and Monuments*, which similarly refers to the primitive time of the Church:

> Thus the catholike churche in her infancy, was innoce[n]t, in her child hode, she grew and multiplyed, in her youthe she increased and gat strength. And in her midle age she wrastled with sondrie sectes, schismes and shismatickes, especially such as contended for supremacie.
>
> Thus the churche coming to her midle age about. viii. or ix hundreth yeres after Christ, began again to decay, by litel & litel.[8]

While this is completely clear about *when* the Church arrived at its middle age, it also strongly suggests that what is intended is *not* a reference to a period of history but rather, in a biological metaphor, a phase of life. The concept of human "middle age" was well known at the time. The classical and medieval notion of the seven ages of man was rivalled, in the late Middle Ages, by the tripartite concept we are more familiar with today: youth, middle age, and old age. The *OED* cites *Piers Plowman* as giving the earliest instance of "middle age" in this sense. Also around the same time, Trevisa, in his translation of Bartholomaeus Anglicus, uses the same term. We can compare this with the early fourteenth-century romance *Arthour and Merlin*, which refers to noble knights "of midel liue" (line 5392). In this sense, biological middle age

---

[6]  John Foxe, *Acts and Monuments* (1570), Book 3, p. 217; cited from www.johnfoxe.org.

[7]  Reinhart Koselleck, "The Eighteenth Century as the Beginning of Modernity," in Koselleck, *The Practice of Conceptual History: Timing History, Spacing Concepts*, trans. Todd Samuel Presner et al. (Stanford: Stanford University Press, 2002), 163.

[8]  *Acts and Monuments*, 1563, book 1, pp. 24, 25. Cited from www.johnfoxe.org.

was usually regarded positively (counterposed to decrepit old age), and it continued to be regarded in this way throughout the sixteenth century.

Foxe, in subsequent editions of *Acts and Monuments*, never uses "middle age" other than in reference to the middle age of the Church. Hence it looks as if there is some semantic contamination so far as vernacular terminology is concerned between the concept of the *medium aevum* with the earlier and still prevalent concept of "middle age" as a phase of life: Foxe could envisage the Church as having a middle age, just like a person; he does not seem to have generalised a period of history from this notion. Indeed, in the late sixteenth century, the use of "middle age" as a period seems to have been more general than particular: for instance, in Lodowick Lloyd's *The Consent of Time Disciphering the Errors of the Grecians in their Olympiads …* (1590), the middle age of the world is placed in Old Testament time, at some point between the earliest patriarchs and classical antiquity.

It is not until the early seventeenth century and William Camden that we have, in English, what looks more securely like the sense of a general historical period nominated by "Middle Ages." In his 1605 *Remaines of a Greater Work, Concerning Britaine*, Camden cites a poem he says is "of the middle age."[9] We appear here to be on surer ground. And there is no question that thereafter, in English, "Middle Age(s)" becomes a commonplace general historical term, referring to the period between classical antiquity and the sixteenth century, usually in a negative sense. In Europe more widely in the seventeenth century, the terminology was becoming settled. The German classical scholar Christoph Cellarius is usually credited with the clear division of history "in Antiquam et medii Aevi ac novum," in 1685. Even so, according to Koselleck, the triad of antiquity, Middle Ages, and modernity was not generally accepted in the eighteenth century (though the idea that 1500 was some form of threshold was).[10]

It appears initially curious that no one seems to have found it necessary to construe an adjective from either the Latin or the English noun. The adjective "medieval" did not appear in English until about 1817, when the minor antiquarian Thomas Fosbroke used it in a book on monasticism and continued to use it in scholarly articles over the following decade.[11] Fosbroke seems to have been unaware that he had coined a new term and it may well be that he unconsciously invented the word by automatically translating *medium aevum* and converting it into an adjective. His coinage took about a decade to enter wider scholarly discourse; it can be traced in various appearances in scholarly journals of the 1820s and 1830s. English led the way here, with the French *médiéval* and German *mittelalterlich* following later in the nineteenth century.

Prior to what appears to be Fosbroke's linguistic innovation, we see writers using cumbersome periphrases such as "of the Middle Age," apparently because they lack the simple adjective. But as I have already warned, the appearance of a word is not

---

[9]   London, 1605, STC 4521 (5).

[10]   Reinhart Koselleck, "'Neuzeit': Remarks on the Semantics of Modern Concepts of Movement," in *Futures Past: On the Semantics of Historical Time*, trans. and intro. Keith Tribe (New York: Columbia University Press, 2004), 222–54 (234).

[11]   Matthews, "From Mediaeval to Mediaevalism: A New Semantic History," *Review of English Studies* 62 (2011): 695–715.

an inauguration but a culmination. George Gordon credits the humanist Joachim von Watt of St. Gall with the first vernacular use of a cognate of "medieval" – *mitteljärigen* – in the sixteenth century. He notes that the term appears not to have caught on in German and later had to be reinvented.[12] Meanwhile in English it was reasonably common to use either "middle-aged" or "middle-age" – meaning what we denote by "medieval" – as far back as 1611. (Furthermore, although it would be rare to hear either expression used in this sense today, the *OED* shows the persistence of these synonyms beyond the coinage of "medieval" and right up until the early twentieth century [*OED* s.v. middle age, *n*. and *adj*. B.1; s.v. middle-aged, *adj*. 2]). Many writers use either "feudal" or "Gothic" as a synonym for the absent "medieval" in the eighteenth century. As Clare Simmons notes, David Hume, in his *History of England*, refers to the "feudal period" and once says "of the middle age."[13]

Hence, it seems likely that "medieval" was only construed from *medium aevum* at what appears to be a late date because before then, nobody needed it. The reason it came into use around 1817, as I have argued in an earlier article,[14] is because of its neutrality. "Medieval" came with no baggage, no prior assumptions about the nature of the period it denoted, whereas such terms as "feudal" and "Gothic" came with a great deal of baggage. But it is important to clarify that in 1817, this was not the neutral adjective that everyone had been waiting for. It was rather that descriptive neutrality had only just become desirable, at the same time as "Gothic" was becoming a pejorative term.

This was the logical outcome of a period of several decades in which, under the influence of French scholars and German Romanticism, British writers had returned to the Middle Ages not, like Foxe and so many commentators thereafter, to vilify the period, but to retrieve from it what was thought to be valuable. It was in the context of this rise in interest – which was checked but certainly not halted by the Napoleonic wars – that Fosbroke came up with his new adjective, one which separated the nascent study of medieval culture from, for example, such conceptions of medieval culture as were delivered by the "Gothic" novel.

The last of the terms under review here to arise was the most pertinent to the current context: "medievalism" itself, which is obviously a fresh noun derived from the newish adjective. This term was, for a long time, thought to be a coinage by John Ruskin in 1853. In fact it arose in the early 1840s, a period which, while it saw a general rise in interest in medieval culture, was also fraught with fears about resurgent English Catholicism. The Oxford Movement and the turn to neo-Gothic in architecture were welcomed by some but led others to decry this fresh turn to the Middle Ages. In this context, the hitherto neutral adjective "medieval" began to be used in pejorative senses and the negative sense of the word was born.

In 1841, John Henry Newman wrote the ninetieth and last of the Oxford Movement's tracts, arguing for the close compatibility of the Anglican Church's Thirty-Nine

---

[12]  Gordon, "Medium Aevum and the Middle Age," *Society for Pure English Tract* 19 (1925): 3–28 (23).

[13]  Clare A. Simmons, "Medievalism: Its Linguistic History in Nineteenth-Century Britain," *Studies in Medievalism* XIII (2009): 28–35 (30).

[14]  "From Mediaeval to Mediaevalism."

Articles with Catholicism. Reactions against the Oxford Movement in the early 1840s label it very specifically as "Mediaevalism," and with clear derogatory intent. The earliest such reference in print that I have been able to find is in 1844.[15] Another, in a long critique of Newman's *Essay on the Development of Christian Doctrine* (1845), appeared anonymously in the *Quarterly Review* in March 1846, by which time its author would have known that Newman had resigned his Oxford fellowship, left the Church of England, and been received into the Catholic Church. For this author, "Mediaevalism" is a synonym for Catholicism and it is used in such a way as to suggest the term was well known.[16] It seems probable, then, that at some point between the first of the tracts in 1833 and the mid-1840s, renewed Catholicism had been labelled as "medievalism." The new noun encapsulated precisely what was wrong with the Middle Ages.

The period between about 1817 and 1844, then, was in general a fruitful one for the development of medieval studies, witnessing a shift in which the "middleness" of the Middle Ages was first taken in a newly neutral sense (a "middle" only in that it appears between two other things). But by the end of the same period, this new view of "middleness" was elided with the Reformation view of periodization, so that a "middle" age is also a dark age. By the end of the 1840s the word "medievalism" appears to have come into general use, and in 1851 we even find Dante Gabriel Rossetti referring to his own "medievalisms" in self-mocking tones, but at the same time using the word in the way modern scholars do, to refer to self-conscious recreations of medieval culture in the modern age. In England in the 1850s, the word "medievalism" occurs most often in writings on architecture, very often with the intention of denigrating neo-Gothic buildings. But quite quickly, "medievalism" came to have a more general sense and some of its pejorative force was lost. In the second half of the century it is common to see "medievalism" referred to neutrally or favorably; such works as Tennyson's *Idylls of the King* were seen, in a good sense, as a form of medievalism. A reviewer of *Idylls of the King* in 1859 refers to Tennyson's turning "to the purely objective side of mediaevalism, to which his sympathies have evidently been long directed."[17]

The different trajectories traced here indicate the deep ambiguity associated with the Middle Ages as a period in nineteenth-century thought, even as medievalist literature and medieval studies consolidated themselves in the second half of the century. First used as a newly objective scholarly term, "medieval" was adopted as part of a shift away from the sixteenth-century construction of a dark age. Yet rapidly, the word took on a negative sense and was re-associated with the sixteenth-century sense of the Middle or Dark Ages. Conversely "medievalism," first used to denigrate renewed Catholicism, rapidly spread in use and took on positive coloring.

This history clearly matters today, in that it has shaped common perceptions of the period we study, as both medievalists and those working in medievalism studies.

---

[15] See "From Mediaeval to Mediaevalism."

[16] Review of Newman, *An Essay on the Development of Christian Doctrine*, *Quarterly Review* 77.154 (March 1846): 404–65 (448).

[17] Anonymous review of Tennyson, *Idylls of the King*, *Universal Review* 2 (August 1859): 251–68 (260).

As I suggested at the outset, periodizing adjectives do not simply describe, but impute a character to the period in question. Nevertheless, these adjectives can also become neutral and inert, with long use. This, I would suggest, has happened with the "middling" character of our period. Today, "middle" is no longer truly pejorative. Indeed, in some quarters, it is almost a badge of honor. To be "in the middle," after all, could be thought of as being at the heart of the matter, in the thick of things, which is certainly how the medievalist blog "In the Middle" portrays it (http://www. inthemedievalmiddle.com/). In the popular view it is perhaps no longer the *medium* of *medium aevum* that is the problem, but the *-eval*. This has lost its etymon and is instead a homophone, inviting such titles as that of the action-adventure video game "MediEvil." The longstanding associations of this period with darkness are ultimately the most difficult to avoid.

Even that association, however, is not uniformly regarded in negative terms: not in an era in which modern Goths stroll the streets, in which Viking culture is enthusiastically praised, in which amateurs with metal detectors find spectacular hoards from the earlier medieval centuries. Perhaps the old and inescapable sense that a middle age must chiefly be something "middling," something designed to hold two other things apart, is no longer a concern over which modern scholars need obsess. The Middle Ages has always been associated with nostalgia; living as we do in what we are constantly assured are the end times, those middling days now seem like a good thing to take into the future.

## Further Reading

De Grazia, Margaret. "Anachronism." In *Cultural Reformations: Medieval and Renaissance in Literary History*. Ed. Brian Cummings and James Simpson. Oxford: Oxford University Press, 2010. 13–32

Gordon, George. "Medium Aevum and the Middle Age." *Society for Pure English Tract* 19 (1925). 3–28.

Koselleck, Reinhart. *The Practice of Conceptual History: Timing History, Spacing Concepts*. Trans. Todd Samuel Presner et al. Stanford: Stanford University Press, 2002.

——. *Futures Past: On the Semantics of Historical Time*. Trans. and intro. Keith Tribe. New York: Columbia University Press, 2004.

Matthews, David. "From Mediaeval to Mediaevalism: A New Semantic History." *Review of English Studies* 62 (2011). 695–715.

Mommsen, Theodor E. "Petrarch's Conception of the Dark Ages." *Speculum* 17 (1942). 226–42.

Robinson, Fred C. "*Medieval*, the *Middle Ages*." In *The Tomb of Beowulf and other Essays on Old English*. Oxford: Blackwells, 1993.

## Related Essays in this Volume

Christianity, Continuity, Modernity, Gothic, Presentism, Lingua, Monument, Primitive, Play

# 17
## Modernity

*Tom Shippey*

**M**EDIEVALISM IS SELF-EVIDENTLY a modern invention. One cannot have a middle without two ends, and the very phrase "the Middle Ages" implies a prior and a later period to frame those ages. The nature of European and American childrearing over many centuries further implied, very strongly, an earlier period of classical civilization which had produced the Latin and Greek texts which formed the basis of young male education and a later contemporary period which posed itself as a successor to that period. The time in between was inevitably seen as a trough between two peaks. Whether that perception was correct remains contested, both by historians and in popular awareness.

One may say that "medievalism," in the modern sense, began when that perception began to be contested. The immediate point, however, is that no literary work of medievalism can avoid some interaction with modernity. Literary medievalism, and movie medievalism as well, must always be in some sense contrastive, if only because the reader is aware of his/her own surroundings.[1] Every writer, of course, finds his/her own way of dealing with this, and multiple ingenuities may make it impossible to frame any wholly satisfactory general categorization of modernity in medievalism. Some generalizations may, however, be put forward as a first suggestive stage.

Three factors seem to be strongly involved in determining an author's interaction between the modern and the medieval. The first is, very evidently, the author's own attitude to the medieval: at one extreme, contemptuous, at the other, adulatory. A second factor is the author's attitude to his/her imagined readers: at one extreme superior, hortatory, ready to deliver information not expected to be challenged, at the other, tentative or ingratiating. A third factor, rather harder to assess, but of particular importance in movie medievalism, is the author's relationship to the well-developed general awareness of "the medieval imaginary," in which crusaders, friars, Robin Hood, Normans and Saxons, and much else, exist in a permanent anachronistic stew.

---

[1] This may not be the case with, for instance, architectural medievalism.

One can indeed imagine a three-dimensional model of modernity in medie-valism, with factor 1 above occupying the horizontal axis, factor 2 the vertical, and factor 3 at 90 degrees. All authors and directors could in theory be placed within this model, which would no doubt show first, the striking differences between approaches and second, probably, a slow creep away from the contemptuous, supe-rior, undifferentiating position which would occupy (in chiastic order) the far upper right corner of our hypothetical box.

The obvious work to place in that multiply extreme position is Mark Twain's *A Connecticut Yankee at King Arthur's Court* (1889). Twain views the Middle Ages with open horror, compounded by ethnocentric nationalism. His hero, Hank the Yankee, is at once an engineer, a Protestant, and a Republican/Democrat, all three self-positionings felt to be peculiarly American. Well-meaning critics have attempted to clear Twain of such charges of naïve culturocentrism by pointing to the gruesome debacle with which the work ends – thousands of knightly corpses rotting as a result of mass electrocution by Hank – but the ending does not succeed in making the many previous open statements seem suitably ironic.

Nor is there any good evidence for distinguishing Hank's views from Twain's, or from the views likely to be popular with the work's first American audience. Hank (who in his own time worked for Samuel Colt) establishes supremacy at King Arthur's court by predicting an eclipse, inventing blasting powder and the lightning rod, and going on with revolvers, bicycles, printing presses, and electric power.[2] Several of these devices are also the stock-in-trade of nineteenth-century British romances set in "darkest Africa," and Hank makes the same assumption of cultural superiority by referring to the Arthurian nobles as "white Indians ... merely modified savages." Special disapproval is reserved for the Catholic Church, "death to human liberty." And it is surely the well- if mis-informed voice of Twain (relying here on William Lecky's *History of European Morals*, 1869), not half-educated Hank, which repeats several of the legendary features of the feudal system, not quite ending with the notorious *ius primae noctis*: "if the freeman's daughter – but no, that last infamy of monarchical government is unprintable."[3]

Twain is then modernistically contemptuous of the Middle Ages, which he furthermore regards in a markedly undifferentiating way. His idea of sixth-century King Arthur is that of fifteenth-century Sir Thomas Malory, the intervening thou-sand years being regarded as one whole, without change or development, and all of it in simple opposition to late nineteenth-century America. Hank's superior

[2]   It was soon realised, and pointed out, that even making "blasting powder" is not just a case of happening to know the formula. For a modern to impose himself on a medieval society would be much harder than Twain thought, or affected to think. This is the basis for such ripostes to "Connecticut Yankee" as L. Sprague de Camp's famous "back in time" novel, *Lest Darkness Fall* (New York: Henry Holt, 1941). I should state here that many years ago de Camp informed me that in writing that novel he was not responding directly to Twain, but to an inferior imitation of "Connecticut Yankee" published in *Astounding Science Fiction*. I have never been able to trace this perhaps justly forgotten work.

[3]   Mark Twain, *A Connecticut Yankee in King Arthur's Court*, ed. M. Thomas Inge (World's Classics edn., Oxford: Oxford University Press, 1997), 21, 88, 69, 91 (chs. 2, 13, 10, 13 respectively).

role as first-hand observer also allows Twain to slide into his imagined Middle Age one feature from his own nation and century: a very prominent institution of slavery. This probably passed unchallenged with his original audience, for whom there was much to be gained by projecting a detested institution of their own time and civilization onto another continent and into the past, so universalizing it. But the only slight palliation of Hank/Twain's multiple assumptions of superiority is the admiration they nevertheless express for both King Arthur and Sir Lancelot: figures too deeply embedded in popular awareness to be utterly dismissed.

In all this, Twain was clearly counterpunching to an already established vision of the Middle Ages which he disliked, and which he thought had proved disastrous for the Southern aristocracy of his own time, and so for the United and Confederate States all together. This was the collective image created by Walter Scott. In our imagined 3D model, Scott would be approximately central on the horizontal axis: aware of his own time's technological and intellectual superiority, but markedly sympathetic to medieval romantic ideals. He would, however, be just as high as Twain, or even a notch higher, on the vertical axis, because of his readiness to address the reader *de haut en bas* in terms of information, through footnotes, endnotes, direct address in text, and often integrated into characters' conversation: it sometimes seems that no-one has ever forgotten the exchange between Gurth and Wamba in chapter one of *Ivanhoe*, in which Wamba points out to Gurth the peasant that words for animals are Saxon (swine, ox, calf and one could add sheep), but become Norman (pork, beef, veal, mutton) when the same animals become meat on the table.

As for the third axis, Scott may almost be said to have created it. The Scott medieval universe, most markedly in *Ivanhoe*, brings together King Richard I (died 1199), Robin Hood (not certainly heard of till c. 1370), Friar Tuck (friars not established till post-1215, and later in England), and Norman–Saxon antipathy (hard to date, but surely faded by the late twelfth century). Scott's errors were pointed out in his own time, but have remained hegemonic ever since, especially in "movie medievalism." Scott would then be almost as far as Twain toward the undifferentiated/unchallenged end of the hypothesized 3D axis.

Two further authors may help to provide a framework for our model of the medieval/modern interaction: William Morris and T. H. White. Both are much further to the left of the first or horizontal axis. Both, in different ways and for different reasons, find much to be admired in the Middle Ages and much to be regretted in the modern world. Neither shares the tacit or open belief in the superiority of his own time and culture seen in Scott and Twain. Both furthermore admired the medieval world for the many skills required to survive in it, which both men also spent time and effort in recovering, where they could. Examples in White's *The Sword in the Stone* (1938) include the skill of falconry (White wrote a long account of his own re-learning of this skill, in *The Goshawk*, 1951) and the woodcraft which his boy-heroes learn from Robin Hood and Maid Marian.

An unexpected addition to the list is haymaking, described in some detail in chapter one. Mowers work the 200-acre field with scythes, women follow up to rake the hay into strips, boys with pitchforks turn the hay inwards to be picked up, and men pitch the hay up to a cart, loading in strict rotation under the supervision of a foreman on the cart, and the contents of the cart are then pitched up on to a hayrick. White notes, "It came up easily because it had been loaded systematically – not like modern hay." The scene gives an image of friendly collective co-operation very far removed from Twain's image of the feudal system, for in White's scene Sir Ector is scrambling about on top of the hayrick and the young aristocrats Wart and Kay are pitchforking along with everyone else. White reinforces this with idealized images of the collective Forest Sauvage celebration of Christmas and the all-classes boar-hunt following: "All the villagers were there, every male soul of the estate from Hob the austringer down to old Wat with no nose, every man carrying a spear or a pitchfork," their loyal assembly reinforced not only by the king's huntsman and visiting nobility, but also by Robin Hood, somewhat incognito.[4] These idealized images are also deliberately anachronistic. White's "Middle Age" is a playful version of the modern world as he would like it to be.

William Morris also, and with notable real-world impact, admired and recreated medieval skills. In his *Dream of John Ball* (1888), almost the first thing which the narrator notices when he finds himself somehow projected back into the medieval world (like Hank) is not strange men in armor but "a certain unwonted trimness and handiness about the enclosures of the garden and orchards," far different from the "tumbledown bankrupt-looking surroundings of our modern agriculture." Morris's narrator is also puzzled by the church spire he sees, "white and brand-new, but at once bold in outline and unaffectedly graceful." It looks new, but its beauty makes the narrator ask himself "how it could have been designed by a modern architect."[5]

Such remarks place White and Morris close together on our factor 1 axis, as far to the left as Twain was to the right. They are reasonably close together also on factor 2, where, once again, they are markedly different from Twain and Scott, with their (respectively) overbearing lectures and paratextual foot- and end-notes. Morris's rather bewildered I-narrator, in *John Ball*, allows his descriptions of events to speak for themselves, and this remains broadly true even in Morris's more deliberate creations of a lost tribally collective past in romances such as *The House of the Wolfings* (1889). White is more inclined to put himself forward and address the reader directly, but the tone is ingratiating rather than expository. Describing the ruins of the Castle of the Forest Sauvage, he suggests that the modern visitor should "spend days there, possibly weeks, working out for yourself by deduction which were the stables, which the mews, where were the cow-byres, the armoury, the lofts" (etc.). The task would be to recreate the old life – just as real and just as complex as any modern one – and to put oneself in the medieval person's mind, and even role: "On this tower the look-out hoved. From here he kept the guard over the blue woods towards Wales. His clean old bones lie beneath the floor of the

---

4    T. H. White, *The Once and Future King* (New York: Ace Books, 1987), 13, 145 (chs. 1, 16 respectively).

5    *Three Works by William Morris*, ed. A. L. Morton (London: Lawrence and Wishart, 1973), 37 (ch. 1).

chapel now, so you must keep it for him."[6] Every effort is made to avoid Twain's sense of complete dissociation from the medieval.

Close together though they are in some ways, however, White and Morris are markedly far apart on our third or 3D axis. White is very deliberately "writing into a gap," in a story already familiar, that of King Arthur: the gap being the unexplained period between Merlin taking the baby Arthur from his mother and Arthur reappearing as Sir Kay's squire to draw the Sword from the Stone and be proclaimed King of England. The gap is filled by White's thoroughly modern idea of an appropriate princely education, carried out by the animals. The playful nature of this experiment, however, means that all resources of the overall medieval "imaginary" can be exploited, without care for anachronism. White indeed deliberately points out his own anachronisms: "they were drinking Metheglyn, not port, but by mentioning the modern wine it is easier to give you the feel."[7]

By contrast Morris, in *John Ball* and even more in his heroic romances, was trying to correct or to expand modern images of the medieval. And here Morris was far more in agreement with Twain than with Scott or White. The latter two are tolerant or even admiring of old aristocratic virtues, while Morris, early socialist that he was, has no more time for the feudal nobility or established Church than his American contemporary. Yet Morris, a learned man, knew too much real history to repeat the kind of self-flattering images which still dominate modern "imaginaries." He knew the Peasants' Revolt did not succeed. And while he tells John Ball that some of his wishes will come true in the future, notably the extirpation of "abbey and priory" and the ability of poor men to become lords and masters, poor men in a capitalist system will make no better lord than lords in a feudal system, so that Ball comments, "Woe's me, brother, for thy sad and weary foretelling!"[8] Morris's works as a whole are much more differentiated than White's, and though he creates what I have called elsewhere "asterisk-realities,"[9] these do not derive from mass-awareness but often (and often unnoticed) from the very latest philological discoveries. A further conclusion to draw, however, perhaps unnecessarily, is that even fairly close proximity in our 3D model of "medievalist modernity" does not preclude major differences of attitude and approach. Every writer has his or her own point to make, his or her own tricks to make it.

If the authorial presence in a work is the most direct method of injecting modernity, one just as familiar is the device of creating a modern character, a character with at any rate modern attitudes, within the plot, as a kind of reader-surrogate. Twain's Hank is once again the most extreme example of this kind of insertion: modern person thrust into (imaginary) medieval world. But the trick may be reversed. In *That Hideous Strength* (1945), C. S. Lewis brings a medieval person, Merlin, into the modern world, so that we see the modern world through

[6]  White, *Once and Future King*, 42 (ch. 5).
[7]  White, *Once and Future King*, 10 (ch. 1). This aside was added to the revised version of *The Sword in the Stone* published as the first part of *The Once and Future King* (1958).
[8]  *Three Works*, 109 (ch. 12).
[9]  See Tom Shippey, *The Road to Middle-earth*, 4th edn. (London: HarperCollins, 2005), 22–6.

medieval eyes for a moment. It may be said that Lewis was strongly sympathetic
to the medieval world (like White), but better than anyone else at disguising his
own learning: a lecturing voice appears in his text, but mediated by a character
(Dr. Dimble) and conversational rather than assertive. What Lewis's Merlin does
is permit an effectively neutral view of medieval/modern differences. By modern
standards, Merlin comes across as a violent and bloodthirsty person: he recom-
mends the beheading of Jane Studdock, for having used contraception, and the
flogging of MacPhee, for insubordination. But he rejects the charge indignantly:
he practices charity on a scale unusual if not unknown in the modern world, he
is in some ways greener than any modern member of the Green Party, aspects of
the modern world strike him as intolerably cruel. His anachronism is not there for
comedy, but to challenge received opinion, notably the modern sense of cultural
(because technological) superiority.

One variation on the technique is to use a kind of pairing, following in the
footsteps of Don Quixote/Sancho Panza. The best examples of this come from
historical fiction not set in the modern world, notably C. S. Forester's "Hornblower" stories (Hornblower presents a modern sensibility, his lieutenant Bush a
kind of Nelsonian average). The device works by forcing the reader to consider
how he/she would cope in such (usually adverse) circumstances. Lewis used the
device several times in his later "Narnia" stories. Two books present one or more
child-heroes accustomed to the Narnian medieval conventions, contrasted with
another child to whom they are unfamiliar (Lucy and Edmund vs. Eustace in
*Voyage of the Dawn Treader* (1952), Eustace vs. Jill in *The Silver Chair* (1953)). In
each case the representative of modern times comes off worse and has to learn
better. In *Prince Caspian* (1951) a similar effect is achieved by having the child-
characters, who have been in Narnia before but then reverted to their real-world
child-selves, "grow back" into their more mature and more medieval behavior: in
chapter thirteen Peter, sending a challenge to "combat and monomachy," "leant
back with half-closed eyes and recalled to his mind the language in which he had
written such things long ago in Narnia's golden age,"[10] which is also the pastiche-
medieval in which Lewis excelled.

Yet one further variation in methods for bringing the modern into contact
with the medieval is to have a character move slowly from recognizable to wholly
unfamiliar surroundings. Of this the best example must be Bilbo Baggins, who
starts *The Hobbit* (1937) in the identifiably Victorian/Edwardian world of the Shire
(as also of Tolkien's youth), but who moves steadily into a fairy-tale world, and
then one might say the saga-world of Middle-earth: though even at the end, and
after he has earned his place in the company of heroes, Bilbo retains markedly
modern and even bourgeois qualities, including reliance on a written contract,
and more admirably, a kind of moral courage which even the physically brave
inhabitants of Middle-earth come to recognize. At the end, in the scene between
Gloin the dwarf and Bilbo the hobbit, it is clear that both parties are saying the

---

[10]   C. S. Lewis, *Prince Caspian* (Harmondsworth: Puffin Books, 1962), 151 (ch. 13).

same thing, if in conspicuously different language: one archaic/ceremonious, one contemporary/familiar.

Yet if modern readers are reluctant to accept the minatory or directing approach normal in the earlier years of historical fiction and are more at ease following the adventures of someone with whom they can identify, there is still the permanent problem of simply conveying information. The solution, in modern times, has often been to have the story told by a narrator who is a member of the medieval world but in some way out of place in it, perhaps because of a more analytic and questioning temperament. Examples include Alfred Duggan's *The Conscience of the King* (1951), told by King Cedric of Wessex, a Machiavellian politician who spends his whole life trying to conceal his intelligence; Robert Graves's "Claudius" novels, where once again Claudius – a disabled person generally regarded by his family as an idiot – is allowed to explain himself to the sympathetic modern ears he does not encounter in his lifetime; or in more modern times, the "Saxon series" of Bernard Cornwell, whose protagonist is Uhtred of Northumbria, a character caught between Christian Anglo-Saxon and heathen Viking cultures, and so capable of judging both – with a particularly hostile judgment on King Alfred, one of the few Anglo-Saxon kings to have found a regular and normally laudable place in popular (and remarkably also in scholarly) awareness.

As said above, every author has a different placing within our overall scheme or three-dimensional box (which represents relations between author, reader, medieval world, and medieval "imaginary"), and every author is similarly at pains to find a different means of approach to reader–character relations. Nevertheless, in even the most determined medieval pastiche, modernity will always enter, directly or indirectly, openly or concealed.

## Further Reading

Brewer, Elisabeth. *T. H. White's The Once and Future King*. Cambridge: D. S. Brewer, 1993.

Foote, Bud. *The Connecticut Yankee in the Twentieth Century: Travel to the Past in Science Fiction*. New York: Greenwood Press, 1991.

Haydock, Nickolas. *Movie Medievalism*. Jefferson, NC: McFarland, 2008.

Pugh, Tison, and Angela Jane Weisl. *Medievalisms: Making the Past in the Present*. London: Routledge, 2012.

Rigney, Anne. *The Afterlives of Walter Scott*. Oxford: Oxford University Press, 2012.

## Related Essays in this Volume

Presentism, Middle, Continuity, Purity, Myth, Lingua, Memory, Feast, Spectacle, Simulacrum, Transfer

# 18
# Monument

### E. L. Risden

L ATIN *MONUMENTUM*, "MEMORIAL," from *monere*, "to remind" or "to warn,"
implies an important idea with respect to both medieval artifacts/construc-
tions and those of medievalism that draw from them: a tension between
the structure as at once something of the past and something of the present, a
significant public artifact with a purpose ambiguated by time. An object of once
significant use may have fallen out of use, or it may remain in use: it may have
less "presence" than it once had, or it may have as much or even more; that is, its
emotional effects and cultural appreciation may change with time. Cultural change
may have made it obsolete as more than a vague memory or feeling of things
past, or it may have increased the object's value as something of more thoroughly
embedded cultural significance and power. Alois Riegl wrote that what we call a
monument may have been "erected for the specific purpose of keeping particular
human deeds or destinies [...] alive and present in the consciousness of future
generations" – it has a deliberateness in its creation and persistence of artistic
and historical value (70), and it may also have "commemorative value" (77) or
"use value": as a construction or a location it retains an unusual weightiness of
*affect*.[1] Philipp Fehl has remarked that in the monument "the work of the artist
and service to the public good are most intimately joined," though in our time
"the whole idea of erecting monuments has become somewhat scandalous" (vii)
– they involve enormous expense and imply dubious polemic.[2] While Fehl notes
that "the monument holds up the mirror to our fonder hopes concerning the true
nature of man" (63), we must add that "[n]either revealed religion nor philosophy
has taken kindly to monuments erected in praise of individuals" (50) – while they

---

[1] "The Modern Cult of Monuments: Its Essence and Development," trans. Karin
Bruckner and Karen Williams, *Historical and Philosophical Issues on the Conservation of
Cultural Heritage*, ed. N. S. Price, K. K. J. Talley, and A. M. Vaccaro (Los Angeles: Getty
Institute, 1996), 69–83 (originally published in 1903). Thanks to Elizabeth Emery for alerting
me to this essay.
[2] *The Classical Monument: Reflections on the Connection between Morality and Art in
Greek and Roman Sculpture* (New York: New York University Press, 1972).

may not intend vanity, but rather an admiration for statecraft or inspiration, they may as well represent a falsification of history.

Beyond a simple call to memory,[3] a monument may also "admonish": it may warn against errors past or keep present our sense of mortality. It may prepare us for an Apocalypse or a Second Coming or gird us against war or social upheaval. It may recall others' sacrifices and warn us that if we lack care, we may need to make those of our own. Monuments in medievalism both remind us of their medieval antecedents and warn us of essential textual concerns; they tie us across time to their roots in the past and their branches in our own present. They move us from the awe of a fictional world that has passed to the tensions of the world of the present. As Umberto Eco asserts in *Art and Beauty in the Middle Ages*, the "elementary form of aesthetic response" amounts to a "liking for anything giving us immediate pleasure," and the "Medievals allowed the imagination free rein instead of fastening it to the unique art object before them." [4] They also insisted on art's "didactic function," seeing beauty and utility as connected (15). Again a tension arises between "earthbound pleasure and a striving after the supernatural" (6), also between spiritual inspiration and excess, as with St. Bernard's "criticizing churches that are too big and cluttered up with sculpture" (7). The "technical literature" of the age was "filled with observations on colour, light, and proportion" (100) as notions of beauty moved from a sense of "ideal order" to one focused much more on the details of "concrete particulars" (117). In their time the medieval monument makers aimed for both the beautiful and unusual, but not for too much of either: not to the exclusion of practical spiritual use. In *Beowulf*, the mead-hall, Heorot, is, for a time, a monument to civilization, but a useful one (though not to Grendel), as is Camelot, for a time, in Arthurian literature; Stonehenge was once a useful monument, but for the medievals and for us it remains a monumental mystery, but no longer useful. Monuments (in the medieval world and in medievalism) tend to have spiritual and imaginative magnitude as well as, or more importantly than, physical magnitude.

This brief essay will consider two sets of two monuments, one set medieval and one set from the fictional world of medievalism: the Gosforth Viking Cross in Cumbria, England, and Notre-Dame Cathedral in Paris; the statues of the Argonath and the Minas Tirith/Minas Morgul paired towers in *The Lord of the Rings*. One could choose any number of possible monuments both actual and fictional, but these four provide excellent examples of how monuments draw past (actual or fictional) and present (actual or imagined) into instantaneous experience, creating an interpretable sense of awe that can move an audience both

---

[3]  Of course a call to memory need not be simple: it may, for instance, invoke the *ubi sunt*, or *dustsceawung*, to use the Old English term – see John R. Holmes, "Tolkien, *Dustsceawung*, and the Gnomic Tense: Is Timelessness Medieval or Victorian?" in *Tolkien's Modern Middle Ages*, ed. Jane Chance and Alfred K. Siewers (New York: Palgrave Macmillan, 2005), 43–58.

[4]  Umberto Eco, *Art and Beauty in the Middle Ages*, trans. Hugh Bredin (New Haven: Yale University Press, 1986), 14.

emotionally and intellectually – ideally they move us to spiritual experience and immediate productive action. Like all medievalism, those monuments blend the medieval with the present to make something at once infused with tradition and yet fully awe-inspiring in the present.

The Gosforth Cross is a mid-tenth-century monument featuring the inter-lacing of pagan Germanic and Christian thought with images that suggest both the Norse eschatological myth of Ragnarök and the salvific crucifixion of Christ. It stands about sixteen feet high in a churchyard in a small town in the west of the Lake District of England. Parts of it now prove difficult to interpret exactly, but its maker probably aimed to assist in the conversion of locals to Christianity. While now it may remind more than admonish, it retains considerable ability to move a viewer because of its syncretism and diachronic immediacy. It retains a powerful presence as an impressive (though not imposing) indicator of times past in an obscure though beautiful churchyard. In contrast, while the high medieval Notre-Dame de Paris stands as a monument to the power and majesty of Gothic architecture and to the centrality of Catholicism in medieval daily life, it remains in use as a cathedral with the magnitude and presence to effect parallel spir-itual experience in our own time: Catholics continue to worship there daily, and "pilgrims" come from all over the world to experience its wonder and spiritual immediacy. Both physical monuments remain medieval *and* present: if the exact effects they produce have changed, their capability to affect has not, and part of their power comes in the remnant presence of a medieval world as well as their persistent physical beauty.

We can find a similar parallel in monuments that Tolkien builds in his Middle-earth. The enormous statues of Isildur and Anárion that stand beside the Anduin as it flows into Gondor remain impressive and imposing, but insufficient to stop – though sufficient to daunt – any invaders or visitors.[5] Rather like the Gosforth Cross, they represent a power of times past that has not disappeared, though it has diminished because of the distance in time and culture from its creation. The towers, Minas Tirith and Minas Morgul, remain in Tolkien's story in present and powerful use. Neither is exactly what it was: Minas Tirith, "Tower of Guard," was built by Anárion as Minas Anor, "Tower of the Setting Sun"; it remains the great guardian of the West. Minas Morgul, "Tower of Sorcery," was built by Isildur as Minas Ithil, "Tower of the Moon" – Sauron has perverted its use from outpost of Gondor to forewarning and watchtower of Mordor, a place of terror rather than of glory. Yet both remain in Middle-earth fully functional, monuments *to* past times but *of* the present. They show the idea of *monument* as flexible yet persistent in time and space, transitory as icons of the exact culture and idea they aimed to create, but powerful in their capability to move viewers in their own time. Like the historical monuments, the fictional monuments retain *presence*: the capacity to inspire awe, to make viewers stop in their tracks and change how they think and act. They also show how monuments, however good the intention in their building, can fall to evil use: the sacred may become profane or even worse. Alter-

5   J. R. R. Tolkien, *The Fellowship of the Ring* (New York: Ballantine, 1965), 508–9.

natively, they can gain a new kind of sacredness – their value as historical artifacts – or they may simply change as culture changes and time wears them down.

The Gosforth Cross, for example, draws the parallel between two sets of characters, one Germanic and one Christian, but it "disambiguates" (in Mark Roskill's term) its identifications by pointing the viewer from the Norse antecedent to the Christian meta-landscape as the "true" background behind the "imaginative" Norse cosmology.[6] The artifact as icon encourages a specific interpretive choice, which remains an Apocalyptic and therefore admonitory choice: the monument, from whichever tradition we view it, retains its capacity to draw our thoughts to explosive end times. Similarly, the story of Odin on the World Tree, as we learn it in the Old Norse *Hávamál*, explains that the king of the gods sacrifices himself to himself, hanging heroically on the Tree for nine days, so that he may achieve the boon of the runic letters for his suffering: that gift he gives to humanity. As a gift it parallels but hardly matches the gift of Christ, Salvation, though the act of the sacrifice itself remains undiminished – the move toward which the experience of the object points us. Both sacrifices appear simultaneously, for comparison, the likely purpose of the monument as monument. In that sense it represents the medieval world doing medievalism: the present Christian medieval world is commenting on the past or departing Germanic medieval world. The interpretive monument functions through the "sublime" terror it invokes. The terror of end-times urges us to consider where the ends will lead us and to choose the more appealing of the possible results, while it also connects us to its physical context, a hill in the west of Cumbria's dramatic lake country just three miles to the west of the Irish Sea. The natural landscape, pastoral and beautiful, reinforces the scene, with its tall cross, as a "crucifixion upon a hill" and yet a fixture amidst natural surroundings, resettling the event as still extraordinary and yet settled within space and time.

As so many medieval monuments, the cross blends the *contemplative sublime* with the *apocalyptic sublime*, to invoke at once fright, heroic agency, and spiritual experience. It has four flat sides that reveal a narrative as one walks around it. The narrative begins with a devil-type figure (probably Loki) at the bottom, bound, an upright rider raising a spear, a leaping wolf, a hart, and a monster with its mouth bound and another with an open mouth ready to bite. It continues with the lower figure still bound, the rider turned upside-down, and a horizontal human figure with a horn holding off two attacking beasts, with the beast-head recapitulated at the top of the panel. The third segment shows no bound devil, but an interlace decoration in his place; two riders appear next, one upside-down and one upright, the latter being attacked by a beast with its mouth open. The fourth (east) face of the cross (facing the rising sun), which concludes the narrative, includes a crucifixion scene (representing probably both Jesus and Odin) above a male and a female human figure, with a dragon at the bottom and a figure with a spear (probably Vithar) killing a beast (probably Fenrir the wolf) at the top – and one more

---

[6]    Mark Roskill, *The Languages of Landscape* (University Park: Penn State University Press, 1997), 227.

animal face with the mouth still opened for attack. The scenes pictured on the cross appear in the Eddic *Völuspá* and in *Snorra Edda*; they relate events of the fall of the reigning gods and the end of the age while throwing particular attention on the crucified figure, which we reinterpret as Christ rather than Odin, turning the medievalism of the narrative to its "contemporary" purpose. Time will not allow the world infinite respite: the event, the Second Coming and following Judgment, can happen anytime, and when it does, it will affect the whole universe, each of us with it – thus the object's history and immediacy.

The great Gothic cathedral Notre-Dame de Paris, perhaps the greatest of them all, may well embody the imagination's perfect medieval monument – yet it, too, has its elements of medievalism. Begun in 1163 and completed in 1345, it bears all the signs of the Gothic ideal: pointed arches, ribbed vaults, flying buttresses (applied there for practical rather than decorative purpose, but fulfilling both), towers and spires, gargoyles and chimeras, cruciform plan, tall stained-glass windows – the awe-inspiring blend of height and light. Its construction began in the "middle of the Middle Ages," but by the time of its completion the Renaissance had already begun, at least in Italy, and its final touches bear a sense of harkening back. Any restoration (particularly, for instance, in its statues and bells), too, has necessarily involved medievalism, a desire to look back to what the cathedral should have or do given its provenance. As well as its "use value," it must, beyond the immediate emotional effects of its presence, draw the intellect back to considerations of its genesis and context.[7] Both the cathedral and the cross represent medieval medievalism: the look back on earlier times from within later times in their own age.

In fantasy fiction the use of monuments of one sort or another appears nearly ubiquitously, but Tolkien's instances exhibit notable use of all the various aspects of the monumental in ways essential to the texture of his world.[8] While Weathertop, in its natural grandeur and as an example of human failure, is a monument to loss and ruin, the Argonath (in *The Fellowship of the Ring*), which the remaining members of the Fellowship reach as they row down the Anduin from Lothlórien, threatens, yet suggests profound loss, though not ruin: the kings of old have fallen, but a new king will return, and the stalwart figures of Isildur and Anárion remind anyone who comes into that land by water of power and majesty past, passing, and to come. Tolkien describes them as pillars, giants, towers, guardians, and even Boromir bows his head to them. They guard the chasm that moves the travelers into Gondor, and they represent the chasm of the past with a mixture of terror, awe, and hope. Aragorn has in his face the same majesty as the sculpted figures, and the figures give way to the path to Amon Lhaw and Amon Hen, the Hill of Hearing and the Hill of Sight: those powers have faded in the interregnum, but

---

[7]   A related instance of medievalism comes in the Anglican St. Peter's Cathedral of Adelaide, Australia, begun in 1869 and completed in the early years of the twentieth century: its south face follows the structure of Notre-Dame.

[8]   For a curious, different use of the notion of monument in fantasy medievalism, see Ian Graham's dark and gritty *Monument* (New York: Ace, 2002). Or see Mark Strand's book of poems *The Monument*, where the "monument" of literary history speaks to the reader (New York: Ecco Press, 1991).

Aragorn revivifies them. While for Sam the figures bring fear, for Aragorn they bring a yearning to see the city of Minas Tirith.[9] Their age and magnitude give them presence and a kind of awful beauty, and their majesty gives them utility: they truly embody the medieval/medievalism understanding of *monument* by means of what they communicate.

Minas Tirith and Minas Morgul represent complements that have become opposites. The reader meets the former first through the gaze of Gandalf and Pippin in the first chapter of *The Return of the King*, where the white Ered Nimrais meet the dark Mount Mindolluin as purple shadows give way to breaking day. The city rises, glimmering like crystal or pearl, amidst a trumpet hail, in seven levels carved right out of the mountain, spiraling up in gleaming stone to the High Court, the Fountain, and the White Tower with its banner flying a thousand feet above the plain.[10] Minas Tirith is not only a citadel, but a monument to the ancient people who built it, a living, functional sculpture that represents the last, greatest remnant of a nearly extinct race of monarchs. We must imagine what sort of effect it would have on Pippin, whose Shirefolk prefer buildings either built into hillsides or flat; having seen Rivendell, Lothlórien, Moria, and Orthanc he would have experience of the organic and masonic architecture of elves, dwarves, and humans, but he would have seen nothing like the proud magnitude of the great city built upward from a mountainside, the greatest outpost of the last of a fallen yet redeemable race. In our time the person who has grown up in a large city may not quite be able to empathize – the person who has grown up in a rural or small-town environment just may. The monument in this case has the utility of defense, of supporting a large number of persons, and of providing hope and courage to all those humans who know of it and believe in it. One of the great monuments of medievalism, it has both great antiquity and enormous presence.

Its parallel monument, Minas Morgul, while exhibiting a similar awe, represents exactly the opposite impulse. Of lesser magnitude, it yet inspires a similar level of emotion in the terror not of sublime presence and sustenance, but of good perverted to evil, of fall and slavery and suffering and of imminent destructive attack rather than heroic defense. It is a monument of fear, horror, intimidation, and subjugation. Once Isildur's city, it has become the dwelling of Nazgûl and their orcs. Its gate recalls the Hell-mouth of medieval manuscript illuminations, and it disgorges the armies that attack Minas Tirith in Sauron's greatest military campaign. It drives those who approach it, unless they are already under the power of Sauron, to madness. Frodo and Sam come before it in "The Stairs of Cirith Ungol" in *The Two Towers*.[11] Like Minas Tirith it rises from the root of a mountain, but it radiates darkness instead of light, a sickening deadness void of illumination. The tower at the top revolves slowly, allowing a more panoramic view, but the eyes of the tower seem only dead (or un-dead) and menacing, and the surroundings stink of filth and decay. Sauron's monument to his intention to conquer and enslave, Minas Morgul is both monument and anti-monument, a promise more

---

9   *The Fellowship of the Ring*, 508–9.
10   J. R. R. Tolkien, *The Return of the King* (New York: Ballantine, 1965), 24–7.
11   J. R. R. Tolkien, *The Two Towers* (New York: Ballantine, 1965), 396ff.

than a remembrance, a threat rather than a warning. Worse than Ozymandias's trunkless legs of stone because it remains alive with the thrill of true horror rather than dead in the dust, Minas Morgul will take years to cleanse – if cleansing of such a haunting lies within the power of any of the mortals of Middle-earth.

The notion of *monument*, like the misunderstanding of *prophecy*, lives among the roots of medievalism. In the Old World, to *prophesy* meant to speak out according to inspiration, but we have tried to turn it into something we wish it were: the ancients giving us esoteric hints about our future – in that endeavor they have even less success than meteorologists. Similarly we reconfigure the purpose of monuments; whatever the aims of those who built them, we who remain to admire, interpret, and perhaps use them impose on them our own hopes and fears, our own directives or warnings.

## Further Reading

Eco, Umberto. *Art and Beauty in the Middle Ages*. Trans. Hugh Bredin. New Haven: Yale University Press, 1986.

Fehl, Philipp. *The Classical Monument: Reflections on the Connection between Morality and Art in Greek and Roman Sculpture*. New York: New York University Press, 1972.

Nichols, Marianne. *Man, Myth, and Monument*. New York: Morrow, 1975.

Riegl, Alois. "The Modern Cult of Monuments: Its Essence and Development." Trans. Karin Bruckner and Karen Williams. *Historical and Philosophical Issues on the Conservation of Cultural Heritage*. Ed. N. S. Price, K. K. J. Talley, and A. M. Vaccaro. Los Angeles: Getty Institute, 1996. 69–83.

Roskill, Mark. *The Languages of Landscape*. University Park: Penn State University Press, 1997.

## Related Essays in this Volume

Presentism, Gothic, Memory, Christianity, Authority, Modernity, Spectacle, Co-disciplinarity, Resonance, Trauma

# 19
## Myth

*Martin Arnold*

"**M**YTH" IS A controversial term, especially in respect of medievalism, for retrospective interpretations placed on medieval and pre-medieval cultural products are often colored by contemporary political and ideological agendas. In order to avoid any confusion with continuing, institutionalized credos, in this essay "myth" is applied to signify defunct belief systems, whereas the term "religion" is used to refer to extant belief systems: in this case, Christianity. The main focus will be on the successive medievalisms involved in the reception history of Old Norse myths. Some brief introductory remarks concerning European mythological systems during the Christian conversion period will help to provide a broad context.

The legitimization of Christianity by the Roman emperor Constantine in the early fourth century, then its adoption as the official religion of the Roman Empire in the late fourth century, greatly facilitated its northward spread. As Christianity carried with it Greek and Latin learning, it was mainly in this way that Greco-Roman classical literature and its associated mythology survived the fall of the Roman Empire in the late fifth century and became esteemed throughout medieval Europe. By contrast, European mythological systems, which came into contact with Christian missions in the early medieval period, were the products of non-literate cultures, and relations between followers of these mythologies and Christianity's messengers frequently involved violence, including the destruction of sacred pagan sites.

Apart from what was written by contemporary Roman and Christian commentators, much of what we now know about the mythological beliefs of the Celtic, Slavic, and Germanic tribes is due to the linguistic and philological recovery period beginning in the nineteenth century. Our knowledge of Finnish mythology is almost entirely due to nineteenth-century recovery projects.[1] Inevitably, the reconstruction of mythologies during periods that were far removed from the

---

[1]  In respect of Finnish mythology, pride in national origins rests to a great extent on Elias Lönnrot's *Kalevala* (1835). Lönnrot both aestheticized and contributed to the oral material he gathered.

times in which they were societally current raises questions about whether authenticity was achievable or even if that was the main intention. The medievalism in such cases is typically improvisational and romanticized. In respect of Old Norse mythology, however, matters were somewhat different, in as much as manuscripts concerning Scandinavian myths and legends set down in the Middle Ages were plentiful and increasingly available to scholars from a much earlier date.

Old Norse paganism, as practiced in Norway, Denmark, Sweden, and Iceland, had lain outside the jurisdiction of the Roman Empire and did not attract the attention of the Church until the ninth century. The subsequent conversion of the Scandinavians during the tenth and eleventh centuries entailed several interlocking elements: the persuasive power of the monotheistic message; a gradual lowering of resistance to Christianity through increased contact; the intimidation of the populace by the converted aristocracy; the prospect of increased trade with Christendom; and what might be called a rebranding exercise – for example, the superimposition of Christmas onto the pagan midwinter festival of Yule (O.N. *jól*). Yet, were it not for the Church's importation into Scandinavia of the Roman alphabet, we would know very little about Old Norse mythology. That we do know rather a lot about it is mainly thanks to the preservation instincts of two Icelanders more than two centuries after Iceland's official conversion to Christianity in 1000AD.

First, there were the remarkable efforts of Snorri Sturluson (d. 1241), who sought to temper the Church's disapproval of Norse paganism through the principles of euhemerization; that is to say, the rationalization of myth as a distortion of real historical events. According to Snorri's systematized mythological compendium known as the *Prose Edda*, Norse mythology came into being through a combination of Ancient Greek warriors venturing northward and the awed gullibility of the Scandinavian natives they encountered, initially in Sweden. Secondly, there was an unknown medieval Icelander who, in or around 1270, set down or, more likely, copied down what has become known as the *Poetic Edda* since the discovery of its manuscripts in the seventeenth century.[2] The *Poetic Edda* is a collection of more than thirty myths and legends in verse form, ten of which concern the deeds and wisdom of the Norse gods, and many of which had been composed in, or at least originated from, western Scandinavia's pre-Christian oral culture. It is reasonable to assume that Snorri Sturluson had to hand an earlier manuscript collection of the same and, it would seem, other eddic verses when he wrote the *Prose Edda*, as he makes reference to mythological beings and episodes that are otherwise unknown. Nonetheless, so far as wider European culture was concerned, Norse myth was to remain relatively unknown outside Scandinavia until the onset of the Romantic revival over 500 years later, when it was considered by many intellectuals and artists to be a key aspect of north European identity.

Eddic myth tells of the origin of the Norse gods, their struggles against monstrous creatures leading eventually to mutual destruction at Ragnarök, the

---

[2] The precise meaning of the term *edda* is unknown but it might conceivably mean "grandmother's tales."

ultimate battle, and, according to the eddic poem "The Prophecy of the Sibyl" (*Völuspá*), the seemingly ill-starred recovery of the gods. The eddas provide by far the greatest information about three particular gods, all of whom are male. These are Odin, the wise and wily chief of the pantheon; Thor, Odin's warrior son, bane of giants and protector of mankind; and the initially mischievous but ultimately treacherous Loki. It is the various significances that have been attached to these gods, along with certain legends associated with their adherents, that inform much of the reception history of the Old North; however, such interpretations often had little direct association with what we know of the gods' original mythic functions.

The postmedieval influence of Norse myth can be characterized as having four overlapping phases. The first was what could be termed an insular phase stretching from the Renaissance to the Enlightenment. This phase almost exclusively concerned Scandinavian scholarly activity, mainly in respect of manuscript evidence for Scandinavian culture in the pre-Christian era. The second was a pre-Romantic phase beginning in the mid-eighteenth century, during which knowledge about, and commentary on, Norse myth and legend reached a much wider European audience. The third was a phase encompassing National Romanticism, a potent aspect of the Romantic revival, and the emergence of aggressive nationalism, which lasted from the early nineteenth century through to the end of World War II. The fourth was, or rather is, a popular culture phase beginning, in this case, in the 1940s with chiefly Hollywood-inspired anti-Nazi propaganda cartoons and continuing in post-war years through the media of superhero comic-books and, most recently, video games. A fifth phase might also be identified in the recent enthusiasm for all things Viking among far-right groups. This, however, can better be regarded as a legacy of the third phase.

The recovery of the mythico-legendary past and the ideologically driven significances conferred on it by Scandinavian scholars was a particularly fraught project. On the one hand, there were national rivalries which, during the sixteenth century, led to failed attempts at Scandinavian union and a series of wars between a Dano-Norwegian coalition and Sweden. Beyond this, with the establishment of Lutheranism across Scandinavia from the latter half of the sixteenth century, there lay wars with Roman Catholic countries in the seventeenth century and further territorial rivalry between Sweden and Denmark. On the other hand, there was the problem of national identity versus religious identity, in as much as taking pride in the pre-Christian past could not include any suggestion that Old Norse mythology had ever had any religious credibility. This combination of overwrought patriotism and biblical orthodoxy led to some rather extravagant claims about national origins.

For the Swedes, much inspiration came from Adam of Bremen's eleventh-century *History of the Archbishops of Hamburg-Bremen* (*Gesta Hammaburgensis Ecclesiae Pontificum*). This they readily combined with early Roman histories, such as Tacitus's sometimes positive first-century ethnographic study of the Germanic tribes, *Germania*, and Jordanes's sixth-century *Getica*, a history of the Gothic tribes that the Swedes assumed to mean them. Lending further help to the Swedish cause were certain fantastical Icelandic sagas with settings in Sweden, all of which were regarded as true histories. Inspiring Danish scholars were Saxo Grammaticus's early thirteenth-century *History of the Danes* (*Gesta Danorum*) and the vast store of medieval manuscripts to be found in Iceland, a Danish colony since 1380. Adding significantly to the resources for both Swedish and Danish scholars were printed versions of Snorri Sturluson's history of the Norwegian kings, *Heimkringla*, his *Prose Edda*, and the *Poetic Edda*, all of which emerged throughout the seventeenth century.

The sixteenth-century Swedish Gothicists, the brothers Johannes and Olaus Magnus, set the tone for future arguments between Danish and Swedish historians by claiming that the Goths were originally led by Magog, a grandson of Noah, who took them to Sweden before the destruction of the Tower of Babel. As a result, the Goths spoke the language of God and had later gone on to promulgate civilized values in Ancient Greece and on through to the birth of Christ. It was this divinely ordained status that allowed the Goths repeatedly to overcome the Roman legions, as had been reported by Jordanes. More such claims came in the following century from Olof Rudbeck in his *Atlantica* (*Atland eller Manheim*; published in 4 vols., 1679–1702). For Rudbeck, Sweden was the cradle of civilization that Plato had named Atlantis. Thus, Greco-Roman mythology originated in Sweden, and, for instance, where Plato refers to elephants, he actually means Swedish wolves. According to Rudbeck, Norse mythology is a palimpsest that rather obscures these historical truths.

Danish attempts to enshrine their own ancestors' role in the founding of Western civilization were, by comparison, slightly more sober. In the seventeenth century, Ole Worm had argued that runes were a Danish derivation of ancient Hebrew script and, later that century, Thomas Bartholin, a fierce opponent of Olof Rudbeck, had lionized Danish character in the legendary personages of certain Viking warriors and their gods; for example, the Danish fondness for drinking bouts can be traced to the god Thor. However, Danish scholars had always been better aided by manuscript evidence than had the Swedes, and for this they were chiefly indebted to two Icelanders, Magnús Ólafsson and Árni Magnússon, who, respectively, had provided the source materials for Ole Worm and Thomas Bartholin.

Although often bizarre and ill-judged, the politically motivated medievalism concerning Old Norse myth during this period helped lay the basis for what was to follow from the mid eighteenth century onwards. This was particularly helped by the manuscripts that the Icelanders noted above had assiduously collected. So it was that, in 1752, when King Frederick V of Denmark commissioned a reputation-enhancing history of his realm from the Swiss writer and pedagogue Paul Henri Mallet, a new aesthetic of Old Norse mythology was provided, one which largely avoided both partisanship and tortuous religious historicizing.

Mallet's successive editions of his *Histoire de Dannemarc* gave increasingly detailed accounts of the Norse gods and included his own euhemerized account of how Odin came north from the Black Sea.[3] All this chimed well with the spirit

---

[3]     Mallet regarded Old Norse and Celtic myths as being from the same source. This error was corrected in the English translation of 1770: see Thomas Percy, *Northern Antiquities*, 2 vols. (Edinburgh: C. Stewart, 1809), I: i–xxxii.

of pre-Romanticism, which included Edmund Burke's analysis of the northern sublime (1756) and Jean-Jacques Rousseau's idea of the "noble savage" (1755). It also coincided with James Macpherson's sensationally populist and allegedly authentic Ossianic poetry (1760–63), a wildly anachronistic account of the Celts' third-century defense of their territory against aggressive Scandinavian Odin worshippers. Set together, Mallet's histories and Macpherson's fraud were central in inspiring a northern Renaissance, a movement which would go on to stimulate national pride across northern Europe, most notably in Germany, where Johann Gottfried von Herder's studies of indigenous folklore established the basis for a singularly Germanic culture.

Mining Old Norse myth and legend for contemporary messages about Danish identity and the prospects for Scandinavian unity was the playwright Johannes Ewald, whose *The Death of Balder* (*Balders Død*; final revision performed in 1778) was the first public airing of a drama based on Nordic antiquity. Urging him on was the Copenhagen-based ex-patriot German poet Gottlieb Friedrich Klopstock, whose own Ossianic and subsequent Nordic enthusiasms fortified his fierce belief in the need for a pan-Germanic literary nationalism. As the century turned and the Romantic revival swept across revolutionary Europe, the intricacies of Norse myth became a kind of theater in which to enact the uplifting dramas of national pride, a typifying example of how medievalism often functions as a buttress for patriotic sentiment. In Denmark, the chief advocates were the gifted poet Adam Oehlenschläger and the theologian, poet, and Lutheran minister N.F. S. Grundtvig, both of whom sought to extol the virtues of Norse mythology as a fundamental aspect of Danish patriotism; whilst in Sweden, it was the literary group known as the *Fosforists* who, stimulated by Rudbeckian ideas and seeking to match the Danes, developed a cosmogonic schematization to explain the significance of the Norse gods. Spurred on in all cases by anti-Roman Catholic sentiment, it was the god Thor, the people's god, who epitomized the spirit and genius of the North, while his perceived opposite, Loki, represented all the impositions on Nordic culture that had originated from Rome.

In itself, revivifying the Old North might well have been no more than expansion of cultural reference points, as was the case in Victorian England, where a less tendentious enthusiasm for Norse myth enlivened artistic possibilities and, by historical association, lent metaphorical weight to imperialist derring-do. However, in mainland Europe, where northern nations were generally less secure than the English about their place in history, the arguments about ownership of the Nordic past began to take a more sinister turn. Much of this was a result of investigations into linguistic origins, and the key figure here was Jacob Grimm.

Grimm's hugely influential studies of the origins of the German language and the vestiges of ancient German mythology that could still be found in place-names and folklore led him to conclude that not only were the Scandinavian languages derived from German but also, for this very reason, that Norse myth had had its origins in Germany.[4] Not surprisingly, the likes of N.F. S. Grundtvig were

---

4   See, for example, James Stephen Stallybrass, trans., *Grimm's Teutonic Mythology*, 4

outraged by this claim, for it was suspected that this was the thin end of the wedge of belligerent German nationalism. As the Danes discovered in the years 1848–64, when Prussian forces invaded and eventually seized the Danish-owned but largely German-speaking territories of Schleswig-Holstein, pan-Germanicism was somewhat more than an academic argument.

As the Scandinavian nations receded in European political significance throughout the nineteenth century, so did their assertions about the importance of their past, this subject having become a largely private matter. Some signs of Nordic pride in the past continued among those of north European stock settled in the USA. Notable in this regard were the musings on Old Norse myth by the New England 'Fireside poets' – Henry Wadsworth Longfellow, James Greenleaf Whittier, and James Russell Lowell – and the belief held by many in a widespread founding Viking presence in north-east America during the eleventh century.

In Germany, however, which did not become a unified nation until 1871, the eddas, sagas, and early Scandinavian histories rapidly became both an essential subject for study and a central plank of German artistic endeavor. One notable, relatively early, example of the attraction of Norse mythology for German writers was Ludwig Uhland's imaginatively interpreted *The Myth of Thor from Nordic Sources* (*Der Mythus von Thor nach Nordischen Quellen*, 1836). Yet, without doubt a defining moment in late nineteenth-century European culture was Richard Wagner's operatic tetralogy the *Ring Cycle* (*Der Ring des Nibelungen*; first performed in full in 1876). Drawing with considerable erudition on Old Norse sources and recent academic studies of them, Wagner delivered a monumental creation that sought to unify the arts into a single expression of Germany's exalted place in world history: past, present, and future. In as much as it is acknowledged to be a timeless work of art, in late nineteenth-century Germany the *Ring Cycle* amounted to an ideological statement, one which embraced ultra-nationalism, virulent racism, and military expansionism.

With the rise of Nazism in Germany after the disaster of World War I, Norse mythology became regarded as the most complete expression of the superior character of the Germanic peoples. Advocating this in its most extreme form was Heinrich Himmler, Hitler's appointed leader of the elite Waffen SS. Bolstered by theories concerning the growing evidence for the common origins of the Indo-European group of mythologies, and surrounding himself with Nordicist fanatics of highly doubtful mental health, Himmler commissioned far-reaching scientific expeditions in pursuit of evidence for the real existence of the Norse gods, whom he had come to believe were the original Aryan master race. Toward the end of World War II, with German military forces in desperate straits, Himmler had an army of scientists working on how they might replicate the power of Thor's lightning-bolt-emitting hammer.

For Nazi ideologues, Norse mythology had helped legitimize global war, and it is therefore understandable that the subject of early Germanic belief systems fell

vols., from Jacob Grimm, *Deutsche Mythologie* [1835], 4th ed. (London: George Bell and Sons, 1882–88).

into disrepute for some time afterwards, for not only did this signify dangerous ideas concerning race but, due in large part to Wagnerian readings of it, it had also become associated with the elitist and prejudicial sonorities of high culture. During and after the war, Hollywood cartoons, often featuring Bugs Bunny or Donald Duck, sought to satirize high-culture elitism, affirming instead the values of the hard-working common people, the unpretentious tastes of Middle America. One notable example of this was Chuck Jones's *What's Opera, Doc?* (Warner Brothers, 1957). In this merciless send-up of Wagner's *Ring Cycle*, the hapless Elmer Fudd takes the roles of both the god Thor and the legendary human hero Siegfried, and Bugs Bunny assumes the role of Odin's exiled Valkyrie, Brünnehilde. For those seeking an antidote to high culture, *What's Opera, Doc?* was perfectly judged.

It was not until 1962 that Norse mythology once again caught the popular imagination. Marvel Comics' *The Mighty Thor* is based on, rather than faithful to, eddic mythology and Icelandic saga legends. Nonetheless, irrespective of the authenticity of the storylines, the immediate attraction of Marvel's version of Thor was exactly what it had always been: his stalwart defense of humanity against all its enemies, including Loki, who in Marvel's version of the myths is a son of Odin and so Thor's sibling rival. Over 600 issues of *The Mighty Thor* have been published to date and have led to two Paramount Pictures box-office hits: *Thor* (2011, dir. Kenneth Branagh), which can be interpreted as a thinly veiled metaphor for post-9.11 anxieties about US interventions in the Middle East; and *The Avengers* (2012, dir. Joss Whedon), a superhero gallimaufry, including Thor, in which Loki is once again a threat to the human race. Further sequels are imminent.

Apart from a plethora of fantasy fiction novels, often taking their lead from J. R. R. Tolkien's *The Lord of the Rings* (1954–55), and, on the big screen, what has been termed "Vikingism,"[5] the current popular craze for Norse myth and legend rests largely on an abundance of video game improvisations. Some recent games that have drawn the attention of those researching the reception history of Norse myth include: *Odin Sphere* (Vanillaware, 2007); *Tomb Raider: Underworld* (Crystal Dynamics, 2008); *Viking: Battle for Asgard* (The Creative Assembly, 2008); and *The Elder Scrolls V: Skyrim* (Bethesda Softworks, 2011). One may well be right in thinking that Old Norse myth set free from troublesome ideologies is now, for the main part, in safer hands.

## Further Reading

Abram, Christopher. *Myths of the Pagan North: Gods of the Norsemen*. London and New York: Continuum, 2011.

Arnold, Martin. *Thor: Myth to Marvel*. London and New York: Continuum, 2011.

Lupack, Alan. "Valiant and Villainous Vikings." In *The Vikings on Film*. Ed. Kevin J. Harty. Jefferson, NC: McFarland, 2011. 46–55.

---

5   See Alan Lupack, "Valiant and Villainous Vikings," in *The Vikings on Film*, ed. Kevin J. Harty (Jefferson, NC: McFarland, 2011), 46–55.

O'Donoghue, Heather. *From Asgard to Valhalla: The Remarkable History of the Norse Myths*. London and New York: I. B. Tauris, 2007.

Wawn, Andrew. *The Vikings and the Victorians: Inventing the Old North in Nineteenth-Century Britain*. Cambridge: D. S. Brewer, 2000.

## Related Essays in this Volume

Purity, Play, Continuity, Authenticity, Authority, Christianity, Lingua, Spectacle, Trauma, Resonance

# 20

## Play

*Kevin Moberly and Brent Moberly*

W HEN WE THINK about the Middle Ages, we do not usually think of play. Famously characterized as a "thousand years without a bath" by the nineteenth-century French historian Jules Michelet, the period is imagined as an uninterrupted spectacle of violence and brutality, one in which the ordeals of everyday life preclude anything as frivolous as play.[1] Take, for instance, the opening episode of the Swedish mini-series *Arn: the Knight Templar*.[2] After the obligatory introductory sequence in which Arn is shown riding down Saracens in the deserts of the twelfth-century Holy Land, the episode shifts to an equally familiar, though in many ways antithetical, version of the medieval: the snowy forests of West Gothia some twenty years earlier. There, the audience discovers a markedly younger Arn playing a spirited game of Folkungs versus Sverkers with his friend Knut. The boys have no sooner begun to play, however, when they are discovered by armed riders who bear them back to their parents' bleak village. Admonished never again to play in the woods, the boys endure a night of half-understood political conversation, and, on the following day, are carted to the courtyard of a nearby church. Caught in an ambush, they watch as Knut's father, King Ericsson, is beheaded. Play is thus constructed as a prerequisite to violence in *Arn*; it is a fundamentally transgressive activity that lures participants outside the protective confines of civilization and, in doing so, exposes them to a hyper-adult, hyper-traumatic world in which childhood, like everything else, is represented as "serious business."

By the same token, however, many of these medieval worlds are not imagined as mature or complete, but instead represent the contemporary era in its childhood. This is very much the case with *Arn*, which is adapted from Jan Guillou's *Crusades Trilogy*, a series of novels that, according to Sandra Ballif Straubhaar,

---

[1]  Jules Michelet, *La Sorcière: The Witch in the Middle Ages*, trans. Lionel James Trotter (London: Simpkin, Marshall, and Company, 1863), 118.
[2]  *Arn: The Knight Templar*, "The Beginning," directed by Peter Flinth (Toronto: Entertainment One Group, 2012).

presents readers with "A Birth Certificate for Sweden."[3] This is also the case with medievalism in general, which, according to Umberto Eco, often stages a return to the pre-modern in an attempt to diagnose the complexities of the present.[4] It is not surprising, then, that the medieval makes for such fantastic play. A staple of mass culture, it allows participants to stage a return to what is, in essence, a particularly traumatic childhood, yet does not require them to endure the trauma of acting like children. Participants are instead interpellated as thoroughly contemporary and, especially in the case of medieval-themed computer games, thoroughly techno-logical subjects: digital Yankees newly arrived in King Arthur's court.

Brian Sutton-Smith describes the result of the oftentimes contradictory, ambig-uous nature of play as a "positive, the sum of two negatives":[5]

> play is a paradox because it both is and is not what it appears to be. Animals at play bite each other playfully, knowing that the playful nip connotes a bite, but not what a bite connotes [...] a playful nip is not only not a bite, it is also *not* not a bite. That is, it is a positive, the sum of two negatives. Which is again to say that the playful nip may not be a bite, but it is indeed what a bite means. (1)

Much of the same holds true for the terms that are the focus of this chapter: play and medievalism. Although the imagined worlds of popular medievalism are not, as many scholars have pointed out, the "real Middle Ages," they are neverthe-less also "not *not*" the real Middle Ages. That is, they provide participants with the metaphorical equivalent of what the Middle Ages is often imagined to be, a version of an imagined past that functions to reify the present as real, absolute, and beyond question. These imagined medieval worlds function in much the same way that Jean Baudrillard describes Disneyland, as "deterrence machine[s] set up to rejuvenate the fiction of the real in the other camp."[6] They offer participants privileged access to worlds that "[want] to be childish in order to make us believe that the adults are elsewhere, in the real world, and to conceal the fact that true childishness is everywhere – that it is that of the adults themselves who come here to act the child in order to foster illusions as to their real childishness" (13). They thus encode one of the crucial differences between traditional medievalisms and the digital or neomedievalisms of the present: a "new" medievalism that, as manifested through the spectacular technologies of the culture industry, does not critique or otherwise offer an antidote to the excesses of late capitalism, but

---

    [3]  "A Birth Certificate for Sweden, Packaged for Postmoderns: Jan Guillou's Templar Trilogy," *The Year's Work in Medievalism, 2002*, ed. Jessie G. Swan and Richard Utz (Eugene, OR: Wipf & Stock, 2003), 64.

    [4]  Umberto Eco, "The Return of the Middle Ages," *Travels in Hyperreality*, trans. William Weaver (San Diego: Harcourt Brace Jovanovich, 1986), 65.

    [5]  Brian Sutton-Smith, *The Ambiguity of Play* (Cambridge: Harvard University Press, 2001), 1.

    [6]  Jean Baudrillard, *Simulacra and Simulation*, trans. Sheila Faria (Ann Arbor: University of Michigan Press, 2002), 13.

instead demonstrates its power to commodify everything, even our most fantastic dreams.[7]

Understood in this sense, the relationship between play and medievalism is more fraught and traumatic than it first appears. Articulated through a seemingly endless number of games, movies, books, and similar productions, all of which evince a larger cultural desire to play with, in, and through the Middle Ages, this relationship is implicated in what, to Baudrillard, is a larger desire for a "reality principle" that, as he writes about Disneyland, allows us to perpetuate the fantasy that it is still possible to distinguish the real from its representations (12–13). Our chapter approaches the relationship between play and the medieval through this lens. Recognizing that, as Sutton-Smith observes, the "word *play* stands for a category of very diverse happenings," one used interchangeably to discuss a sometimes contradictory array of experiences and performances, we examine a critical definition of play that directly impinges on the medieval: that which Johan Huizinga offers in his 1938 *Homo Ludens*.[8]

Paying particular attention to Huizinga's notion of the "magic circle," we want to challenge the predominant view of play as a fundamentally pedagogical strategy – one that, through a clearly articulated system of rules, attempts to persuade audiences to take meaningful action towards specific and usually positive outcomes.[9] We wish to suggest that the opposite is also true – that as manifested through contemporary medievalism and similar instances of simulational culture, play serves a much less positivist, though equally political, purpose. Play, in short, is one of the primary means through which the inequalities of late capitalism are constructed as inevitable and unassailable.

Although the emergence of computer games as a medium has prompted a resurgence of interest in the theory of play that Huizinga outlined in *Homo Ludens*, he established his reputation with his 1919 *The Waning of the Middle Ages*.[10] Subtitled, "A Study of the Forms of Life, Thought, and Art in France and the Netherlands in the Fourteenth and Fifteenth Centuries," Huizinga's ostensibly historical treatment presents readers with a version of the Middle Ages that would be instantly recognizable to fans of *Arn*, George R. R. Martin's *Song of Ice and Fire*, or any number of other medievalist works that, as described earlier, present the Middle Ages as a sort of traumatic childhood constructed in the image of more complex contemporary struggles. Huizinga, for example, begins his preface to Fritz Hopman's 1924 English translation of the work by explicitly stating that the Middle Ages represents not a beginning but an end, an "epoch of fading and decay" synonymous with the end of childhood.[11] He repeats this thesis in the

---

[7]   See Kevin and Brent Moberly, "Neomedievalism, Hyperreality, and Simulation," in *Studies in Medievalism* XIX (2010): 12–24.

[8]   Sutton-Smith, *The Ambiguity of Play*, 3; Johan Huizinga, *Homo Ludens: A Study of the Play Element in Culture*, trans. unknown (Boston: Beacon Press, 1955).

[9]   Huizinga, *Homo Ludens*, 10.

[10]   Johan Huizinga, *The Waning of the Middle Ages*, trans. Fritz Hopman (Toronto: General Publishing Company, 1999).

[11]   Huizinga, *Waning*, v.

work's first chapter, arguing that the lived experiences of medieval peoples were more vivid, more pure, or, as Baudrillard might say, "more real" than our own. Again, invoking childhood as a delimiter, he writes, "To the world when it was half a thousand years younger, the outlines of all things seemed more clearly marked than to us. [...] All experience had yet to the minds of men the directness and absoluteness of the pleasure and pain of child-life."[12]

Edward Peters and Walter P. Simons observe, however, that Huizinga did not simply wish to describe this essentially pre-modern subjectivity to readers, but to "immerse [them] in a sensuous re-creation of late-medieval experience that set the stage for the further argument that unfolded slowly, relentlessly, and with an unyielding logic that was far more consistent than many have given him credit for."[13] Laura Kendrick offers a similar assessment in her "Games Medievalists Play: How to Make Earnest of Game and Still Enjoy It."[14] As her title suggests, she argues that Huizinga's *Waning of the Middle Ages* asks readers to engage in a game of sorts, one that demands that "modern interpreters accept the absolute alterity of the medieval, setting it within a kind of magic circle, defining it as definitely *not* our ordinary life."[15] For Kendrick, Huizinga's work is significant because it establishes the rules of a larger game of interpretation, one in which all medievalists engage as they attempt to make the medieval real for audiences. As she explains:

> The most fundamental rule that medievalists play is "Mind the Gap." We must remember that "they" (medieval people) saw and experienced differently from "us." Yet, at the same time we mind this gap – or chasm – we are encouraged to bridge it imaginatively. [...] We are encouraged to understand the medieval text by imagining what it meant to medieval players (performers and audiences); in other words we are encouraged to play the role of a medieval interpreter, to pretend. (44)

To Kendrick, then, *The Waning of the Middle Ages* embodies many of the key principles of the definition of play that Huizinga would later develop in *Homo Ludens* – a definition that Kendrick quotes in its entirety in her essay: "Play is a voluntary activity or occupation executed within certain fixed limits of time and place, according to rules freely accepted but absolutely binding, having its aim in itself and accompanied by a feeling of tension, joy and the consciousness that it is 'different' from 'ordinary life.'"[16]

Yet as becomes clear from her admonition to "Mind the Gap," Kendrick's discussion of *Homo Ludens* focuses primarily on Huizinga's concept of a "magic circle": an enclosed ritualistic, "hallowed" space whose boundaries are defined by

---

[12]   Huizinga, *Waning*, 1.

[13]   Edward Peters and Walter P. Simons, "The New Huizinga and the Old Middle Ages," *Speculum* 74:3 (1999): 587–620 (592).

[14]   Laura Kendrick, "Games Medievalists Play: How to Make Earnest of Game and Still Enjoy It," *New Literary History* 40:1 (2009): 43–61.

[15]   Kendrick, "Games Medievalists Play," 44.

[16]   Huizinga, *Ludens*, 28.

the implicit and explicit rules of the game being played.[17] Fraught with religious and occult symbolism, Huizinga's notion of a magic circle is certainly relevant, as Kendrick argues, to the serious scholarly work of reconstructing the Middle Ages – work that, as a sort of "earnest game," is "regulated by using historical contexts as boundaries and chiefly involves trying to avoid 'out-of-bounds' anachronism."[18] Huizinga's magic circle, however, is perhaps even more relevant to the playful medievalisms of mass culture: medievalisms that are not constrained by the need to be historically or, as Kendrick also insists, semantically accurate, and thus better exemplify the spirit of freedom that, to Huizinga at least, is a prerequisite to play.

J. R. R. Tolkien, for example, explicitly imagines the Middle-earth of his *Lord of the Rings* as a "forbidden spot," one that, as Huizinga writes, is "isolated, hedged round, hallowed, [and] within which special rules obtain" – rules that simultaneously determine how the characters within the works are allowed to behave and how the audience should approach the work in relationship to their experiences as subjects.[19] Much of the same can be said for C. S. Lewis's Narnia and many of the other imagined worlds of so-called classic works of medievalism, as well as for those that define neomedieval fiction, film, and television: the Wizarding World of J. K. Rowling's *Harry Potter* and George R. R. Martin's Westeros, to name just two.[20] In comparison to more realistic modes of mass culture that attempt to establish their representational authority by reproducing a presumably external "reality" as accurately as possible, these works use topography to separate themselves, to designate the boundaries of a fictional playing field that is imagined without paradox as simultaneously existing within and separate from the exigencies of a so-called "real" world.

This effect is even more pronounced in medieval-themed computer games. As Ken McAllister argues, one of the crucial differences between computer games and traditional forms of media is that games ask players to work to improve their performances as subjects in respect to the game. The result, he explains, is very similar to the way that Huizinga discusses winning in *Homo Ludens* in that mastering a game confers a sense of what becomes a marker of more than simply in-game expertise.[21] In medieval-themed computer games such as *World of Warcraft*, *Skyrim*, or *Neverwinter Nights*, this emphasis on performance requires players to acknowledge and constantly validate the rules within which the magic circle of the game is constructed, through questing, character configuration, combat, and almost every other aspect of game play. At the same time, however, it also means that players have a heightened awareness of the limits of the magic

[17]  Huizinga, *Ludens*, 10.

[18]  Kendrick, "Games Medievalists Play," 48.

[19]  Huizinga, *Ludens*, 10. J. R. R. Tolkien, *The Lord of the Rings*, 50th Anniversary Edition (New York: Houghton Mifflin, 2004).

[20]  C. S. Lewis, *The Complete Chronicles of Narnia* (New York: HarperCollins, 1998); J. K. Rowling, *The Harry Potter Collection* (New York: Scholastic, 2006); George R. R. Martin, *A Song of Ice and Fire* (New York: HarperCollins, 2012).

[21]  Ken McAllister, *Game Work: Language, Power, and Computer Game Culture* (Tuscaloosa: University of Alabama Press, 2004), 59.

circle – of a theoretical point in which it is possible to beat the game, to emerge victorious and, in a sense, whole, into the larger reality that surrounds and informs the game. Medieval-themed computer games thus foreground an aspect of play that is perhaps not immediately obvious in movies or novels: that the relationship between the imaginary world of the magic circle and the presumably non-imaginary world in which it is contained is oftentimes adversarial, one that is defined as much by possibility and promise as difference and lack.

This is especially the case with the medieval-themed worlds of popular culture, many of which use the difference between childhood and adulthood to designate the boundary or, as Kendrick phrases it, the "gap" between the imaginary and the real.[22] Tolkien's Middle-earth, for instance, is explicitly constructed as a nascent world, one whose magical conflicts anticipate a fourth and presumably modern age dominated by men. Yet as both Bilbo and Frodo discover, exploring Middle-earth requires them to leave the relative security of the Shire for a world of increasingly adult responsibility. Much the same is expected of readers, who are interpellated into and therefore expected to approach the fantastic events of the texts as modern subjects, an assumption that Tolkien foregrounds early in *The Hobbit* when he explains that the modern game of golf, with which he presumes readers are familiar, was invented in the fictional world of the novel when Bandobras "the Bullroarer" Took clubbed an invading goblin king with such force that his head was knocked off into a nearby gopher hole.[23]

The difference between the "real" adult world and the "imaginary" child world is even more pronounced and traumatic in C. S. Lewis's Narnia series and J. K. Rowling's Harry Potter books. There, a number of child-protagonists learn that it is possible, through magic, to make the transition back across the gap separating adulthood from childhood. Yet they have no sooner stepped through the wardrobe or reached the end of Diagon Alley when they discover that they are no longer allowed to act as children – that the only way that they can save these permanently imperiled worlds of childhood is to assume the role of an adult: a role that, if played successfully, guarantees the survival of the very childhood in which they are no longer allowed to participate.

Many medieval-themed computer games present their players with a similar conundrum, requiring them not only to witness and approve tacitly this loss of childhood, but to facilitate it through their game play. *World of Warcraft*, for example, presents players with a seamless world, one that, if the game's packaging can be believed, promises the ultimate in medievalesque play: a fantastic realm that is as fraught with danger and adventure as anything that Tolkien or Lewis might have imagined, but which is also distinctly juvenile in its frequent recourse to popular culture and scatological humor. Yet while players are inducted into this world as children of sorts – level one characters who are equally short on experience, skills, and equipment – they are nevertheless tasked with the in-game equivalent of growing up.

---

[22] Kendrick, "Games Medievalists Play," 44.
[23] J. R. R. Tolkien, *The Hobbit* (New York: Ballantine Books, 2012), 18.

Rewarded with experience, gold, and equipment for completing quests, vanquishing monsters, and performing other tasks that the game deems worthwhile, players watch in the third person as their characters gradually achieve the maximum level possible, the so-called "end game." At this point, much of what passes for play in *World of Warcraft* begins to look suspiciously like work, and is often described by players in terms that recall labor: as "farming" or "grinding."[24] Players thus find themselves in much the same position as Harry Potter at the conclusion of the first two or three books, or as Bilbo and Frodo upon returning to the Shire. Players discover that their play has become a heroic vocation of sorts, one that requires them to pay $14.99 a month to confront a series of dungeon and raid bosses, all of whom threaten, without irony, to visit all kinds of "serious business" on the otherwise child-like realms of Azeroth.

Understood in this sense, the fantastical playgrounds of contemporary medievalism do not instantiate but simulate Huizinga's concept of play. Explicitly constructed as self-contained worlds, they promise audiences a retreat to a childhood of sorts, an escape to fantastic realms explicitly imagined as isolated from the exigencies of the larger and presumably more adult realities of the material world. Yet while what takes place within their boundaries is undeniably fun, it ultimately bears little resemblance to the way that Huizinga understands play – that is, as a fundamentally generative activity, a "*significant* function" that, with characteristic romanticism, he describes as existing prior to and transcending culture, as the well-spring from which all civilization originates.[25]

Instead, these worlds construct play as an end-point: an activity that, like childhood, is imagined as temporary, terminal, and ultimately unsustainable. Play, as such, functions as a disciplinary rather than a liberatory construct in neomedievalism. Quantified, commodified, and increasingly conflated with work, it is not just the means through which audiences are interpellated into the larger systems of economic and cultural production that are relentlessly packaged and sold as magical by the culture industry; it is the means through which these systems of production are constructed as natural, inevitable, and beyond question. Contemporary medievalism, in this sense, is implicated in what Baudrillard understands as a larger strategy of deterrence. "[M]etamorphosed into its opposite to perpetuate itself in its expurgated form," it promises participants the ability to escape the present tense through privileged participation in the childish excesses of an imagined medieval past.[26] What participants discover, however, is that the opposite is true: that such desires ultimately lead them back through the wardrobe to the place where they began – a place that, unlike Narnia, has not changed in their absence, but which looks all the more desirable for the trauma of having left.

[24] See Kevin and Brent Moberly, "'For your labor I will give you treasure enough': Labor and the Third Estate in Medieval-Themed Role-Playing Games," in *Neomedievalism in the Media*, ed. Carol L. Robinson and Pamela Clements (Lewiston: Edwin Mellen Press, 2012), 307–38.

[25] Huizinga, *Ludens*, 1, emphasis in original.

[26] Baudrillard, *Simulacra and Simulation*, 19.

## Further Reading

Huizinga, Johan. *Homo Ludens: A Study of the Play Element in Culture*. Boston: Beacon Press, 1955.

Kline, Dan, ed. *Digital Gaming Re-Imagines the Middle Ages*. New York: Routledge, 2014.

McAllister, Ken. *Game Work: Language, Power, and Computer Game Culture*. Tuscaloosa: University of Alabama Press, 2004.

Robinson, Carol L., and Pamela Clements, eds. *Neomedievalism in the Media*. Lewiston: Edwin Mellen Press, 2012.

Sutton-Smith, Brian. *The Ambiguity of Play*. Cambridge: Harvard University Press, 2001.

## Related Essays in this Volume

Spectacle, Simulacrum, Reenactment, Humor, Modernity, Resonance, Presentism, Authenticity, Authority, Memory, Co-disciplinarity, Gesture, Heresy, Trauma

# 21

# Presentism

*Louise D'Arcens*

I N THE 1988 film *The Navigator: A Medieval Odyssey*, a group of miners from
fourteenth-century Cumbria attempt to ward off the Black Death by obeying
a vision that tells them they must dig through the Earth and attach a crucifix
to a cathedral in the "celestial city" that is their destination. Emerging from their
tunnel not just on the other side of the world but in 1987 Auckland, they encounter
a world which, despite its miraculous modernity, exists, very much like their own,
under the parallel threats of global pandemic and military mass destruction.[1]

By drawing parallels between medieval apocalyptic fears and modern anxieties
about the AIDS virus and nuclear force, literally linking them via the time portal
unwittingly dug by the miners, this film uses a common medievalist technique
known as "presentism." Presentism is widely understood to mean the practice of
representing, interpreting, and, more importantly, evaluating the past according
to the values, standards, ambitions, and anxieties of a later "present." It is a core
concept for medievalism studies, this being because it is arguably the essence of
medievalism itself, unifying the enormously varied ways the Middle Ages has been
represented in its postmedieval cultural afterlife.

Presentism as a mode of historicist reception has proven contentious within the
larger field of medieval studies over the last three decades, where its virtues and
vices have been debated as part of a wider querying of the field's methodological
assumptions. These debates have, according to Kathleen Biddick in *The Shock of
Medievalism* (1998), revolved around the irresolvable "double bind" between alternative perceptions of the European Middle Ages as either the origin or "nonorigin"
of modern Western culture. This double bind, she argues, "has divided medieval
studies into camps of pastists and presentists." "Pastism" is described as "a position that argues for radical historical difference between the Middle Ages and the
present. Pastism regards the past and the present as bounded temporal objects that
cannot come into contact for fear of scholarly contamination."[2]

---

[1] *The Navigator: A Medieval Odyssey*, dir. Vincent Ward (Arena Film, Australian Film
Commission, John Maynard Productions, 1988).
[2] Kathleen Biddick, *The Shock of Medievalism* (Durham, NC: Duke University Press,
1998), 83.

Presentism, conversely, "looks into the mirror of the Middle Ages and asks it to reflect back histories of modernist or postmodernist identities."[3] While Biddick concedes that "more neutral versions of this model of historiographic temporality" have developed that focus on "questions of 'continuity' and change" between the medieval and the modern, she still places these explorations of the relationship between the two periods under the general rubric of presentism.

In stating that medieval studies has "cycle[d] repetitiously" between acceptance or rejection of presentism, Biddick alludes to the continuing legacy of polemics around the in/commensurability of the medieval with the modern that gathered force in the 1970s. While this conversation had begun in the early 1970s, the parameters of the polemic are most starkly drawn in the landmark suite of essays published in a 1979 special issue of *New Literary History*, in which leading scholars of medieval literature, including Paul Zumthor, Hans Robert Jauss, Brian Stock, and Eugene Vance, weighed the merits of pastism and presentism under the aegis of debating the "alterity" and "modernity" of the Middle Ages.[4] Within this debate, defenders of medieval alterity argued that recognizing the true modernity of the Middle Ages lies in acknowledging its radical difference from what we take to be the modern; others argued for the value, and indeed the unavoidability, of viewing the medieval from within modern critical paradigms. The continuing legacy of the tension documented in this polemic is evident in the fact that almost two decades later, Louise O. Fradenburg pointed to the clear moral inflection of the discipline's subscription to pastism, arguing that its insistence on "responsibility to the temporalized other"[5] situates presentist scholarship as, contrastingly, irresponsible and indulgent, a point that has been adopted and finessed in twenty-first-century scholarship.

The debate around presentism has not been limited to medievalism studies. Discussing the field of intellectual history, for instance, Carlos Spoerhase has anatomized the disagreement between adherents to the "historical availability thesis," in which "no acceptable historical interpretation may use knowledge, descriptive terms or classification schemes which were not available or accessible to a certain era," and those who argue for analogies and/or continuities between past and present.[6] The general applicability of such debates notwithstanding, one reason they have had particular potency within medieval studies is that the field's development as an institutional *régime du savoir* has – as argued by many, including most recently Carolyn Dinshaw – involved the suppression of engagements with medieval culture that are amateur, imaginative, or fail to mask their cultural affiliations.[7] This occlusion has been explored in numerous genealogical accounts

---

[3]   Biddick, *Shock*, 84.

[4]   See the essays in "Medieval Literature and Contemporary Theory" special issue, *New Literary History* 10:2 (Winter 1979).

[5]   Louise O. Fradenburg, "'So that we may speak of them': Enjoying the Middle Ages," *New Literary History* 28 (1997): 205–30 (209).

[6]   Carlos Spoerhase, "Presentism and Precursorship in Intellectual History," *Culture, Theory and Critique* 49:1 (2008): 49–72 (59).

[7]   Carolyn Dinshaw, *How Soon is Now? Medieval Texts, Amateur Readers, and the Queerness of Time* (Durham, NC, and London: Duke University Press, 2012).

of the discipline's professionalization since the nineteenth century, which have also demonstrated that an enduring, though mostly unacknowledged, presentist impulse has persisted beneath the field's "official" subscription to positivistic method.[8]

The 1990s saw a heightened interest in this genealogical self-reflection: Norman Cantor's *Inventing the Middle Ages* (1991), which, as Richard Utz has pointed out, was a watershed in its emphasis on the impact of scholars' biographies on their scholarship, was the first of numerous studies which have collectively exposed the deeply presentist ideological and personal underpinnings of medieval studies.[9] While these studies initially dwelt on the influence of nationalist and patriarchal agendas on philological research, more recently this has broadened out to examine the role of colonialism on the scholarly reception of the Middle Ages. Together these theoretical and genealogical interventions have demonstrated what philologist Joseph Bédier claimed a century ago in his *Légendes épiques*: that medievalist scholars who believe themselves "impervious" to presentism fail to acknowledge the extent to which the currents and movements of "the spirit of the time" actually determine their practice.[10]

At the same time as medieval studies was deliberating on scholarly presentism in the 1970s, the adjacent field of studies in medievalism was gaining momentum. The impetus behind pioneering studies such as Alice Chandler's *A Dream of Order* (1971) led to wider interest and the foundation by Leslie Workman of the journal *Studies in Medievalism* in 1976.[11] By examining the abundance of medievalism that has been produced over several centuries up to the present, research in this field places particular critical pressure on the notion of the absolute alterity of the Middle Ages by performatively exposing the limitations of pastism. Biddick's criticism that presentist scholarship's privileging of the present means that it "forgets […] to question institutional and personal investments in understanding the

---

[8]  See, for instance, the essays in R. Howard Bloch and Steven G. Nichols, eds., *Medievalism and the Modernist Temper* (Baltimore and London: Johns Hopkins University Press, 1996), and Allen J. Frantzen, *Desire for Origins: New Language, Old English, and Teaching the Tradition* (New Brunswick: Rutgers University Press, 1990).

[9]  Norman Cantor, *Inventing the Middle Ages* (New York: William Morrow, 1991); Richard J. Utz, "Resistance to the New Medievalism? Comparative Deliberations on (National) Philology, *Mediävalismus*, and *Mittelalter-Rezeption* in Germany and North America," in *The Future of the Middle Ages and Renaissance: Problems, Trends, and Opportunities for Research*, ed. Roger Dahood (Turnhout: Brepols, 1998), 151–70 (155). Other biographical studies include Helen Damico and Joseph B. Zavadil, eds., *Medieval Scholarship: Biographical Studies in the Formation of a Discipline* (New York: Garland Publishing, 1995/98) and Jane Chance, ed., *Women Medievalists and the Academy* (Madison: University of Wisconsin Press, 2005).

[10]  Joseph Bédier, *Les légendes épiques: Recherches sur la formation des chansons de geste* (Paris: Champion, 1908–13), 3: 287. Quotation translated in Hans Aarsleff, "Scholarship and Ideology: Joseph Bédier's Critique of Romantic Medievalism," in *Historical Studies and Literary Criticism*, ed. Jerome McGann (Madison: University of Wisconsin Press, 1985), 93–113 (109).

[11]  Alice Chandler, *A Dream of Order: The Medieval Ideal in Nineteenth-Century English Literature* (London: Routledge and Kegan Paul, 1971); *Studies in Medievalism* (Cambridge: D. S. Brewer, 1976–).

past as a mirror"[12] does not apply readily to the study of medievalism, because this field's primary object is, in fact, the myriad of modern "investments" in the medieval past. Rather than debating the *validity* of presentist engagement with the Middle Ages, the study of medievalism sets out to analyze the *fact* of presentist medievalism in its many iterations, taking as its fundamental premise that presentism is vital to the postmedieval afterlife of the Middle Ages, and key to its continued potency and relevance within the modern.

Although the proliferation of presentist engagements with the Middle Ages is almost uncontainable, I will nevertheless discuss three key modes through examples taken from medievalist time-travel films. The genre of time-travel narrative is illuminating because in dramatizing the uncanny encounter between the past and present, and the mutual befuddlement this generates, it offers an amusing reflection on the medieval past from a postmedieval perspective. In the majority of cases this involves characters from the present finding themselves transported into the past, although occasionally, as in the case of *The Navigator*, it is medieval people who must negotiate the strangeness of the future. Amusement is generated from the split perspective demanded of the viewer, who needs to move between modern and medieval world-views but with the ironic omniscience of one who can see beyond both. The trans-temporality of this scenario has, as William McMorran has observed, "obvious satirical possibilities,"[13] as the received beliefs and values of both medieval and modern periods are defamiliarized, and hence opened up to scrutiny.

The first kind of presentism subscribes to a progressivist model of history, in which the medieval past has been superseded by modernity; the Middle Ages is depicted using the standards of the present and found wanting. This approach can be detected in *A Connecticut Yankee in King Arthur's Court*, American humorist Mark Twain's 1889 satire on post-Walter Scott romantic medievalism, in which the hard-nosed Hank Morgan, courtesy of a blow to the head, finds himself back in Camelot in 528. Camelot is ridiculed by the novel's time-travelling Yankee as being pompous, credulous, coarse, and inequitable. Its courtiers attract Hank's derision for their mindless acceptance of oppressive hereditary rule and their childish faith in the bogus "magic" of Merlin. Twain's novel, widely regarded as the template for comic medievalist time travel, spawned a cinematic tradition in its wake. Looking through its many cinematic adaptations, it becomes apparent that despite their tweaking of Twain's template, they consistently feature time travellers who are contemporary Americans, and the destination is always the Middle Ages, whether it is 528, as in Tay Garnett's 1949 iteration, or 1328, as in Gil Junger's looser 2001 adaptation, *Black Knight*.[14]

The cultural work being done by these films' representation of the Middle Ages is the affirmation of modern American self-congratulation. Twain's intention to sati-

---

[12]  Biddick, *Shock*, 83.

[13]  William McMorran, "Les Visiteurs and the Quixotic Text," *French Cultural Studies* 19 (2008): 159–72 (164).

[14]  *A Connecticut Yankee in King Arthur's Court*, dir. Tay Garnett (Paramount Pictures, 1949); *Black Knight*, dir. Gil Junger (20th Century Fox, 2001).

rize his *bête noire*, nineteenth-century Romantic medievalism, no longer pertains, but his novel's historical progressivism is reproduced, particularly in scenes where the time traveller's contact with modernity imparts a significant advantage over medieval people, who are still mired in ignorance and superstition. In most cases the modern protagonists, despite being ordinary people, are granted elevated status in their medieval settings as a result of their contact with quotidian scientific innovations. In Tay Garnett's version, Hank Martin (Bing Crosby) astonishes the people of Camelot with his use of a magnifying glass, matches, a paperclip, and a magnet. In later versions such as *A Kid in King Arthur's Court* (1995), a portable CD player, rollerblades, and laptop computers all lead to their owners being regarded as powerful wizards by the credulous medieval innocents.[15] The films add ideological advancement to technological progress in their modern protagonists' subscription to democratic rather than autocratic government, and their rejection of medieval gender inequality.

Tay Garnett's adaptation evades the satiric critique of modern America implicit in parts of Twain's novel. Instead, this Hank is an unqualified subscriber to American entrepreneurialism. It is difficult to spot any evidence that this film critiques modernity in any way. Other versions, however, are more ambivalent. Russ Mayberry's 1979 *Unidentified Flying Oddball*, produced in the developmental phase of space shuttle travel, takes a light-hearted swipe at the neo-colonialism of the NASA space program by having an aeronautical engineer, Tom Trimble, and his android double (both Denis Dugan) land in Camelot as a result of a malfunctioning space mission. Nevertheless, despite the backfiring of a number of Tom's attempted technological interventions in the medieval setting, the film's modern techno-fetishism, featuring jet-packs and the like, ultimately prevails. While modernity is ridiculed up to a point, the film's narrative retreats in the final instance into an affirmation of modern values.[16]

In the second presentist approach that can be identified, the medieval past becomes a nostalgic corrective to modernity. While this can have the appearance of an alterist vision of the past ("it was different, and better, back then"), it does not subscribe unproblematically to a notion of discontinuity between past and present. Rather, it reflects anxieties about modernity as a culturally impoverished age that is a feeble echo, or decadent successor, of a nobler past. A time travel film that captures this anxiety is Jean-Marie Poiré's *Les Visiteurs* (1993).[17] In this film, the twelfth-century Count Godefroy de Montmirail (Jean Reno) and his squire Jacquouille le Fripouille (Christian Clavier) are mistakenly sent forward from 1123 to 1992, where Godefroy encounters his distant descendant Béatrice. The plot of *Les Visiteurs* is based on a looped temporality in which Godefroy must get back to the moment in 1123 just before he mistakenly shot his fiancée Frénégonde's father and lost her love, in order to prevent this calamity and thus guarantee the survival of his patrimony into the future (the film's present). The fact that Béatrice

---

[15]  *A Kid in King Arthur's Court*, dir. Michael Gottlieb (Tapestry Films, Trimark Pictures, Walt Disney Pictures, 1995).

[16]  *Unidentified Flying Oddball*, dir. Russ Mayberry (Walt Disney Productions, 1979).

[17]  *Les Visiteurs*, dir. Jean-Marie Poiré (Alpilles Productions, 1993).

still bears his name, and is identical to Frénégonde, reassures the audience that he will ultimately succeed.

*Les Visiteurs*' presentist approach to the medieval past is complex. Guy Austin has noted the heavy emphasis the film places on the bodies of the medieval characters, especially that of Jacquouille, whose testicular name and repeated association with excrement aligns him with the lower bodily stratum celebrated by Mikhail Bakhtin,[18] and situates the medieval as the abject other of modern hygiene and technology. On the other hand, the modern world, despite its hygienic conveniences, is arguably critiqued more pointedly than the Middle Ages. Modernity is presented as a world of convention and bourgeois complacency, qualities epitomized by Béatrice's unappealing husband, Jean-Pierre the dentist. While modern France does boast the material remains of an *in situ* Middle Ages, this past has been thoroughly commodified and bourgeoisified: Godefroy's castle still stands, but has been converted into a hotel run by Jacquouille's descendant, the aspirational Jacquard.

Stumbling into this sterile environment, the two medieval characters, for all their grotesquery, are symbolic of a lost world of passion and human vitality. Godefroy in particular becomes a compelling figure of nostalgic masculinity, in contrast to the ineffectual Jean-Pierre. Although it is essential to the plot that Godefroy return to medieval France in order to safeguard the modern present, the audience is left pondering whether this present, with its heritage hotels, Range Rovers, and crockery sets, is the one that should have come to be. Unlike the *Connecticut Yankee* films, then, *Les Visiteurs* uses the Middle Ages in service of a sustained satire of modern life. This, however, does not make it any less presentist, for although it is critical of modernity, its representation of the Middle Ages is still fundamentally informed by modern anxieties, and the medieval period is valued only insofar as it can address those anxieties.

The third kind of presentism is an ingenious and playful variety that queries linear models of temporality, depicting the medieval past as alive and present within modernity. A film in which "the medieval" becomes a paradoxical and relativized category is the two-way time travel comedy *Bill and Ted's Excellent Adventure* (1989).[19] In this film two high school friends (Alex Winter and Keanu Reeves) are gifted with a time machine from the future that allows them to collect people from the past for a history assignment that tasks them with explaining what three people from history would think of their home, San Dimas, California, in 1988. Although the friends visit several epochs, the Middle Ages features most prominently, as they visit three distinct medieval contexts: fifteenth-century England, Mongolia in 1209, and France in 1429, bringing back with them Genghis Khan and Joan of Arc. As they set out to discover what the historical characters think of modern America, Bill and Ted bring their own modern perspectives to bear on the Middle Ages. As they struggle to adjust their behavior and to suit their medieval

---

[18] Guy Austin, "Body Comedy and French Cinema: Notes on *Les Visiteurs*," *Studies in French Cinema* 6 (2006): 43–52 (49).

[19] *Bill & Ted's Excellent Adventure*, dir. Stephen Herek (De Laurentiis Entertainment Group (DEG), 1989).

surrounds, their modernity is most evident when they address fifteenth-century dignitaries as "royal ugly dudes," while their rescue of two "historical babes" from arranged marriages reflects their modern masculinity, as does their flight from the medieval ultra-violence favored by the English knights and by Genghis Khan. As becomes apparent in the anarchic scene when the historical characters run amok in the San Dimas mall, it is this violent pre-modern energy that ultimately makes the medieval characters unassimilable within civilized modernity: while Genghis Khan terrifies onlookers with his brutal beheading of a shop mannequin, Joan of Arc's overzealous hijacking of an aerobics class leads to her arrest.

The film is more ambivalent about the present than it appears, however. One vital difference between this and the *Connecticut Yankee* films is that the modern characters are more ignorant than their historical forebears, their only advantage being that they know about the posthumous fame of the people they are collecting. Furthermore, the reassertion of Joan's medieval unruliness in the aerobics scene is unflattering to modernity, for it suggests that if Joan were a modern woman her heroic drive might have been domesticated into feminine self-disciplinary regimes carried out in bland consumer spaces. The privileging of the present is further compromised, moreover, in the part of the film when Bill and Ted's time machine takes them forward to the year 2688, and they discover that they are destined to become the revered ancestors of a utopian society 700 years into the future; that is, they are the "medieval" people of the future, an identity reinforced by their repeated alignment, as Lynne Lundquist observes, with oral rather than literate culture.[20] This ingenious, historically relativizing plot device means that while modernity appears to be the standard against which the past is measured in the film, the present itself becomes subject both to the bemused appraisal of the past and the knowing judgment of the future.

It is virtually impossible, then, to think about medievalism without recourse to the capacious concept of presentism. Applied across the expansive history of medievalism, it discloses a story of twofold temporal mobility; for the idea of the medieval past constantly changes because the present itself is ever moving, receding into the past – perhaps becoming the Middle Ages of some future that will also call itself "the present."

## Further Reading

De Groot, Jerome. *Consuming History: Historians and Heritage in Contemporary Popular Culture*. London: Routledge, 2009.

Fender, Lynn. "The Upside of Presentism." *Pedagogica Historica: International Journal of the History of Education*, 44:6 (2008). 677–90.

Finke, Laurie A. and Martin B. Shichtman. *Cinematic Illuminations: The Middle Ages on Film*. Baltimore: Johns Hopkins University Press, 2010.

---

[20] Lynne Lundquist, "Myth and Illiteracy: Bill and Ted's Explicated Adventures," *Extrapolation* 37 (1996): 212–23.

Gajowski, Evelyn. "Beyond Historicism: Presentism, Subjectivity, Politics." *Literature Compass*, 7/8 (2010). 674–91.

Groth, Helen and Paul Sheehan. "Introduction: Timeliness and Untimeliness." *Textual Practice*, 26:4 (2012). 571–85.

Pugh, Tison and Angela Jane Weisl. *Medievalisms: Making the Past in the Present.* London: Routledge, 2012.

### Related Essays in this Volume

Middle, Modernity, Trauma, Play, Memory, Primitive, Purity, Co-disciplinarity, Humor, Lingua, Genealogy, Transfer, Gothic

# 22
# Primitive

*Laura Morowitz*

I N THE MEDIEVALIST imaginary of the nineteenth century the medieval artist was often considered either as "primitive" or as a *primitif*. Although closely related, each of these terms was associated with specific values, and was in many ways directly opposed to the other. Until the age of modern scholarship the notion of the primitive and the *primitif* colored the reception of medieval works, the historiography of medieval art, and the practice of contemporary artists who attempted to emulate the spirit of the Middle Ages in their own productions. Moreover, the child-like and unsophisticated nature of the medieval artist was seen as an embodiment of the entire medieval mindset.

First and foremost, we must understand the formation of these tropes as part of the larger Western fascination for the primitive, arising in response to modern industrialized culture.[1] Mark Antliff and Patricia Leighten have noted of the primitive that "The condition of 'timelessness' bestowed on the primitive also connotes the 'primeval,' for by not changing, the 'primitive' is necessarily in opposition to all that does change or develop, namely the 'civilized.'"[2] The child-like and ahistorical nature attributed to Western civilization's Other is very much at play in these constructions.

Although the term *primitif* is French, it was utilized in Germany and Italy, as well as many other European nations, in the nineteenth century. The *primitif* was characterized above all by his *naiveté*, his innocence, and his profound Catholic devotion. Most often a painter-monk or manuscript illuminator, the *primitif* was thought to create art out of a sense of spiritual piety, and in an environment free from material temptation, indifferent to individual recognition. In 1894, the Dutch artist Jan Verkade, once a member of the avant-garde Nabi group, wrote:

---

[1]   In contrast to the ideas taken up in this essay, a 1966 book by George Boas, *Essays on Primitivism and Related Ideas in the Middle Ages* (London: Octagon Press, 1966), attempts to locate a kind of "primitivism," specifically Christian concepts of the fall of mankind and original paradise, in the writings of medieval Church fathers and intellectuals.

[2]   Mark Antliff and Patricia Leighten, "Primitive," in *Critical Terms for Art History*, ed. Robert S. Nelson and Richard Shiff (Chicago: Chicago University Press, 1996), 170–84 (170).

The Middle Ages believed in God, put their trust in the merits of Christ and the intercession of the Blessed Virgin and Saints, and found joy in their festivals. Of this the cathedrals, the paintings of the Madonna, the figures of the Saints, and the mystery plays all tell us.[3]

Not surprisingly, such discourse often focused on medieval artists who had entered the monastery or Church, the better to serve their Christian inspiration.

Many nineteenth-century scholars, writers, and artists held that the *primitifs* artistic production was entirely the result of Christian inspiration. This motivation was reflected in a naive style which eschewed realism and detail in favor of a simplified, but soothing visual appearance. Artists viewed in this manner included Gothic sculptors, manuscript illuminators in various scriptoria, and the early Renaissance artists of Italy. The *primitifs* also made their appearance in the novels of writers such as Émile Zola, J.-K. Huysmans, and Léon Bloy, as well as in the writings of the Schlegel brothers in Germany.[4] The concept of the *primitif*, applied in particular to artists we now categorize as early Renaissance, or fifteenth-century, was widely spread through the writings of Alfonse Rio, in his *De l'art chrétien* of 1861–67. Rio argued that the style of these *primitifs* was inseparable from their Catholicism.[5] In Germany, the popular essay of Wilhelm Heinrich Wackenroder, *Outpourings of an Art-Loving Friar* (*Herzensergießungen eines kunstliebenden Klosterbruders*, 1797), created an exemplum of the pious artist-monk.

In 1809 the brotherhood or *Lukasbund* of the Nazarenes moved into the San Isidoro monastery in Rome, believing they were resurrecting the purity of the original circle of Christ's apostles. As was so often the case in the nineteenth century, they viewed the works of fifteenth-century artists as part of the medieval world. Their models – like those of the pre-Raphaelites – were the early Renaissance artists of Italy, who were seen as child-like innocents enthralled with the beauties of the natural world, but devoid of any sensuality. The ultimate model for these artists, as for those working throughout the nineteenth century, was the painter-monk Fra Angelico, whose soft colors, humble settings, and doll-like

---

[3]   Dom Willibrord (Jan) Verkade, *Yesterdays of an Artist Monk*, trans. John Stoddard (London: P. J. Kennedy and Sons, 1930), 25.

[4]   On novels featuring *primitif* artists see Elizabeth Emery and Laura Morowitz, "Packaging the *Primitifs*: The Medieval Artist, the Neo-Primitif and the Art Market," in *Consuming the Past: The Medieval Revival in Fin-de-Siècle France* (Aldershot: Ashgate Publishing, 2003), 37–60. On the Schlegel brothers' writing see "Friedrich Schlegel: From *Descriptions of Paintings from Paris and the Netherlands in the Years 1802 to 1804*," trans. Peter Wortman and Gert Schiff, in *German Essays on Art History*, ed. Gert Schiff (New York: Continuum, 1988), 59–72. Originally published as "Gemäldebeschreibungen aus Paris und den Niederlanden in den Jahren 1802–1804," in *Sämtliche Werke*, 6 vols. (Leipzig, 1910).

[5]   Alfonse Rio, *De l'art chrétien* (Paris: Hachette, 1861–67). For two studies of the fascination for early Renaissance artists in nineteenth-century France see Paul Michael Driskel, *Representing Belief* (University Park: Pennsylvania State University Press, 1992), and Bruno Foucart, *Le renouveau de la peinture religieuse en France: 1800–1860* (Paris: Arthéna, 1987). For an interesting discussion of the British and French collecting of the Italian *primitifs* see Francis Haskell, *Rediscoveries in Art: Some Aspects of Taste, Fashion and Collecting in England and France* (Ithaca: Cornell University Press, 1976).

figures stood as a perfect embodiment of the *primitif*. Artists who followed in these footsteps could themselves be seen as modern *primitifs*, most especially Pierre Puvis de Chavannes.[6]

The term reached a high point with the *L'Exposition des Primitifs français*, held at the Musée du Louvre and the Bibliothèque nationale in 1904 (Figure 8).[7] In addition to exposing the concept of the *primitif* to a wide public, the exhibition firmly linked these artists with a nationalist agenda.[8] "The French masters of the Middle Ages," claimed the curators, "had nothing to learn from anyone."[9] Such ideas had deep roots: in his magisterial *L'Art religieux du XIIIe siècle en France* (1898) Émile Mâle had noted "we are also certain that nowhere was Christian thought expressed with such breadth and richness as in France ...".[10] By the 1904 exhibition poetic musings on the *primitif* had begun to be supplemented with archival research, and a preliminary attempt made to correct the notion that such artists lacked sophistication.

In contrast to the positive nature of the *primitif*, discourse about the Middle Ages also abounds with tropes of the medieval primitive: the image of the medieval artist – and medieval man – as half-savage, crude in appearance, appetites, and lifestyle. Often linked closely with the barbaric tribes of Germany and Eastern Europe, the medieval primitive held either pagan or vaguely Eastern spiritual beliefs. The (often mistaken) social practices and worldview of barbarian tribes were conflated and extended to all periods of the Middle Ages.

The concept of the medieval artist as primitive took on currency in the later part of the nineteenth century, not surprisingly when other "primitive" forms, such as those of Africa, Oceania, and South America, were discovered, and it often overlapped with them. It may, in fact, be understood as a sub-category of the ubiquitous fascination for the primitive which appears with such frequency at the dawn of the twentieth century. The primitive could be located both abroad (such as in the examples of colonial booty on display at the Musée du Trocadéro) or found in the cultures of peasant society and untrained visionaries like Henri (Le Douannier) Rousseau.[11]

---

[6]   Armand Point, "Les Primitifs et les symbolists," *L'Ermitage* (July 1985): 11–19.

[7]   *Exposition des primitifs français au Palais du Louvre (Pavillon de Marsan) et la Bibliothèque nationale* (Paris: Palais du Louvre and Bibliothèque nationale, 1904).

[8]   For a discussion of this issue see Laura Morowitz, "Medievalism, Classicism and Nationalism: The Appropriation of the French *Primitifs* in Turn-of-the-Century France," in *Nationalism and French Visual Culture: 1870–1914*, ed. June Hargrove and Neil MacWilliam (Washington DC: Trustees of the National Gallery of Art/New Haven: Yale University Press, 2005), 225–40.

[9]   "Ils n'avaient rien à apprendre de personne en fait de sincerité, délicate ou brutale ...": Georges Lafenestre, introduction to *Exposition des primitifs*, xviii.

[10]   Émile Mâle, *L'art religieux du XIIIe siècle en France: étude sur l'iconographie du moyen âge et sur ses sources d'inspiration* (Paris: Leroux, 1898). For an English translation see *Religious Art in France: The Thirteenth Century. A Study of Medieval Art and Its Iconography*, ed. Harry Bober, trans. Marthiel Mathews (Princeton: Princeton University Press, 1984).

[11]   The Musée d'Ethnographie du Trocadéro existed in Paris from 1878–1935. For an excellent discussion of the "primitive" reception of African art in early twentieth century France see James Clifford, "Histories of the Tribal and Modern," in *The Predicament of*

8. Enguerrand Quarton, *La Pieta de Villeneuve-lès-Avignon*.

In the field of art history, by far the most important proponent of the primitive Middle Ages was the historian and curator Louis Courajod, who founded the Département de la sculpture du moyen âge et de la Renaissance at the Louvre in 1893. Through his series of lectures at the École du Louvre, as well as his publications and his collecting activities, Courajod proposed *all* medieval art as having barbaric roots (he spoke of "les arts barbares"). He traced the style and spirit of medieval art to the Christian East: "For us the source of light was neither Greece nor Italy, but the bottom of the Black Sea, and further back, Persia and Assyria ..."[12] For him, the reigning spirit of Gothic artists was rooted in their Celtic heritage and had nothing to do with the gentle, sweet style of the *primitifs*. It is

*Culture: Twentieth-Century Ethnography, Literature and Art* (Cambridge: Harvard University Press, 1988), 189–214. On Rousseau's reception as primitive see Nancy Ireson, *Interpreting Henri Rousseau* (London: Tate Publishing, 2006).

[12] "... Le foyer de lumière a été, pour nous, non la Grèce ou l'Italie, mais le fond de la mer Noire, and dans le lointain, la Perse et l'Assyrie." Louis Courajod, "Les origines de l'art gothique," *Leçon d'ouverture au cours d'histoire de la sculpture française* (10 December 1890). On Courajod see Laura Morowitz, "'Une guerre sainte contre l'Académisme': Louis Courajod, the Louvre and the Barbaric Middle Ages," in *The Year's Work in Medievalism* XVII, ed. Jesse G. Swan and Richard Utz (Eugene, OR: Wipf and Stock: 2003), 56–63. See also the pages on Courajod in Francis Haskell, *History and its Images: Art and the Interpretation of the Past* (New Haven: Yale University Press, 1993), 442–4.

9. Plate 32, Frédéric Moreau, *Album des principaux objets recueillis dans les sépultures de Caranda (Aisne) pendant les années 1873, 1874 et 1875.*

hardly surprisingly that Courajod was notably absent from the 1904 Exposition des Primitifs.

The burgeoning field of archaeology, and the excavation of Merovingian and Frankish sites in particular, contributed to a growing fascination with the early medieval or "barbaric" periods of history, and the objects they produced. The publications of archaeologists Jules Pilloy (1830–1922) and Frédéric Moreau (1798–1898), especially *l'Album Caranda* (1877–93) made available abundant colored plates showing an array of weaponry, jewelry, and pottery with powerful, abstract vigorous designs (Figure 9).[13] Pilloy, trained in the fine arts, provided the drawings of the thousands of pieces excavated from Merovingian tombs by Moreau. Many of the objects displayed complex interlace design and strong geometric patterning.

[13] For scholarship on the importance of Merovingian excavations and French national identity in the nineteenth century see the works of Bonnie Effros, for example, *Uncovering the Germanic Past: Merovingian Archaeology in France 1830–1914* (Oxford/New York: Oxford University Press, 2012).

10. Paul Gauguin, *The Green Christ*, 1889. Inspired by the "calvaires," the calvary-sculptures of Brittany.

The spread of the "primitive" Middle Ages was due in no small part to contemporary artists, who had a vested interest in championing the non-naturalistic and seemingly virile art of artists outside the Western and post-Renaissance canon. Paul Gauguin, Émile Bernard, and their circle, working in the remotest corners of Brittany, believed that they had returned to the distant Middle Ages. Visible beneath the layers of Catholic ritual and Christian piety were the remnants of a far older "barbarian" culture.[14] Bernard wrote, "Atheist that I was, it [Brittany] made of me a saint ... it was the gothic Brittany which initiated me in art and God."[15] The forests of the Druids, the crude stone menhirs, and even the language of the Celtic populations of Brittany seemed to provide a continuous link to a pre-Christian past that formed the foundation for medieval Brittany. In their images of Breton peasants, these artists mapped Eastern features onto their faces, to imply their barbaric heritage (Figure 10). Their very physiognomy was witness to the mingling of Celtic populations and Eastern tribes, while the green crucifix "imagined" by the peasant in Gauguin's painting mixes Romanesque iconography with the crude stylization associated with the art of that region.

The lure of the primitive medieval artist also held appeal for the German Expressionists working at the beginning of the twentieth century. In the fifteenth-century woodcut they found an art form both inherently Germanic and tied to the art of the indigenous peoples of the non-Western world. The art critic Wilhelm Worringer (1881–65) firmly tied the art of the Expressionists to the German Gothic tradition, in particular the expressive art of Matthias Grünewald (c.1470–1528), whose works were rediscovered in the nineteenth century. The German Gothic artists and the Expressionists produced art that was restless, expressive, and "masculine."[16]

Despite their prevalence during these two centuries of medievalism, both the "primitive" and the *primitif* were constructions created to serve the needs of the modern societies that embraced them. How do the notions they put into circulation stand up against what we understand from modern scholarship about the workshop production, social practice, and motivations of artists working in the Middle Ages?[17]

Decades of research by scholars such as J. J. G. Alexander and Leslie Ross have disproven the notion of the medieval artist working in inspired isolation, relying solely on imagination and fervor. Artistic workshops of the Middle Ages were highly organized, deeply hierarchical spaces. There was often a great deal of collaboration: knowledge and working models were shared and absorbed. Artists were trained in the most up-to-date techniques and with developing tools and both model and recipe books. While many scriptoria were located in monasteries, the majority of artists were not members of religious orders. The workshop was hardly a meditative space of inspired and spontaneous production, but alive with multiple artisans, voices, and projects.

---

[14] On Brittany as a locus of both primitivism and medievalism see Gill Perry, "The Going Away," in Charles Harrison, Francis Frascina, and Gill Perry, *Primitivism, Cubism, Abstraction* (London/New York: Yale University Press, 1993).

[15] Bernard quoted in Perry, "The Going Away," 16.

[16] For a good discussion of German Expressionism and German Gothic art see Peter Selz, *German Expressionist Painting* (Berkeley: University of California Press, 1974), 12–19.

[17] For a good overview of recent scholarship on the medieval artist see "Artists," chapter two in Veronica Sekules, *Medieval Art* (Oxford/New York: Oxford University Press, 2001); Jonathan J. G. Alexander, *Medieval Illuminators and their Methods of Work* (London/New Haven: Yale University Press, 1994); Leslie Ross, *Artists of the Middle Ages* (Westport: Greenwood Publishing, 2003).

Nor was the medieval artist negligent or indifferent about issues of money and status. Many artists were attached to courts, and earned significant sums. Distinct ranking held between apprentices, journeymen, and masters. The "anonymous" *imagier* is largely a fiction. Artists often did sign their names (for example in the colophons of medieval manuscripts) and even when this was not the case, many works were attributed to them and widely recognized (although we cannot always assume the name to be that of the artist; it was often that of the patron). Anonymity was often due to the multiple hands at work on a given commission rather than the product of humility.

Lack of adherence to anatomical correctness or perspective was the result of a different set of accepted conventions. Whatever crudeness may appear to us in the work of artists of "barbaric" origin, they worked within a set of accepted conventions, and their products often reveal incredibly advanced technical skills, for example in metal working. Artists in the Middle Ages were hardly "innocents," but skilled craftsmen, the better among them often well travelled.

Finally, what functions did such artistic conceptions serve? Both "primitive" and *primitif* were understood and structured in opposition to the successful artists of the late eighteenth and nineteenth centuries. How do the fictions of these two terms shed light on modern attitudes and fears about the commercialism, detachment, and commodification of art-making and provide an alternative vision set within the mythic Middle Ages?

The creation of the medieval "primitive" and *primitif* was a response to wider social conditions within the industrial nations of Europe. They must be understood in opposition to modern man – time-bound, urban, urbane, and cynical. These figures require social isolation – for example the cloistered painter-monk – and took on currency at a time when capitalism began to link various networks and a "realm apart" became nearly impossible to locate.

It is hardly coincidental that the Christian *primitif* reached enormous popularity in the decades just before the separation of Church and State in France (and this insistently Christian element helps to explain why this myth had less currency in England, where William Morris and John Ruskin's medievalism edited out the hegemonic Christianity of the period). The insistence on a link between Catholicism and art is echoed by contemporary artistic groups moving into monasteries, and by the formation of artistic associations demanding Christian belief.[18] Suppressing the individual nature of the artistic productions created by the primitive and the *primitif* allowed their works to become signifiers of collective religious beliefs: thus the works were thought to express *all* medieval artists, and by extension, *all* medieval men and women.

The development of the primitive and *primitif* also responded to changes within the structure of the art world and in the development of artistic style. It is not hard to understand the lure of these figures in a climate focused on the marketing of the individual artist. These medievalist tropes created a phantasmagoric image

---

[18] Such was the case with the artists in the Salons de la Rose+Croix, who had to be Christian in order to exhibit. See Robert Pincus-Witten, *Occult Symbolism in France: Jósephin Péladan and the Salons de la Rose+Croix* (New York: Garland Publishing, 1976).

in which art was produced out of sheer inspiration, detached from any monetary concerns. Such features help to explain, for example, the primitive flavor of Vincent van Gogh's dreamed-of Studio of the South, in which Gauguin would serve as abbot and all resources would be pooled.

As untrained artists with goals counter to realism, the primitive and the *primitif* provided legitimacy and a legacy for artists breaking from Renaissance ideals. After decades of Academic ideals, based on a faithful and detailed reproduction of the "real world" – such as including a rational perspectival system, an accurate use of scale, and convincing sensory details – the medieval artist provided a profound alternative.[19] To embrace the crude, "unsophisticated" art of the barbaric tribes, for example, was a radical re-envisioning of the entire value system of Western art. This applies of course equally to the simultaneous fin-de-siècle embrace of plain-chant in music, or epic poetry in literature.

Against jaded modern man – self-conscious, worried about social approval and material gain, intellectual – stood the "primitive" medieval inhabitant. In an age of doubt, the primitive and *primitif* engaged in a world in which there was no thinking outside spirituality. They were tied to the world of the senses and unconcerned with larger social forces. Above all, the medieval primitive and *primitif* were seen as creatures of *instinct* – their invention belongs to the world of Nietzsche, of the Romantics, and even of Freud. This instinct might take the form of violence, of child-like joy, or of an outpouring of religious fervor. In the medievalist schema, man was not a passive inhabitant of the world, but an active member, *homo fabricans*, who turned the act of living into the greatest art of all.

## Further Reading

Antliff, Mark and Patricia Leighton. "Primitive." In *Critical Terms for Art History*. Ed. Robert S. Nelson and Richard Shiff. Chicago: Chicago University Press, 1996. 170–84.

Effros, Bonnie. *Uncovering the Germanic Past: Merovingian Archaeology in France 1830–1914*. Oxford/New York: Oxford University Press, 2012.

Emery, Elizabeth and Laura Morowitz. *Consuming the Past: The Medieval Revival in Fin-de-Siècle France*. Aldershot: Ashgate Publishing, 2003.

Driskel, Michael Paul. *Representing Belief: Religion, Art and Society in Nineteenth Century France*. University Park: Pennsylvania State University Press, 1992.

Haskell, Francis. *Rediscoveries in Art: Some Aspects of Taste, Fashion and Collecting in England and France* Ithaca: Cornell University Press, 1976.

Morowitz, Laura. "Medievalism, Classicism and Nationalism: The Appropriation of the French *Primitifs* in Turn-of-the-Century France." In *Nationalism and French Visual Culture: 1870–1914*. Ed. June Hargrove and Neil MacWilliam.

---

[19] For a thoughtful discussion of this issue see Madeleine Caviness, "Broadening the Definition of Art: The Reception of Medieval Works in the Context of Post-Impressionist Movements," in *Hermeneutics and Medieval Culture*, ed. Patrick J. Gallagher and Helen Damico (Albany: State University of New York Press, 1988).

Washington DC: Trustees of the National Gallery of Art/New Haven: Yale University Press, 2005. 225–40.

Thiebaut, Dominique, Philippe Lorentz, and François-René Martin. *Primitifs français: Découvertes et redécouvertes.* Exh. Cat. Paris: Musée du Louvre, 2004.

## Related Essays in this Volume

Continuity, Gothic, Christianity, Heresy, Play, Presentism, Purity, Trauma, Transfer, Resonance

# 23

## Purity

*Amy S. Kaufman*

W
HEN EDMUND SPENSER wanted to write an epic that could "fashion a gentleman or noble person in vertuous and gentle discipline," he produced the *Faerie Queene*, a poem that drew on medieval romance tropes, medieval allusions, and the medieval mode of allegory to edify a Renaissance audience.[1] Eighteenth-century Gothic novelists like Horace Walpole and Ann Radcliffe summoned readers to a mystical, occult past while their own world lost its mysteries to the Enlightenment. William Blake and Sir Walter Scott became entranced with the Middle Ages as their environments darkened with the grit and smog of industry, and Tennyson and Swinburne hung their poetry on idyllic visions of beautiful, virginal maidens and brave, boyish conquerors from the past even as England's imperial subjects rebelled against their colonization. The Middle Ages has represented a period of innocence and moral purity to writers and artists throughout modernity; even Mark Twain's *A Connecticut Yankee in King Arthur's Court*, which mocks medieval credulousness as ignorance, has longing mixed with its loathing, longing for a retreat from cynicism and scientific certainty, and for a world full of wonder.

And yet, there has always been a darker side to humanity's nostalgia for the "unspoiled" past. The same purity imagined by Spenser, Tennyson, and their counterparts has also been embraced by the Ku Klux Klan, Nazi Germany, and fundamentalist sects of religious movements, all of which imagine the medieval era as a pristine space in which whiteness and masculinity assume a prevalence naturalized by the soft focus of medievalism's pseudo-historical lens. For each of these authoritarian cultures, medievalism is the symbolic medium through which members are encouraged to perform according to prescribed roles, falling into place based on the imagined historicity of class, race, and gender.

While the English under Victoria's reign gloried in Pre-Raphaelite paintings and misty poetic tributes to the Lady of Shalott, the other side of the pond became enamored with the Middle Ages as well. This was particularly true of the American South, which imagined itself as a neo-feudal empire crushed into

---

[1] Edmund Spenser, "Letter to Sir Walter Raleigh," in *The Faerie Queene* (1589).

ruin by northern barbarians during the Civil War. A number of southern writers, including Thomas Nelson Page, Thomas Dixon, Sidney Lanier, and George Washington Cable, framed their characters' virtues with medieval tropes: heroes dueled to prove their manhood and defend just causes, and damsels in distress were rescued by knights clad in the shining armor of moral righteousness, knights who often developed into wise, kingly patriarchs who were born to rule. Tales of the medieval *bel inconnu*, or fair unknown, experienced a renaissance especially evident in the renewed popularity of King Arthur, history's most famous *bel inconnu*, whose supernatural ability to pull a sword from a stone belied his peasant upbringing. The reassuring fiction of genetic aristocracy in which one's power naturally equaled one's virtue was an appealing narrative for a white elite in danger of losing its privilege.[2]

The nineteenth century was a period of upheaval and national redefinition in the American South: industrialization, the feminist movement, and the emancipation and reconstruction following the Civil War combined to create a level of anxiety that compelled Americans, especially southerners, to seek stability in the past.[3] Slaveholders once considered themselves feudal lords whose ancestors created a new courtly society in a fertile promised land, thus conveniently rationalizing slavery. But now that Southern gentlemen faced the prospect of competing with black men politically, economically, and even romantically, they clung even more fiercely to an ideology of genetic white chivalry, a myth enabled both by historical nostalgia and pseudoscience. The trend of purified medievalism that had seized the nineteenth-century imagination – sanitized, bowdlerized tales cleansed of blood, sex, and moral ambiguity – provided the "historical" narrative of an inherited system of moral superiority, one in which virtue adhered to bloodlines.[4] Social Darwinism provided the "science": proponents of this theory argued that white Anglo-Saxon Protestants were superior to other races by virtue of their position of power. It was a markedly circular argument for social "natural" selection. The American South, a culture anxiously obsessed with whiteness and racial purity after emancipation, had shattered the fiction of racial boundaries and used this cocktail of medievalism and pseudoscience as a foundation from which to preach the rhetoric of racial superiority and genetic purity and, eventually, to legislate both.

---

[2]   The American South certainly did not invent this practice. Europe had already seized on its own form of medievalism as justification for perpetuating a genetic aristocracy far earlier in the nineteenth century. See for instance, Zrinka Stahuljak, *Pornographic Archaeology: Medicine, Medievalism, and the Invention of the French Nation* (Philadelphia: University of Pennsylvania Press, 2013) on medical theories of hereditarianism in nineteenth-century France.

[3]   Kim Ileen Moreland, *The Medievalist Impulse in American Literature: Twain, Adams, Fitzgerald, and Hemingway* (Charlottesville, VA: University Press of Virginia, 1996), 1–5.

[4]   Morton W. Bloomfield, "Reflections of a Medievalist: America, Medievalism, and the Middle Ages," in *Medievalism in American Culture: Papers of the Eighteenth Annual Conference of the Center for Medieval and Early Renaissance Studies*, ed. Bernard Rosenthal and Paul E. Szarmach (Binghamton: Center for Medieval and Early Renaissance Studies, SUNY, 1989), 13–27 (21).

Few writers employed medieval tropes to market racist propaganda as blatantly as Thomas Dixon, author of the 1905 novel *The Clansman: An Historical Romance of the Ku Klux Klan* (the novel that inspired one of the country's most racist films, D. W. Griffith's 1915 *The Birth of a Nation*). In *The Clansman*, emancipated slaves rise up and take over government, banking, and law enforcement, roaming the streets in unruly gangs, extorting citizens, destroying crops, and living on government rations.[5] The rape of a young virgin, Marion, finally inspires a group of young white men with ancestral roots in medieval Scotland to form the Klan, a vigilante order of self-styled knights who will purge their land of color and restore its purity. Dixon's Klansmen dress in medieval costumes and his narrator compares them to crusaders, taking care to emphasize the pure white blood of his heroes.[6] The motivation Dixon gives his chivalric characters – the protection of their women and the restoration of social order – romanticizes the actual origins of the Ku Klux Klan (KKK), which began as a group of young hooligans pulling pranks, mostly on black families.[7] Despite these ignoble beginnings, the Klan believed its own whitewashed mythology. Members of the KKK in the 1920s even went on regular "purity campaigns" to cleanse their towns of vice.[8]

Dixon's novel also models the ways in which racial hierarchy and gender divergence are inextricably connected within the medievalist impulse for purity. His knights are inspired to manly action by the need to protect white female bodies. After Marion's rape, "A gale of chivalrous passion and high action, contagious and intoxicating, swept the white race. The moral, mental, and physical earthquake which followed the first assault on one of their daughters revealed the unity of the racial life of the people."[9] Dixon's female characters, such as the heroine Elsie, who renounces her feminism in order to be a proper mate for the Grand Dragon, are forced to submit to white patriarchal rule in order to earn chivalric protection and to inspire greatness in their men. White male identity, medievalism reveals, is symbiotic: its power is elevated by white female vulnerability.

The inverse was also held to be true: female independence and autonomy were thought to weaken men. Social Darwinism proposed that white racial purity was contingent upon gender divergence; in other words, men and women became more opposite the higher up the evolutionary ladder they climbed. Effeminacy in men and assertiveness in women were signs of atavism, falling out of nature's favor through racial contamination, miscegenation, weakness of spirit, or the inappro-

---

5    Thomas Dixon, *The Clansman: An Historical Romance of the Ku Klux Klan* (Lexington: University Press of Kentucky, 1970). For further discussions of Dixon's medievalism, see Amy S. Kaufman, "Anxious Medievalism: An American Romance," *The Year's Work in Medievalism* 22 (2009): 5–13 (9–11); and Tison Pugh and Angela Jane Weisl, *Medievalisms: Making the Past in the Present* (London: Routledge, 2012), 142–3.

6    Dixon, *The Clansman*, 316.

7    Michael Newton, *The Ku Klux Klan: History, Organization, Language, Influence and Activities of America's Most Notorious Secret Society* (Jefferson, NC: McFarland & Co., 2007), 6.

8    Nancy MacLean, *Behind the Mask of Chivalry: The Making of the Second Ku Klux Klan* (Oxford/New York: Oxford University Press, 1994), 98–9.

9    Dixon, *The Clansman*, 341.

priately gendered behavior of one's partner. And as nineteenth-century America struggled with economic and racial change, it also faced suffragettes and women entering the workforce, agitating for emancipation. It is therefore no surprise that alongside fears of racial impurity and the loss of aristocratic power, American culture was in a panic over the "end" of masculinity, terrified that the American male was turning into a "Miss Nancy Man" and would lose his privileged place in the social and evolutionary ecosystem.[10]

The solution to this perceived crisis was to get medieval: countless fraternal orders with medieval names and medieval initiation rituals sprang up across America, including the Knights of Columbus, the Knights of King Arthur, the Knights of Pythias, the Holy and Noble Order of the Knights of Labor, the Knights of the Golden Circle, and even, for a short time, the Knights of Ben Hur.[11] The other side of this equation was that women would need to play the "angel in the house," remaining sheltered in their homes and serving as moral and spiritual centers of the family in order to enable the nobler sensibilities and chivalrous instincts of their sons and husbands.[12] Suffragettes were lampooned as ugly and masculine, their male supporters chided as effeminate weaklings. Women were warned of the terrible toll that work, politics, or heavy intellectual endeavors could take on their wombs, their appearance, and their desirability to men. But this idea of the sexes as "complementary" was never just about gender: whiteness was also the preexisting condition for pure femininity, as Sojourner Truth famously pointed out in 1851.

Thus, "purity" in nineteenth-century American medievalism was often code for white male authority, female submission, and the disappearance of people of color who could be "cleansed" out of the southern gentleman's paradise just as they appear to be absent from Western medieval narrative. Dixon's novel provides a lens (albeit a magnifying one) to view the reactionary beliefs of his historical moment. But problematic employment of medievalism is not limited to one period in history. Perhaps the most infamous abuse of medievalism occurred several decades later in Nazi Germany, where Teutonic fantasies of purity emerged from the same climate of medievalism that fueled the revisionist histories of the American South.

As England and the American South chased their armor-clad fantasies of gender and racial purity, continental Europe underwent its own passion for medievalism. Medieval Germany was rediscovered and celebrated by nineteenth-century artists,

---

[10] Anthony E. Rotundo, *American Manhood: Transformations in Masculinity from the Revolution to the Modern Era* (New York: BasicBooks, 1993), 472–3.

[11] The Knights of Ben Hur renamed themselves the Supreme Tribe of Ben Hur when they were reminded that there were no ancient knights. Mark C. Carnes, *Secret Ritual and Manhood in Victorian America* (New Haven: Yale University Press, 1989), 5.

[12] Famous feminist critiques of the Victorian "angel in the house" include Virginia Woolf, "Professions for Women," in *The Death of the Moth and Other Essays* (New York: Harcourt Brace, 1974), 235–42; Kate Millett, *Sexual Politics* (Champaign, IL: University of Illinois Press, 2000), 106–7; and Sandra M. Gilbert and Susan Gubar, *The Madwoman in the Attic: The Woman Writer and the Nineteenth-Century Literary Imagination* (New Haven: Yale University Press, 1979), 1–106.

composers, writers, and scholars as a national Golden Age.[13] Wagner brought new life to the medieval German *Parsifal* and *Nibelungenlied*, which were increasingly used for nationalist ends in political propaganda, and linguistic and folklore studies by Jacob Grimm, Franz Bopp, and Max Müller posited that the shared history, language, and sentiment of English, Germanic, and Norse cultures pointed to humanity's original, purest, and noblest state of existence.[14]

The fervor of medievalist memorialism and nationalist medievalism that had swept the nineteenth century gave the twentieth-century Third Reich everything it needed to manipulate the past and fuel its dream of a pure, Aryan future. Nazi folklorists conflated Norse, Scandinavian, and Germanic medieval legends and argued for a single original ancestor; the Nazi party claimed that the links between these cultures had decayed because of "foreign elements" and it was the mission of good scholars to re-establish the Aryan purity of a Proto-Germanic history.[15] Nazi propaganda and rhetoric painted portraits of party elites as chivalric knights; they even created "Order Castles," schools for party officials intended to model medieval knightly and monastic orders.[16] Wagner had already elevated the *Nibelungenlied* to the status of national epic; thanks to its popularity, the Siegfried type – the proto-Germanic, übermasculine warrior – became an all-important figure in Nazi revisionist ethnography and historiography. He was, according to Nazi Party official guidelines, the picture of "loyalty, courage, honesty, endurance under trying circumstances, a readiness to fight against enemy forces, and a manly mastery of difficult situations."[17] It goes without saying, perhaps, that the neo-Germanic warrior was also a paragon of whiteness and heterosexuality; like the Crusaders whose blood supposedly surged through his veins, he would cleanse Germany, and indeed all of Europe, of the taint of Judaism, racial degradation, and homosexuality.

Like his American counterpart, the übermensch required submissive female purity to inspire his personal (and racial) perfection. The Third Reich encouraged women to leave the labor market to make room for men; emancipation was dismissed as a Jewish scheme.[18] *Mein Kampf* (1925) warns repeatedly against the compromised racial purity of Germany, jeopardized by black men brought to the Rhineland by Jews and by Jews themselves, all of whom plotted to seduce

---

[13]   Francis G. Gentry, "The Politicization of the Middle Ages: Nationalism and Festivals in Nineteenth-Century Germany," *Studies in Medievalism* III.iv (1991): 467–88.

[14]   See Christa Kamenetsky, *Children's Literature in Hitler's Germany: The Cultural Policy of National Socialism* (Athens, OH: Ohio University Press, 1984), 4–12; and Martin Arnold, *Thor: Myth to Marvel* (London and New York: Continuum, 2011), 126–36.

[15]   Kamenetsky, *Children's Literature*, 72; and Heather Pringle, *The Master Plan: Himmler's Scholars and the Holocaust* (New York: Hyperion, 2006), 43–6, 78–81.

[16]   Laurie A. Finke and Martin B. Shichtman, *King Arthur and the Myth of History* (Gainesville: University Press of Florida, 2004), 190; and Richard J. Evans, *The Third Reich in Power* (New York: Penguin, 2006), 287.

[17]   Kamenetsky, *Children's Literature*, 76.

[18]   Evans, *Third Reich*, 331.

Aryan women.[19] Once in power, Hitler called on German women to stay home and nurture their children rather than "interfere" with the world of men.[20] Joseph Goebbels agreed, arguing that "The mission of the woman is to be beautiful and to bring children into the world [...] The female bird pretties herself for her mate and hatches the eggs for him. In exchange, the mate takes care of gathering the food, and stands guard and wards off the enemy."[21] National purity depended not only on the strength of men but on the isolation and disempowerment of women. Siegfried can only be Siegfried if Brunhild learns to submit and get out of the way. (In this sense, at least, Nazi propaganda was markedly faithful to medieval epic). The view of the Middle Ages as an era of purity is hardly just the concoction of bygone racist, sexist, violent eras, however. The Nazi Proto-Germanic hero and the Klan's chivalric warrior, hybrid fantasies steeped in cross-cultural medieval symbolism, supported by the submission of women and charged with maintaining national purity, remain what is often identified in contemporary cultural fantasy as the ideal medieval model for manhood.

Contemporary anxieties over the supposedly precarious status of masculinity, Christianity, and whiteness continue to promote medievalism as the solution to society's ills. The twenty-first-century Christian Patriarchy movement, for instance, encourages knightly masculinity in boys and purity in young women through toys and educational materials.[22] Its adolescent girls attend annual purity balls in which young women are led under an archway of crossed swords by their fathers to take a "purity pledge," vowing to remain virgins until their fathers find a suitable husband.[23] Their brothers undergo knighthood ceremonies in which they are presented with swords made to medieval standards.[24] King Arthur and William Wallace are this movement's heroes, just as they were to the nineteenth-century fraternal orders and the Klan. Such activities come in response to perceived threats against the sexual purity of young women, the perceived marginalization of paternity, and the declining birthrate among whites (known to alarmists as the "demographic winter").[25] The fantasy of the medieval past as a pure and natural model for humanity also governs less radical spaces: as recently as July 2013, the *New York Times* published a debate entitled "Resuscitating Chivalry" in which one of the columnists expresses much the same sentiment about "natural" gender relations as Joseph Goebbels. Brett McKay, author of the 2009 book *The Art of Manliness*, argues in this debate that chivalry "can foster mutual respect and remind us of

---

[19] Adolf Hitler, *Mein Kampf*, trans. Ralph Manheim (New York: Houghton Mifflin, 2001), 249–89.

[20] *Frankfurter Zeitung*, 9 September 1934, qtd. in Evans, *Third Reich*, 331–2. See also Pringle, *Master Plan*, 92.

[21] Qtd. in Evans, *Third Reich*, 332; and Pringle, *Master Plan*, 106–7.

[22] Kaufman, "Anxious Medievalism," 5–13 (5–8); and Laurie Finke and Martin B. Shichtman, "Who's Your Daddy?: New Age Grails," *Arthuriana* 19.3 (2009): 25–33.

[23] Amy S. Kaufman, "'His Princess': An Arthurian Family Drama," *Arthuriana* 22.3 (2012): 41–56.

[24] Kaufman, "His Princess," 52–3.

[25] Kathryn Joyce, *Quiverfull: Inside the Christian Patriarchy Movement* (Boston: Beacon Press, 2009), 192–6.

our underlying biological differences and the complementary nature of the sexes. Some women will bear children, and some men will step up to be protectors should danger arise."[26]

Popular media such as the television show *Game of Thrones*, video games derived from the *Dungeons and Dragons* universe, and even the cinematic renditions of *The Hobbit* and *The Lord of the Rings* seem to amplify the oppression of women and revel in racial stereotypes when people of color appear (if they appear at all). The defense provided by producers and fans alike is almost always a claim of authenticity: these fantasy worlds are medieval and political correctness is far less important than fidelity to the past.[27] But authenticity is, in fact, where medieval records and medievalism diverge. People living in the Middle Ages neither dwelled in an uncorrupted sea of whiteness nor submitted to an unflinching patriarchy. Medieval westerners actually did interact with the world around them – consider the literary, philosophical, and scientific exchanges between France and Al-Andalus during the twelfth-century Renaissance or the Saracen heroes and heroines of medieval romance. Nor were gender roles as fixed as contemporary fantasy would like to believe. There were many circumstances in which medieval women could own property, get divorced, read and write, govern, be religious leaders, or even lead armies. Women often remarried more than once and were considered desirable for their wealth or their childbearing ability rather than their virginity. Thus, it is not the purity of the Middle Ages audiences invoke when they want their medievalism to be authentic, but the purity of a fantasy of the Middle Ages – a brand of medievalism with a violent, devastatingly destructive lineage.

It is a strange phenomenon indeed that a period etymologically identified as *medium aevum*, the "middle age," should so often be imagined as primeval, as the beginning of things, an era in which Western civilization might locate its purest origins and, therefore, prescriptions for proper human relations. Perhaps the same Renaissance revisionist historiography that denigrated the Middle Ages as "dark" and celebrated the advanced wisdom of the ancients did its job too well: in this asynchronous timeline of human progress, the ancient moves forward and the medieval moves back, more *primitus* than *medius*. But those who believe their own propaganda about history and purity hope that their vision of an unspoiled past – a world of whiteness, chivalry, masculinity, and monolithic Christian faith – will be the paradise of the future.

[26] Brett McKay, "Respecting Our Differences," *New York Times* (31 July 2013), http://www.nytimes.com/roomfordebate/2013/07/30/can-chivalry-be-brought-back-to-life/chivalry-is-a-nod-to-differences-between-the-sexes (accessed August 2013).

[27] See, for instance, the many defenders of George R. R. Martin's depictions of race and gender in James Lowder, ed., *Beyond the Wall: Exploring George R. R. Martin's* A Song of Ice and Fire, *from* A Game of Thrones *to* A Dance with Dragons (Dallas, TX: Smart Pop/BenBella Books, 2012).

## Further Reading

Aronstein, Susan. *Hollywood Knights: Arthurian Cinema and the Politics of Nostalgia*. New York: Palgrave, 2005.

Kamenetsky, Christa. *Children's Literature in Hitler's Germany: The Cultural Policy of National Socialism*. Athens, OH: Ohio University Press, 1984.

Moreland, Kim Ileen. *The Medievalist Impulse in American Literature: Twain, Adams, Fitzgerald, and Hemingway*. Charlottesville: University Press of Virginia, 1996.

Pringle, Heather. *The Master Plan: Himmler's Scholars and the Holocaust*. New York: Hyperion, 2006.

Rosenthal, Bernard, and Paul Szarmach, eds. *Medievalism in American Culture: Papers of the Eighteenth Annual Conference of the Center for Medieval and Early Renaissance Studies*. Binghamton: Center for Medieval and Early Renaissance Studies, State University of New York, 1989.

## Related Essays in this Volume

Myth, Christianity, Genealogy, Primitive, Heresy, Troubadour, Trauma, Presentism, Authenticity, Gothic, Middle, Modernity, Transfer

# 24
# Reenactment

*Michael A. Cramer*

THEY ARE WEIRD, let's face it: those who dress up and pretend to be something else; grown men and women who play make-believe. Let's start with that point, that they are weird. Popular culture mocks reenactors, calls them "nerds" or "dorks." Their hobby is ridiculous. It has no value. It is escapism pure and simple: and escapism is, as we all know, for losers who can't handle the real world. Academics treat them with scorn because they are amateurs who have not paid their scholarly dues and yet have the temerity to speak like experts. They are depressed melancholic losers: thousands of Miniver Cheevys living out pathetic fantasies.[1] In a recent article in *Maxim Magazine*, Laura Morreale, associate director of the Center for Medieval Studies at Fordham University, said,

> There is a tension between academic historians and SCA [Society for Creative Anachronism] folks [...] It took me 10 years to get my degree, and there's a notion that they just have to go out and live it and it's more real. But from a business perspective, we need people who are passionate about history.[2]

Ah! But in a postmodern world, where professionalism and expertise are devalued, monoculture has been replaced by various sub-cultures, and nerds rule; the tables have been flipped. These amateurs have often been studying their period for years, sometimes decades, sometimes for a whole life. They perform incredibly well-designed experiments in experimental archeology or performance reconstruction. They are often more invested in the field, in terms of time and money, than are some tenured professors. Besides, "weird" is the new "normal," which means they can't be weird. Recently, through the efforts of Ken Mondschein of

---

[1]   Miniver Cheevy, "born too late," is the eponymous character of an Edward Arlington Robinson poem: "Miniver loved the days of old / When swords were bright and steeds were prancing": http://www.poetryfoundation.org/poem/174244.

[2]   Ben Detrick, "Game of Dorks: Inside the World of Medieval LARPing," *Maxim*, 5 June 2013. Available from http://www.maxim.com/tv/game-of-dorks-inside-the-world-of-larping (accessed 28 June 2013).

the Higgins Armory, as well as the Chicago Sword Guild, and La Belle Compagnie (a reenactment company), reenactment has been making serious headway gaining entry into academia, in a series of panels at the International Congress on Medieval Studies in Kalamazoo that have focused on the intersection between academia and reenactment.[3] Reenactment is suddenly legitimate.

Why do they do it? (Ok, confession time: we.[4]) Why dress up and pretend to be Elizabeth or Bayard or a twelfth-century peasant blacksmith? What can be gained from this form of play and, more importantly, how are we (academics) supposed to write about it? This chapter looks at reenactment as both an activity and as a critical term for scholars of medievalism.

Of course, reenactment is not exclusively medieval. In the United States the most popular form is American Civil War reenactment. Every past military era, from Ancient Persia to the Vietnam War, has its enthusiasts who dress up and play soldier. There is a nationalist or patriotic style of reenactment as well, wherein important non-military historical events, like the founding of a town or the signing of a treaty or document, are reenacted. Examples would be reenactments at the Fourth of July of the signing of the Declaration of Independence, or the Victorian civic pageants invented by Louis Napoleon Parker.[5] Medieval reenactment can include battle reenactments, costumed interpreters at castles and cathedrals, medieval-style feasts and dances, some carnival parades, role playing re-creation,[6] Historical European martial arts, costumed fairs, and performance reconstruction. If we expand our era to the sixteenth century, the list can include Renaissance faires and the performances at the Globe Theatre.

Reenactment in its purest sense involves acting out documentable historic events, such as the battle of Hastings or Leif Erickson's voyage to Vinland. There is usually a premium put on historical accuracy, and the object from the point of view of the reenactors is to get as close to a "medieval moment" as possible, to make somehow a temporal transference so that they can actually come to know what it was like to live in the Middle Ages. Such a transference is, of course, impossible. At all times the medieval person is a character, an object being manipulated by the modern subject portraying him.

At its most basic, reenactment is a form of make-believe. It shares a number of qualities with a theatrical performance, such as costume and mimesis, but it is different as well. It is less formal. It is less likely to have a script. It sometimes does not even have an audience. Reenactment is therefore a type of proto-theater that has as its object not (or not only) the edification of an audience, if any, but, often more so, the edification of the players themselves.

---

[3]  See Ken Mondschein, ed., *Can These Bones Come to Life?* (Chicago: Freelance Academy Press, 2014).

[4]  I have been a medieval re-creationist, what some people call a reenactor, for thirty-five years and an academic for twenty.

[5]  For information on the Victorian pageants, see Louis Napoleon Parker, *Several of my Lives* (London: Chapman and Hall, 1928).

[6]  I always prefer to hyphenate re-creation to distinguish it from recreation, as in a leisure activity, but many people writing about re-creation leave the hyphen out, and since re-creation is a type of recreation it can be rather confusing.

The biggest problem with the use of reenactment as a critical term is that it is used haphazardly. It is interchangeable with a number of other terms, each of which describes an activity that could be said to be a sub-category of reenactment. The most common of these is re-creation. Re-creation is distinct from reenactment in that it is a game in which modern people pretend to be made-up medieval people interacting in a made-up world. It includes some live action role playing and groups such as the Society for Creative Anachronism and the Adrian Empire, in which people interact within a faux-medieval social structure. Richard Schechner uses the term "historical restorations" to describe all types of historical performance.[7] To Schechner, historical restorations are an entirely postmodern activity that likely arose out of the existence of film portrayals of history, giving people a visual frame of reference as to what history might look like. Schechner sees this as a nostalgic longing for an authentic identity in a fragmented world, a common desire within the postmodern condition.

"Living history," an equally popular term, is an activity in which people create an impression of a particular time as opposed to reenacting a specific event. This would include people who act as historical interpreters at sites such a Carcassonne or Hampton Court Palace. However, people who perform at Renaissance faires, commercial activities that are usually far less interested in historical accuracy, also call what they do "living history." In theater studies, Robert Sarlos uses the term "performance reconstruction" to describe his attempts to re-create famous theatrical performances, such as the first performance of *The Triumph of Peace*, right down to re-creating the class relationships between the audience members.[8] As a theater historian, Sarlos sees this as an important element of the study of theater history, an effort to understand not only the technologies that went into theatrical production in different periods but also audience responses. Historical dance reconstruction, historical costuming, early music performances, experimental archeology, and HEMA or "historical European martial arts" are also terms that should be considered here, since the people who do these things are often referred to as "reenactors" if, within their various performances, they dress up in historical garb.

Reenactments of historical events are narrative performances with established roles and scripted outcomes based on the historical record. If, when reenacting the battle of Agincourt, the French somehow win, then it has ceased to be a reenactment and become a re-creation. In this way, reenactment is tied directly to historical narrative. As all history is told from a particular political perspective, so all historical reenactment will follow either an official narrative or a counter-narrative. Usually, it is the former. A reenactment of the battle of Hastings will for the most part ignore the complex social and political issues that surrounded the succession crisis of 1066 and simply show the fight. The official narrative of

[7]   Richard Schechner, *The End of Humanism* (New York: Performing Arts Journal Publications, 1982), 106.
[8]   See Robert Sarlos, "Performance Reconstruction," in *Interpreting the Theatrical Past: Essays in the Historiography of Performance*, ed. Thomas Postlewait and Bruce McConachie (Iowa City: University of Iowa Press, 1989), 198–229.

the battle of Hastings is that it was part of the right, just, and inevitable march of progress toward the coronation of Elizabeth II, because it is part of British history ("1066 And All That"). There is an imperialist element to battle reenactment, and to most other reenactment of historical events as well – although on occasion reenactments will be staged from a postcolonialist perspective, such as reenactments of the colonization of North America that adopt the perspective of native peoples.

With other forms of reenactment, such as living history or re-creations, and even performance reconstructions, the audience–actor relationship is blurred. "These places," Schechner writes of living history sites (and of theme parks), "are large environmental theaters."[9] Reenactment constitutes what Schechner called environmental theater because of its use of space. "The first scenic principle of environmental theater is to create and use whole spaces."[10] In other words, there is no separation between audience and actor. Everyone becomes part of the performance. In *Between Theater and Anthropology*, Schechner notes of the preparation for performance at Plimoth Plantation, "Interestingly, there is very little group rehearsal – for this is not a play the performers are preparing for but a more improvisational world of interaction not only among performers but with the tourists who visit the plantation daily."[11] While what actors would recognize as rehearsal is not taking place, there is a lot of preparation. The reenactors must be steeped in the period they are interpreting. In another study of Plimoth Plantation, Stephen Eddy Snow writes, "Like singers, dancers, dramatic performers, storytellers and reenactors of other societies, the actor/historians of Plimoth Plantation are what Milton Singer calls 'cultural specialists.'"[12] While the scripted portions of the performance at Plimoth Plantation represent a fairly typical actor–audience relationship, at least recognizable when compared to other forms theater, they are not actually the "main show."

Most of the performance at a living history event is the interaction that happens around and between the set pieces, the conversations between reenactors and their audience. In this way the very idea of theater gets broken down. As Schechner said of his most famous experiment in environmental theater, *Dionysus in 69*, "Two Points should be made clear regarding the participation in Dionysus. First, participation occurred at those points where the play stopped being a play and became a social event – when spectators felt they were free to enter the play as equals [...] The second point is that most of the participation in Dionysus was according to the democratic model: letting people into the play to do as the performers were doing, to 'join the story.'"[13] This is the nature of reenactment in living history situations (including Renaissance faires).

[9]   Richard Schechner, *Between Theater and Anthropology* (Philadelphia: University of Pennsylvania Press, 1985), 78.

[10]   Richard Schechner, *Environmental Theater* (New York: Hawthorne Books, 1973), 2.

[11]   Schechner, *Between Theater and Anthropology*, 84.

[12]   Stephen Eddy Snow, *Performing the Pilgrims: A Study of Ethnohistorical Role-Playing at Plimoth Plantation* (Jackson: University of Mississippi Press, 1993), 121.

[13]   Schechner, *Environmental Theatre*, 44.

Nikolai Evreinov, like Sarlos, sought to recreate not just the style but the total experience of earlier styles of theatrical performance, which he hoped would be an antidote to nineteenth-century realism.[14] As Marvin Carlson writes, "The Theatre, said Evreinov, 'is not dramatic literature' but a totality of drama, acting, staging, and audience; a proper revival of past works should attempt to revive 'a whole complex of the social and intellectual life of a given epoch, where the spectacle itself occupies only a part of the scene.'"[15] Evreinov, like William Poel in England and later Sarlos in California, recreated total theatrical events, staging plays in appropriate venues, such as banqueting halls or existing town squares, and providing costumes for the audience.

Evreinov's writings on theatricality touch more directly on the impulses behind reenactment than any other works. To Evreinov, theater does not come from other forms of art, from music, or from dance, nor does it come from religious practice. The urge for theater comes from man's natural urge for transformation, to become something else. This, he points out, is a game children play before they have a sense of any aesthetic. It is a mind-set that exists before there is art:

> The instinct of theatricalization, which I claim the honour to have discovered, may be best described as the desire to be "different," to do something that is "different," to imagine oneself in surroundings that are "different" from the commonplace surroundings of our everyday life. It is one of the mainsprings of our existence, of that which we call progress, of change, evolution and development in all departments of life. We are all born with this feeling in our soul, we are all essentially theatrical beings. In this a cultured man differs little from a savage, and a savage from an animal.[16]

This need for theatricality can manifest itself in many ways, but one of the most obvious is in the realm of make-believe. Just as a young boy might make believe that he was a knight, so too might a grown man. This, in essence, is reenactment. Evreinov coined an important term for understanding theatricality (and it is useful in understanding reenactment): the theater of oneself. In the end, Evreinov believed that we are all drawn toward privacy and to creating our own play worlds. Instead of sitting in a dark room watching other people pretend to be something else, acting out a preposterous story for our entertainment, it is better to amuse ourselves through make-believe.

Evreinov did not anticipate postmodernism. Where Evreinov's isolationist theory of theatricality ultimately fails in helping us to understand reenactment, postmodernism succeeds. One hallmark of postmodernism is a fragmentation of culture into various taste groups, groups which can form their own hierarchies, their own self-contained sub-culture. Evreinov's theater for oneself assumes that

---

[14] Marvin Carlson, *Theories of the Theatre* (Ithaca: Cornell University Press, 1984), 326.
[15] Nikolai Evreinov, *Histoire du théâtre russe*, trans. G. Walter (Paris: Brentanos, 197), 383–4, quoted in Carlson, *Theories*, 326.
[16] Evreinov, *Histoire*, 23.

everyone wishes to be isolated, while postmodernism assumes that each person will become the intersection of different sub-cultures.

Medieval re-creation is far removed from reenactment, even though the people who take part in these activities are often referred to as "reenactors" and they, as a frame of reference, often compare themselves to Civil War reenactment. This is usually for contextual reference, since Civil War reenactment is the best-known variety in the United States. Members of the SCA, Medieval Scenarios and Recreations, the Adrian Empire, Empire of Chivalry and Steel, Amptgard, et al. (most of these latter groups are groups that, for one reason or another, splintered away from the SCA) do not seek to reenact actual historical events. Members of these groups create alternate worlds in which to live out their medieval fantasies, part of a large medievally coded counter-culture set up in opposition to the banal realities of "mundania."[17] Their re-creations are essentially postmodern versions of the old medieval king game, in which a person becomes king of the group through a contest – in this case combat. Groups imprint their own geography onto the world by dividing it into kingdoms or empires. They create their own social hierarchies by setting up rigid social systems based on medieval titles of nobility, which must be earned from and awarded by a king or prince. Because these are not true reenactments, members are able to change things about the Middle Ages that they do not like and imbue their version of the Middle Ages with modern sensibilities. Such groups are usually secular, which makes them anti-medieval in one of the most important ways. Because of their use of "persona," the identity members adopt for their performances, race and gender are somewhat fluid. There are Caucasians who portray Samurai, Black men who portray French knights, and women whose personas are men (although women whose personas are women can still fight and become knights).

In the first chapter of *Don Quixote*, Cervantes wrote:

> You must know, then, that the above named gentleman, whenever he was at leisure (which was mostly all the year around) gave himself up to reading books of chivalry with such ardor and avidity that he almost entirely neglected the pursuit of his field sports, and even the management of his property; and to such a pitch did his eagerness and infatuation go that he sold many an acre of tillage-land to buy books of chivalry to read, and brought home as many of them as he could get.[18]

Such was the passion of Cervantes's literary medieval reenactor, and such is the life of chivalric reenactors today, whether in the SCA or HEMA or as members of battle reenactment companies. It is a reasonable generalization to say that they read copiously about chivalry and the Middle Ages. They study all the secondary sources and as many of the primary ones as they can obtain. They examine and

---

[17] It is reasonable to ask, however, whether or not a counter-culture can exist in a postmodern society. The lack of a true social hierarchy means there is nothing to resist.

[18] Miguel de Cervantes, *Don Quixote*, trans. John Ormsby. Available from classiclit. about.com/lirary/bl-mdecervantes-p1–1.htm (accessed 27 July 2013).

argue about the medieval *fechtbucher* and Charny's questions. Those who prac-tice the gentler arts do the same with sources in cooking or clothing and other pursuits, so that among SCA members (and this is probably true among reenac-tors in general) there are more people who have read *The Art of Carvyng*, or *Le Ménagier de Paris*, or Jordanus Rufus's *The Care of Horses* than you will find in any department of medieval studies in any university.

The Fordham professor quoted at the beginning of this article is, in fact, dead wrong. She is working from a paradigm that has been outdated for at least a decade. Reenactment has made serious inroads into the academy. At the annual International Medieval Congress at Kalamazoo in 2013 reenactment events were the most obvious feature of the conference. For the seventh year, The Higgins Armory organized sessions on reenactment. The Chicago Sword Guild presented a reenactment of a judicial duel. In the next room there was an interactive chant session going on. La Belle Compagnie put on an armored fashion show. AVISTA – the Association Villard de Honnecourt for Interdisciplinary Study of Medieval Technology, Science, and Art – organized an iron-smelting demonstration by a Viking reenactment group from Canada. Discussion, Interpretation, and Study of Textile Arts, Fabric, and Fashion – or DISTAFF – presented their usual series of papers on medieval textile arts. The brewers' guild held their popular mead and beer tasting.

All of these sessions involved collaboration between professional scholars and hobbyist reenactors. All of this has happened because, in the years since the SCA was founded in 1966, many reenactors and re-creationists have turned their love of the Middle Ages into their profession. They turn the projects they began as reenactors into scholarly research, and end up writing dissertations on medieval culinary arts, or literary representations of chivalry, or on the *fechtbucher*. Reen-actment now influences the academy as much as the academy influences reenact-ment, because Evreinov was correct: people love playing make-believe.

## Further Reading

Blackson, Robert. "Once More … With Feeling: Reenactment in Contemporary Art and Culture." *Art Journal* 66 (2007). 28–40.

Cramer, Michael. *Medieval Fantasy as Performance: The Society for Creative Anach-ronism and the Current Middle Ages*. Baltimore: Scarecrow Press, 2009.

Esty, Joshua D. "Amnesia in the Fields: Late Modernism, Late Imperialism, and the English Pageant Play." *ELH* 69 (2002). 245–76.

Gilsdorf, Ethan. *Fantasy Freaks and Gaming Geeks: An Epic Quest for Reality Among Role Players, Online Gamers, and Other Dwellers of Imaginary Realms*. Guilford: The Lyons Press, 2010.

Horowitz, Tony. *Confederates in the Attic*. New York: Pantheon Books, 1998.

La Belle Compagnie. *1381 – The Peel Affinity: An English Knight's Household in the Fourteenth Century*. Harrisburg: Schumacher, 2007.

Merrington, Peter. "Masques, Monuments, and Masons: The 1910 Pageant of the Union of South Africa." *Theatre Journal* 49 (1997). 1–14.

## Related Essays in this Volume

Spectacle, Play, Authenticity, Simulacrum, Co-disciplinarity, Authority, Humor, Feast, Resonance

# 25

# Resonance

*Nils Holger Petersen*

WHILE THE METAPHOR of resonance can be applied beyond sound, this essay limits itself to discussing the idea of the resonance of medieval music and ritual in modern music and ritual practices. Depending on one's understanding of the notions of music and ritual (and the Middle Ages), it must first be acknowledged that modern practices directly access neither medieval music nor medieval rituals; at most they can sometimes be found to resonate. Any attempt to reconstruct a medieval ritual practice or musical performance encounters fundamental obstacles that make the reconstruction as much a creative as a scholarly effort. Even the most reliable and detailed sources (musical scores, liturgical manuscripts, narrative sources, or combinations of such documents) provide only vague notions of tempo, timing, sound, or of movements and gestures in the performative event constituted by the ritual or musical performance. Therefore, musicians and musicologists do not assume or expect authenticity of modern performances of medieval or other so-called "early" music (this may include music up to the time of Mozart, Beethoven, and the early Romantics). Today, in the so-called early music revival, the term "historically informed performance practice" characterizes modern attempts to implement current knowledge about earlier practices of music in contemporary performances.[1]

The problems concerning medieval ritual are of a similar order. Not only is it difficult to get close to details about how specific rituals were actually carried out

---

[1]  See Daniel Leech-Wilkinson, *The Modern Invention of Medieval Music* (Cambridge: Cambridge University Press, 2002), Anette Kreutziger-Herr, "Imagining Medieval Music," *Studies in Medievalism* XIV (2005): 81–109, and Paul C. Echols and Maria V. Coldwell, "Early-Music Revival," *Grove Music Online* (http://www.oxfordmusiconline.com [accessed 25 July 2013]). See also Daniel Leech-Wilkinson, "The Good, the Bad and the Boring," in *A Companion to Medieval and Renaissance Music*, ed. Tess Knighton and David Fallows (Oxford: Oxford University Press, 1997, orig. published London: Dent, 1992), 3–14. General theoretical discussions of the notions of music, the musical work, performance, and performance practice are found for instance in José A. Bowen, "Finding the Music in Musicology: Performance History and Musical Works," in *Rethinking Music*, ed. Nicholas Cook and Mark Everist (Oxford: Oxford University Press, 1999), 424–51, and Stanley Boorman, "The Musical Text," in *Rethinking Music*, 403–23.

(for similar reasons as medieval musical performances), but as with "music," it is not clear how to define or delimit the notion of the "ritual."[2] Nevertheless, the problems become less daunting when one leaves behind abstract discussions and focuses on specific and well-defined areas. Looking at medieval music connected to medieval liturgical practices like the mass or the Divine Office provides a framework for discussing the impact of such rituals and their music on modern composers and even on modern liturgical practices.[3] Furthermore, the chant of medieval liturgical ceremonies has traditionally been understood as the beginning of Western music history in academic musicology.[4]

In this article I shall deal with resonances of medieval chant and hymns in three areas of music performance: 1) within modern Protestant Lutheran mass liturgy; 2) among composers of so-called avant-garde music; and 3) within modern performance practice of medieval liturgical music. I shall do this by way of three short case studies. The first presents an attempt around 1900 by a composer and church musician, Thomas Laub (1852–1927), to reform hymn singing in the Lutheran Church of Denmark. The second case study briefly discusses the *Black Angels: Thirteen Images from the Dark Land for Electric String Quartet* (1970) by the American contemporary composer George Crumb (born 1929). Finally, I shall point to the resonances of medieval mass ritual in a historically informed CD performance of medieval chant.

Thomas Laub carried out his reform efforts as a composer of (mainly) liturgical music (hymn melodies and other liturgical songs) and through his theoretical writings. He published two books, *Om Kirkesangen* (*On Church Singing*, 1887) and *Musik og Kirke* (*Music and Church*, 1920),[5] in addition to practicing his ideas through newly composed hymn melodies and musical appropriations of medieval (including Reformation) hymns for congregational singing in Danish. He only set

---

[2]   Concerning the lack of a commonly agreed definition of "ritual," see Catherine Bell, *Ritual: Perspectives and Dimensions* (Oxford: Oxford University Press, 1997), see esp. 1 and 21. Bell points out that scholars do not agree, and that "ritual is not the same thing everywhere; it can vary in every feature" (81). See also Philippe Buc, *The Dangers of Ritual: Between Early Medieval Texts and Social Scientific Theory* (Princeton: Princeton University Press, 2001), esp. 247–8, for a criticism of the use of the notion of ritual in medieval studies, and the discussion in Nils Holger Petersen, "Ritual. Medieval Liturgy and the Senses: The Case of the Mandatum," in *The Saturated Sensorium: Principles of Perception and Mediation in the Middle Ages*, ed. Hans-Henrik Lohfert Jørgensen, Henning Laugerud, and Laura Skinnebach (Aarhus: Aarhus University Press, forthcoming).

[3]   The notion of liturgy as understood today is not medieval and does not completely correspond to any term used in the Middle Ages. See Nils Holger Petersen, "Liturgy and Ritual in the Middle Ages," in *Cantus Planus: Papers Read at the Twelfth Meeting, Lillafüred, 2004*, ed. László Dobszay (Budapest: Hungarian Academy of Sciences, 2006), 845–55.

[4]   See Leo Treitler, *With Voice and Pen* (Oxford: Oxford University Press, 2003), 103–18, and Nils Holger Petersen, "Carolingian Music, Ritual, and Theology," in *The Appearances of Medieval Rituals: The Play of Construction and Modification*, ed. Nils Holger Petersen, et al. (Turnhout: Brepols, 2004), 13–31, esp. 25–9.

[5]   Thomas Laub, *Om Kirkesangen* (København: Reitzel, 1887), and Thomas Laub, *Musik og Kirke* (Herning: Poul Kristensen Forlag, 1997), reprinting the original 1920 edition with a new introduction by Peter Thyssen and also reprinting an introduction to an edition from 1978.

Danish language hymns including re-writings of medieval hymns and sequences by Danish poets, not least by N.F. S. Grundtvig. Although he was initially much criticized and his hymn melodies have never won complete acceptance in congregations, he gradually came to exert a huge influence on church singing and hymn melodies in Danish Lutheran churches, primarily through followers among organists and Lutheran Church ministers.[6]

Laub's reaction against the romanticized hymns in the Danish nineteenth-century Lutheran Church was to a large degree based on his own theologically informed interpretation of Western music history, not least his theological criticism of major-minor tonality as it evolved after c. 1600. Laub's critique may in a certain way be characterized as premodern because of its attempt to distinguish between subjective individual feelings and less subjective, corporate responses to the preaching of the Gospel. This involved stating the "yes and amen of the congregation," something which Laub believed could be found in medieval (and Reformation) singing and which he deemed to be the true (theological) function of music in church services.[7] The following statement summarizes Laub's musico-theological distinction between medieval and Reformation music and music after c. 1600:

> A composer from that time [the pre-1600 era] – a church composer foremost – was not about to depict his own personal feelings as resulting from the words he would set in music. He wrote for a congregation of which he was a member himself and for whom the words were central; his music was an expression of the congregation's humble reception of what the words contained; it was the yes and amen of the congregation [...] After 1600 music became sentimental, feeling became central; words were now primarily a pretext for the music, that is one had a predilection to choose words which gave the music the richest occasion to display all its strengths and one was consciously absorbed in human emotions and passions.[8]

Laub's point is that the "new" tonality of the Baroque period (thought to have

---

[6]  There seems to be almost no literature in English about Thomas Laub. For a brief biographical introduction, see Niels Martin Jensen, "Laub, Thomas (Linnemann)," *Grove Music Online* (http://www.oxfordmusiconline.com accessed 25 July 2013).

[7]  Laub, *Om Kirkesangen*, 9; Laub, *Musik og Kirke*, 91–2.

[8]  Translations are mine throughout this article. Laub, *Om Kirkesangen*, 9: "En komponist fra den tid – en kirkekomponist, for det var han først og fremmest – gik ikke ud på at skildre sine personlige stemninger, som var fremkomne ved de ord, han havde at sætte i musik. Han skriver for en menighed, af hvem han selv er et medlem, og for hvem ordene er hovedsagen; hans musik er et udtryk for menighedens ydmyge modtagelse af det, som ordene indeholder, den er dens ja og amen [...] Efter 1600 er musikken sentimental, stemningen er bleven hovedsagen, og ordene er nu væsentlig anledning for musikken, d.v.s. man vælger med forkærlighed de ord, der giver musikken den rigeste lejlighed til at udfolde alle sine kræfter og går med fuld bevidsthed ud på at fordybe sig i de menneskelige sindsbevægelser og lidenskaber." Laub includes a footnote making it clear that he does not use the notion of sentiment negatively, just as he also emphasizes that it is only with respect to church music that the "old" music is superior to the "new" (tonal as opposed to modal) music.

developed between Monteverdi and Bach) was well equipped to express feelings, but that, in his opinion, was irrelevant to the situation of a church congregation. Discussing how a composer could go about setting a psalm of David, for instance, he comments critically on a potential setting of the psalm which tries to express David's feeling while writing the psalm (Laub assumes the Book of Psalms to have actually been written by David):

> The churchgoers do not assemble at the service to feel emotions about the emotions of another person, even if they are ever so beautifully expressed; they assemble to state the words of the liturgy and thereby their own praises and prayers, stating them in the common tone that expresses the mental position of the whole congregation, not of the individual, in relation to the words (in the hypothetical case, the psalm of David), the unanimous voicing of the congregation to unite with the words – briefly, as said before, the yes and amen of the congregation, honestly, simplemindedly, without ulterior motives.[9]

What Laub did in practice was to avoid modulations, leading notes, and to write melodies and settings informed by medieval melodies, especially the church modes, although he was far from completely consistent in avoiding what he called "modern chords," by which he seems to have meant harmonies that emphasized "modern" tonality.

Indeed, Laub wrote tonal music in a "modern" way, but avoided overt Romantic devices and emotional appropriations of tonality. A medieval sequence melody (*Veni, sancte spiritus*) can be clearly recognized in Laub's setting of *Kom, Gud Helligånd, kom brat* (Come, God the Holy Spirit, Come Fast); still, his setting is undeniably contemporary, and not a pastiche. Also, Laub's understanding of medieval liturgical music is unmistakably modern. There are, certainly, insights that accord with medieval thought and practice. It is, for instance, a reasonable interpretation of medieval chant in general to claim that it does not (normally) express individual feelings. But Laub's juxtaposition of two possible ways of setting words for the liturgy, one subjective, based on individual feelings, the other communal as a general response to the biblical or liturgical text, establishes a critical question for Laub's own time and situation which does not seem to have much to do with medieval liturgical situations. As exemplified in a number of so-called liturgical dramas from the Middle Ages, one would sometimes juxtapose general congregational statements of praise and prayer with representations of Rachel's laments over her lost children in ceremonies about Herod's massacre of the Innocents (Matt 2:16–18; for Holy Innocents) or with Daniel's lament as he entered the lions' den in the famous *Danielis ludus* and – even more importantly – with Marian

---

[9]  Laub, *Musik og Kirke*, 92. "Kirkefolket kommer jo ikke sammen ved gudstjænesten for at føle rørelse over andres følelser, selv om de er nok så smukt udtrykt, det samles for selv at frembære kirkeordene og derigennem sine egne lovsange og bønner, frembære dem i den fællestone der udtrykker, ikke den enkeltes, men hele menighedens sjælelige stilling overfor ordene (i det tænkte tilfælde Davids salme), dens stemthed til at gøre sig til ét med dem, – kort, som før sagt, dens ja og amen, redeligt, énfoldigt, uden bagtanker."

1  Christian Barnelow's setting (1859) of N.F. S. Grundtvig's hymn *Kom, Gud Helligånd, kom brat*. In: *Menighedens Melodier*, 2 vols, ed. by L. Birkedal-Barfod, O. Madsen, and S. Widding (Copenhagen and Leipzig: Wilhelm Hansen, 2nd edn. 1920), I, p. 254.

2  Thomas Laub's setting (1914) of N.F. S. Grundtvig's hymn *Kom, Gud Helligånd, kom brat*. In: *Menighedens Melodier*, 2 vols, ed. by L. Birkedal-Barfod, O. Madsen, and S. Widding (Copenhagen and Leipzig: Wilhelm Hansen, 2nd edn. 1920), I, p. 253.

laments, explicitly intended to invoke the compassion of churchgoers.[10] The ritual in such ceremonies consisted – to a large extent – in confrontation with and identification with biblical narratives, thereby reinforcing the liturgical "answer" to the message contained in the narrative.[11]

[10] See Susan Boynton, "From the Lament of Rachel to the Lament of Mary: A Transformation in the History of Drama and Spirituality," in *Signs of Change: Transformations of Christian Traditions and their Representation in the Arts, 1000–2000*, ed. Nils Holger Petersen, et al. (Amsterdam: Rodopi, 2004), 319–40; Margot Fassler, "The Feast of Fools and *Danielis ludus*: Popular Tradition in a Medieval Cathedral Play," in *Plainsong in the Age of Polyphony*, ed. Thomas Forest Kelly (Cambridge: Cambridge University Press, 1992), 65–99; Nils Holger Petersen, "Devotion and Dramaticity in the Bordesholmer Marienklage (1476)," in *Dies est leticie: Essays on Chant in Honour of Janka Szendrei*, ed. David Hiley and Gábor Kiss (Ottawa: The Institute of Mediæval Music, 2008), 413–27.

[11] See Nils Holger Petersen, "Representation in European Devotional Rituals: The

Laub must have known that his hymn melodies were not (strictly) modal (in the church modes), and he did acknowledge that he chose to use medieval liturgical music to resonate in his ecclesiastical context around 1900 in order to deal with what he conceived of as problems in the church life of his own time. He seems, on the other hand, to have transposed back to the Middle Ages his own (modern anti-Romantic) idea of an opposition between individual feelings and communal liturgy. Just as medieval liturgical music can, in some measure, be said to resonate in Laub's reformed church music by way of modality and the appropriation of medieval melodies, Laub's modern liturgical ideology resonates in his understanding of medieval liturgy and music.

My second case study belongs to the modern avant-garde concert sphere. George Crumb is a contemporary composer who uses sounds and traditions from many cultures and many periods of the Western music tradition; he "composes in the historical and geographical universe occupied by humans."[12] Thus, medieval musical elements as well as medieval ritual elements are far from alone among historical borrowings in Crumb's music. In *Black Angels* for electric string quartet there are references to medieval symbolism, applied to the Vietnam War, but more generally to the struggle between good and evil, between God and the Devil. Crumb explicitly points out that his use of religious symbolism is pre-religious rather than an expression of his adherence to a specific religion. He sees myths as "poetic truths."[13] In *Black Angels*, Crumb quotes music and verbal phrases from various times, including Schubert's *Death and the Maiden* string quartet (1824) as well as the medieval *Dies irae* sequence (thirteenth century) evoking the ultimate judgment and its associations to the medieval Requiem Mass. In *Black Angels* Crumb also gives brief references to elements from non-European (including Tibetan, Japanese, and African) cultures in a context of advanced and innovative modern sounds extending the use of the instruments beyond traditional sounds.

The music does not sound altogether "medieval," but in addition to the use of the *Dies irae* and references (sometimes verbal) to other classical music, it uses a concept of form which draws on a basic Christian narrative, expressed in the three-part division of the work: "I: Departure (fall from grace)" – "II. Absence (spiritual annihilation)" – "III. Return (redemption)." These are further subdivided in 5 + 4 + 4 short movements which sometimes clearly deepen the overall headline (like "Devil music," the fourth movement, part I; or "Black Angels," movement 7, part II; or "God-music", movement 10, part III), but at other times are more ambiguous.[14] The main point I wish to make is that medieval music and a biblical notion of salvation history, which was basic to medieval theology and liturgy and

---

Question of the Origin of Medieval Drama in Medieval Liturgy," in *The Origins of Theater in Ancient Greece and Beyond: From Ritual to Drama*, ed. Eric Csapo and Margaret C. Miller (Cambridge: Cambridge University Press, 2007), 329–60, esp. 336–48.

[12]    See Nils Holger Petersen, "Quotation and Framing: Re-contextualization and Intertextuality as Newness in George Crumb's *Black Angels*," *Contemporary Music Review* 29 (2010): 309–21 (311).

[13]    Petersen, "Quotation and Framing," 312.

[14]    For a fuller analysis, see Petersen, "Quotation and Framing."

was received into musical forms in fundamental ways in Western music,[15] resonates through the composition of Crumb's *Black Angels* in ways that can be heard directly in the sounds of the work, but also perceived in other, more subtle, intellectual ways, which also influence the way the music is heard, notably in the sweet reminiscences of tonality and melodiousness in the God-music. I interpret this to be an expression of redemption not as mental or religious hope, but as musical hope for "creating a recognizable order in the huge, chaotic musical sound universe in which modern – conscious – man lives."[16]

Many other composers appropriate medieval music, sometimes in other, more direct ways. In all such cases, whether the medieval notes are more or less clearly audible or not, there is re-signification and re-contextualization, so that the medieval melodies or ritual connotations resonate through the modern music, but they are no longer there as their original selves.

The third and last example I would like to discuss concerns the performance of music from a medieval ritual. A CD I often use to show what I believe medieval chant may have sounded like is Dominique Vellard's recording, with his Ensemble Gilles Binchois, of music and poetry from the medieval mass as preserved in medieval manuscripts from the Swiss monastery of St. Gall.[17] Here, tropes and sequences for various masses taken from early (ninth-century) manuscripts from St. Gall are performed, applying the most recent knowledge about medieval notation and liturgical practice to a modern artistic performance. The performances are historically informed in their music, but reflect little of the ritual context. The music appears as music does in typical modern consumption practices such as recordings of Chopin nocturnes, Bob Dylan songs, or other music anthologies. Listening carefully to the chants and to the words, one may perceive some resonance of what constituted a ritual of confrontation with divine words, angelic songs, and sacraments in the medieval mass, but it is obvious, even when such performances take place in a concert setting, or even in the rare event of a reconstruction of a medieval mass, that it is a re-contextualized and re-signified event, something which no longer can be expected to constitute a meeting place between "the world as lived and the world as imagined," in the words of Clifford Geertz.[18]

Applying and extending Geertz's understanding of "ritual" to broader categories of more or less ritualized performative events, including concerts and even individual listening practices, or to published performances of music through electronic media, it is clear that such practices only work if a correspondence of some kind is perceived between a general sense of what constitutes meaning and the experience of the performance. Hence, performances of medieval music or

---

[15] Nils Holger Petersen, "Classical Music," in *The Encyclopedia of the Bible and its Reception*, vol 5, ed. D. C. Allison, Jr., et al. (Berlin: De Gruyter, 2012), col. 391–7.

[16] Petersen, "Quotation and Framing," 320.

[17] *Musique et poésie à Saint-Gall: Séquences et tropes du IX^e*, Ensemble Gilles Binchois, Dominique Vellard. Harmonia Mundi/Schola Cantorum Basiliensis 905239, recorded in 1996, with liner notes by Wulf Arlt.

[18] Clifford Geertz, "Religion as a Cultural System," in *Anthropological Approaches to the Study of Religion*, ed. Michael Banton (London: Tavistock, 1966), 1–46 (28).

of a medieval ritual, even to the small and problematic extent they are possible as discussed above, can only be meaningful if they also resonate in some way with a modern experience. This may be through the experience of their alterity (cf. the German philologist Hans Robert Jauss[19]), but even such alterity must in some way or other be experienced as fruitful. To the extent it is possible at all, medieval sounds – like other past sounds – are received by modern ears through appropriation and resonance.

## Further Reading

Aubert, Eduardo Henrik. "Historicizing Neumatic Notation: Medieval Neumes as Cultural Artifacts of the Early Modern Times." *Studies in Medievalism* XXI (2012). 65–88.

Buc, Philippe. *The Dangers of Ritual: Between Early Medieval Texts and Social Scientific Theory.* Princeton: Princeton University Press, 2001.

Flanigan, C. Clifford. "Medieval Liturgy and the Arts: Visitatio Sepulchri as Paradigm." In *Liturgy and the Arts in the Middle Ages: Studies in Honour of C. Clifford Flanigan.* Ed. Eva Louise Lillie and Nils Holger Petersen. Copenhagen: Museum Tusculanum Press, 1996. 9–35.

Kreutzinger-Herr, Annette. "Imagining Medieval Music. A Short History." *Studies in Medievalism* XIV (2005). 81–109.

Leech-Wilkinson, Daniel. *The Modern Invention of Medieval Music.* Cambridge: Cambridge University Press, 2002.

Østrem, Eyolf, et al., eds. *Genre and Ritual: The Cultural Heritage of Medieval Rituals.* Copenhagen: Museum Tusculanum Press, 2005.

Petersen, Nils Holger. "Quotation and Framing: Re-contextualization and Intertextuality as Newness in George Crumb's *Black Angels*." *Contemporary Music Review* 29 (2010). 309–21.

## Related Essays in this Volume

Presentism, Reenactment, Spectacle, Lingua, Gesture, Christianity, Myth, Continuity, Simulacrum

---

[19]   Hans Robert Jauss, "The Alterity and Modernity of Medieval Literature," *New Literary History* 10.2 (1979): 181–229.

# 26

# Simulacrum

*Lauryn S. Mayer*

J EAN BAUDRILLARD'S DEFINITION of the simulacrum as "a copy without an original" is deliberately paradoxical and provoking.[1] If there is no original, how could there possibly be a copy, since the term "copy" depends for its meaning on the idea of an original for comparison (a "good" or "bad" copy). Although the term was designed to describe the hyperrealistic nature of twentieth-century Western or Westernized culture, the definition has even more resonance for the study of medievalism, since there *can be no* original. Imagine, for example, that you could go back to the tenth century and attend a celebration in a mead hall; you could even bring a video camera. Nonetheless, you could not bring back an original; your presence itself would change the past, and even if you were invisible, a recording would be necessarily subjective, and probably reveal more about you than it would about the period, the event, or the participants, no matter how much you presented it as authentic history. The presence of the simulacrum haunts traditional medievalism and its desire to re-create the period. For postmodern or neomedievalism, the same impossibility of accessing an original provides a way of critiquing or challenging traditional medievalism and creates a space for neomedievalism's deliberate play with the inevitably constructed nature of all re-creations of the Middle Ages.

Before addressing the specific importance of the "simulacrum" for the study of "neomedievalism," both terms should be defined and elucidated. Put as simply as possible, a simulacrum is something that subverts our ability to distinguish between what is real and what is represented. Moreover, it calls into question the hierarchy of reality over representation. Think, for example, of the public unease caused when several fashion photographers decided to stop using expensive and necessarily imperfect human models and instead to rely on digitally created ones, or the inversion of hierarchy implied when one sees a beach and says, "It looks just like a postcard!" This simplified definition of the simulacrum, however, cannot address the levels of complexity the term has acquired over centuries of use, study,

---

[1]   Jean Baudrillard, "The Precession of Simulacra," in *Simulacra and Simulations*, trans. Sheila Glaser (Ann Arbor: The University of Michigan Press, 1984), 1–42 (1).

and debate. "Medievalism" and "neomedievalism" are similarly problematic terms, particularly since some writers use them interchangeably. However, the consensus is to use medievalism as a blanket term describing a cultural re-creation of the Middle Ages, while considering neomedievalism as a subset of medievalism that comments directly on the *process* of that re-creation, playing with the entire idea of accessing the past. Like the term "simulacrum," however, this basic description is insufficient to describe the various modes of medievalism and the way the term changes in the array of contexts in which it is used. Finally, the word "neomedievalism" *seems* simple (a "new" variant of medievalism), but in fact refers to a far different practice: a medievalism that takes earlier medievalist texts (history, popular culture representations, conventions, tropes, and the like), fragments them, and playfully repurposes those fragments, all in the process of calling attention to the created nature of any representation of the past.

Given the protean nature of all three terms, the attempt to analyze the importance of a concept like the simulacrum for a phenomenon like neomedievalism seems rather like trying to escape quicksand with a rope made of water. In grappling with this difficulty, this essay will first focus on the tendency of critics after Deleuze and Baudrillard to limit and caricature two divergent patterns of thought about the nature of the simulacrum. One tendency of these critics is to center on the loss of transcendence in Jean Baudrillard's characterization of the simulacrum and to equate this loss of transcendence with a loss of inherent coherence or logic in a neomedievalist work. Another critical tendency is to confuse Gilles Deleuze's refusal of transcendent reality in favor of immanent reality with a lack of reality itself; the critic, consequently, has no ground for a discussion of neomedievalism other than a compiling of *exempla*. To examine the underlying motivations for these approaches and create a more productive model to examine the intersections of term and phenomenon, we must first explore the interweaving of the simulacrum, the practice of historiography, and the multivalent aspects that comprise the term "neomedievalism."

To see how unsettling the idea of the simulacrum can be, we need to look to the puzzle that images raise for Western metaphysics: what kind of a thing is an image? It is obvious that images are not *what* they represent; we do not touch a seascape and expect to feel water. However, they would be meaningless if they did not refer to something other, something they are not, but something *from* which they come and *to* which they point back: the model. The essence of an image lies in this tension between itself and the model. We only recognize *that* something is an image when we recognize *to what* the image refers. However, this recognition of an image entails recognition that the model is absent, that this image is something very different from the model, even as it purports to represent its model. It is this tension which makes images inherently suspicious. To create a likeness one must divorce oneself from the true and divine; in the *Sophist*, Plato claims that "in works either of sculpture or painting [...] there is a certain degree of deception."[2]

---

[2]  Plato, *The Sophist*, trans. Benjamin Jowett, http://classics.mit.edu/Plato/sophist.html (accessed August 2013).

The seascape refers back to the sea, but it cannot contain all of the elements that comprise the sea. A world of truth would be a world without images.

Images, however, are redeemed by the fact that their very existence presupposes a "truer" reality. In a Platonic account, an image, even a copy (an indirect one, like a print of the seascape), is justified by virtue of its participation in a higher order of being. Some images, however, disrupt this order; they belong neither to the top level of the hierarchy (the unrepresentable source of all that is) nor to the lowest unformed matter. They are not *in the image of* a model; rather, they seem to be both image and original. In this kind of image, deception overcomes resemblance. Called "simulacra," these are neither reality nor pointers to a more real order because they create something that cannot be classified in a logic of representation: namely, a *quasi-reality*. The simulacrum here is a dangerous phenomenon that threatens the hierarchy and order of this logic.

This monstrous combination of image and original, like all monstrosities, questions by its very existence the categories themselves, a challenge taken up by contemporary philosophy, with two distinct paths. In "Plato and the Simulacrum," Gilles Deleuze questions the Platonic desire to distinguish between the pure and the impure, the authentic and the inauthentic, the image and the model. Plato's continual search for the true lover, the true philosopher, or the true friend reveals his desire for "the triumph of the copy over the simulacra, of repressing the simulacra, of keeping them chained in the depths, of preventing them from rising to the surface, and 'insinuating' themselves everywhere."[3] The simulacrum is not a degraded copy of a copy, but the product of the encounter of disparate elements, and cannot be defined in relation to a paradigm. In *Difference and Repetition*, Deleuze defines simulacra as "those systems in which different relates to different *by means of* difference itself. What is essential is that we find in these systems no *prior identity*, no *internal resemblance*."[4]

The second contemporary path appeals to the same notion of "simulacrum" for very different reasons. For Baudrillard, late capitalism has created a form of consumerism that primarily produces not commodities but mediatic images and signs (films, videos, television, the Internet, brands, etc.) with no referent but themselves. "It is no longer a question of imitation, nor of reduplication, nor even of parody. It is rather a question of substituting signs of the real for the real itself."[5] Confronted by hyperreality, we become unable to tell the difference between reality and simulation; or rather, this difference becomes ultimately irrelevant. Disneyland (a case discussed by Baudrillard and Umberto Eco) transplants visitors to a fantastic past of knights, princesses, and castles that can "give us more reality than nature can."[6] We have at our fingertips a massive amount of informa-

---

3   Gilles Deleuze, "Plato and the Simulacrum," trans. Rosalind Krauss, *October* 27 (1983): 45–56 (48).
4   Gilles Deleuze, *Difference and Repetition*, trans. Paul Patton (New York: Columbia University Press, 1995), 299.
5   Baudrillard, "The Precession of Simulacra," 2.
6   Umberto Eco, *Travels in Hyperreality*, trans. William Weaver (New York: Harcourt Brace, 1990), 44.

tion but no meaning. In this context, "the simulacrum is never what hides the truth – it is truth that hides the fact that there is none. The simulacrum is true."[7] In other words, the simulacrum is neither real nor copy, but an image that has become truth in its own right; its value depends solely on its being in circulation.

This second conceptualization of the simulacrum mourns a posited lost order and stability. In Baudrillard's account, meaning demands a permanent center, an ultimate referent. In its absence, all turns to chaos and indifference. Fredric Jameson, too, approaches the simulacrum with the intention of mourning a loss when he mentions as an instance of simulacrum the case of "photorealism" where a painting is created by copying a photograph that is itself a copy of the real.[8] By treating the simulacrum as a twice-removed reality (an image of an image), Jameson still refers the simulacrum to an original, only to one that is falsely identified. Likewise, by identifying the era of simulation with the latest technologico-informational phase of capitalism, Baudrillard implies that "once upon a time" the order of copies and reality was clearly delineated. Then, meaning was fixed and stable and things were whatever they were by reference to a genuine normative original in relation to which they were (more or less faithful) images. The nihilism Baudrillard sees at the core of our modern condition is the loss of an ultimate meaning-granting referent.

The difference between these two antithetical conceptualizations of the simulacrum (Baudrillard and Deleuze) rests in the fact that Deleuze does not define the simulacrum as a move *away* from the real (this would presuppose that some transcendent reality was already there, had always already been there). Deleuze's account "overcomes the polarity between the model and the copy by treating them both as a second-order productions, as working-parts in the same machine [...] Reality is nothing but a well-tempered harmony of simulation."[9] This kind of simulation is a matter of extracting and combining potentials, abilities to affect and be affected, rather than the frenzied production of "signs of the real," a production designed to hide the absence of the real. This is not, of course, to imply that Deleuze is an anti-realist, but to underscore that he does not acknowledge a transcendent reality, but an immanent one.

The change in thinking about the simulacrum (from a glitch in a stable ontology to a sign of freedom or loss) goes hand in hand with the drastic change in approaches to the study and writing of history. Early historiography, for the most part, anchored itself in a variety of ways: first, the idea that there existed such a thing as a retrievable past that could be accessed for the most part by sufficient rigor and judgment on the part of the historian. Eyewitness accounts, the weighing and sifting of primary documents, and the skilled examination of earlier histories would enable the historian to get at the "truth" of a particular event or person,

---

7    Baudrillard, "The Precession of Simulacra," 1.

8    Fredric Jameson, *Postmodernism, or the Cultural Logic of Capitalism* (Durham: Duke University Press, 1991), 30.

9    Brian Massumi, "Realer than the Real: The Simulacrum According to Deleuze and Guattari," http://www.anu.edu.au/hrc/first_and_last/works/realer.htm (accessed August 2013).

and even in cases where accounts were wildly differing or the evidence unavailable, historians excused themselves with variations on the phrase "the matter is so dark."[10] This is a statement telling in its assumptions: there is a "matter" that could be accessed (and may be in the future), but at present a lack of consensus or sufficient evidence renders it not undecidable, but "dark" or "hidden" – matter that might be visible with sufficient illumination.

Ranulf Higden's *Polychronicon*, for example, argues against King Arthur's existence on the ground that his exploits are not mentioned in French or Latin chronicles, despite Arthur's supposed conquest of France and Rome. John Trevisa, who translated the work from Latin in 1387, argues that lack of evidence does not equal lack of truth:

> The reasons Ranulf moves against Geoffrey (of Monmouth) and Arthur no clerk should move that knows how to frame an argument, because the conclusion does not follow. St. John in his gospel tells many things and doings of which Mark, Luke, and Matthew do not speak in their gospels, ergo, we should not believe John in his gospel. He would be an idiot who believed that this argument was worth a bean.[11]

Differing accounts do not render any or all of those accounts false, any more than the different accounts of Christ's life and passion in the Gospels of John, Mark, Matthew, and Luke put the divine truth into question. Trevisa's scriptural analogy summarizes a second argument for the truth of history, one that appears first in Romans 15:4 ("[f]or all that was written of old was written for our instruction") and is later further articulated in Augustine's theory of signs. While accounts may be contradictory or evidence missing, there exists a truth more important than simple historical accuracy: a divine truth.

A third approach sees history as heuristic; the object of history is to create an ideal future by giving readers exemplary figures and actions; Anglo-Saxon writing gains much of its power by the juxtaposition of good kings and bad, wisdom and folly, bravery and cowardice. William Caxton, England's first printer, understood the ways in which past histories could be more productive of virtue because they demanded the active exercise of imagination: "the works of the ancient and old people are for to give us example to live in good and virtuous behavior [...] and also in recounting of noble histories common understanding is better served by imagination than by the simple submission to authority."[12]

In all of these approaches, a common practice was to narrow – consciously or unconsciously – the subjects history should present. The *Polychronicon* summarizes a traditional list of appropriate subjects for historiography:

---

[10] Lauryn S. Mayer, *Worlds Made Flesh: Reading Medieval Manuscript Culture* (New York: Routledge, 2004), 12–15.

[11] Ranulf Higden, *Polychronicon*, trans. John Trevisa (Manchester: Chetham's Library MS 11379), f. 114r. (author's modernization of Trevisa's prose).

[12] N. F. Blake, *Caxton's Own Prose* (London: Andre Deutsch, 1976), 66.

> Take heed of seven manners of famous acts: building of cities, victory
> over enemies, making of laws, punishment of law-breaking, aiding in the
> common profit, government of people and households, and the rewarding
> of good men and punishment of evil men.[13]

Such assumptions about the proper subjects and objects of history came into
question as traditional historiographical values and practices were attacked for
being too narrow, for ignoring large sections of the field, and for championing an
ideology that served the dominant classes of society. In addition, the idea that one
could recover the past came into serious question. In the field of anthropology, it
became more and more clear that the study of a culture was inevitably affected by
the culture and values of those doing the research. In the same way, any attempt
to recover "the past" *qua* past could not help but be compromised by the presence
of the scholar, who could not help focusing her attention on particular aspects of
a document, bringing her own cultural values and assumptions into her research,
and compiling evidence in a way that provided, at best, a limited and partial view.
Despite fierce rearguard action from traditional historians, the study of history
now included the study of hitherto marginalized groups (such as homosexuals)
and practices frequently ignored or simply condemned (the thriving economy
of the underworld, superstitions and their cultural logic, the treatment of the
mentally ill, or the daily life in smaller communities such as villages or rural
parishes). Even greater was the blow struck to historiographical presumptions;
one could not simply write a history or analyze an event. Now it was necessary
to acknowledge, at least implicitly, that one's participation in a moment in time
and space would inevitably affect one's analysis. The historian must content herself
with a self-conscious attempt at recovering aspects of the past and acknowledge
the inevitable distorting qualities of any lens. All historiographical work shares the
methods used in the creation of the Disney princesses and the Las Vegas Excalibur
hotel that Baudrillard cites as quintessential examples of simulacra.[14]

   In these cases, the *existence* of a grounding past is not questioned. Each
approach assumes either: a) a complete account of the past exists in some form,
but the presentation of that past is incomplete; or, b) a past whose *existence* is not
questioned, but which is irrevocably distorted by the very process of attempting to
describe and analyze it. Although critics may see these approaches as dangerously
relativistic, they hardly constitute a step towards the kind of nightmarish ground-
lessness depicted in Baudrillard's darkest imaginings or the productive harmony
of the Deleuzian simulacrum. Cultural history relies on the *idea* of a model, even
while it acknowledges that the model itself is inaccessible and the copy necessarily
degraded.

   When we turn to neomedievalism, however, we are stepping off the ledge: how
does one talk about a phenomenon whose name invokes at once model and copy
(the prefix neo- implying as it does an intelligible Deleuzian difference between

---

13  *Polychronicon* f.36v
14  Baudrillard, "The Precession of Simulacra."

model [medievalism] and copy [neomedievalism]) and a "model" too amorphous to be articulated as such, let alone to exist?

First, we cannot responsibly position neomedievalism (despite the chronology implied in the term) as a continuous historical progression like that from Plato to Deleuze or from objectivist history to more self-conscious and contingent historiographical approaches. In fact, the terms "medievalism" and "neomedievalism" are often used interchangeably: if we take the term "medievalism" as referring to the beliefs and practices, the culture of the Middle Ages as invoked or represented in the culture of later periods, then the very generality of the term "referring" can encompass early modern antiquarian interests, the Gothic Revival, Keats's 'Eve of St. Agnes,' and the chain-saw swords, techno soundtrack, and Victoria's Secret costumes of Graham Baker's 1999 film *Beowulf*, as well as the purportedly realistic quests for dominion in the *Medieval: Total War*, *Stronghold*, and *Guild* computer games. In addition, taking its cue from the pejorative use of the term "medieval," political theorists have warned of particular developments they see as medievalist or neomedievalist.[15]

Given the expansive meaning of the term "medievalism," can we say there is a specific quality inherent to neomedievalism? The definition offered by the MEMO (Medieval Electronic Multimedia organization) group outlines the characteristics that make a text, practice, or consciousness "neomedieval," as opposed to "modernist" or "postmodern" medievalism, although, as they note, these definitions are the beginning of a continuing intellectual conversation, not the result thereof.[16] The modernist longing for a simpler or more harmonious past seen in modernist medievalism, and the acknowledged futility of trying to access the medieval past (which we see in postmodern medievalism and its debt to cultural historiography) are gone, replaced by what Carol Robinson describes as "a gleeful embrace of the absurd" that is predicated on "the denial of reality" in the task of creating "a conscious vision of an alternative universe (a fantasy of the medieval that is created with forethought)" and "lacks the nostalgia of earlier medievalisms" by its refusal to buy into the fantasy of retrieving a medieval past. In doing so, it allows current values and issues to "rewrite the traditional perceptions of the European Middle Ages."[17]

Thus far, we appear to have a concept that should work very well with the definition of the simulacrum; the neomedieval text as a copy (the invocation of the "medieval" in the conscious creation of an alternative universe) that has no extant "original" (because of both the admitted inaccessibility of the medieval past and the inscribing of current issues and ideas onto that already-lost Middle Ages). We could also term neomedievalism's sense of playfulness as a variant on the free play of the Deleuzian simulacrum and its endless recombinations.

---

[15] Bruce Holsinger, *Neomedievalism, Neoconservatism, and the War on Terror* (Chicago: University of Chicago Press, 2007).

[16] Carol L. Robinson, "Some Basic Definitions," http://medievalelectronicmultimedia.org/definitions.html (accessed August 2013).

[17] Robinson, "Definitions," n. 14.

This is not to say that neomedievalism is chaotic; "a conscious vision of an alternative universe" implies, in fact, the "well-tempered harmony of simulation" Deleuze posits as the essence of the simulacrum. We do not have a hierarchical model/copy pattern in neomedievalism; rather, we have a system, a "second-order" harmony between the *matter* of neomedievalism and the *dynamic of interaction* that expresses itself in the combination of this matter.[18] The matter is defined in the medieval sense of the term: the accumulation of representations that create the ever-growing body of a subject (in this case, what we recognize as "medieval/ medievalist"), while the specific interaction is the way in which elements of this matter are combined. As a final twist, in medievalist and neomedievalist practices the simulacrum itself appears as a harmony between Deleuzian immanence and a process of combination that dates back to medieval memory practice itself, the necessity of making a text one's own in order to "read" it fully.[19] The only Middle Ages within our grasp is the neomedieval.

## Further Reading

Baudrillard, Jean. *Simulacra and Simulation*. Trans. Sheila Faria Glaser. Ann Arbor: University of Michigan Press, 1994.

Deleuze, Gilles. *Difference and Repetition*. Trans. Paul Patton. New York: Columbia University Press, 1995.

Holsinger, Bruce. *Neomedievalism, Neoconservatism, and the War on Terror*. Chicago: University of Chicago Press, 2007.

Pugh, Tison and Angela Jane Weisl. *Medievalisms: Making the Past in the Present*. New York: Routledge, 2013.

Robinson, Carol L. "Neomedievalism in a Vortex of Discourse: Film, Television and Video Games." In *Neomedievalism in the Media*. Ed. Carol L. Robinson and Pam Clements. Lewiston: Mellen Press, 2012. 1–14.

## Related Essays in this Volume

Authority, Play, Spectacle, Authenticity, Archive, Reenactment, Modernity, Memory, Heresy

---

[18] Lauryn S. Mayer, *"Dark Matters and Slippery Words*: Grappling with Neomedievalism(s)," ed. Karl E. Fugelso, *Studies in Medievalism XIX: Defining Neomedievalism(s) II* (Cambridge: D. S. Brewer, 2010): 68–76.

[19] Mary Carruthers, *The Book of Memory: A Study of Memory in Medieval Culture* (Cambridge: Cambridge University Press, 1990), 8–10.

# 27

# Spectacle

*Angela Jane Weisl*

S PECTACLE: "A SPECIALLY prepared or arranged display of a more or less public nature (esp. one on a large scale), forming an impressive or interesting show or entertainment for those viewing it," reads the *Oxford English Dictionary* (*OED*). The first offered example, from Richard Rolle's 1340 Psalter, describes "Hoppynge & daunceynge of tumblers and herlotis, and oþer spectakils."[1] Although the context here is specifically English, this medieval notion of spectacle as a kind of exotic performance carries into the present; much medievalism, intentional or accidental, takes the form of a spectacle, a creation to be both observed and experienced, although it exists alongside other, less exotic visions of spectacle. Spectacle's etymology in the Latin *specere*, "to look at," suggests that all observed phenomena can be spectacles.

This might suggest an Anglo–American tradition distinct from other models whose view of spectacle is more general and less, perhaps, spectacular, and to some extent, many ideas of spectacle, most of which inform contemporary medievalism, do hearken to that tradition. Yet these more general understandings, such as Guy Debord's notable analysis which shows spectacle to be a condition of life rather than an excessive evocation of it, also offer valuable insight into the ways that medievalism functions as spectacle.[2] It is important to see the ways that these two ideas intersect. Spectacle shares many features with "real" life, particularly in its intersection of the past and its building of communities; however, critics are not mistaken in suggesting that to be a spectacle, the phenomenon must offer more than an opportunity for mere looking. John MacAloon, for instance, observes:

> Not all sights, however, are spectacles, only those of a certain size and grandeur, or as the dictionary puts it, "public displays appealing or intending to appeal to the eye by their mass, proportions, color, or other dramatic qualities." For example, only films employing a "cast of thousands," impressive scenery, and epic historical or religious themes are designated as spectacles.[3]

---

[1] "Spectacle," *Oxford English Dictionary*, online edition.
[2] Guy Debord, *Society of the Spectacle*, trans. Ken Knabb (London: Rebel Press, 2009).
[3] John J. MacAloon, "Olympic Games and the Theory of Spectacle in Modern Societies,"

This perception limits the view of spectacle too much; yet we can view many acts of medievalism in this context; much of what we think of as medievalism does involve public displays appealing to the eye through a range of dramatic qualities, whether that medievalism is a Renaissance faire (an ironic title, perhaps), an historical reenactment, a Viking Metal concert, a joust (either theatrical or "real"), or a film whose mechanically produced scenery, historical and/or religious themes and proportions certainly draw the observer's attention. All participants engage the theatricality of the experience, whether as performers or spectators. MacAloon notes, "Spectacles institutionalize the bicameral roles of actors and audience, performers and spectators. Both sets are normative, organically linked, and necessary to the performance. If one or the other set is missing, there is no spectacle."[4]

The past cannot be resurrected; it can only be represented, and all roles (including spectating) within a representation are performances as they act outside of the real, in a created time and space which can connect present and past, time and timelessness, the transcendent moment of theater and of transcendence. This temporal interaction, inherent in medievalism, offers "insights into contemporary social and cultural life that contemplation of the spectacle uniquely affords."[5] Medievalism, Richard Utz notes, is performative at its very essence, as he calls the term's history a "linguistic performance responding to particular pressures in and outside of the academy as well as to the almost coeval emergence of competing terms and practices related to the study of the past."[6] Medievalism – both the popular culture phenomena that seek to recreate, revise, revisit, or remake the Middle Ages in the present, and the study of these responses to the Middle Ages – he suggests, engages various kinds of performances. In "encompassingly register[ing] and embody[ing] all the elements and forces shaping our ongoing *re-present-ations* of the medieval past" (emphasis his),[7] medievalism, or perhaps *medievalisms*, as that plural term encompasses the large range of activities popular and scholarly, embodies the elements of spectacle – representing, shaping, embodying, and displaying the past within the present as something to be observed and interpreted. David Marshall comments that "medievalisms are constructs by which individuals (sometimes collectively) articulate their own discursive selves";[8] that articulation lies at the heart of spectacle, a performance of the self in a context separate from its own real world. For Elizabeth Emery medievalism is "a constantly evolving and self-referential process of defining an always fictional Middle Ages";[9] it is additionally

in *Rite, Drama, Festival, Spectacle: Rehearsals Toward a Theory of Cultural Performance*, ed. John J. MacAloon (Philadelphia: Institute for the Study of Human Issues, 1984), 241–80 (243).

[4] MacAloon, "Olympic Games," 243.

[5] MacAloon, "Olympic Games," 265.

[6] Richard Utz, "Coming to Terms with Medievalism," *European Journal of English Studies* 15:2 (2011): 101–13 (103–4).

[7] Utz, "Coming to Terms," 111.

[8] David W. Marshall, "Neomedievalism, Identification, and the Haze of Medievalisms," *Studies in Medievalism* XX: *Defining Neomedievalisms* (2011): 21–34 (22).

[9] Elizabeth Emery, "Medievalism and the Middle Ages," *Studies in Medievalism* XVII: *Defining Medievalism(s)* (2009): 77–85 (85).

this fictionality from which its spectacle emerges. The intersection of a performance of time, a performance of place, and a performance of the self, tied to an essential fiction that the Middle Ages can be recreated in our time, is what makes medievalism spectacle.

But what is the context of that spectacle? In his seminal work on the spectacle, Guy Debord opens with the observation that "in societies dominated by modern conditions of production, life is presented as an immense accumulation of spectacles. Everything that was directly lived has receded into a representation."[10] Although Debord would reject MacAloon's definition above, because he sees spectacle created out of a tension between reality and unreality, he does perceive it as having distinct defining qualities: "the spectacle cannot be abstractly contrasted to concrete social activity [...] the spectacle that falsifies reality is nevertheless a real product of that reality. Conversely, real life is materially invaded by the contemplation of the spectacle, and ends up absorbing it and aligning itself with it."[11] Medievalisms, at least in the popular culture sense, are inventions of reality created out of real life; the contemplation of them, whether the thoughtful engagement of academic medievalism or the mere experiencing of these spectacles, is absorbed and aligned with the spectacles created and observed. For instance, full-contact jousters might be playing a medieval sport, but they are really injured by unhorsing one another; furthermore, anyone watching, no matter how academic his or her interest, becomes part of the audience, an audience which is then medievalized by its attendance at a tournament simultaneously representational (because it takes place at a medieval festival or Renaissance faire) and real. Whether one cheers for one of the "knights" or merely watches, one cannot remove oneself from this audience position.

Ironically Debord viewed the historical Middle Ages as the point at which this specularity began, moving out of a mythical unity into a fragmented social world. This trend is cemented with the rise of early modern capitalism, which is also the point at which the Middle Ages ends and medievalism begins – the nostalgic, and performed recreation of medieval past, as well as its contemplation, can be seen to begin in the Renaissance, in Shakespeare's plays that draw their subjects from medieval literature and history; in Spenser's purposeful archaism, and in the work of historians like Leonardo Bruni and Flavio Biondo who create the period as "dark" or "middle," distinct from their own, and therefore a locus for various kinds of fantasy.[12]

We may therefore see spectacle as a range of performances, which John MacAloon notes are "constitutive of social experience and not something merely

---

[10]  Debord, *Society*, 7.
[11]  Debord, *Society*, 8.
[12]  Petrarch named the period the "Dark Ages" in the 1300s; Bruni, in *History of the Florentine People* (1442), and Flavio Biondo, in *Historiarum ab Inclinatione Romanorum Imperii* (1483), invented the term "medium aevum" to distinguish the period between the classical past and their own "enlightened" present.

additive or instrumental."[13] This does not diminish spectacle's value or make it any less vital than other forms. Cultural performances, in and of themselves:

> are more than entertainment, more than didactic or persuasive formula-
> tions, and more than cathartic indulgences. They are occasions in which
> as a culture or society we reflect upon and define ourselves, dramatize our
> collective myths and history, present ourselves with alternatives, and eventu-
> ally change in some ways while remaining the same in others.[14]

Victor Turner suggests that cultural performances create a kind of ideological *communitas* that demonstrates or creates a deep commonality, suggesting it exists as a model of human connectedness.[15]

It is productive to consider medievalism in the same way. Every medievalist spectacle creates a community, whether it is the 40,000 people attending the annual Medieval Festival at the Cloisters in Fort Tryon Park each October, the group of players engaging in a medieval live-action or massive multi-player online role-playing game, the audience at the latest medieval movie, or the audience at the Waverly Consort's Christmas concert performed "in the spirit and pageantry of the medieval church dramas and mystery plays," to which "many have come in a yearly pilgrimage to hear this beautiful seasonal music from the great cathe-drals of Europe in an original setting."[16] While there are examples of medievalism experienced more privately, even those create communities of shared interest that exist in a similar liminality, a space where the past is used to interrogate, or at least become an antidote to (and therefore a commentary on), the present. Indeed, it is this intersection that seeks to define both spectacle and medievalism.

Medievalist spectacle is distinguished in its combining of these two cultural performances, as each embodies both past and present simultaneously. Medieval performance finds its origins in religious rites and celebrations, both ecclesiastical and popular, the *quem quaeritis* trope and the carnival; medievalist performance draws on those past antecedents, yet it also looks directly into the present by setting the contemporary world up against the past, often showing it as wanting. Sometimes this dichotomy is marked by a tension between nostalgic yearning and presentism; the past can be longed for or it can be incorporated into the present moment in a way that does not privilege what *was* over what *can be*, which again

---

[13] John J. MacAloon, "Introduction: Cultural Performances, Cultural Theory," in *Rite*, ed. MacAloon, 1–18 (2).

[14] MacAloon, "Introduction," *Rite*, 1.

[15] Victor Turner, "Liminal to Liminoid in Play, Flow, and Ritual: An Essay in Comparative Symbology," *Rice University Studies* 60:82 (1974): 53–92 (75).

[16] The Waverley Consort, "The Christmas Story," http://www.waverlyconsort.org/concerts.php (accessed 28 July 2013). This concert is performed annually at the Cloisters, the Metropolitan Museum of Art's medieval collection, housed in a building made up of fragments of various medieval buildings put together, and located in Fort Tryon Park on a bluff above the Hudson River, providing a location both "authentic" and created, a spectacle in itself.

brings the spectacle not just to medieval performances but to the heart of the discipline itself.[17]

So at what level is medievalism itself a spectacle? Nickolas Haydock defines medievalism as "characterized [...] as a discourse of contingent representations derived from the historical Middle Ages, composed of marked alterities to and continuities with the present."[18] An act of medievalism is by necessity an image rather than the thing; as David Marshall notes,

> recognizing that we cannot "be" medieval and that any attempt to re-create the medieval amounts to play-acting a dream, producers and participants in this sort of medievalism assert an autonomous expression of the medieval that is contingent upon its own cultural context. In effect, within this identification producers and consumers introject the medieval as a symbolic signifier within their own cultural systems.[19]

Medievalisms take place at the intersection of performance and invention; they use the past to act upon and within the present; the act of taking on any kind of medieval identity, whether in the nostalgic poetry of William Morris or a medieval character in a game of *Assassin's Creed*, is inherently specular: the actor or author inhabits the identity; the audience observes and engages with that inhabiting. If one spectacle is primarily an image, something observed (a film, a concert, a book), while the other is more participatory and lived (a video game, a festival), they both by nature create a kind of community, even if it is only a community of shared interest and engagement; this is, all the same, a connection to others who also read medievalist novels, watch medieval films, or play medieval games. This engagement can be more or less active, but even the most passive observer still joins in medievalism's spectacle for the time period of his or her observation.

To draw from one example, we can find these actions taking place in contemporary jousting. Many people experience jousting at a Medieval Times Dinner and Tournament™. This form relies heavily on pageantry, both from the performers and the audience, who are asked to take on the role of a medieval audience, supporting certain knights with cheers and/or favors; there is no doubt that this creates a kind of spectacle both of the kind that the *OED* defines and of the kind Debord describes. Filled with elaborateness, excess, and energy, it is ultimately an empty representation; whatever claims it may make to authenticity, it is essentially a

---

[17] At the heart of this discussion is the distinction between "medievalism" and "neomedievalism," which David W. Marshall discusses in detail in his previously cited essay. Although less vital for this particular consideration of spectacle, these terms are becoming increasingly considered in discussions of contemporary representations of the past, "medievalism" coming to stand for a more nostalgic response that generally makes some pretense towards authenticity, while "neomedievalism" consciously discards both the nostalgia and the authenticity in place of a more patchwork (and in certain ways, postmodern) approach to the medieval past.

[18] Nickolas Haydock, "Medievalism and Excluded Middles," *Studies in Medievalism* XVIII: *Defining Medievalism(s) II* (2009): 17–30 (19).

[19] Marshall, "Neomedievalism," 29.

fiction. Visitors may eat with their hands, but they are eating potatoes and tomato soup, both new world foods unknown to medieval diners; the jousting may be exciting, but it is entirely scripted, with the various knights knowing who will be unhorsed and who will conquer on any given evening. While this spectacle may well provide people with a created Middle Ages to substitute for the historical Middle Ages, the participation it invites makes it a Middle Ages that extracts both meaning and spontaneity.

In contrast lies full-contact jousting, notably explored by Dashka Slater in a *New York Times Magazine* article, in which much of the pageantry is dropped in favor of fighting. This form of jousting seems to be enjoying a revival because "there's a real possibility of getting hurt," as a spectator at the Gulf Coast International Jousting Championships noted in anticipation.[20] This version offers a different kind of spectacle; instead of scripted theater, there is the spontaneous excitement of a sporting event. However, the theatrical remains no less present; it simply offers a different kind of drama with different kinds of performance. The spectators still play the role of a medieval audience, they revel in the destruction as did their predecessors: David Couch offers Jacques Bretel's description of the tournament at Chauvency in January 1280: "when one pair were badly bloodied, the ladies commented how the jousting that day was 'impressive and fine,' and when two lances simultaneously burst into fragments that 'it was jolly well done.'"[21] Contemporary jousters take on medieval names and titles, and while the focus may be the violence, there is also a version of the code of chivalry in place, an attempt to adapt medieval ideology in a living way for a contemporary setting. This spectacle may have elements of the authentic in the fighting, but it loses the authenticity of the pageantry found at medieval tournaments; in all cases, medievalist spectacle can escape neither its theatricality nor the dangerous emptiness of its signifiers as, detached from real time, it can only represent, and not be, authentic. Although MacAloon would argue that not all representations are spectacles, it is possible to recognize, at least in many examples of popular medievalisms, that these representations operate on the grandiose scale necessary to meet his definition.

In a pointed study of the specular nature of a particular facet of medievalism, Michael Cramer explores the theatrical and performative nature of the Society for Creative Anachronism, demonstrating how the "central activities of the SCA mirror theatrical activities common to the Middle Ages – tournaments, processions, coronations, courts plus mimetic activities such as masking and the performance of plays. They constitute, for all intents and purposes, an ongoing, roving work of performance art, which has been running nonstop since 1966."[22] The spectacle doubles or triples itself, a modern performance that recreates a medieval performance, in which the act of performance itself becomes a performance. This

---

[20]  Dashka Slater, "Can a Band of American Knights Turn 'Full Contact' Jousting into the Next Action Sport?" *New York Times Magazine* (11 July 2010): 24–9 (25).

[21]  David Crouch, *Tournament* (London: Hambledon and London, 2005), 124.

[22]  Michael Cramer, *Medieval Fantasy as Performance* (Plymouth, UK: Scarecrow Press, 2010), xxix.

is clearly not a neutral activity; Cramer views this performance of identity as more than just a nostalgic reenactment, and rather, as constructive of a postmodern counterculture. However, as Lev Grossman observes, "a darker, more pessimistic attitude toward technology and the future has taken hold, and the evidence is our new preoccupation with fantasy, a nostalgic, sentimental, magical version of a medieval age."[23] Cramer evaluates Grossman's point, noting that the SCA allows us to examine "some ways how and reasons why that fantasy is being played out, as well as allowing us to analyze the dissatisfaction with contemporary culture that leads people into the realms of fantasy."[24] The reproduction of this specifically medievalist set of spectacles demonstrates a protest against modernity, in both its critical and material form.[25] What medievalist spectacle offers is an alternative to modernity, an engagement with a different identity, of an alternative world, whether the spectacle requires engagement or demands a more participatory performance.

Contemporary scholarship shows that many things constitute medievalism, but for those who choose to experience this contemporary fantasy of the past, things seen – whether a jousting tournament, an art exhibit, or the background of a video game – come to create and define that past, making a princess hat with a floating scarf, a wizard, a display of aquamanilia in a reconstructed chapel, or a performance of medieval music in a Gothic revival church that which both simultaneously represent and make the Middle Ages. Specular medievalism need not even look medieval to enact it: pilgrims on the road to the National Baseball Hall of Fame in Cooperstown, New York, or to Graceland replicate and engage in as much medievalism as attendees at Renaissance faires. Medievalism is a rich world, but its spectacle, which reflects the past and holds a mirror up to the present, is one of the most potent loci for the function and use of the medieval period in the contemporary world.

Medievalisms by nature "explicitly or implicitly, by comparison or by contrast, comment on the artist's milieu."[26] Therefore, the spectacle becomes a *speculum humanae*, a related and most medieval term, a mirror that reflects far and wide its own society and its own creation. In the spectacle of medievalism, we see both a longing for the past and a longing to make it present, a desire to make the fantasy of the spectacle into a kind of reality, just as that image retreats again into the imaginary. Or, as Debord would have it, "cyclical time was the really lived time of unchanging illusions. Spectacular time is the illusorily lived time of a constantly changing reality."[27]

If we join John MacAloon in asking "what spectacle points toward, what gener-

---

[23] Lev Grossman, "Feeding on Fantasy," *Time* (2 December 2002): 90. Qtd. in Cramer, *Medieval Fantasy*, ix

[24] Cramer, *Medieval Fantasy*, ix.

[25] Cramer, *Medieval Fantasy*, 65.

[26] Tison Pugh and Angela Jane Weisl, *Medievalisms: Making the Past in the Present* (London: Routledge, 2012), 1.

[27] Guy Debord, *Society*. Kindle edition, location 1926 of 2510.

ative potentials and auspicious beginnings might lie within it, certain facts previ-ously mentioned emerge in a new light."[28] Medievalist spectacles, through their pageantry, reveal nostalgia for real living, for an (imagined) unity and constancy lost with the advent of modernity and technological reproduction, an invention of the past as an antidote to a fragmented and unstable reality. It hardly needs saying that this Middle Ages is itself an illusion, a fantastic creation, an anachronistic and exotic invention – indeed, in whatever form it takes, a spectacle.

## Further Reading

Cramer, Michael A. *Medieval Fantasy as Performance*. Plymouth, UK: Scarecrow Press, 2010.

Debord, Guy. *Society of the Spectacle*. Trans. Ken Knabb. London: Pebel Press, 2009.

MacAloon, John J., ed. *Rite, Drama, Festival, Spectacle: Rehearsals Toward a Theory of Cultural Performance*. Philadelphia: Institute for the Study of Human Issues, 1984.

Pugh, Tison and Angela Jane Weisl. *Medievalisms: Making the Past in the Present*. London: Routledge, 2012.

Scala, Elizabeth and Sylvia Federico, eds. *The Post-Historical Middle Ages*. New York: Palgrave Macmillan, 2009.

Weisl, Angela Jane. *The Persistence of Medievalism: Narrative Adventures in Contemporary Culture*. New York: Palgrave, 2003.

## Related Essays in this Volume

Reenactment, Play, Feast, Authenticity, Simulacrum, Gothic, Resonance, Presentism, Middle

---

[28] MacAloon, "Olympic Games," 267.

# 28

## Transfer

*Nadia Altschul*

I N THE CORE geographical areas studied within the Studies in Medievalism collective, keywords for medievalism have been more readily associated with nostalgia and origins than with transfer and translation.[1] In this essay, I will examine some of the issues detected when ideas of the medieval are carried across continents and cultures, focusing on the Spanish and Portuguese American colonies as an area generally left out from medievalism studies in the English-speaking academy.[2] This discussion on medievalism and transfer also highlights my own view that the Middle Ages is not a global historical time – leading to concepts like a Chinese or a pre-Columbian Middle Ages – but a local European time span. This local historical time has gathered its meaning from engagement with particular parts of Europe – mainly France, England, and German-speaking countries – to the detriment of the more hybrid, multi-confessional, and multiracial societies of the Mediterranean. Such is the case of medieval Iberia, my own disciplinary base, but also the European cultural matrix that conquered and colonized most of the Americas, including large tracts of what is currently the United States. Within this context, this essay on transfer as a critical term in medievalism studies will consider three aspects that relate to postcolonial medievalism in and of Ibero-America: "transfer" in relation to its close relative "translation" and the older term "influence"; the concept of "misplaced" or "out of place" ideas that circulate within

---

[1]   For the study of origins the reader should peruse volumes of *Studies in Medievalism*; for a complementary take on nostalgic and traumatic forms of medievalism, see Kathleen Biddick, *The Shock of Medievalism* (Durham: Duke University Press, 1998). See also the special issue *The Medievalism of Nostalgia*, eds. Helen Dell, Louise D'Arcens, and Andrew Lynch, *postmedieval* 2.2 (2011).

[2]   Besides the contents of the journal *Studies in Medievalism* the reader may consider monograph series such as *Making the Middle Ages*, which is sponsored by the University of Sydney, Australia, and specifies that "Works in the series focus on the interpretation of the Middle Ages in history, literature, art, scholarship, and popular culture in England, continental Europe, and North America from the 16th century to the present day": http://www.perspicuitas.uni-essen.de/medievalism/making.htm (accessed 27 July 2013). This is also the series that opened the field of Australian medievalism with Stephanie Trigg, ed., *Medievalism and the Gothic in Australian Culture* (Turnhout: Brepols, 2005).

Ibero-American criticism; and the notion of a transfer of the Middle Ages into Spanish and Portuguese America by its conquerors.

A close relative of "translation," "transfer" incorporates the former's etymological meaning of carrying across or spatially transporting and relocating, recognized by medievalists from *translatio studii et imperii*.[3] In its sensitivity to postcolonial topics, translation now takes into account "the migration of texts and discourses between the mother country and its former colonies" and has increasingly recognized similarities with other types of representations of source texts like editions, literary criticism, or retellings.[4] Postcolonial translation in particular is currently viewed as "part of an ongoing process of intercultural transfer" that can be likened to the medievalist cross-cultural and cross-temporal act of transferring the medieval to a different place or time.[5]

At first sight, then, especially due to its spatial meaning, "transfer" seems like a felicitous term in the context of postcolonial medievalism studies. Yet "transfer" maintains the core problems observed in the older term "influence": the indication of an active giver of ideas and a passive receiver of those ideas. Although comparative to "influence," the ideological underpinnings of "transfer" are not as close to the surface; cultural transfers are not innocuous events. Critics have identified "flow" as a main metaphor of globalization; it "thrives on the illusion that no material conditions – political or economic – are at work in fostering certain kinds of movement but not others."[6] The key questions to be asked of global flows – what is transferred, from where to where, by whom, for what purposes and with what means – are thus significant indications of the pitfalls and challenges of "transfer" as a serviceable term in medievalism, especially outside the so-called first world or the core geographical areas that defined the European Middle Ages.

Postcolonial translation studies is a field that tackles directly the power-related questions that dwell at the core of postcolonial theories and reappraises, for starters, the well-known paradigm of a translation as a lesser linguistic copy of an original text. Postcolonial translation is thus currently recognized not as a simple linguistic transfer, but as "a highly manipulative activity" that "rarely, if ever, involves a rela-

---

[3]  Maria Tymoczko, "Post-Colonial Writing and Literary Translation," in *Post-colonial Translation: Theory and Practice*, ed. Susan Bassnett and Harish Trivedi (London: Routledge, 1999), 19–40 (19).

[4]  See Monika Gomille, "Translating the Caribbean: Issues of Literary and Postcolonial Translation," *Anglistik & Englischunterricht* 67 (2007): 283–96 (284), and for similarities with other representations, like editions, Maria Tymoczko, "Translation: Ethics, Ideology, Action," *The Massachusetts Review* 47.3 (Fall 2006): 442–61 (448).

[5]  Bassnett and Trivedi, "Introduction: Of Colonies, Cannibals and Vernaculars," in *Post-colonial Translation*, ed. Bassnett and Trivedi, 1–18 (2). In terms of the cross-temporal and cross-cultural, medievalism studies tends to think of its essence as cross-temporal but the Middle Ages, as the saying goes, is a foreign country, such that medievalisms are cross-cultural as well, even more starkly outside Europe. As we will see, the cross-temporal aspect of medievalism also comes into question when the Middle Ages is seen as alive in the present, as in many parts of the non-hegemonic world.

[6]  João Ferreira Duarte, "The Trials of Translation: From Global Cultural Flow to Domestic Relocation," *Journal of Romance Studies* 11.1 (2011): 51–62 (56); discussing work by Mary Louise Pratt.

tionship of equality between texts, authors or systems."[7] Neither is medievalism an innocent activity or a simple temporal or geographic transfer. The power imbalance of "copy" versus "original" is perhaps inherent to medievalism as a latter-day copy of a purportedly real Middle Ages. And in the former colonies this power imbalance additionally involves the notion that postcolonial lands copy an original Middle Ages that has happened both earlier and elsewhere. Postcolonial transfer in terms of cultural power relations might also be found, for instance, in how a now hegemonic postcolony like the United States becomes a global expert in Chaucer medievalism studies; or in how medievalism in geographical peripheries like non-hegemonic Chile shows the persistent value of the cultural matrix brought in by conquest and colonization.[8]

Tellingly for thinking of medievalist transfer in the postcolony, the already quoted book on postcolonial translation by Bassnett and Trivedi starts its introduction highlighting issues of cultural (mis)appropriation through Brazilian anthropophagy.[9] As is well known among Latin Americanist scholars, cultural mistranslations and misappropriations in Ibero-America became intensely debated with Roberto Schwartz's essay on misplaced or out-of-place ideas in Brazil. Research might find other ideological uses, but in broad strokes the Middle Ages and medievalism in Ibero-America have been part of the local assertion of Europe's cultural hegemony over the area, fostering an association with outside locations and times as well as a cultural imbalance between European center and Ibero-American periphery. Schwartz's misplacement of ideas was generally taken to mean that certain ideas brought into Ibero-America did not belong where they had been transported. In this short essay I will approach his positions through the detailed critique of Elías Palti's "The Problem of 'Misplaced Ideas' Revisited," an attempt to consider the dynamics of cultural exchange in peripheral areas through Schwartz's essay.[10]

Palti notes that the heart of Schwartz's position was to tackle the dynamics of local cultures in the peripheries without falling either into the dualistic schemes of a precapitalist periphery that needed modernizing – a core principle from the field of dependency theory that Schwartz was applying to the cultural realm – or into the nationalist positions that rejected incorporated ideas as foreign to the

---

[7]  Bassnett and Trivedi, "Introduction," in *Post-colonial Translation*, ed. Bassnett and Trivedi, 1–18 (2).

[8]  See Richard Utz, "The Colony Writes Back: F. N. Robinson's *Complete Works of Geoffrey Chaucer* (1933) and the *Translatio* of Chaucer Studies to the United States," *Studies in Medievalism* XIX (2010): 160–203; and Nadia Altschul, *Geographies of Philological Knowledge* (Chicago: University of Chicago Press, 2012). In comparison, in the medieval *translatio studii* the power was in the hands of the receivers, who could claim to be continuing the learning of Rome, and for whom the copy was as good as, and due to its Christianity better than, the Roman original.

[9]  Interested scholars should read on the Antropofagia movement in Brazilian arts, which I will not discuss here.

[10]  Elías Palti, "The Problem of 'Misplaced Ideas' Revisited: Beyond the 'History of Ideas' in Latin America," *Journal of the History of Ideas* 67.1 (2006): 149–79. For an English version of the original essay, see Roberto Schwartz, "Misplaced Ideas: Literature and Society in Nineteenth-Century Brazil," *Comparative Civilizations Review* 5 (1980): 33–51.

national essence (158). As Palti specifies, however, the notion of "misplaced" or "out-of-place" ideas is a misnomer because, as researchers of medievalism are well aware, even apparently irrelevant themes and topics tend to show local functions despite their dislocation from the local ideological mainstream.[11] Allegedly foreign or out-of-place concepts are therefore always local and in-place because "Brazil" or "Argentina" or "Mexico" today would not be what they are without them. Put differently, the colonizers did not strictly import something foreign – a view that leads to Amerindian cultures as the only elements that are in-place – but made the Americas what they are through conquest and colonization. As Palti summarizes, while all ideas are always in-place because they have local functions in their new locations, the notion of misappropriation of ideas arises from the fact that within any culture there are many different contradictory ideas circulating and many ideologically different groups that are assimilating or rejecting them (176). As the reader will have noticed, this thinking bumps directly into key issues of ideology. While some of us might disagree in ideological terms with much Ibero-American medievalism, the desire to connect to a quintessential Europe through the Middle Ages is local, regardless of how allegedly foreign or imposed the initial concept might have been. Ideology here is also a question of "time" because there is a time when a location is viewed as already formed such that the (contradictory) elements incorporated after that time are the ones perceived as foreign and misplaced. But when do "Brazil" or "Argentina" or "Mexico" become what they are? In this essence-in-time, when does one cut the cord – before the Conquest, after Christianity, after Marxism, after neoliberal so-called modernization or democracy?

Another interesting implication of the ill-named concept of misplaced ideas for medievalism studies is that it creates the illusion that medievalist ideas are well-placed in Europe while ill-placed in Ibero-America. The Middle Ages recuperated as origin, as the truly local European indigenous customs, fits the search for essences of old world nationalisms. We should therefore underscore again that in its original geography the Middle Ages is as much an ideological construction as it is in Ibero-America, and that in Europe the Middle Ages has been invented and made-up according to the dictates of particular places and local power groups. This construction by ideologically specific groups has led, for instance, to the exclusion of other types of Middle Ages from the generalized definition. As mentioned above, the so-called Middle Ages that so much medievalism presumably recuperates was invented on the back of the hybrid Islamicate societies of the Mediterranean such that for many postcolonial medievalists, artistic as well as academic medievalism is not a reworking of medieval themes and topics, but the construction of these themes and topics as constitutive of an entity known as "the Middle Ages."

---

[11]   One would be expected to state that *all* forms of medievalism have a local function. At this stage, however, I wonder whether some forms of private obsession and antiquarianism run in parallel to their physical surroundings, specifying at most the local existence of economically privileged groups.

The transfer and relocation of the Middle Ages in places like Ibero-America does not merely involve the misplacement of ideas, but has a more concrete meaning in terms of an actual physical displacement and relocation of the medieval in this (and other) peripheries and postcolonial locations.[12] In a colonization happening mainly during the early modern or Baroque period of the Iberian Peninsula, the colonization of Spanish and Portuguese America was nevertheless purportedly carried out by medieval sectors of the originating society that literally transferred a medieval mentality to the colonized lands. For instance, the foremost medieval historian of his generation, the conservative Claudio Sánchez Albornoz, explained the conquest of Spanish America as "a projection of the Hispanic Middle Ages in space and in time," and Luis Weckmann expanded his vision in two hefty books, stating in an earlier *Speculum* article that in the Americas "the Middle Ages found their last expression," whereas Spain transmitted her Middle Ages "as a living product and not as a dead tradition."[13] Leslie Workman, the foundational figure of medievalism studies as we know it today, could therefore state in his first editorials for the journal *Studies in Medievalism* that "The society which Spain planted in the New World was medieval by almost any definition."[14]

This is especially important for the field of medievalism studies because the continuation of the medieval in non-hegemonic parts of the world was not only noted by Workman in early issues of *Studies in Medievalism* but given as an example of that which would be excluded from this newly founded field of studies. Workman started from the position that in different parts of the world and for different groups of society "medieval patterns of thought and behavior ended at different times [...]"[15] Medievalism itself, however, was instituted through the conscious separation from these survivals of medieval worldviews and lifestyles and it depended on a Middle Ages that had both ceased to exist and was viewed through the lens of historical distance. Thus according to Workman in *Studies in Medievalism* I.1:

> medievalism could only begin, not simply when the Middle Ages had ended, whenever that may have been, but when the Middle Ages were perceived to have been something in the past, something it was necessary to revive or desirable to imitate. This consciousness of an historical watershed grew in

[12] This geographic translation of the Middle Ages to the colony also means that the postcolonial location is in a way a (distorted) copy of the European original, as is the belief in the premodern character of colonial lands and their inhabitants that I discuss below.

[13] Claudio Sánchez Albornoz, *Spain, a Historical Enigma* (Madrid: Fundación Universitaria Española, 1975), II: 1059; Luis Weckmann, "The Middle Ages in the Conquest of America," *Speculum* 26 (1951): 130–41 (130), *La herencia medieval de México* (México: Fondo de Cultura Económica, 1984), and *La herencia medieval del Brasil* (México: Fondo de Cultura Económica, 1993).

[14] Workman, "Editorial," *Studies in Medievalism* I.1 (1979): 1–4 (2).

[15] Workman, "Editorial": 1–4 (2). Besides a medieval Spanish America, Workman noted that French feudal law "survives today in the formerly French provinces of Canada," while "the social ideas as well as the agricultural technology which the Puritans took to New England were similarly medieval" (2).

the sixteenth and seventeenth centuries, and our concern extends from that time to the present, if not into the future.[16]

From the lens of postcolonial medievalism, it is clear that this form of theorizing maintains the structure of a medieval–modern divide that postcolonial theory is especially keen to reexamine critically. Medievalism becomes richer when it evaluates the ideological paradigms on which it has been founded and is commonly practiced. For the practitioner of medievalism in a world that openly values modernity it is particularly useful to note that "the modern" is necessarily constituted against the "not modern." The medieval thus plays an essential part in the constitution of modernity itself, and a part that medievalism studies would be particularly well poised to assess. The main tenets laid out for the field of medievalism are also telling because Schwartz's essay is an attempt to reject the dualistic views of society that are almost absentmindedly constituted in Workman's version of medievalism studies: in areas treated as peripheral, medieval patterns of thought and behavior have continued even after the alleged end of the Middle Ages, and in modern metropolitan centers medieval lifestyles and worldviews have been left behind, opening the way to medievalism.[17] In other words, in the premodern peripheries the Middle Ages continues to exist, disallowing a medievalism that involves revival and desire, while in the modern centers medievalism can instead begin with the nostalgic slant referred to in the opening of the essay.

Dualistic temporal views are a form of medievalism, however, and I have examined elsewhere the ways in which this form has been instrumental in Ibero-American foundational narratives. Nineteenth-century texts like Domingo Faustino Sarmiento's *Civilization and Barbarism* in Argentina and Euclides da Cunha's *Os Sertões* in Brazil use dualistic views discursively to implement the medieval as a retrograde past that lives within and needs eradication before the true modern nation can emerge.[18] As in these cases, in Ibero-America the idea that regions and groups of its local inhabitants belong to the medieval period was used by conservative groups and by modernizing elites with exclusionary and belittling consequences for large populations in these regions, thus providing a non-nostalgic and politically troubling use of medievalism.

The critical notion of transfer within medievalism studies, with its attendant attention to physical dislocation and ideological misplacement, is a welcome change in a field of studies that had been instituted as predominantly Anglo-American and intra-European. Schwartz's application of dependency theory opens dialogues between medievalism studies and so-called third world cultural contexts

---

[16]  Workman, "Editorial": 1–3 (1).

[17]  Workman also states that until 1926 "feudalism was not banished from the English statute book," but this reads differently than his comment that feudal law *survives* in parts of French Canada ("Editorial": 1–4 [2]).

[18]  Nadia Altschul, "Medievalism and the Contemporaneity of the Medieval in Postcolonial Brazil," forthcoming in *Studies in Medievalism*; and "Writing Argentine Premodernity: Medieval Temporality in the Creole Writer-Statesman Domingo F. Sarmiento," forthcoming in *Interventions: International Journal of Postcolonial Studies*.

and provides an Ibero-American theorization on cultural transfers that should be on par with theorizations from former English colonies like Australia and the United States, which have been far more thoroughly studied in our discipline. Most importantly in a programmatic volume on critical terms that seeks to direct the disciplinary field in the future, this essay on "transfer" proposes that this field should expand the investigation of medievalism beyond Workman's definition of a Middle Ages that can be manipulated and desired from the safety of a temporal divide. As practitioners of medievalism we are all ideologically caught up in the medieval–modern divide and yet the temporalities of medievalism, especially when taking into account the transfers of the medieval to postcolonial lands, are openly more complex and ethically implicated than those allowed in our field's foundational definitions.

### Further Reading

Altschul, Nadia. "Medievalism and the Contemporaneity of the Medieval in Post-colonial Brazil." In *Studies in Medievalism* (forthcoming).

——. *Geographies of Philological Knowledge: Postcoloniality and the Transatlantic National Epic.* Chicago: University of Chicago Press, 2012.

Dell, Helen, Louise D'Arcens, and Andrew Lynch, eds. *The Medievalism of Nostalgia. postmedieval* 2.2 (2011).

Ferreira Duarte, João. "The Trials of Translation: From Global Cultural Flow to Domestic Relocation." *Journal of Romance Studies* 11.1 (2011). 51–62.

Davis, Kathleen and Nadia Altschul, eds. *Medievalisms in the Postcolonial World: The Idea of "The Middle Ages" Outside Europe.* Baltimore: Johns Hopkins University Press, 2009.

Palti, Elías. "The Problem of 'Misplaced Ideas' Revisited: Beyond the 'History of Ideas' in Latin America." *Journal of the History of Ideas* 67.1 (2006). 149–79.

Utz, Richard. "The Colony Writes Back: F. N. Robinson's *Complete Works of Geoffrey Chaucer* (1933) and the *Translatio* of Chaucer Studies to the United States." *Studies in Medievalism* XIX (2010). 160–203.

Weckmann, Luis. "The Middle Ages in the Conquest of America." *Speculum* 26 (1951). 130–41.

### Related Essays in this Volume

Presentism, Modernity, Middle, Co-disciplinarity, Heresy, Trauma, Archive, Lingua, Simulacrum, Authenticity, Authority

# 29

# Trauma

*Kathleen Biddick*

W HEN SIGMUND FREUD famously took up the question of trauma in *Beyond the Pleasure Principle* (1920) and asked why individuals unconsciously repeat patterns of suffering in their lives, he exemplified such
traumatic repetition with a scene drawn from Torquato Tasso's epic of the First
Crusade, *Gerusalemme Liberata* (1581), penned by the poet in the triumphant wake
of a Christian victory over the Ottoman navy at the Battle of Lepanto (1571).[1] Tasso
used the matter of pagan epic as an imperial mirror and repetitiously sought to
annex to his imaginary Christian Jerusalem (*translatio imperii*) things Trojan (the
matter of Homer's *Iliad*), and things Roman (the matter of Virgil's *Aeneid*). Freud,
too, thought epically. He conceived his *Interpretation of Dreams* as an epic: "[it]
becomes in effect, Freud's *Aeneid* because of its recurrent focus on 'the matter of
Rome.'"[2] Freud was also intent on the matter of Troy as explicated by his hero
Heinrich Schliemann, the excavator of Troy, whose archaeological account, *Ilios:
The City and the Country of the Trojans*, first appeared in German in 1881.[3] The
utter confusion of Turks and Trojans, whose entangled genealogy dates to the
medieval period, and which was revived contentiously in Renaissance histories of
the Ottoman Turks, traumatically haunts Freud's matter of Rome in *The Interpretation of Dreams*, and, I shall argue, haunted Tasso's epic as well.[4] Both are medieval-

---

[1]  For an introduction to the structure of trauma see Cathy Caruth, *Unclaimed
Experience: Trauma, Narrative and History* (Baltimore: Johns Hopkins University Press,
1996), and more specifically on the traumatic structure of medievalisms see Kathleen
Biddick, *The Shock of Medievalism* (Durham NC: Duke University Press, 1997). For an
important recent study with a useful bibliography see Patricia Clare Ingham, "Chaucer's
Haunted Aesthetics: Mimesis and Trauma in *Troilus and Criseyde*," *College English* 72 (2010):
226–47.
[2]  Elizabeth J. Bellamy, *Translations of Power: Narcissism and the Unconscious in Epic
History* (Ithaca NY: Cornell University Press, 1992), 42.
[3]  Richard H. Armstrong, *A Compulsion for Antiquity: Freud and the Ancient World*
(Ithaca NY: Cornell University Press, 2005), 114.
[4]  For an indispensable study of the entanglements of Trojan and Turkish genealogies
see Margaret Meserve, *Empires of Islam in Renaissance Historical Thought* (Cambridge
MA: Harvard University Press, 2008); Nancy Bisaha, *Creating East and West: Renaissance*

isms that mobilize the tropes of massacre and martyrdom that fueled Christian accounts of the overthrow of Muslim rule in Jerusalem in 1099.

Epic and psychoanalysis are closely bound; yet, students of Freudian trauma have reflected more on the traumas of medievalism than on the medievalisms of Freud's theory of trauma. They have not questioned the entanglement of *translatio imperii* with the unconscious of psychoanalysis. This essay addresses the medievalism of Freud's trauma in an effort to gain insight into what happens when the trauma of *translatio imperii* is foreclosed in the very theory of psychoanalytic trauma.

Freud drafted his dream book in the wake of several excursions in the Balkans. Under Ottoman hegemony since 1463, the western edges of this geopolitical region had only come under Austro-Hungarian rule with the Treaty of Berlin in 1878. Freud collected a series of anecdotes about his Balkan journey in an essay published under the title "Psychic Mechanisms of Forgetfulness" (1898). In an account of a dream from this Balkan holiday (April 1898) sent to Wilhelm Fliess, Freud had imagined himself as a kind of Dante descending into the Inferno, encountering "Tartarus" when he (like Virgil) descended into the cave at St. Cangian: "If Dante saw anything like this, he needed no great effort of imagination for his inferno."[5]

Freud tells a more complicated Balkan story in the published essay. Posing as a Habsburg ethnographer, Freud describes how a colleague, who treated Turkish patients, informed Freud of their fatalism and the over-riding importance "these Bosnian [Turks] attached to sexual enjoyments." Here Freud ventriloquizes the colonial psychiatry of his day, epitomized by the influential Algerian school of French psychiatry. These doctors disseminated a scientific literature that measured the psychiatric difference between Muslims and Europeans by the sexual violence of the former. The exclusion of colonized Muslims as psychiatric subjects also had the effect of leaving them behind in the high stakes of fabricating a psychiatric and psychoanalytic discourse of trauma after World War I.[6] French colonial psychiatrists examined a large number of "colored" (Muslim) regiments who served under the French flag in Northern Africa and argued that they were to be exempted from

*Humanists and the Ottoman Turks* (Philadelphia: University of Pennsylvania Press, 2004); and J. Harper, "Turks as Trojans and Trojans as Turks: Visual Imagery of the Trojan War and the Politics of Cultural Identity in Fifteenth-Century Europe," in *Translating Culture: Postcolonial Approaches to the Middle Ages*, ed. A. J. Kabir and Deanne Williams (Cambridge: Cambridge University Press, 2005), 151–79.

  5   J. M. Masson, ed. *The Complete Letters of Sigmund Freud to Wilhelm Fliess, 1877–1904* (Cambridge MA: Belnap Press/Harvard University Press, 1985), 309; Sigmund Freud, "The Psychical Mechanism of Forgetfulness (1918)," in James Strachey, trans., *The Standard Edition of the Complete Psychological Works of Sigmund Freud*, vol. 3 (London: Hogarth Press, 1962), 287–97.

  6   Freud's stereotypes need to be read within their powerful discursive frame of medical medievalism in the nineteenth-century metropolis and colony: Zrinka Stahuljak, *Pornographic Archaeology: Medicine, Medievalism, and the Invention of the French Nation* (Philadelphia: University of Pennsylvania Press, 2013), 71–98; Richard C. Keller, *Colonial Madness: Psychiatry in French North Africa* (Chicago: University of Chicago Press, 2007); Didier Fassin and Richard Rechtman, *The Empire of Trauma: An Inquiry into the Condition of Victimhood*, trans. Rachel Gomme (Princeton NJ: Princeton University Press, 2009), 51–7.

a more humane treatment of traumatic war injury because these Muslim soldiers played out an impoverished emotional life imprisoned by basic instincts.[7]

Here is how Freud condenses the Balkan dream matter in *The Interpretation of Dreams*. He dreamt, he tells the reader, that he entered a great hall of machines, which reminded him of an "Inferno." He saw a colleague strapped onto an apparatus. As the dream unfolds, Freud is told that he can go, but because he cannot find his hat, he cannot leave. The dream prompts Freud to make an important revision of his dream theory to include the possibility of negation. At this juncture Freud adds a footnote that refers to a primal scene. First, he associates the permission to leave to a famous quotation from his beloved Schiller: "The Moor has done his duty, the Moor *may go*." He continues in the footnote: "And then follows the waggish question: 'How old is the Moor when he has done his duty? One year, then he may go'. It is said that I came into this world with so much black curly hair that my young mother declared me to be a Moor."[8]

Freud thus inserts into this vision of a mechanical inferno a fantasy of Muslim infantile sexuality (and recall that his birthplace in Moravia had been seized by the Ottomans in the seventeenth century). Since, according to Freud, infantile sexuality is the site of amnesia, he thus assigns the lack, the very traumatic structure that prompts desire, to a Muslim fantasy, an impersonation, and such impersonation, as we shall see, is what drives the epic plot of Tasso in *Gerusalemme Liberata*.

Freud's Muslim fantasy shaped his reading of Tasso. Readers of *Gerusalemme Liberata* will know that Freud truncated the account of the second wounding of the Muslim warrior Clorinda by the Christian crusader Tancred in *Beyond the Pleasure Principle*:

> The most moving poetic picture of a fate such as this can be found in the story told by Tasso in his romantic epic *Gerusalemme Liberata*. Its hero, Tancred, unwittingly kills his beloved Clorinda in a duel while she is disguised in the armor of an enemy knight. After her burial he makes his way into a strange magic forest which strikes the Crusaders' army with terror. He slashes with his sword at a tall tree, but blood streams from the cut and the voice of Clorinda, whose soul is imprisoned in the tree, is heard complaining that he has wounded his beloved once again.[9]

[7] Antoine Porot, "Notes de psychiatrie musulmane," *Annales Médico-psychologiques* 74 (1918): 377–84.

[8] Freud is citing from the Schiller play *Fiesco, Or the Genoese Conspiracy* (1783) (Act 3, Scene 4). Set in Genoa in 1547, it features Muley Hassan, a "wooly pated" Moor of Tunis, who acts as spy and hired assassin and speaks these words. See Patricia Cotti, "Hunger and Love: Schiller and the Origin of Drive Dualism in Freud's Work," *International Journal of Psychoanalysis* 88 (1) 2007: 167–82. Freud thus conflates Islam and race. I am using A. A. Brill's translation of *Die Traumdeuting* (New York: Modern Library, 1950), 225–7.

[9] Sigmund Freud, *Beyond the Pleasure Principle*, in Strachey, trans., *Standard Edition*, vol. 18 (1920–22) (London: The Hogarth Press, 1955), 1–64 (22). Kathleen Biddick, "Unbinding the Flesh in the Time that Remains: Crusader Martyrdom Then and Now," *GLQ* 13 (2007): 197–225, and Sigrid Weigel, "The Symptomatology of a Universalized Concept of Trauma: On the Failing of Freud's Reading of Tasso in the Trauma of History," *New German Critique* 90 (2003): 85–94. For a bibliographic introduction to Tasso and his epic,

In Tasso's version, Clorinda lets Tancred know that she is not alone when she speaks through the wound of the bludgeoned tree. Buried with her, she explains, are fellow martyrs, Christian crusaders and Muslim warriors, who fell with her in the crusader battle for Jerusalem. Tasso fashions the crypt of the tree as a burial place for the archive of the medieval First Crusade – an archive stained as it was with massacre and cannibalism.[10] So successful was his encryption that Freud falls right into its traumatic trap and fails to mention that Clorinda mourns a collective trauma. She is not alone in her leafy tomb, which is also inhabited by Christian crusaders and Muslim warriors. Here is the plaint of collective trauma penned by Tasso, which Freud seems not to have heard when reporting Clorinda's speech:

> How could you [Tancred] be so cruel to resume
> War with your adversaries in the tomb?
> I was Clorinda. Other spirits dwell
> Beside me in this rough, hard plant: for all
> Those fighters, Saracen and French, who fell
> And left their dying limbs beneath the wall,
> Are here pent up by some unheard-of-spell,
> And incarnation, or a burial,
> I cannot say. Their limbs, ensouled, feel pain,
> And if you cut you murder us again. (13.42–43)[11]

Tasso's literary efforts to encrypt the ghosts of crusaders past are deliberate. As a good student of the widely disseminated printed editions of the chronicles of the First Crusade, he knew the generic conventions of crusader martyrdom and used them to stage Clorinda's "first" death at the hands of Tancred.

To appreciate the complexity of Tasso's "martyring" of martyrdom, some plot review will be helpful. In *Gerusalemme Liberata* (as in the First Crusade) Tancred is one of the leaders besieging the city. He has fallen in love with Clorinda, a mysterious female knight, who is one of the city's leading Muslim defenders. Her religious genealogy is as transvestite as her gender. She learns of it from her beloved eunuch as she leaves Jerusalem on a dangerous mission to the Christian camp. The Egyptian eunuch discloses that she was born the white daughter of a black Ethiopian queen. To avoid scandal the queen decided to place her infant in the eunuch's care and to send them into exile. Before their departure, the queen made her eunuch promise to baptize Clorinda. Tasso drew his ethnography of

see Bellamy, *Translations of Power*, as well as Sergio Zatti, *The Quest for Epic: From Ariosto to Tasso*, ed. Dennis Looney, trans. Sally Hill with Dennis Looney (Toronto: University of Toronto Press, 2006); David Quint, *Epic and Empire: Politics and Generic Form from Virgil to Milton* (Princeton NJ: Princeton University Press, 1993); Elizabeth Siberry, "Tasso and the Crusades: History of a Legacy," *Journal of Medieval History* 19 (1993): 163–9.

[10] For an overview of the medieval sources used by Tasso see Siberry, "Tasso and the Crusades," and Quint, *Epic and Empire*.

[11] I have used Anthony M. Esolen's translation, *Jerusalem Delivered* (Baltimore: Johns Hopkins University Press, 2000), and Lanfranco Caretti's Italian edition, *Gerusalemme liberata* (Bari: Editori Laterza, 1967). I cite by canto and stanza.

Ethiopian Christianity from a popular travel account (translated into Italian and widely circulated) of a visit to the court of Atani Tingil (King David of Ethiopia) made in the 1520s by a Portuguese priest, Francisco Alvarez.[12] Alvarez found the Ethiopians practicing a "judaized" Christianity, meaning that they observed the rite of circumcision and the Saturday Sabbath (the Inquisition regarded such Judaized practices as heretical crypto-Judaism). Nor did these Ethiopian Christians practice infant baptism like their orthodox Roman counterparts, hence the queen's request that the eunuch see to Clorinda's eventual baptism. The eunuch failed to fulfill his promise and ended up raising Clorinda in Egypt as a Muslim; she now defends Islam as one of its fiercest warriors. Clorinda thus embodies the fractures of unstable religious identities (Judaized-Christianity – or crypto-Judaism becoming Muslim); the fractures of race (black becoming white); the fractures of gender (she "passes" as a male knight among the Christians as long as she is helmeted; her Muslim comrades know her as a female warrior and deeply value her military leadership).

Tasso martyrs Clorinda, but what exactly does her martyrdom mean when she is so complexly embodied? Who or what is being martyred? To flatten out her fractured identities into a domesticated, feminine, Christian one, Tasso crafts a striptease. This is how the scene unfolds. Tancred mortally wounds a Muslim knight outside the crusader camp, unaware that his foe is his beloved Clorinda. He plunges his "blade" into the breast of his adversary and in a fit of chivalric *jouissance* drinks blood from the wound: "Into her lovely breast he thrusts his blade, drowns it, eagerly drinks her blood" (12.64). For the titillation of the reader (who already knows that the dying knight is Clorinda), Tasso next describes the breast-binder beneath her cuirass, which is "sweetly lined with gold that held her breasts with a light and tender pull" (12.64), and which is now filling with blood.

In this scene of the first death of Clorinda, Tasso closely parallels crusader narratives to stage his medievalism. He draws on the accounts of cannibalism and martyrdom to be found in medieval crusade chronicles such as that of Raymond d'Aguilers.[13] He revels in the seduction of martyr narratives; he draws attention to Clorinda's underclothes just as the story of St. Pelagius has the young Christian boy disrobe in front of the caliph in protest at the lavish clothing in which the caliph had dressed him.[14] Tasso also inverts the trope of impending rape by a Muslim in the story of Pelagius, since it is Tancred, the Christian warrior, who bludgeons ("rapes") and vamps ("cannibalizes") his Muslim victim.

The scene continues. The dying Muslim knight begs Tancred for baptism. It is only when he removes his enemy's helmet to minister the sacrament that Tancred

---

[12] I rely on David Quint's superb reading of Tasso and his sources in his *Epic and Empire*.

[13] Raymond d'Aguilers, *Historia Francorum Qui Ceperunt Iherusalem*, trans. John Hugh Hill and Laurita L. Hill, *Memoirs of the American Philosophical Society* 71 (1968).

[14] Mark D. Jordan, "Saint Pelagius, Ephebe and Martyr," in *Queer Iberia: Sexualities, Cultures, and Crossings from the Middle Ages to the Renaissance*, ed. Josiah Blackmore and Gregory Hutchinson (Durham NC: Duke University Press, 1999), 23–47. The story is set in the caliphate of al-Andalus.

realizes that it is Clorinda whom he has killed. He manfully holds off his grief until he performs the baptism. Clorinda then dies and later appears to the bereaved Tancred in a dream in which he can hear her words and behold her transfigured martyrial body: "Behold how beautiful I am, and blessed, my faithful lover. Let your sorrows rest. I am so by your grace" (12.91–2).

Clorinda's apparition as a martyr accomplishes several important theological supersessions in this epic of the Catholic Counter-Reformation. The normalization and medievalizing of her fractured religious identities disarm the threat of theological undecidability (Protestants who look like Catholics, Catholics who look like Protestants, crypto-Jews, crypto-Muslims). The infidel Muslim Clorinda, by birthright a questionable "judaized" Christian or crypto-Jew, is converted by Tasso to orthodox Roman Christianity. The conversion settles once and for all the triumph of Christian martyrdom over Muslim martyrdom and permits Tasso to use the Middle Ages as a crypt in which he strives to bury the First Crusade forever and in so doing buries also the contemporary enemy, the Ottoman Turks that haunt his epic.

So powerful is Tasso's traumatic spell of encryptment that Freud repeats this traumatic pattern and encrypts the First Crusade in his own paradigm of Western trauma in *Beyond the Pleasure Principle*. Like Tancred, Freud medievalizes his Muslim fantasy and thus represses the Turko-Trojan *translatio imperii* that conflicted with his epic interest in the matter of Rome. My reading does not ask the ghost of Freud to get over the trauma of the First Crusade and the trauma of his Muslim fantasy. It asks instead what happens when, as I have argued, the trauma of *translatio imperii* is foreclosed in the very theory of psychoanalytic trauma.

Let the Byzantine historian Michael Critoboulos, who served as governor under Sultan Mehmed II (1430–81), Ottoman conqueror of Constantinople (and also, of Bosnia), have the last word. He wrote in his *History of Mehmed the Conqueror* (c. 1467) that the Ottoman sultan, like Xerxes, Alexander, and Caesar before him, travelled to Ilium to pay his pious respect: "He observed the ruins and the traces of the ancient city of Troy ... He also inquired about the tombs of the heroes – Achilles, Ajax and the rest."[15] By disentangling the medievalisms of Tasso and Freud and understanding the Christian expedition to Muslim Jerusalem in 1099 as a collective trauma that repeats itself in the very heart of psychoanalytic theory, we are able to understand the implications of a contemporary psychoanalytical impasse which stages *translatio imperii* as the "clash of civilizations." Take, for example, the complaint of the Lacanian pundit Slavoj Žižek who imagines that the "Balkans is structured like the unconscious of Europe" – and the critique of contemporary Muslim psychoanalysts (for example, Fethi Benslama) who ask what psychoanalysis would look like if it worked through its traumatic foreclosure of Islam.[16]

---

[15]    Michael Critoboulos, *The History of Mehmed the Conqueror*, ed. and trans. Charles T. Rigg (Princeton NJ: Princeton University Press, 1954), 181–2; also, Meserve, *Empires of Islam*,43.

[16]    For Žižek on the Balkans as the unconscious of Europe, see Euronews 9: http://www/

## Further Reading

Bellamy, Elizabeth J. *Translations of Power: Narcissism and the Unconscious in Epic History*. Ithaca NY: Cornell University Press, 1992.

Benslama, Fethi. *Psychoanalysis and the Challenge of Islam*. Trans. Robert Bononno. Minneapolis: University of Minnesota Press, 2009.

Biddick, Kathleen. *The Shock of Medievalism*. Durham: Duke University Press, 1998.

Bjelić, Dušan. *Normalizing the Balkans: Geopolitics of Psychoanalysis and Psychiatry*. Burlington VT: Ashgate, 2011.

Caruth, Cathy. *Unclaimed Experience: Trauma, Narrative and History*. Baltimore: Johns Hopkins University Press, 1996.

Fassin, Didier and Rechtman, Richard. *The Empire of Trauma: An Inquiry into the Condition of Victimhood*. Trans. Rachel Gomme. Princeton NJ: Princeton University Press, 2009. 51–7.

Meserve, Margaret. *Empires of Islam in Renaissance Historical Thought*. Cambridge MA: Harvard University Press, 2008.

## Related Essays in this Volume

Genealogy, Christianity, Heresy, Love, Myth, Transfer, Continuity, Co-disciplinarity, Gesture, Purity, Authority, Troubadour

euronews.net/2008/09/12/euronews-talks-films-and-balkans-with-slavoj-zizek/ (accessed 17 April 2013). Bjelić and Benslama provide a critical overview: Dušan Bjelić, *Normalizing the Balkans: Geopolitics of Psychoanalysis and Psychiatry* (Burlington VT: Ashgate, 2011); Fethi Benslama, *Psychoanalysis and the Challenge of Islam*, trans. Robert Bononno (Minneapolis: University of Minnesota Press, 2009).

# 30

# Troubadour

*Elizabeth Fay*

THE LATE EIGHTEENTH century in Britain and continental Europe was a period in which a rebellion against both Hobbesian pessimism and Enlightenment rationalism manifested as a reinvestment in the sentiments and the passions. If the Enlightenment was characterized by a renewed appreciation for classical stoicism and Socratic reason, the following period of Romantic reaction found that the medieval period offered previously disregarded terrain for affective investment; if the Enlightenment embraced a cosmopolitan ethos in philosophy and political theory, the Romantic period experienced a deeply nationalistic tendency. Nationalist feeling swept across Europe and throughout Britain, colliding with the more global purview of cosmopolitan urbanity; reexamination of earlier, especially native, histories, accompanied by the new focus on aesthetic theory and aesthetic appreciation, revealed that in pre-Roman artifacts and medieval ruins lay the clues to one's own and one's nation's cultural past.

While antiquarians labored to recover, decipher, catalog, and reinterpret relics of the pre-Roman and medieval past, writers and the public at large, particularly in Britain, felt freer imaginatively to resuscitate the past in ways that could exploit the aesthetic elements of surviving historical spaces such as ruined abbeys and castles. At the same time this cultural labor provided a reconstructed cultural lineage that could embellish newly important published peerages and other reference works documenting family genealogies. Arms and armor not necessarily from the family storerooms became fashionable décor for estates, while lesser ranked families made do with painted medieval scenes or print versions such as John Boydell commissioned for his Shakespeare Gallery.

This essay will first survey the more general approach to medievalism in the British Romantic period, and then address the more specific appeal of the troubadour to both Romantic poets and their readers. Indeed, the link between a vaguer medieval sensibility and the figure of the troubadour poet was a strong one, beginning in the 1760s and lasting until chivalry came to stand in for medieval culture by the 1840s and 1850s. For the reading public Petrarch represented the very person of the troubadour; he was as much a literary touchstone as Shakespeare, his love sonnets appealing to the late eighteenth-century cult of sensibility, with this appeal hardly lessening in subsequent decades. He who could write love verses and sing or recite well had the requisite accomplishments of a modern troubadour, the successful ladies' man; such a figure is recognizable in Jane Austen's Willoughby (*Sense and Sensibility*, 1811), Henry Crawford (*Mansfield Park*, 1814), and Frank Churchill (*Emma*, 1815). But the troubadour also appeared as the poetic-I and as a medieval-era figure in a broad range of lyric and narrative verse. Porphyro, the lover in John Keats's "The Eve of St. Agnes" (1820), evinces major characteristics of the type even though he clearly intends to elope with Madeline, in a deviation from the standard plot of courtly love:

> ... he took her hollow lute,–
> Tumultuous, – and, in chords that tenderest be,
> He play'd an ancient ditty, long since mute,
> In Provence call'd, "La belle dame sans mercy"[.][1]

The Romantic poet in particular was intrigued and compelled by the figure of the medieval troubadour who was at once a free agent, moving from court to court to perform, and enslaved to his beloved, a resistant or unavailable object of intense desire. Both concepts – that of free agency, unbeholden to a patron or to a literary marketplace, free to produce art as the nightingale does (the medieval troubadour's metaphor of choice for his own performative art), and that of entanglement, of being enmeshed in a web of artistic and sensuous compulsions and transgressive passions – combined to make the troubadour figure a powerful model for the Romantic poet. The troubadour situated the sense of peril that poets felt as the literary marketplace turned increasingly toward prose fiction, the sense of impending self-dissolution resulting from loss of readership coming at a time when serious verse was never more necessary.

Poetry remained a powerful medium for addressing the disastrous political outcomes of Britain's response to continental revolution and its aftermath, but was faced with fierce competition from more popular genres. While novelists such as Austen took the conservative view in characterizing the troubadour figure as a deceitful rake and social menace, poets like Keats self-identified with the rebellious, politically compromised, and emotionally frustrated troubadour (many of Keats's works use an I-speaker in the troubadour position, and we have two extant versions of "La Belle Dame sans Merci" [1819], the song Porphyro sings to Madeline).

For women poets such as Mary Robinson, the female troubadour or trobaritz offered a gendered model for voicing these same concerns while also emphasizing the difficulties that sexual power relations bring to the mix. Robinson's sonnet sequence *Sappho and Phaon* (1796) explores the loss of voice, social alienation, and female loss of agency in sexual relations to engage the general sense of political disenfranchisement in an international arena and to critique the masculinist

---

[1]    *The Complete Poems of John Keats*, ed. Jack Stillinger (Cambridge, MA: Harvard University Press, 1978), 229–40 (ll. 289–92).

assumptions underlying the troubadourian beloved – that by holding the power of denial over her lover she dominates the love relation.

The major conceit the troubadour offered Romantic poets – that the female object of desire enslaves the poet-I while it orients his sense of self-loss and dissolution – creates the conditions for the myth of "true love." This phantasm seductively masks investigations into the existential angst poets felt as subjective fracture, cracks in self-identity produced by disempowerment of the poetic voice. R. Howard Bloch discusses the twelfth-century troubadour's intense awareness of a differential space opening up in the self with each act of speaking and writing; medieval sign theory sets the conditions for such self-alienation.[2] The revival of interest in troubadourian lyrics allowed Romantic poets an ideal figuration of this sematic disorientation and for their own reenactment of it.

For the British reader, contemporary troubadourian lyrics appealed through their sensibility. Sensibility was a major expression of aesthetic appreciation under the new regime of affective response, allowing for a greater immersion in present experience as well as a greater imaginative play for "romance," meaning historical scenes particularly as relating to medieval lays and ballads. Although late eighteenth-century sensibility was clearly a development of a new interest in the sentiments and passions, it was propelled by developments in nerve science, which focused on the interactions between external stimuli, sensory input, the nervous system, and cognition – as well as philosophical theories concerning faculties of the mind, cognitive mechanisms, and the relation of ideas to memory and emotions. What troubled nerve scientists as well as philosophers, basing their theories as they were on Enlightenment principles, was the role of emotions in this sensory circuit.

Somehow nerve stimulation could produce affective responses both positive and negative, just as imaginative stimulation could. Moreover, the new aesthetic appreciation allowed for a way to interpret emotional response rather than disregarding it as inappropriate. It was now possible to sigh over a ruined abbey, allowing its physical irregularities, disastrous history, and haunting losses to play on the senses in order to evoke a melancholy mediation on the loss of historical knowledge or the downfall of regimes; similarly, such melancholic nostalgia might produce a pleasurable reimagining of life within those walls, of valiant knights and their ladies, beneficent overlords and their courts, and poets singing of unobtainable love – a reconstruction that could at the same time lead to equally pleasurable thoughts of haunted buildings, tyrannous villainy, and oubliettes. Not surprisingly, viewing Shakespeare's plays and reading Gothic novels were hugely popular leisure pursuits during the Romantic period. While Romantic poets saw the troubadour as expressing angst and self-alienation, the courtly love lyric an apt form for exploring presence and absence, the reading public interpreted the troubadour and his lyric through its seductive appeal to sensibility, as well as the pleasures of historical reconstruction.

---

[2]   R. Howard Bloch, *Medieval Misogyny and the Invention of Western Romantic Love* (Chicago: University of Chicago Press, 1992), 149–51.

Positive reconstruction of the past went hand-in-hand with the antiquarian collection of lays and metrical romances, an important part of the work of the new nationalism; new versions of such romances allowed the public to bypass antiquated language, facilitating the absorption of medievalism as a strand in the cultural imaginary by evoking a brave and loyal yeomanry, and the stout-heartedness of a new figure of patriotism, John Bull.[3] An icon of supposedly historically based patriotism, he was a useful political tool for countering the caricature of the effete Gaul. John Bull's staunch beef-and-beer symbolism was also an anodyne for the negative reconstruction of medieval life as the nightmarish foundation of modern progressivism, which is how Gothic novels portrayed the medieval ruins of haunted abbeys at home and tyrannically ruled castles located in Catholic countries such as France and Spain.

In Protestant England, the negative aspects of medievalism – murderous schemes, punishment-oriented monasteries, and claustrophobic spaces – were invasive in the cultural imaginary; artists and the public alike delighted in the new craze for the Gothic. An architectural style that gave birth to a literary genre, the Gothic was characterized by a darker mood than melancholic nostalgia since it was predicated on the idea of haunting and a return of the repressed: repressed memories, repressed ideologies, and a repressed Catholic theology. In contrast, the pleasant imagining of courtly life characterized a nostalgia for a medieval England that contrasted sharply with contemporary England's most pressing social issues: dispossessed agrarian workers, poorhouse laws, and disabled veterans. The craze for all things Gothic, on the other hand, was deeply invested in the explorations of terror as an aesthetic release through thrilling experiences brought on by introducing "Gothic" elements into new buildings, by exploring medieval ruins, or, best of all, by reading Gothic literature.

Together melancholic nostalgia and terror provided a way to confront the underside of the sublime. The positive sublime brought aesthetic appreciation to new heights (and a revised cosmopolitanism), lifting the spirit to an epiphany of cosmic understanding by lifting one out of oneself very briefly into a divine or universal communion. By contrast – indeed, by very opposition – melancholy and terror focus very explicitly on inner feeling and subjective experience; because of the religious implications of an Anglican public engaging in a medievalism that exploited the worst aspects of the Catholic Church's (real and imagined) practices, the subjectivity engaged while reading nightmarish plots and scenarios could only reinforce nationalistic identification when the English and Protestant protagonist either succeeded or succumbed in the finale.

The thrills of the Gothic, or negative sublime, are not only easier experiences to evoke, extremely accessible through the commonality of nightmares and ghost stories, but much more gratifying as well. Romantic poets interested in the positive sublime, and looking for ways to combat what they considered the ill effects of "sickly" Gothic novels, as William Wordsworth puts it in his Preface to *Lyrical*

---

[3]   The origins of the "John Bull" character of Britons is first discussed by John Abuthnot in his pamphlet of 1712, *The Law is a Bottomless Pit*; his treatment of the figure can now be found online at Project Gutenberg as *The History of John Bull.*

*Ballads* (1800), quickly realized the efficacy of one aspect of medieval cultural history that could provide sublime uplift as well as subjective, internal feelings, and even pleasing melancholy. This historical phenomenon was the courtly love poetry of the troubadours, imaginatively recovered not through archival research of Occitan poetry and historical records, but through a revival and revivifying of Petrarch's love for Laura and Dante's "la vita nuova."

What served poetic needs so well in the Romantic period, particularly in the decades that began to experience backlash from the French Revolution – and a virulent anti-Gallic ideology – was that courtly love poetry is ideal for a non-ideological, non-nationalistic excursion into soulfulness and states of alienation. For literary artists concerned to return to a cosmopolitan idealism and imaginative agency, the courtly love poem provides a paradoxical format well suited to querying self–other constructions.

The courtly love poem is at once externally oriented and internally obsessed: the troubadour lover sings his plaint to a lady who has denied him her love, a scenario that allows the poet to paint his internal feelings while praising the lady, and to praise her while leaving her voice to be imagined by the reader. By casting himself as alienated from her love and thus from society, the lover-poet asks his reader – who must identify with him as subject-self – to wonder about the state of being alien, of being rejected and therefore an "other" – and to experience imaginatively that othered state himself. If alienation can be read politically, poets asked their readers instead to read this state as existential: what does it mean to be so entirely alone, so lost to oneself? The close affinity between rejected love and the loss of self as the kind of self-alienation associated with a transcendent, or sublime, moment allowed poets to exploit the potential for the lyric to be something vastly more than a mere love song. The greatest expression of this achievement may well be John Keats's odes, some of which he titled as "ode," but all of which are of a mixed genre, a combination of sonnet, ode, and address.

British poets in particular, then, exploited the lyric's transcendent possibilities by creating a re-imagined troubadourism, in which love for the exalted but unattainable lady could be translated into a quest for the sublime. With the failure of human love, the poet engages the Romantic imagination as a supremely creative act to transcend the frustration of the moment, and to achieve sublime communion with a divine power far in excess of the lady's capacity to gratify. This transcendent act replicates the imaginative act necessary to transform a landscape scene of an alpine mountain or other sublime locale into communion with the cosmic soul; by exploring courtly love and the transformative love song of the troubadour, Romantic poets could use the lyric song in the same way as they had used the ode. The effect, in a moment when poetry's greatest competition was the increasingly successful novel, was to cultivate the privacy implicit in the longings of a rejected lover as a form of the seductive titillation associated with the Gothic. The public enthusiasm for intensely subjective states induced by wallowing in medieval affect could be exploited for a more serious mission: that of teaching the reader how to desire transcendence rather than terror, and how to imagine transport rather than abduction.

But Romantic poets were versed in Chaucer and Shakespeare, not troubadour poetry, and even so they were more fluent in the Latin and Greek poets taught at schools and universities. Although the British public was just being introduced to Dante through Henry Francis Cary's 1805 English translation of the *Divine Comedy*, which caused interest in other historical and contemporary Italian writers, Renaissance courtly love was still not that of the Provençal troubadours; this rich history, however, was dormant in English culture through the inheritance of Eleanor of Aquitaine, who brought the arts to which she was accustomed and a high regard for those arts to the rough-and-tumble world of English twelfth-century life which she encountered upon her second marriage, to her third cousin, who two years later was crowned Henry II of England. She patronized poets as accomplished as Wace, Benoît de Sainte-Maure, and the great troubadour Bernart de Ventadorn. Ventadorn was a contemporary of romance writers like Chrétien de Troyes, who cemented the literary conventions of courtly love in the popular romances.

The transition from troubadour chansons with their envois to English courtly love poetry in the form of the sonnet is one that left its mark on the sonnet form, particularly in the Shakespearean variant where the final couplet queries the beloved's silence. That query echoes the gesture of the envoy but also the troubadour's plea for his lady's "gift," doing it so well that Romantic poets could resurrect that structure of desire and resistance for their own explorations of the self–other dynamic. At the same time, the tradition of medieval English ballads and romances was revived in literature that celebrated the heroic bards of medieval Wales and Scotland, as in ballads such as Sir Walter Scott's 1805 *Lay of the Last Minstrel*, while Scott's Waverley novels, although set in the recent Jacobite period, derived much of their interest from the depiction of a chivalrous Highland culture. Scott was only one of many writers taking advantage of the renewed interest in earlier British culture spawned by antiquarian research, including the collecting of popular romances and ballads by Sir Thomas Percy and by Scott himself.

Other writers considered the philosophical ramifications of revisiting life in the high medieval period: Percy Bysshe Shelley's "Julian and Maddalo: A Conversation" (c. 1818, pub. 1824), for instance, contains an incident that suggests the poem takes place in the time of Tasso, one of the great figures in the literary tradition of courtly love. Similarly, Lord Byron's popular "Turkish Tales," metrical romances set in the time of the Venetian Republic, assimilate contemporary issues concerning subjectivity and otherness to concepts of courtly love, female roles under patriarchy, and chivalry. But it is not the subject matter of these works so much as the role of the poet-narrator in them that suggests an interest in the troubadour figure himself. Shelley's Julian is an idealist whose goals are transcendent; unlike the cynical Count Maddalo, the Shelley-like Julian strives for a sublime vision of man's potential.

Count Maddalo's cynicism, by contrast, can be taken as an alignment with what Simon Gaunt argues is the deep irony of Provençal poetry, and as a philosophical marker of the worldview that structures the Gothic.[4] As the underside of the

---

[4]   Simon Gaunt, *Troubadours and Irony* (Cambridge, UK: Cambridge University Press, 2008), 10–12.

sublime, the Gothic typically – and ironically – punishes both its ladies and its troubadour poets, and even chivalrous heroes have difficulty subduing the forces of patriarchal tyranny. Interestingly, the Gothic flourished not just in novel form, but also in dramas and poems, and women writers as well as men tried their hand at it. Few, with the exception of Ann Radcliffe, achieved much success, but that women such as Charlotte Dacre and Anna Batten Crystall sought to do it suggests that they were resisting the role of courtly love's silent beloved.

In *Valperga: or, the Life and Adventures of Castruccio, Prince of Lucca* (1823), Mary Shelley takes up the challenge of her husband's transcendent medievalism and Scott's historical novels, but also the dark implications of the Gothic, to integrate detailed historical research with historical figures so as to shed light on current social and political issues. Her heroine, Countess Euthanasia, is an enlightened ruler who patronizes the arts much as Eleanor of Aquitaine did, and who is governed by reason and sensibility. Her rule contrasts sharply with the self-interests of aggressive and cynical male characters, opening up a space for the female voice of the beloved, which is silenced or absent in troubadour poetry. Mary Shelley thus contests the sentimental attitudes of her time toward romances and poetry that celebrate medieval, and especially troubadour, values. As in her first novel *Frankenstein*, she questions the ethics of transcendent poetic visions, particularly in the political realm. Yet it is the political realm that harbored Romantic identifications of the sublime: Edmund Burke, William Wordsworth, and Percy Shelley located the power of the sublime to transform human lives in its political efficacy. All three major figures understood this efficacy to be translated for human absorption by the poet (or in Burke's case, by the aesthetic more generally).

Like Mary Shelley, other women interested in female voice also used the troubadour tradition to explore what that voice might say if given space. Mary Robinson, for instance, deliberately reverses the role of male lover and female beloved in the courtly dynamic in her sonnet cycle *Sappho and Phaon* (1796). The form itself harkens back to troubadour genres, and although the setting is classical Greece, Sappho is imagined as both a love poet and a beloved who speaks her love back; moreover, it is she who is loyal and pleading for a gift, while her love-object, Phaon, is the one who rejects, denies, and is silent. In a less ardent, more melancholy self-framing, Letitia Elizabeth Landon created celebrity for herself by writing poems with troubadour settings and characters, published in volumes with titles such as *The Improvisatrice* (1824) and *The Troubadour* (1825).

Together with her publications, Landon promoted herself as a female troubadour by wearing white robes of a vague historical fashion to literary salons. Her volumes of poetry and her own social appearances allowed her to explore the beloved's voice and experience; to sound out what women might have said back and what the troubadour poet might not have wanted to hear. By situating that voice in the role of the beloved, Landon moved the focus even further away from the poetic transcendence that Mary Shelley had questioned but Mary Robinson had left as a viable path for women poets. Landon's achievement was admired by Victorian successors such as Elizabeth Barrett Browning and Christina Rossetti, who also wrote poems in the voice of the female troubadour poet.

By shutting down the possibility for female transcendence, and thus access to the sublime, Landon's late Romantic poems helped pave the way for a Victorian-era resurgence in medieval sentimentalism that veered away from a political and aesthetic sublime to locate medieval chivalry and courtly love fully in the religious sphere. This movement was articulated early on by Dante Gabriel Rossetti and his Pre-Raphaelite Brotherhood; their poetry and paintings depicted despairing lovers, longing poets, and a focus on a highly detailed immediacy that has more in common with Gothic traditions than with the troubadourian sublime. The Romantic period had evinced a movement in the opposite direction, from senti-mental historical scenarios to the troubadour as visionary seer, from an Ivanhoe to a Dante, and thus from a regressive to a progressive use of medievalism.

Yet at the very end of the Romantic period poets began to conflate sentimental with transcendent medievalism, revealing the Victorian reversal of direction already in play. John Keats offers a case in point; his first achievements were in the Spenserian vein, but he quickly began to experiment with alternating between a Grecian imaginary and a high medieval one. In 1819, his *annus mirabilis*, he realized the transcendent effects of troubadourian sublimation in his great odes, particularly "Ode to Melancholy," "Ode to Psyche," and "Ode to Indolence"; at the same time, he also experimented with medieval pathos and troubadourian irony in his ballad "La Belle Dame sans Merci," and his romances "The Eve of St. Agnes," "The Eve of St. Mark," and "Isabella, or the Pot of Basil," the last of which deeply influenced the Pre-Raphaelite Brotherhood and then Victorian culture more generally. Keats as himself the troubadour who is engrossed with issues of self-alienation, absence or loss, and transcendence is most evident in his six odes, but his romances, such as "The Eve of St. Agnes," were too compellingly seduc-tive in the portrayal of a troubadour poet at work. It was this vision of sensuous medievalism and of courtly love's tribulations that could immediately appeal to Victorian writers and painters; sentimentality became the way to understand the troubadour's appeal.

### Further Reading

Bloch, R. Howard. *Medieval Misogyny and the Invention of Western Romantic Love.* Chicago: University of Chicago Press, 1992.

Biddick, Kathleen. *The Shock of Medievalism.* Durham: Duke University Press, 1998.

Esterhammer, Angela. *Romanticism and Improvisation, 1750–1850.* Cambridge: Cambridge University Press, 2008.

Fay, Elizabeth. *Romantic Medievalism: History and the Romantic Literary Ideal.* New York: Palgrave Macmillan, 2002.

Labbe, Jacqueline. *The Romantic Paradox: Love, Violence and the Uses of Romance, 1760–1830.* Basingstoke: Macmillan, 2000.

Lowenthal, David. *The Past is a Foreign Country.* Cambridge: Cambridge University Press, 1999.

Simmons, Clare. *Popular Medievalism in Romantic-Era Britain.* New York: Palgrave Macmillan, 2011.

## Related Essays in this Volume

Gothic, Love, Monument, Lingua, Humor, Memory, Presentism, Genealogy, Christianity, Spectacle, Trauma, Transfer, Heresy, Primitive, Continuity, Resonance

# Index

Medievalism

I

*Anglo-Saxon Culture and the Modern Imagination*
edited by David Clark and Nicholas Perkins

II

*Medievalist Enlightenment: From Charles Perrault to Jean-Jacques Rousseau*
Alicia C. Montoya

III

*Memory and Myths of the Norman Conquest*
Siobhan Brownlie

IV

*Comic Medievalism: Laughing at the Middle Ages*
Louise D'Arcens

V

*Medievalism: Key Critical Terms*
edited by Elizabeth Emery and Richard Utz

VI

*Medievalism: A Critical History*
David Matthews

VII

*Chivalry and the Medieval Past*
edited by Katie Stevenson and Barbara Gribling

VIII

*Georgian Gothic: Medievalist Architecture, Furniture and Interiors, 1730–1840*
Peter N. Lindfield

www.ingramcontent.com/pod-product-compliance
Ingram Content Group UK Ltd.
Pitfield, Milton Keynes, MK11 3LW, UK
UKHW020048280125
454293UK00006B/123